WHAT IN THE WORLD IS MUSIC?

ALISON E. ARNOLD
NORTH CAROLINA STATE UNIVERSITY

JONATHAN C. KRAMER
NORTH CAROLINA STATE UNIVERSITY

Routledge
Taylor & Francis Group

NEW YORK AND LONDON

First published 2016
by Routledge
711 Third Avenue, New York, NY 10017

and by Routledge
2 Park Square, Milton Park, Abingdon, Oxon, OX14 4RN

Routledge is an imprint of the Taylor & Francis Group, an informa business

Library of Congress Cataloging-in-Publication Data
A catalog record for this book has been requested

ISBN: 978-1-138-79025-4 (pbk)

Typeset in Berkeley Oldstyle
by Apex CoVantage, LLC

Senior Editor: Constance Ditzel
Assistant Editor: Denny Tek
Production Manager: Mhairi Bennett
Marketing Manager: Amy Langlais
Copy Editor: Ruth Jeavons
Proofreader: Nikky Twyman
Cover Design: Jayne Varney

To our teachers, with gratitude:

Gordon Epperson

David McAllester

Bruno Nettl

"When you pray...you thank God, you thank your ancestors, and you thank your teachers, whether they are alive or not alive."—Henk Tjon, "The Griot of Suriname"

Thanks, Henk. This is for you, too.

CONTENTS

MAPS

PREFACE

What in the World is Music? is an exploration of music's materials, contexts, and purposes. We approach music as a global phenomenon and a fundamental mode of expression of all people, as basic to our common humanity as language. *What in the World is Music?* considers the nature of musical sound, and examines the shared ways people engage with music, in worship, courtship, entertainment, etc. It shows on the one hand the enormous variety and ingenuity of human musical invention and on the other the similarities in the ways humans use music to express their emotions and organize their social interactions.

What in the World is Music? was created for undergraduate courses in Music Appreciation and World Music. Yet it differs from conventional approaches in the ways information is organized and delivered. Our course explores the ways humans organize sound, the many roles music plays in human life, and the situations both live and mediated in which music takes place. Genres, styles, performance contexts, and artists from all parts of the world and various time periods exemplify fundamental patterns of engagement, making no distinction between Western and non-Western music and music making.

This curriculum grew out of a Music Appreciation course called "Understanding Music," which was originally taught as a chronological survey of Western art music. It gradually became more and more a hybrid, more and more like a World Music course as we attempted to respond ever more fully to the question, "What does it mean to understand *all* music?" Western art music constitutes only a very small percentage of human musical engagements. Music is an extraordinarily diverse and complex universal category of human expression that has neurological, psychological, mythological, metaphysical, acoustical, social, and cultural dimensions and ramifications. We found that neither the historical and chronological survey of Western art music nor the regional survey of World Music was methodologically adequate to foreground the larger questions we wanted our students to explore: What is music for? When does music happen? Who are the music makers? What else is going on when people make and listen to music? How and why is musical skill taught and learned? Furthermore, the material in existing textbooks, although excellent for traditional undergraduate survey courses, provided insufficient or inappropriate illustrations for the discussions we were generating, and so over a decade of research and writing we developed this curriculum.

We felt that these larger questions needed to be considered before asking students to differentiate between Baroque concerto and concerto grosso, or between North Indian *khyal* and *thumri*. This kind of factual knowledge, easy to test and grade, becomes more relevant in the context of a broader inquiry into the nature of music as a fundamental form of human expression. To deepen student understanding, we sought and developed case studies that demonstrate humanity's extraordinary diversity and creativity. Over time the course curriculum evolved thematically. Academic distinctions between Western and non-Western music lost their primacy. Juxtaposing Ludwig van Beethoven with Salif Keita shed greater light on the creative processes of musical innovators than considering Beethoven in a stylistic period and Keita in a world region. Similarly, juxtaposing Bollywood with Hollywood, and Buddhist chant with Gregorian chant, both accentuated our common humanity and liberated music from the boxes and categories of time and place, and even academic disciplines.

The following introduction to our innovative text uses a rephrasing of the main four questions that form the lesson headings of our first unit: What is Music? What is Music Made Of? Where does Music Come From? What is Music For?

WHAT IS IT?

What in the World is Music? is a curriculum presented in an online e-text format with integrated resources for undergraduate non-Music Majors. Music majors will also benefit from the global perspectives that this textbook offers. Central to the organization of the text is a fully integrated multimedia program that includes over three hundred video clips and audio tracks. This is an essential feature that allows students to understand performances, styles, and traditions as expressions of human engagement with music, as well as the social occasions and contexts in which these engagements take place.

Students access the text and streaming media online through the token and passcodes provided by the publisher. With the purchase and access of the interactive eBook, a print book is provided as an ancillary to the course website, for the convenience of re-reading and studying offline.

WHAT IS IT MADE OF?

The curriculum consists of fifteen lessons divided into four units.

1. THE FOUNDATIONS OF MUSIC

Unit 1 deals with four fundamental questions for musical understanding. The first lesson, asking the question "What is Music?" discusses definitions from a variety of cultures and ways for engaging with musical sound. The second question, "What is Music Made Of?" is divided into two Lessons. Lesson 2, "Voices and Instruments," surveys the sounds that music is made from and how these sounds are produced. More than eighty videos from around the world present students with a rich experience of people engaged with musical artistry. Lesson 3, "The Elements of Music," explores the ways in which these sounds are organized, in terms of melody, harmony, rhythm, etc. with examples drawn from many of the world's music traditions. Lesson 4, "Where Does Music Come From?" uses origin myths from around the world and origin theories from the scientific and anthropological literature to examine possible explanations for music's universality. Finally in Lesson 5, "What Is Music For?" the text presents functions of music and the different ways people use it in their lives.

The rest of the curriculum considers in depth three fundamental ways in which people engage with music: to project their identities, respond to the sacred, and enhance their social lives.

2. MUSIC AND IDENTITY

In the four lessons of Unit 2 the discussion is organized around broad conceptual frames: the individual, the group, hybridity, and conflict. In Lesson 6, "Music and Individual Identity," the career of Ludwig van Beethoven is juxtaposed with those of Ravi Shankar, Salif Keita, Bulgarian bagpipe player Maria Stoyanova, and Chinese rock star Cui Jian. Lesson 7, "Music and Group Identity," explores national and regional forms of music, song, and dance, and includes discussions of the Argentine tango, Egyptian superstar Umm Kulthum, Bohemian composer Bedřich Smetana, and the expression of ethnic identity in multicultural Suriname (former Dutch Guyana). In Lesson 8, "Music and Hybrid

Identity," Cajun culture in Louisiana, the Montagnard refugee community in North Carolina, and Indo-Trinidadian music are among the case studies presented. In Lesson 9, Latin American protest songs (*Nueva Canción*), music during South African Apartheid, and Global Hip-Hop exemplify "Music and Oppositional Identity."

3. MUSIC AND THE SACRED

Unit 3 explores sacred music in Hindu, Buddhist, Islamic, and Christian contexts as well as in folk and syncretic traditions. Lesson 10 deals with forms of sacred chant including Vedic, Plainchant, and Qur'anic recitation; and with singing devotional verses (Islamic *qawwali* and Christian hymnody). Lesson 11, "Sacred Embodiment and Sacred Enactment," discusses the roles music plays in inspiring religious experience such as ecstasy and trance, and in conveying religious expressions through dance and drama. The lesson draws from traditions in China, Zimbabwe, Côte d'Ivoire, Japan, Bali, and India. In Lesson 12, "Sacred Space and Sacred Time," case studies examine life-cycle and calendrical rituals, pilgrimages and processions, and the demarcation of sacred locales in Myanmar, Cape Verde, Ethiopia, and elsewhere.

4. MUSIC AND SOCIAL LIFE

Unit 4 begins with two lessons (13 and 14) that explore music in narrative traditions: bardic, theatrical, and cinematic. Epic narration from the Balkans and West Africa, storytelling from Korea and China, puppet theater from Japan and Java, and Western opera exemplify bardic and theatrical traditions. The discussion of film music (Hollywood and Bollywood) is prefaced by a general introduction to audio, video, and digital technologies and mass media. Music in the public contexts of urban nightlife, sporting events, ceremonies, and festivals, constitutes the subject matter of the final Lesson 15, "Music in Public Spaces." Examples are drawn from Brazil, Canada, Mexico, Nigeria, Trinidad, the United States, and elsewhere.

SPECIAL FEATURES

- Unique thematic organization designed for both World Music and Music Appreciation curricula.
- A bank of nearly three hundred videos linked directly to the e-text.
- A Video Index arranged by lesson, theme, and world region.
- A Spotify channel for audio files integrated into the lessons.
- More than a hundred photographs, many taken in the field during research expeditions, appearing in color on the website.
- Twenty-six maps showing geographical locations for the traditions that the lessons present.
- Case studies drawn from thirty-seven countries representing every continent except Antarctica.
- "Thinking About Music" questions that tie lesson material to students' own musical experiences.
- Endnotes containing bibliographic information.
- Three-hundred-word glossary.
- Instructors' test bank.
- End-of-lesson self-quiz questions.

WHERE DOES IT COME FROM?

We began developing this curriculum for our course "Understanding Music" in the early 2000s, when North Carolina State University was exploring innovative undergraduate teaching strategies funded by a grant from the Hewlett Foundation. The focus of these educational reforms was inquiry-guided learning, and increased attention to developing critical thinking skills in students. Faculty members were invited to create teaching plans for traditional courses that incorporated these new initiatives. Our common interests in Western classical music and other musical traditions of the world, and the lack of an appropriate textbook that combined both, inspired us to create a new curriculum. Statements of fact became questions for analysis and discussion. The initial interrogative lesson titles reflect this change in approach, with the rest of the curriculum exploring the implications of the fourth question: What is Music For?

Several years later, NC State University began to encourage faculty to develop Distance Education formats for general education courses. In 2004 and 2005, we received grants from the university's LITRE Fund (Learning in a Technology-Rich Environment) to create an online platform for "Understanding Music" with streaming multimedia capabilities. In 2006 the online course was first offered, and since that time more than a thousand students have taken it both in the traditional classroom setting and through distance education. Ongoing collaborative work—writing and revising lessons, adding new field research materials, and locating relevant video and audio recordings—has resulted in the e-text *What in the World is Music?* Together we have presented papers on this online curriculum and its innovative approach to undergraduate music education at both national and international conferences, including meetings of the College Music Society, Cultural Diversity in Music Education, the International Council for Traditional Music, and the Society for Ethnomusicology.

WHAT IS IT FOR?

What in the World is Music? can be used either in Music Appreciation or World Music courses by instructors who wish to take a fresh, new approach to these subjects. Our purpose in writing it was to help students think about music not in terms of categories defined by Western scholars—repertoires, styles, time periods, geographical regions—but in the shared ways people (including the students themselves) engage with music. There is little technical analysis of musical forms and genres with mandatory charts for guided listening. Rather, students engage with musical sound as it is embedded in social contexts, frequently presented through media resources that serve as a parallel learning environment. We have attempted to eliminate the disciplinary boundaries between Western and non-Western music and between Music Appreciation and World Music curricula by presenting case studies that best exemplify universal concepts without regard to these distinctions. Like Music Appreciation texts, *What in the World is Music?* provides discussions of instruments and elements (such as melody, rhythm, and harmony), and includes a number of Western art music examples. Like World Music courses, the curriculum examines traditions of music, dance, theater, and religious practice from many parts of the world.

TO THE INSTRUCTOR www.routledge.com/cw/arnold

What in the World is Music? can be used as a self-sufficient curriculum for online Distance Education courses. The website contains everything needed for the course, making it unnecessary for students to purchase CD packs or other auxiliary materials. In the traditional classroom setting, instructors may use this curriculum in a variety of ways. We often present the video and audio recordings in class for interactive lectures and discussions before the students read the lessons, which are then assigned through the online platform for out-of-class study and review. Instructor's resources are located on the companion website at the above URL.

We ask students to:

- read the lessons (equivalent to classroom lectures) and engage with multimedia resources linked directly to the text;
- respond to short-answer and "Thinking about Music" questions;
- submit written assignments on the website;
- make connections between unfamiliar, "exotic" sounds heard in the lesson videos and familiar contexts from their own experience, and within their own communities.

Instructors using *What in the World is Music?* for either World Music or Music Appreciation courses may wish to supplement or modify the material based on their individual areas of interest, expertise, or specialization. For example, an instructor might want to give a detailed introduction to the principles of sonata form when students read the section on Beethoven. An instructor with expertise in

African percussion might engage students in a drumming practicum in order to elaborate musical rhythm or other relevant sections of the text. The extensive media resources can be used as a media library. An instructor might illustrate a general discussion of India, for example, with some of the more than twenty videos in the video bank directly related to the music of South Asia.

TO THE STUDENT

We have been teaching this course in various forms for fifteen years, and have found that students taking it have come to a deeper appreciation of why music is important in their lives and in the life of humanity. Despite the importance many of you put on music, others find it easily dismissed as a frill, a mere entertainment, a marginal distribution requirement, as something separate from more significant endeavors. But understanding music from a global perspective, critically engaging with its many and intricate inner workings and connections to the wider world, shows how essential it is. The late Ernest Boyer, former President of the Carnegie Foundation for the Advancement of Teaching, urged students to engage thoughtfully with those aspects of human experience that are shared throughout the world. He called these aspects "core commonalities"—"those universal experiences that are shared by all people and all cultures on the planet and make us truly human." note 1 It is the goal of this music curriculum to provide a deep engagement with music as a universal human activity and communicative code. While forms of musical expression around the world can be radically different from each other, there are also fascinating areas of convergence. These areas of convergence form the foundation of this curriculum. What people around the world do with music is not so different from what you do with music, and this course provides the means for you to actively engage in this core commonality.

This is a course that *requires* your active engagement. *What in the World is Music?* is not a traditional textbook. Text, videos, maps, pictures, and audio files all together constitute a complete platform for learning that you access through the internet. There is a famous quote, variously attributed: "Talking (or writing), about music is like dancing about architecture." Reading about music without hearing it, seeing its context, and engaging with its multiple meanings is inadequate. Music must be experienced in all its complexity for it to be understood as a living force in our lives. By accessing the token that comes with the textbook and setting up your passcode, you will see, hear, and read about musicians throughout the world engaged with instruments, dancers, actors, worshipers, audience members, and even boxers: a world of human expressive culture.

THE AUTHORS

In developing *What in the World is Music?* we draw from decades of experience performing, researching, and writing about music, and teaching college-level music courses. We are both professors of Music and Arts Studies at North Carolina State University. We have traveled extensively and have carried out music research in diverse regions of the world. We have significant backgrounds in Western and non-Western music as performers and scholars, and continue professional lives as instrumentalists outside the university.

ALISON E. ARNOLD

From my earliest memories in Yorkshire, England, music was always a significant part of my family life. My brother took piano lessons, my sister and I followed suit, my dad loved opera, my mom loved classical symphonies, and my parents had an old wind-up gramophone and a stack of 78 rpm records. When I decided to pursue a college degree in music, I took up the flute and had my first college-level flute lessons with the principal flautist of the Royal Liverpool Philharmonic Orchestra, Atarah Ben-Tovim. An undergraduate thesis on Ralph Vaughan Williams and English folk song proved to be the ticket to my first full-time job, as an editorial assistant for *The New Grove Dictionary of Music and Musicians* (ed. Stanley Sadie). Here was my first formal introduction to non-Western music, and after three years working with the ethnomusicology editors under Peter Cooke, I moved to the U.S. for graduate studies at the University of Illinois at Urbana-Champaign. My advisor was the eminent and now emeritus Professor of Ethnomusicology and Anthropology, Bruno Nettl. I spent a year in India carrying out doctoral research on Hindi Film Song (now called the music of "Bollywood"). Teaching positions in subsequent years took me to Colorado, Pennsylvania, and North Carolina, and travel for research, conference participation, and pleasure included trips to Japan, China (the Silk Road), Malaysia, Cambodia, Laos, Vietnam, Trinidad, France, Ireland, Cape Breton, and Newfoundland. In the late 1990s I edited the South Asia volume of *The Garland Encyclopedia of World Music*, and in 2000 joined the Music Faculty of North Carolina State University. Over the past fourteen years I have taught courses in World Music, Music of Asia, Celtic Music, and Multicultural Arts. In North Carolina, with its strong history of Scottish immigration and culture, I began playing traditional Irish and Scottish music on wooden flute and whistles, and now teach and perform Celtic music and direct a local Irish music session.

JONATHAN C. KRAMER

I began the study of the cello in my native Hartford, Connecticut at the age of eight. My six brothers and sisters all sang and played instruments. I discovered the field of Ethnomusicology at Wesleyan University, where I studied "Native American Dance and Vocal Techniques" with David McAllester and South Indian *vina* with Sri Kalyanakrishna Bhagavatar, and continued taking cello lessons at Yale with Aldo Parisot. Later, I attended the University of Arizona where I worked with the great cello mentor and aesthetician Gordon Epperson. While performing with the San Francisco Opera and Ballet Orchestras, I attended Ali Akbar Khan's class in San Raphael, and was awarded a Fulbright to study *dhrupad* on cello at Banaras-Hindu University with Dr. Ritwik Sanyal. I served a second Fulbright in South Korea after completing a Ph.D. in Ethnomusicology and Performance Studies at the Union Institute with a dissertation on bi-musicality. There, I taught cello at Chosun University in Kwangju and studied *haegum* (two-string bowed fiddle) with Shim Im-Taek. I joined the North Carolina Symphony in 1983, and in 1985 was recruited by the Music Faculty of North Carolina State University. Over three decades there, I have taught courses in Western Music History, World Music, and American Popular Music, as well as conducted the university orchestra for ten years. I also teach as adjunct professor of Ethnomusicology at Duke University, offering courses in both South Asian and East Asian music cultures. I continue to perform as a cellist, but my primary interest in that regard is now cello pedagogy. Former students have attended many of America's major music conservatories including Juilliard, Manhattan, New England, Cincinnati, Peabody, and the University of North Carolina School of the Arts. Ethnomusicological research has taken me to India, Korea, China (particularly the Tibetan regions), Suriname, Uganda, and Ethiopia.

Alison E. Arnold
Jonathan C. Kramer
October 1, 2014

NOTE

1 Ernest Boyer, *Selected Speeches 1979–1995* (Princeton, NJ: Carnegie Foundation for the Advancement of Teaching, 1997), p. 109.

ACKNOWLEDGMENTS

In developing materials for this e-textbook, we have relied on the research and writing of many scholars, both of the present and past, known to us personally or by reputation. We do not claim global expertise, but readily acknowledge that we draw on a wide range of texts and other media in order to discuss music as a truly universal human phenomenon. We have corresponded with literally hundreds of musicians, scholars, filmmakers, writers, photographers, and publishers from around the world, and are indebted to the many contributors without whom this project would have been inconceivable. In this Acknowledgments section, we would like to express our enormous gratitude to all those who have supported the project and contributed to making this curriculum available to general students.

During the more than ten years of our collaboration on *What in the World is Music?* we have taught at North Carolina State University and are most grateful for the generosity and friendship of our colleagues there. In particular we would like to thank former Music Department Chair J. Mark Scearce, current Interim Chair Tom Koch, and Faculty; our invaluable Teaching Assistant, friend, and associate Elizabeth Holt; the Caldwell Scholars and Director Janice Odom; Lavon Page and Donna Petherbridge of the LITRE grant program; Melissa Williford of Distance Education; the D.H. Hill Library staff; and Professor Emeritus David B. Greene and the Hewlett Initiative. We have been fortunate to receive travel funds on a number of occasions, notably from the NCSU Division of Academic and Student Affairs, the College of Humanities and Social Sciences, the Music Department, and the NCSU Confucius Institute. Many of our travel arrangements were made with the capable assistance of Program Manager Kathleen Laudate. This project could not have been undertaken without the continuing support of our home institution.

We have received generous support and encouragement from a number of colleagues at regional academic institutions. At Duke University, Louise Meintjes and Paul Berliner provided much appreciated wise counsel, especially at the beginning of this project. Also at Duke, Hsiao-Mei Ku and the Ciompi String Quartet; the late Benjamin Ward; Miriam Cook, Leo Ching, and Eunyoung Kim of the Asian and Middle Eastern Studies Department; Ingrid Byerly in the Cultural Anthropology Department; and graduate assistant Andrew Pester—all made invaluable contributions. From the University of North Carolina system, we greatly appreciate the help of David Garcia and Juan Alamo at UNC-Chapel Hill, and Gavin Douglas at UNC-Greensboro.

Other academics in ethnomusicology and related fields have given indispensable assistance: Juliana Azoubel (UFMG, Escola de Belas Artes, Brazil), Birgitt Drüppel (International School of Düsseldorf), John Baily (Goldsmiths, University of London, Emeritus), Tingting Chen, Alessandra Ciucci

(Northeastern University), the late Marnie Dilling (UC Berkeley), Ellen Dissanayake, Ter Ellingson (University of Washington), Peter Manuel (CUNY), Helen Myers, Don Niles (Institute of Papua New Guinea Studies, PNG), Dale Olsen (FSU, Emeritus), Cathy Ragland (University of North Texas), Ann Rasmussen (College of William and Mary), Tim Rice (UCLA, Emeritus), George Sawa, János Sipos (Hungarian Academy of Sciences), Beth Szczepanski (Lewis and Clark College), and Holly Wissler.

During the course of our research and writing for this project, we have each traveled extensively and would like to express our enormous appreciation to the many scholars, musicians, institutions, and travel organizers for welcoming us into their communities and sharing with us their expertise and firsthand knowledge.

- In Cape Breton, Canada: Paul Cranford, David ("Papper") Papazian, Otis A. Tomas, Mario Colosimo, Brenda Stubbert;
- In China: Frank Kouwenhoven, the late Antoinet Schimmelpennink, and CHIME (European Foundation for Chinese Music Research); Gerald Roche, Tsering Samdrup, Dawa Drolma of the Plateau Music Project; Hsiao Mei and Xiaolin Dai of the Shanghai Conservatory; Wen Xiangcheng, Acko Choedrag, and Xiao Wenli; Steven Zhang of Xinjiang Western International Travel Service, and Baiwei, Liang, Vicky, Jimmy, Jack, YaFan;
- In Ethiopia: Lidetu Shambal, Azmari Gezate, and Imagine Ethiopia Tours;
- In India: American Institute of Indian Studies (AIIS), Shubha Chaudhuri and Saraswati Swaminathan of the Archives and Research Center for Ethnomusicology (ARCE), Pandit Ritwik Sanyal, Shanti Shivani, Raju Bharatan, Adrit Joseph and Holiday India;
- In Korea: Korean-American Educational Commission (Fulbright Korea), Baewon Lee of the National Gugak Center; Shim im Taek, Byon Kyong Hyuk, Jocelyn Clark, Joseph Celli;
- In North Carolina, USA: the Irish community in the Triangle region, especially Julie Gorka and Tim Smith; the Montagnard community of Raleigh and Greensboro, especially Hip Ksor, Mondega (Bom Siu), Dock Rmah, Y Dha Eban;
- In Suriname: Cyriel Eersteling, the late Henk Tjon, the late President Elfriede Baarn-Dijksteel of NAKS (Na Afrikan Kulturu fu Sranan), the American Embassy in Suriname and former Ambassador Lisa Bobby Schreiber-Hughes; the late Granman Belfon Aboikoni of Djoemoe; Ricardo van Varsseveld, Rakieb Waggidhossain, Roy Raghu, Narider Singh, Hilary de Bruin of the Department of Culture Studies, Paremuru Native American Culture Society, Marlene Lie A. Ling of Marlene Dance Company, Wilgo Baarn and Alakondre Dron, and Director Herman Snijders of the Volksmuziekschool;
- In Trinidad: Marilyn Rousseau, Mungal Patasar and Pantar, Wendell Manwaran and 3Canal band;
- In Uganda: Nicholas Sempijje (Makarere University), James Isabirye (Kyambogo University), Nile Beat Artists Troupe, Larry Council of Teaching and Travel Sojourners (TATS); Zziwa Annet and the staff at Adonai House;
- In Vietnam: Dam Thi Thao of Handspan Adventure Travel, Hanoi.

In addition to the musicians and dancers we encountered on our travels, we are indebted to many more we have met via the internet, who have generously shared their artistry and recordings with us in support of World Music education:

Armour Hill Singers (Canada); Ayan Basi Adeleke (Nigeria and USA); Sergio and Odair Assad (Brazil); Maya Beiser (Israel, and New York, USA); Diali Cissokho, Will Ridenhour, and Kaira Ba (Senegal, and North Carolina, USA); Nana Kimati Dinizulu and the Dinizulu Archives (Ghana); Duo Agua Y Vino—Barbara Hennerfeind and Erik Weisenberger (Germany); Karlheinz Essl (Germany); Carolina Eyck (Germany); Bela Fleck (USA); Steve and Kate Fowler (California, USA); Imamyar Hasamov (Azerbaijan); Dan Heymann (South Africa); Naji Hilal (Lebanon and USA); Yoko Hiraoka (Japan); Jorge Choquehuillca Huallpa (Peru); Louis-Daniel Joli (Canada); Kamal Kant (North India); Soheil Kaspar (Lebanon and USA); Areti Ketime (Greece); the late Ali Akbar Khan (North India); Ivan Kovachev (Bulgaria); Ladysmith Black Mambazo (South Africa); Michael Levy (USA); Cosmas Magaya (Zimbabwe); Wu Man (China and USA); Gilbert Mandere (Zimbabwe); Koji Matsunobo (Japan); Randy Max (UK); Nusaiba Mohammad (UK); Sahba Motallebi (Iran and USA); Mauricio Murcia (Colombia);

Nuuk Posse (Greenland); Ricky Olombelo and Salala (Madagascar); Luca Paciaroni (Italy); Karen Panigoniak (Canadian Inuit); Wes Parker and Carolina Brass Band, music director Brian Meixner (North Carolina, USA); Steve Riley (Louisiana, USA); Rabbi Rodriguez Sabino (Israel); Mohammed Reza Shahjarian (Iran); Durian Songbird (USA); Vijayalakshmi Subramaniam (South India); Kayohito Takenaka (Japan); Victoria and Jussef Vasquez (Chile); Glen Velez (USA); Aishu Venkataraman (South India); Wolf's Robe (Native American, USA); Darlene Zschech (Australia).

We are also grateful to the many music and film producers and organizations for sharing with us materials they have developed:

Swami Arun (Balinese *Calonarang*); Centre National de la Recherche Scientifique (CNRS) and the Département d'ethnomusicologie at Musée de l'Homme, Paris; Cat Celebrezze (Ravi Shankar's *Raga*); Jeremy Chevrier (Mali wedding party); Martin Cradick (Baka pygmies); Banning Eyre at Afropop Worldwide; the late Howard Gardner *Altar of Fire*); Michal Goldman (*Umm Kulthum*); Harvard Archive (*Avdo Međedović*); Paul Hodges (Argentine tango), Nic Hofmeyr (*Weeping* music video); International Olympic Committee; Ulf Jägfors (Gambian *akonting*); Susan Levitas ("Shout Bands" in *The Music District*); Antonio Lino (*mbira* musicians); Hari Madathipparambil and Invis.org (*Kathakali*); Manohar Lalas (*Epic of Pabuji*); Lomax Foundation (*Cajun Country*; *Jazz Parades*); Jeremy Marre and Harcourt Films (*Konkombe*; *Rhythm of Resistance*); Peter Miller (*The Internationale*); Bruno Monsaingeon (*Nadia Boulanger*); Shauna Murray and Playing for Change; George T. Nierenberg (*Say Amen, Somebody*); Nobel Prize Committee; Michael Y. Parker and Leda Scearce (Laryngoscopy videos); Fraser Pennebaker (*Monterey Pop*); Marcia Rego (Cape Verde footage); Thomas Roebers and Floris Leeuwenberg (*Foli: There is no Movement without Rhythm*); Chris Simon and Sageland Media (*Oil Barrels, Steel Drums: Pan in Trinidad and Tobago*); Im Kwan Tek (*Sopyonje*); and UNESCO.

We give special thanks to Yoko Ono Lennon for generously granting us permission to include the video of her late husband John Lennon performing "Mother" in concert; Coleman Barks for translations of Jalaluddin Rumi's poetry; the Venkateswara Temple of Cary, NC; and the great friend of music, the late Pete Seeger, with whom we spoke at length in November 2013 regarding his 1966 documentary *Afro-American Work Songs in a Texas Prison*, and whose hope for a world reconciled through music permeates this work.

A number of individuals at Routledge have guided this project since 2013. We would especially like to thank Music Editor Constance Ditzel, Assistants Denny Tek and Aurora Montgomery, and Editors Mhairi Bennett and Ruth Jeavons at Taylor and Francis in the U.K. We also appreciate the assistance of the Design Staff at Routledge and the Technical Support staff at Vital Source.

Finally, throughout the many years of our collaborative work we have enjoyed the love, comfort, and patience of our families. On the Kramer side, beloved wife Debbie; children, their spouses, and grandchildren: Vieve Radha, Jamie P., Kahlila, Anthony, Andreas, Stella, Jaime, Jonathan F., Ava Grace, Brittney, Mike, Olivia, Harrison, and Matthias. Finally, thanks to my six brothers and sisters who taught me nearly everything I know—Stephen, David, Katherine, Susan, Christina, and Paul, and their families (especially sister Christina who maintained enthusiasm for the project when my own flagged, and brother Paul whose wizardry with photo editing saved many of our field photographs). On the Arnold side, sons Adam and Nathan, daughter-in-law Jessica and baby Ember, my mother Cathy and late father James, my brother Nick and sister Gill and her family; and my closest friend and life partner, husband Gordon, whose support has been immeasurable.

Visual Tour of the Interactive eTextbook

Access your Interactive eTextbook at home, on campus or on the move,[1] online or offline. Your eTextbook offers note sharing and highlighting functionalities, as well as exclusive interactive content to enhance your learning experience. The notes you make on your Interactive eTextbook will synchronize with all other versions, creating a personalized version that you can access wherever and whenever you need it.

Throughout the text you will see icons in the margin where multimedia resources are available via your Interactive eTextbook. These include:

 Links to audio files.

 Links to video files.

 Multiple choice and fill-in-the-blank questions.

You can also find additional student and instructor resources at **www.routledge.com/cw/arnold**

NOTE

1 BookShelf will provide access to your eTextbook either online or as a download via your PC, Mac (OS X 10.6>), iPad, iPhone, iPod Touch (iOS 3.2>), Android app, or Amazon Kindle Fire.

UNIT 1
THE FOUNDATIONS OF MUSIC

INTRODUCTION

There has never been a time in history when music was more available, more portable, and more pervasive than today. People of the industrial and post-industrial world wake to music from their clock radios and smartphones. They go about their day accompanied by music delivered directly into their brains by earphones connected to digital devices. They shop in **Muzak**-saturated malls and go to movies where a background music track calibrates their emotional responses. Before the early experiments with sound recording in the late 19th century, music could only be heard live, in the presence of its performers. The electronic and digital technologies of sound recording, amplification, transmission, and broadcast that began only a little more than a century ago have radically altered the way we make and listen to music. These transformational technologies have reached even the remotest corners of the globe. Inuit of the Arctic listen to heavy metal on boom boxes. Tibetan yak-herding songs are posted on YouTube.com. The roofs of shanties and shacks that line the banks of the Mekong Delta sprout a forest of wire TV antennae. As radio, television, CD and MP3 players, laptops, tablets, and cellphones become ever cheaper, the environment is increasingly saturated with recorded and broadcast music, which is now a multi-billion dollar global industry. Never before have so many different kinds of music been available on such a wide scale. The internet is a crossroads of World Music; and song files and music videos from all continents and centuries flash across information superhighways.

This course concerns music as a commonality of human experience, made and listened to by people in every society. We are born with innate and inherited musical competence, to which particular domains within the brain are assigned. Music, like language, is an inherited capacity that then develops after birth in culturally determined ways. While humans are born with the ability to acquire language, they don't grow up speaking language as such, but *specific* languages like French, Swahili, or Korean. Similarly, human groups have created distinctive musical languages that are constantly evolving. As the circumstances in which people live their lives change, they share, transform, and adapt tunes, instruments, and dance rhythms to new purposes. Songs are forgotten, instruments

Fig. 1.1 **Antennae rising from shanties along the Mekong Delta, southeast Vietnam**

become obsolete, and musical fashions change with changing times. Why do humans have musical perception and skill "hard-wired" into their neural circuitry? And how do humans use this inborn ability to create and respond to the infinitely diverse musical experiences that shape and enhance their lives? Whether by nature or nurture, most of us have an appreciation for music, but why this is so is a great mystery. Through this course, you may come to appreciate a wider variety of music than you do now, but more importantly, you will have a deeper understanding of the roles music plays in human life. It is the mysterious power of music to move the heart, along with many less lofty purposes, that we will seek to understand in this course.

Lesson 1
What is Music?

Let us begin our study with the question "What IS music?" From a global perspective, we may wonder if our term "music" refers to a single universal category or many categories each culturally determined. Not all languages have a single term to encompass all the meanings and associations the English word usually carries. On the one hand, as ethnomusicologist Charles Keil noted, some languages have no equivalent term, although they may have many words to identify or describe associated activities and concepts:

> Tiv, Yoruba, Igbo, Efik, Birom, Hausa, assorted Jarawa dialects, Idoma, Eggon, and a dozen other languages from the Nigeria-Cameroons area do not yield a word for "music" gracefully. It is easy to talk about song and dance, singers and drummers, blowing a flute, beating a bell, but the general terms "music" and "musician" require long and awkward circumlocutions that still fall short, usually for lack of abstraction.[1]

On the other hand, some languages have an equivalent term but with a broader meaning. The ancient Greek *musiki* included all the arts under the influence of the nine Muses. Thus, the words of a song along with its melody and rhythm were considered part of this single concept. In certain African languages, music and dance—sounds and the movements that accompany them—form a single, indivisible category. In ancient India, the **Sanskrit** term *sangita*, writes Indian music scholar Lewis Rowell, "is the closest equivalent to the Western concept of music, although the inclusion of dance as one of the three main compartments suggests that in early Indian thought *sangita* was regarded as a composite art."[2] Melody, rhythm, and bodily movement in the forms of dance and theatrical mime, were all considered components of this single broad concept.

Even in English there is disagreement over how to define "music." Coming up with a suitable definition for the purpose of our study that is broad enough to encompass all the world's music yet narrow enough to be workable and precise proves to be a challenge. Music surely has something to do with sound, but not all sound is music. Perhaps we may begin with ethnomusicologist John Blacking's famous definition of music as humanly organized sound. A problem with Blacking's definition is that it is too broad. Language is humanly organized sound, yet an adequate definition of music must differentiate between speech and song. We need to limit the definition further, because speech, as well as car horns, ringtones, shouts, murmurs, and other human-made sounds, would be included in this definition and would make our investigation too large and unwieldy. We clearly recognize differences between speaking and singing, but the exact quantifiable moment when "sing-song" speech becomes "monotone" or "tuneless" singing is ambiguous. Perhaps what identifies a given sound as music lies in the intentions of the person making it. This point can be clarified by considering a car horn. When you use it politely to invite the car in front of you, whose driver is talking on the cell phone, to move when the light has turned green, you are using the horn as a substitute for the word "Move!" and it is therefore not music. If, however, you are driving along a boring stretch of interstate at night and begin entertaining yourself by beeping the horn, perhaps in accompaniment to a tune on the radio, it IS music, because you are using the sound of the car horn AS music. Similarly, if a percussionist in an orchestra accidentally drops the cymbals on the floor, it is not music. When she crashes her cymbals at the appropriate moment in the performance, it IS music because of the musician's *intention* that it is music. Thus it is the purposes of the humanly organized sound that are decisive. Accidental sounds may be intentionally incorporated into music, but music itself is not accidental.

A WORKING DEFINITION

Let us propose a working definition of music: *sounds organized by humans and intended for musical purposes*. This is problematic because it is circular; we include in the definition a form of the word we are defining. Nevertheless, this definition is broad enough to encompass the enormous diversity of all human musical expression. It focuses our attention on musical sounds themselves as well as what is most revealing about them: the purposes they serve and the meanings they convey. After all, in the examples of the car horn and the cymbals, it is not the quality of the sound itself that makes it music, but a human's intention.

Now we consider three examples that may or may not fall within our conceptual limits. First is the famous "**composition**" by the American **avant-garde** composer John Cage (1912–1992) titled *4'33"*. The work consists of four minutes and thirty-three seconds of silence. Is this music? Critic Peter Gutmann describes the work as follows:

4'33" was Cage's favorite work. Written in 1952, it came at the exact mid-point of his 80-year life of discovery and culminated his exploration of indeterminacy, music in which some elements are carefully scripted with others left to chance...4'33" was inspired by Cage's visit

Fig. 1.2   John Cage (1912–1992)

to Harvard's anechoic chamber, designed to eliminate all sound; but instead of promised silence Cage was amazed and delighted to hear the pulsing of his blood and the whistling of his nerves... Here's how one performance went: A tuxedoed performer came on stage, sat at a grand piano, opened the lid, occasionally turned some music pages but otherwise sat as quietly as possible for 4 minutes and 33 seconds, then rose, bowed and left. And that was it.

Although often described as a silent piece, 4'33" isn't silent at all. While the performer makes as little sound as possible, Cage breaks traditional boundaries by shifting attention from the stage to the audience and even beyond the concert hall. You soon become aware of a huge amount of sound, ranging from the mundane to the profound, from the expected to the surprising, from the intimate to the cosmic—shifting in seats, riffling programs to see what in the world is going on, breathing, the air conditioning, a creaking door, passing traffic, an airplane, ringing in your ears, a recaptured memory. This is a deeply personal music, which each witness creates to his/her own reactions to life. Concerts and records standardize our responses, but no two people will ever hear 4'33" the same way. It's the ultimate sing-along: the audience (and the world) becomes the performer.[3]

In 4'33", the composer invites the audience to listen to the sounds around them, for that time interval, the way they listen to music. Setting the time interval and the **context** constitutes a degree of organization, and Cage's intention, that engaged listening will transpire in a public venue designed for such a purpose, meets (perhaps just barely!) our definitional requirements.

Now consider an **Albanian funeral song**. Listen several times. How would you describe what you hear? On first listening, the voices may seem random and disorganized, like the hubbub heard in an athletic stadium. The sound lacks those "ingredients" that we usually associate with music—pitch, melody, beat, instruments, etc. Yet the sonic events seem to follow a predictable pattern. A solo male voice calls; it is joined by a group of men shouting an elongated cry; and then a clamoring chorus of individual voices gradually descends in pitch and intensity, finally dissipating. It begins again with the call of the leader. These events repeat in the same order two more times. Is it music? It is certainly produced by humans and has some degree of organization. The question we need to consider is whether the men *intend* their cries to be music. Crowd noise in a football stadium, which this resembles sonically, is produced by humans but is not intended as musical expression. In Unit 3 of this course, "Music and the Sacred," we will see that rites for the dead the world over have been accompanied by singing, chanting, and other forms of expressive sound intended as public outpourings of grief. Therefore, based on our definition, the Albanian funeral song IS music. Indeed, the respected ethnomusicologist Hugo Zemp describes the Albanian example in musical terms, as "song." How do the participants at the funeral experience these sounds? They may have a category of their own, like "organized wailing," that is separate from other forms of music making in their society. Do they decide; or scholars like Zemp? Or do listeners like us decide, who hear this recording far removed from the funeral in time and space? Perhaps the question cannot ultimately be answered. Nevertheless, is this suitable material for an investigation of the world's music? By our definition, it is.

Finally, listen to this recording of **Swiss cowherds** leading their cattle home from an upland pasture for the evening milking. A most striking feature is the sound of cowbells that provides a steady accompaniment to the shouts and calls of the cowherd—a repeating sequence of shouted syllables, vocal warbling, and **falsetto** singing. Now without the herders' voices, would the cowbells alone be music? Hmm...an interesting question. It is true that the cows moving along the mountain trail have no musical intention, just as the wind has no musical intention when it causes wind chimes to sound. The cowbells ring with the random movements of the animals. However, the cowherds hung the bells around the necks of the animals in the first place. Was the intention of the herders to use the sound of the bells only to locate cows that have strayed? Such a utilitarian purpose is akin to an automobile horn or a fire alarm—an auditory signal substituting for a speech act: in the case of the car horn, "Move out of the way!"; in the case of the fire alarm, "Get out of the building!"; and in the case of the cowbell, "Here I am!" Without knowing the intention of the herders, we might consider if there was an additional *musical* purpose: to beautify the Swiss mountain air with music. Is it possible that the jangling bells, in addition to locating strays, give **aesthetic**, musical pleasure to the human listener? Perhaps in this sense we can consider the cowbells music, as we can likewise consider the wind chimes music. No intention is ascribed to the wind and yet there IS intention on the part of the chimes' designer and the human hand that hung them in a windy spot. As to the voice, the herder is saying in Swiss dialect "Come on, little cow, come on"—surely a speech act. Yet the "**yodeling**" falsetto portions, in addition to encouraging the cows, no doubt entertain the herder and his human companions. In mountainous regions of the world, people have developed highly specialized forms of vocalizing that make use of the acoustical properties of thin atmosphere and narrow valleys. As we will read in Lesson 5, "The Functions of Music," entertainment is universally an important musical function. If the sounds of the Swiss cowherds are marginally music, this kind of cattle calling furnished the raw material for an international singing style. Listen to this **yodeling song**. Now, *that's music!* The intentions of the songwriter and performers are unambiguous. The song, with its yodeling, serves to

1-1

1-2

1-3

Fig 1.3 **Cowbell**

entertain, communicate a story, and symbolize the Swiss Alps—all *musical* purposes.

But what of the sounds of nature? Are the "songs" of birds and whales music? These and other natural sounds, such as pounding surf, whistling wind, and dripping water, have features that resemble many kinds of human music: pitch, rhythmic regularity, etc. Indeed, it has been suggested that bird song and other natural sounds were a source of musical inspiration among early humans. Two of the primary reasons birds "sing"—to mark territory and attract mates—are important in human music making, as evidenced by the sheer number and universality of national anthems, fight songs, and love ballads. For the purpose of this course, however, we will categorize the sounds of nature not as music but as "music-like," since they lack *human* intention, although they can be considered music *under certain circumstances*. There are many examples of music around the world imitating the sounds of nature, such as Vivaldi's *Four Seasons* and Beethoven's *Pastoral Symphony* from the Western symphonic repertoire. Chinese *guzheng* (21-string long zither) pieces also often have evocative titles such as "Autumn Moon Above Calm Lake" and "Fighting the Typhoon," as do Japanese *shakuhachi* (bamboo flute) solos with names like "Bell Ringing in the Misty Ocean." Tuvan singers, who live on

the steppes of Central Asia, manipulate their vocal cords and mouth cavities in ingenious ways to imitate the natural sounds of their environment: wind, mosquitoes, horses, etc.

There are also examples of natural sounds themselves being part of the music. The Finnish composer Einojuhani Rautavaara journeyed to the Arctic and recorded colonies of nesting birds, and composed his *Cantus Arcticus* (concerto for birds and orchestra) around these haunting sounds. Similarly, American composer and musician Paul Winter used recorded whale "songs" in his *Lullaby from the Great Mother Whale for the Baby Seal Pups*. In Afghanistan, musicians bring caged birds with them to their performances in order that the singing of the birds in response to the instrumental music becomes a part of the total musical sound. In some parts of the world, hobbyists bring their caged birds to public parks where they join in the collective avian ensemble; indeed, often the "singing" is competitive and prizes are awarded to owners of the most active songbirds. In this video from Paramaribo, the capitol of Suriname in South America, two judges are scoring competing Amazonian songbirds to determine which bird sings the most times in a fifteen-minute interval. A final example comes from a recording in which the buzzing of a beetle in Papua New Guinea is "turned into" music by a child who holds the insect, tied to a twig, between his lips. By changing the shape of his mouth cavity, he can "play" melodies on the insect. While these examples demonstrate the close connections between music and the natural world, our exploration primarily concerns the human dimensions of musical sounds: how and why they are made, and what understanding them tells us about ourselves, our relationships, and our values.

FOUR APPROACHES TO MUSICAL INQUIRY

In our investigation of music, we introduce four approaches that help us understand human musical behaviors and products in all their richness and complexity, whether a boy playing on a beetle or a Beethoven symphony. Ethnomusicology, the academic discipline that informs this material, is the study of human music making in its cultural context. The kinds of questions that ethnomusicologists ask when confronting music phenomena lead them to finding connections between musical sound and the ways that humans live and organize their lives. Let's examine some of the kinds of questions scholars ask in order to deepen their understanding of the meanings, values, structures, beliefs, and goals that people encode in their music.

We might begin by asking the question, "What is music made of?" This question initiates a process of investigation called **analysis**. This process, so powerful in both science and the humanities, deals with the component elements of musical sound and their interrelationships. Analysis subjects the experience of music to an inquiry into the ways people organize musical sound. What instruments or voices are producing the sound? How can we understand the music we hear in terms of melody, harmony, rhythm, and form? How do these elements relate to each other, and how do they produce such aesthetic qualities as unity, variety, and expressive power? Does a musical style have a grammar like a language? If so, what are the structuring principles that make it recognizable and meaningful to those who use it?

Analysis has its limits for it requires isolating the object of inquiry—music—from its human environment and separating elements that musicians and listeners experience holistically. Music does not exist apart from the people who create, perform, record, experience, and subsidize it. To fully understand music, we must consider it in the **context** of its human environment. Under what circumstances do people sing or play musical instruments or listen to the radio? Who makes music, who listens to it, who pays for it? How and why is it produced and reproduced, taught, remembered, learned, preserved, marketed, etc.? What goes on during music: dancing, eating, exercising, acting, lovemaking, studying, sleeping? The word "context" refers to all these non-musical, social factors that surround musical performance and musical experience.

Analysis and contextual study are powerful tools in understanding music, but are insufficient; at least two other approaches are needed. Because we have defined music as *sounds organized by humans and intended for musical purposes*, we must inquire into these purposes. Music, like other products of the human will and imagination such as poems, pictures, stories, and dramas, is created specifically for the purpose of carrying and conveying **meaning** between and among people. In seeking to understand a song, for instance, we must investigate what feelings, ideas, and values it communicates. What does it mean to those who compose, sing, and respond to it? How does it function as a mode of communication? What messages does it convey? What occasions does it mark? How do song lyrics relate to melody and rhythm? How does music motivate actions, move the body and the emotions, transform consciousness? What does music mean to you as an individual, to us as a society? How might musical forms reflect or symbolize socio-economic organization, modes of religious worship, or the natural environment? How do musical meanings change as contexts change? It is through questions like these that ethnomusicologists seek to "unpack" a musical event to reveal both personal and collective histories, value systems, modes of livelihood, and social structures.

The fourth approach to understanding music deals with **performance**: How do people do it? How and why do they sing songs or play the violin, or participate in or evaluate a performance in the ways that they do? The New Zealand-born **musicologist** and educator Christopher Small proposed replacing the word Music with the verb, "to music," or simply "**musicking**," suggesting that music should be viewed as an act instead of a thing. He explains:

> In that real world where people actually make and listen to music, in concert halls,...in bathrooms and at political rallies, in supermarkets and churches, in record stores and temples, fields and nightclubs, discos and palaces, stadiums and elevators, it is performance that is central to the experience of music.[4]
>
> *To music is to take part, in any capacity, in a musical performance, whether by performing, by listening, by rehearsing or practicing, by providing material for performance (what is called composing), or by dancing.* We might at times even extend its meaning to what the person is doing who takes the tickets at the door or the hefty men who shift the piano and the drums or the roadies who set up the instruments and carry out the sound checks or the cleaners who clean up after everyone else has gone. They, too, are all contributing to the nature of the event that is a musical performance.[5]

In Christopher Small's view, the violinist and the fiddler are musicking, as are the listener, the shopper in the department store, perhaps even the janitor in the stadium sweeping up after the concert. Perhaps even now we are musicking as we write—and you also as you read—this lesson. For Dr. Small, any involvement with music, active or passive, is a kind of performance. To understand music fully, we must take into account the "doing" of it. What human actions bring about, sustain, conclude, and evaluate music? What teaching, learning, composing, rehearsing, and organizing precede a performance? Is it preserved for future performances? How is it preserved, and how does it change as it is notated, recorded, engineered, marketed, sampled, compressed, stored, and played back? What constitutes a good rendition? What is the relationship of a performance or recording to a musical score, template, or ideal? What social relationships are enacted, celebrated, contested, and supported in the processes of performance?

We now have four approaches with which to investigate music in our quest to deepen our understanding of it: analysis, context, meaning, and performance. Intellectual processes of engagement that lead to understanding are open-ended and theoretically infinite. Understanding is never a goal that is ultimately accomplished, but rather a relationship that, once established, may grow over a lifetime. It is the hope that this course will encourage or deepen an already established love of music, one of humanity's most profound and most intimate forms of expression and pleasure.

WHAT IS SOUND?

The fundamental material of music is sound, as in our working definition, *sounds organized by humans and intended for musical purposes*. Therefore we need to understand what sound is and how humans perceive and respond to it. For sound to be present, four conditions are required:

Energy that activates an object
Object that vibrates in an environment
Environment that conducts vibrations to a receiver
Receiver that collects and interprets the vibrations

A singer on a stage provides a simple example. Her muscle and breath power provide the **energy**, which causes her vocal cords, the **object**, to vibrate. The vibrations travel through the **environment**, the atmosphere, and reach the **receiver**, the ears of the audience members, which then channel the vibrations through the hearing system to the brain, where they are recognized and interpreted as musical sounds.

WHAT IS HEARING?

The Ear/Brain system is our primary receiver. Sound waves or vibrations travel into the outer ear, along the ear canal, and through the tympanic membrane (ear drum) into the middle ear. The three connected bones of the middle ear—the malleus (hammer), incus (anvil), and stapes (stirrup)—amplify the force of the vibrations in order for them to pass through the oval window membrane into the more dense fluid in the spiral-shaped cochlea (inner ear). The oval window moves in and out, creating pressure waves that cause hair fibers along the inner ear to vibrate. The vibrating hair fiber cells trigger electrical nerve impulses that then travel along the auditory nerves to the cerebral cortex of the brain. Here is where the real mystery begins as we leave the domain of mechanics and enter the domains of perception and consciousness. It is in the brain that the impulses are interpreted as sounds, and where sound now changes from physical vibrations to psychological information. The manner in which the auditory nerve connects to the brain is much more complicated than the manner in which the eye connects to the frontal lobes. The auditory nerve branches into complex networks of neurons that stimulate the limbic system, balance, the ways we interpret language, fight-and-flight responses, and emotions. It is no wonder that sound provides humans with their most complex channels for communication and interaction with their social and natural environment.

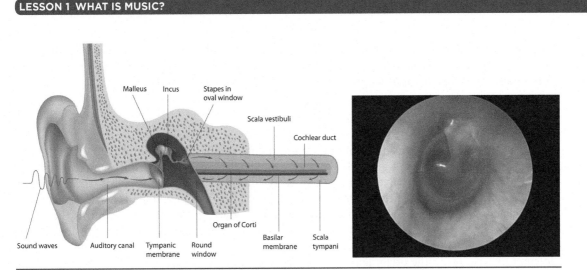

Fig. 1.4   **Diagram of the anatomy of the ear (L), and the human eardrum (R)**

The most important characteristics of sound that our brain distinguishes are:

Volume (amplitude) how loud or soft a sound is
Pitch (frequency) how high or low a sound is
Timbre the quality of a sound
Duration how long a sound lasts

The **volume** of sound can be described subjectively using terms such as "loud" and "soft"; and measured objectively by calculating the physical pressure of sound waves. The scientific measurement of the arc of a vibration measures volume in decibels (dB). A normal speaking voice is approximately 60 dB, while a loud orchestra measures 90–100 dB, and the threshold of human pain is 120–130 dB. Rock concerts can reach a level of 135–140 dB. Long-term exposure to this **decibel** level may cause permanent and irreversible hearing loss.

Pitch too can be described subjectively with terms such as "high" and "low"; and measured objectively by calculating how many times per second an object vibrates through a complete wave cycle. Frequency is measured in cycles per second (cps): the greater the frequency, the higher the pitch. Humans distinguish sounds between approximately 16 cps and 20,000 cps. Animals can hear sounds well beyond 20,000 cps. Most sounds of the world are composites of multiple frequencies, like radio static or white noise. Sounds of a single, measurable frequency—called pitches or tones—are somewhat rare in nature. The sounds many bird species produce, unlike those of most other animals, consist of clear, recognizable pitches. These special sounds, which humans also produce and respond to in many complex ways, are the building blocks of much of the world's music. This is why we attribute "song" to songbirds.

Timbre refers to the tone quality or tone color of a sound. When two sounds of exactly the same volume and pitch are produced, as on a flute and a violin, the difference between the sounds is a difference in timbre. As the object vibrates, it does so as a whole, producing a fundamental tone that the ear hears. The object also vibrates in sections, as two halves, as three thirds, as four quarters, etc. Each of these further vibrations simultaneously produces **overtones**, which are higher and softer than the fundamental tone and are not heard as distinct sounds by the ear. However, the brain interprets these overtones as part of a composite sound with a particular tone quality or timbre. The different sizes, shapes, and materials of musical instruments favor different sets of overtones. The relative strengths and proportions of the overtones in a flute sound, for example, are what determine its characteristic flute timbre. Likewise, a variety of anatomical differences contribute to the uniqueness of each human voice.

Like volume and pitch, the **duration** of a sound can also be described subjectively as in a long or short sound; and objectively as a sonic event measured in minutes and seconds. In the case of music, duration may be described as the time between drum strokes, or in note values such as a quarter note or whole note in Western notation. Another aspect of duration is the decay of a musical tone. A sound may be sustained then abruptly stopped or gradually allowed to decay and dissipate.

CONCLUSION

In this lesson we have provided a definition of music that emphasizes its human and social dimensions, by placing in the foreground the reasons why people engage with artful sound around the world. Unit 1 continues by investigating three more fundamental questions: What is music made of? Where does music come from? and What is music for? Lesson 2 provides a general discussion of the mechanisms that produce musical sound: the human voice and musical instruments. Lesson 3 concerns melody, rhythm, harmony, etc.—the dimensions by which humans organize musical sound. Lesson 4 is also divided into two sections. The first presents myths from a variety of cultures that attempt to account for the origin and presence of music in human experience. The second section discusses music from the perspective of human evolution, presenting theories on why humans are biologically equipped with the capacity to make and respond to musical sound. In Lesson 5 we discuss ten functions of music, which were first identified by anthropologist Alan Merriam. Serving as the "musical purposes" of our definition, these frame the rest of our course material.

KEY CONCEPTS

Defining music cross-culturally	Context	Ear/Brain system
"Music-like" sounds of nature	Meaning	Volume
Analysis	Performance	Pitch
	"Musicking"	Timbre
	Conditions of Sound	Duration

Q THINKING ABOUT MUSIC QUESTIONS

1. Why is music difficult to define? How would *you* define it? What are the strengths and weaknesses of the definition provided by the authors?
2. Consider the example of the Swiss cowherds. Why *is* it music, by our definition? Why *isn't* it music, by our definition?
3. Choose a selection of music that you like and try considering it from each of our four perspectives: Analysis, Context, Meaning, and Performance. Write a few descriptive sentences from each perspective (you may need to do a bit of research). Does this exercise deepen your understanding and appreciation of your selection? How? And if not, why not?
4. Composer Igor Stravinsky said that the sounds of nature are not music, although they are "music-like." What do you think he means by that? Based on the definition of music in Lesson 1, why are the bird songs in Einojuhani Rautavaara's composition *Cantus Arcticus* **music** and not merely "music-like"?
5. Consider Christopher Small's concept of "musicking." Does Small's idea change the way you think of music?

NOTES

1   Charles Keil, *Tiv Song: The Sociology of Art in a Classless Society* (Chicago: University of Chicago Press, 1979), 27.

2   Lewis Rowell, *Music and Musical Thought in Early India* (Chicago: University of Chicago Press, 1998), 9.

3   Peter Gutmann, "John Cage and the Avant-Garde: The Sounds of Silence," *Classical Notes* (1999), http://www.classicalnotes.net/columns/silence.html.

4   Christopher Small, "Musicking: A Ritual in Social Space," (lecture presented at the University of Melbourne, June 6, 1995), http://www.musekids.org/musicking.html.

5   Christopher Small, *Musicking: The Meanings of Performing and Listening* (Middletown, CT: Wesleyan University Press, 1999), 9.

Lesson 2
What is Music Made of?
Voices and Instruments

In Lessons 2 and 3 we explore the major components of musical sound. Here in Lesson 2, we investigate human voices and musical instruments, the means by which musical sounds are produced. Then in Lesson 3, we introduce the concepts by which we analyze music: rhythm, melody, harmony, **texture**, and form.

THE HUMAN VOICE

The primary organ of the human voice is the vocal folds (or cords) located in the larynx or "voice box," which men and some women feel externally as the Adam's apple. We have voluntary control over whether these elastic folds are open or closed. When they are open, we exhale without producing a sound. When they are closed and we force air between them, we produce a sound in the same way that blowing air between two blades of grass produces a buzz. Watch this video clip of the vocal folds vibrating during singing. The amount of air forced through determines the amplitude or loudness of the voice. We also have control over the pitch or frequency of the oscillation by means of a complex neuromuscular mechanism. The sound produced within the larynx is the raw material for both speech and song. Within the mouth the buzzing sound produced by the vocal folds is manipulated and shaped into spoken and musical languages. The sound is then amplified when the vibrations resonate within the nasal and sinus cavities, the mouth itself, and the chest cavity. Thus the human voice is truly a human instrument, consisting of a power source (breath), a vibrator (vocal folds), and a resonator (the oral and chest cavities and sinuses). All humans share this physiology, but there is a great deal of variation in the sounds produced by this apparatus, due both to biological and cultural diversity.

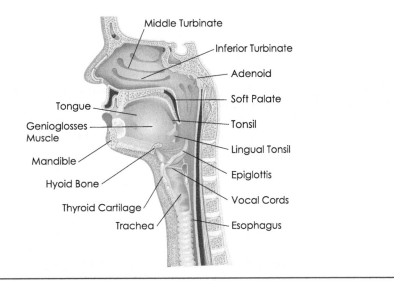

Fig.2.1 **Anatomy of the human vocal apparatus**

DIVERSITY OF HUMAN VOCAL PRODUCTION AND EXPRESSION

Biological Difference

The human voice changes as we grow and develop. There is little difference between the voices of young boys and girls. However, the voices of children are easily differentiated from those of adults, because the smaller vocal folds and resonating chambers produce the timbres or sound qualities that we associate with young voices. The development of the larynx at puberty produces one of the most important human secondary sex characteristics: the differentiated voice. Mature male voices are approximately an octave lower than those of females, because the longer and thicker vocal folds of the male have a lower fundamental frequency. As humans grow older, their vocal folds lose flexibility causing the timbre of their voices to change yet again, into the vocal sound characteristic of senior citizens. Aside from age and gender differences, there is also a great deal of human diversity in terms of anatomical features that affect sound production, such as size and thickness of the skull and vocal tissues, overall stature, lung capacity, etc. Thus there is considerable variance of vocal timbre and pitch both among individuals within a group and among genetically related groups. Characteristic vocal norms are a complex interaction of biological tendencies and socially constructed preferences.

Cultural Difference

The sounds produced by our vocal cords serve as raw material for the qualities of speaking and singing that we learn as children by listening and imitating. Anthropologists call this process of learning "**enculturation**." We use our voices in ways that are considered socially acceptable and "normal" within our families and communities, modifying them according to circumstance or context. We speak with a very different voice in the classroom, for example, than we do at a football game. What is considered normal for speaking and singing differs widely among social groups. Societies tend to favor higher or lower pitches within the normal range of the human voice. High in the Andes Mountains in Peru, Quechua women sing at the top of their vocal range. In this video clip, we see a family of musicians dedicated to preserving the traditional culture of the Andean region, with performances that feature traditional dress, instruments, songs, and dances. The Sioux grass dance songs heard in Native American powwows are sung by men with high-pitched voices in a register that elsewhere would be considered normal for women. Sometimes the voice is stretched beyond its normal range. Tibetan Buddhist monks perform exercises as a religious practice that over years deepen their vocal range. It is with these specially cultivated voices that they recite their sacred scriptures. In Europe in the 17th and 18th centuries, pre-pubescent boys who were recognized for outstanding vocal ability were castrated to preserve the upper (or soprano) range of their voices. These *castrati*, as they were called, sang in the great chapel choirs of the Vatican in Rome, from which women were excluded. There was something of a vogue in 18th-century Spain for the **castrato** voice, and leading roles in **operas** of the time were written for these singers. Where men and women sing together, as in church choirs, the music is divided into parts for high voices (female) and low voices (male). Further subdivision has led to the four standard vocal parts: soprano, alto, tenor, and bass.

 Throughout the world, people have learned to use the vocal apparatus in extraordinary ways. We as humans produce a surprising variety of sounds that are expressive of our identities as members of social groups. Inuit women living near the Arctic Circle make the unique vocal sounds of *katajjaq*, or **throat singing**, as a form of entertainment. In this follow-the-leader game of endurance, the first to laugh or quit is the loser. The sounds the women make imitate those of their natural environment: birds, mosquitoes, wind, and ocean waves. In Lesson 1 we heard the Swiss cattle herders singing in a highly specialized way called *yodeling*, taking advantage of the acoustical properties of their alpine environment. This technique, by which the voice fluctuates between registers, was a popular feature in American country music of the 1930s. Watch this video of the great *Jimmie Rodgers* (1897–1933), the Father of American Country Music, singing the 1928 hit "T for Texas" with his signature yodel. Inscribed on his memorial statue in Meridian, Mississippi, are these words: "His is the music of America. He sang the songs of the people he loved, of a young nation growing strong. His was an America of glistening rails, thundering boxcars, and rain-swept night, of lonesome prairies, great mountains and a high blue sky." Not only the songs he sang, but the quality of his voice, high and lonely, resonated with millions of rural Americans and echoed back to them a sound both authentic and familiar. The quality, or timbre, of a singer's voice carries with it essential aspects of the singer's identity. This love song, sung by an anonymous shepherdess in Tibet, seems to capture and project something essential about her life, her people, and their place in the world. The vocalist sings in a style that was developed out-of-doors in the high plateau of Central Asia, in which singers project their voices into the sky, and court each other across miles of endless grassland.

SPECIALIZATION OF "THE SINGER"

The ability to sing is as universal as the ability to speak. At a baseball game, for instance, everyone is encouraged to participate in the singing of the national anthem for it is assumed that this competence is universally shared. However, often a professional "singer," who has been chosen for her outstanding vocal skill, leads the audience with her amplified voice. Most societies recognize certain individuals for their exceptional vocal ability. Such individuals often receive extensive training from early childhood and cultivate a specialized singing voice that exhibits to an extraordinary degree features that are highly prized within their society, such as volume, range, flexibility, projection, and expressive power. These trained singers serve important roles in ritual, theatrical, and/or entertainment events. In this video, we hear the Reverend Timothy Flemming leading his congregation in an **old time camp meeting song**. Compare his voice with the voices of his church members. This mode of group singing is known as "**call and response**," and metaphorically enacts the role of the preacher as the shepherd leading his flock.

A singing voice, unlike a musical instrument, can convey words; and in the following two examples the verbal skill of the singers, praising a patron or conveying a dramatic narrative, is paramount. In each case a special vocal timbre or color is cultivated to add power to the verbal delivery. The assertive, penetrating voice of **West African praise singer** Diali Cissokho is suited for publicly recounting the genealogies and great deeds of the ancestors of aristocratic families. By the same token, the **Japanese epic narrator** Yoko Hiraoka is trained to produce a high-pitched nasal voice, by which she enthralls her audience with tales of great battles and powerful warlords. In other traditions, Iranian sung poetry for example, following the thread of a narrative is less important than emphasizing particular turns of speech, metaphors, and elevated diction. The voice of this **Iranian classical singer** Afsâne Ziâ'i produces the same intricate and subtle inflections as the accompanying *ney* (flute), which shadows her melodic **improvisation**. Throughout this excerpt, but particularly at 1' 20", the singer ornaments a single syllable in a manner characteristic of this tradition, using a technique called *tahrir*. This level of skill and deep emotional expression are not "natural," but rather require years of training. European operatic singers are trained in a sophisticated pedagogy that is hundreds of years old.

It is characterized by the use of both chest and facial resonance, a careful enunciation of vowels and consonants, a vocal technique called vibrato, the ability to portray a dramatic character through the singing voice, and the projection of the voice into large auditoriums without electronic amplification. In this recording of the tenor **aria** *"Vesti la Giubba"* from Ruggiero Leoncavallo's early 20th-century opera *I Pagliacci* (The Clowns), the character Canio, leader of a circus troupe, has just learned that his wife has been unfaithful. He must now prepare for the afternoon's performance by putting on his clown's makeup and costume. While seated before his mirror, he weeps in anguish, crying "Laugh, Clown, Laugh!" (*Ridi, Pagliaccio!*).

2-4 🔊

MUSICAL INSTRUMENTS

Musical instruments are devices created specifically to produce musical sounds of definite pitch and timbre, and sounds for keeping musical time. *The New Grove Dictionary of Musical Instruments* catalogues more than twelve thousand varieties. Here we highlight both this extraordinary diversity and how few fundamental ways there are for producing musical sound—a vibrating string, reed, skin, or shaped piece of metal or wood. We also examine the diffusion of musical instrument technologies around the world. People have spread these technologies through exploration, trade, conquest, and the global sharing of cultural resources; and have adapted these resources to new purposes and contexts. Sometimes the same instrument goes by different names and is put to very different uses in different cultural settings, like the violin and the **fiddle**, for instance. Musicologist Frank Tenaille, writing about dancehall music of West Africa, states, "Much of modern African music is indebted to the musical instruments of colonization brought over by sailors, soldiers, and missionaries. The bugle, the flügelhorn, the harmonica, the accordion, the banjo, and the harmonium often preceded the teaching of harmony and religious musical education. It was in the bars that these instruments were diverted from their original purposes and adapted to new life."[1] An instrument alone is merely an object. But combined with the skill and knowledge of a human player, it becomes almost a living thing, a voice, a culture bearer, a purveyor of meaning and value, a source of fascination...some would say, an extension of the human soul.

CLASSIFICATION

Classification systems help us understand the enormous variety of musical instruments that exist in our world, and enable us to make comparisons across time and across cultures. They also serve as essential tools for instrument collectors, museum curators, organologists (musical instrument scholars), musicologists, ethnomusicologists, and anthropologists.

You may be familiar with the way instruments of the symphony orchestra are grouped into four main classes:

Woodwinds	piccolo, flute, clarinet, oboe, bassoon
Brass	trumpet, trombone, French horn, tuba
Strings (bowed/plucked)	violin, viola, cello, double bass
Percussion (pitched/unpitched)	cymbals, triangle, timpani, bass drum

In ancient China, musical instruments were classified into eight groups according to the material of which they were made:

Metal	bronze bell, gong
Stone	stone chime
Silk	long zither (with silk strings), bowed fiddle
Bamboo	flute, panpipe
Gourd	mouth organ (bamboo pipes inserted in gourd chamber)
Leather	drum
Clay	ocarina (globular flute), clay pot
Wood	tiger-shaped wooden scraper, woodblock

Fig. 2.2 **Western Symphony Orchestra**

Fig. 2.3 **Ancient Chinese bronze bell chime (L), and Korean traditional orchestra with flutes and stone chime (R)**

The impressive sets of tuned stone and bell chimes that were once part of the ancient court ensemble are no longer played in China (except at tourist venues on modern reproductions), but they are still heard in Korea. In this video from the **National** *Gugak* (traditional music) **Center** in Seoul, you can see examples from a number of the instrument categories: the aforementioned **bell** and stone chimes, silk-stringed zithers and fiddles, bamboo flutes, leather-headed drums, and wooden clappers. Missing are the gourd and clay instruments that completed the traditional ensemble. In the ancient Chinese and Korean courts, the belief was held that when instruments constructed from this variety of materials played together harmoniously in court rituals, their music harmonized the ruling family with the cosmos and the common people.

In the early 20th century, two German scholars, Curt Sachs and Erich Moritz von Hornbostel, developed an elaborate instrument classification system based upon a 2000-year old Indian treatise on drama, music, and dance, the *Natya Shastra*. The **Sachs-Hornbostel** system is based on the means by which sound is produced, and has four major classes, each of which is further subdivided into many subcategories. It has since been widely adopted by organologists, ethnomusicologists, and others.

Chordophones	sound produced by a vibrating string
Aerophones	sound produced by a vibrating column of air
Membranophones	sound produced by a vibrating drum head
Idiophones	sound produced by the material itself vibrating

In 1940 Sachs added a fifth category:

Electrophones	sound produced electronically, and now digitally

While classifying instruments into categories and subcategories has been useful to scholars interested in their historical development, diffusion, adaptation, and structure, such analytical methods may take us away from what musicians find most significant about musical instruments. Jan Mrázek, a Czech musicologist, wrote of his instrumental studies in Thailand and Indonesia:

> I realized that the "standard" scholarly descriptions and classifications of musical instruments—which I learnt first as a teenager studying violin at the Prague Conservatory, and then again a number of times later—are not just unsatisfactory for my purposes, but are in direct conflict with my own experience of what are musical instruments: in separating the instruments from human experience, human bodies, feelings, imaginations, worlds, and applying "universal" methods of "identifying" them, all that I feel is important is methodically ignored. Where are the joy and pain of learning to play an instrument; the feel of the instrument in my hand, as it gives me a magical power to enter the realm of music and opens up for me a whole field of possibilities; the intimate, physical, life-long bond between the musician and his instrument; the respect and gratitude for my teacher for making me suffer through learning; the atmosphere, excitement, magic of being part of a performance? Each kind of instrument is different, not primarily because of what vibrates in or on the instrument (as the standard classification would lead us to believe), but because each grows from and into human lives and worlds differently. Where are these differences between instruments, the different experiences they make possible, the different ways in which they extend and empower human bodies, the different feelings they evoke, the different roles they play in people's lives and in their world, the different associations they accumulate?[2]

In the following catalogue of world instruments, we have tried to strike a balance between the descriptions of the physical objects themselves, and how and why instruments are played by musicians, along with what meanings they hold for them and their audiences.

CHORDOPHONES

Among the many types of **chordophone** are **musical bows** (like a hunting bow), harps (with strings perpendicular to the instrument soundboard), zithers (strings parallel to the soundboard), lutes (strings parallel to a sound box and neck, played with fingers), and fiddles (strings parallel to a sound box and neck, played with a bow).

The strings of chordophones may be set in motion by striking, plucking, bowing, or rubbing. That there were no **indigenous** chordophones used by the native peoples of the Western Hemisphere or Australia suggests that of the four categories of acoustic instruments these developed last. One can imagine the discovery of the sound possibilities of a string under tension coming from the twang of the hunting bow. Perhaps around a campfire at night, our hunter-ancestor related the story of how the game was brought down, accompanying himself by plucking on the bowstring used to shoot the killing arrow. Hunters may have discovered that placing the end of the bow frame against the teeth greatly amplified the sound of the instrument, the mouth serving as a resonating chamber. A hole in the ground, a gourd, or a clay pot attached to the bow served the same function. The !Kung of the Kalahari Desert in southwest Africa used a resonator made from an ostrich egg.

In this video, Chris Haambwiila of Zambia plays a musical bow known as *kalumbu,* accompanying a traditional song. The musical bow from southern Africa was brought to Brazil during the Atlantic slave trade. Known there as the *berimbau,* it became incorporated into a popular Afro-Brazilian martial art called *capoeira,* providing the beat patterns that coordinate the moves of the martial artists.

Harps and Lyres

 Harps and **lyres** have strings stretched perpendicular to the soundboard. Two or three strings of different lengths added to the frame of a bow produced the first **harps.** Harps today exist in a proliferation of forms, from the Celtic **harps** of the Irish that have a lever system to alter the pitch of each string half a step, to the concert grand harps of the Western symphony orchestra with elaborate pedal mechanisms for changing the pitches. The Spanish brought harps to South America where they became popular folk instruments among the indigenous peoples of the Andes regions and elsewhere. The harp is the **national instrument of Paraguay** and Venezuela. In Asia, the largest and most populous continent, all indigenous harps have fallen into disuse, except in Myanmar, where the **Burmese harp** (*saung gauk*) accompanies refined and courtly forms of sung poetry.

Attaching the strings to a yoke—two arms and a crossbar—above the resonating chamber produces a lyre, the instrument the ancient Greeks associated with the god Apollo and the mythical singer Orpheus (See Lesson 4, p. 53; and Lesson 14, p. 212). In this video you can see representations  of the lyre in pottery and sculpture, and hear the sound of a modern replica.[3] Both harps and lyres are abundant throughout Africa. An example of an African lyre is the Ethiopian *krar.* It has the lead role in both traditional and popular ensembles. In this video, an electronically amplified *krar* is heard in a band that plays nightly at a tourist restaurant in Addis Ababa. The *kora* of Mali, Senegal, and The Gambia is a hybrid harp-lute that combines the "one string per pitch" characteristic of the harp with the lute neck, from which the strings are suspended. It is associated with praise singers (*jalolu*) which we will be studying in Lesson 13.

Lutes

Instruments of the lute family have strings stretched along a neck and parallel to the surface of a resonating chamber. The word "**lute**" derives from the Arabic word *al ud* (literally, "wood"), the name of an instrument popular in the Middle East, known by virtuoso practitioners as "The King of Musical Instruments." The modern *ud* has a smooth fingerboard like the violin, which allows the player to bend pitches and glide continuously from one pitch to another. Many types of lute, however, are fitted with raised frets or bars on the fingerboard that control pitch. Instruments of this type are called *tar* and *setar* in Iran, *sitar* in India, and *guitar* in Spain—names indicating a common ancestry by the final syllable *tar,* meaning "string." The *sitar* and other plucked lutes of India have **sympathetic strings** for increased resonance, like the *sarangi* (bowed fiddle) discussed below. The

Fig. 2.4   **Harps from Paraguay (*harpa*) (L), and Myanmar (*saung gauk*) (R)**

dutar ("two strings" in Farsi) is played throughout Central Asia. These long-necked fretted lutes with pear-shaped sound chambers are especially associated with women in the Fergana Valley of Eastern Uzbekistan and Tajikistan. In China, reaching the eastern end of the Silk Road trade routes, the lute became known as the *pipa*. In this video, modern *pipa* virtuoso Wu Man plays an original composition.

Portuguese traders to the Spice Islands brought small four-stringed lutes with them on their voyages, and native Hawaiians adapted them to accompany songs and hula dances, calling the instrument *ukulele* meaning "leaping flea." Similarly, the Spanish conquistadors brought fretted lutes to the New World where they were adapted to new hybrid forms by colonists and indigenous peoples. In the Andes of Bolivia and Peru, the small *charango* is the national instrument. Its body was traditionally made from the hard shell of the armadillo, although more recently most are carved from wood.

Lutes in West Africa, such as the *akonting* in Senegal and The Gambia, were made out of gourd resonators covered with skin to increase resonance. These were brought by slaves to the New World where the instrument took the fretted neck of the guitar and the name banjo. In China, the *sanxian*, a long-necked fretless lute, has python skin covering the resonating chamber. This instrument is popular with blind storytellers (discussed in Lesson 13 below). Its derivative in Japan, the *shamisen*, has delicate cat skin for resonance in the finest models.

Fig. 2.5   North Indian *sitar* (L), and Chinese *pipa* (R)

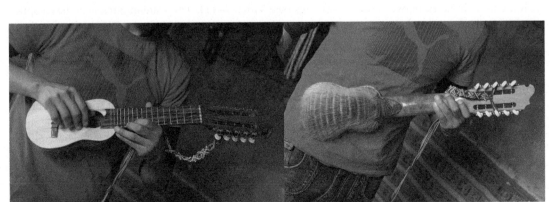

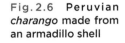

Fig. 2.6 Peruvian *charango* made from an armadillo shell

Fig. 2.7   Senegalese *akonting* (L); blind Chinese storyteller with *sanxian* (C); and Japanese *shamisen* (R)

The lute family of chordophones is perhaps the most dramatic example of the diffusion of a musical technology, and the guitar is the most widespread lute within this family. The acoustic classical guitar as we now know it was developed in mid 19th-century Spain. More portable than the harp or the piano, and able to sound multiple simultaneous pitches, the guitar owes much of its extraordinary adaptability to the spread of chordal harmony and popular song styles. The guitar has proven to be one of the world's most versatile instruments, used to accompany dances, serenades, church services, and campfire sing-alongs. Among the great guitarists of the 20th century are Andres Segovia in Spain, Django Reinhardt in Belgium, Ali Farka Toure and Habib Koite in Mali, **Sergio and Odair Assad** in Brazil, and the list goes on. Efforts to produce instruments loud enough to compete with the saxophones and horns of the dance band led to experimental models of the modern electric guitar, developed in the 1920s. The first successful solid-body model to be put on the market was designed in 1950 by Leo Fender, whose name is still associated with the instrument. It has become a staple of popular music the world over. **Jimi Hendrix**, one of the great innovators on the electric guitar, made use not only of amplification of the strings via electronic pickups but also pedal-controlled distortion and feedback effects. Thus, his guitar became a hybrid chordophone-electrophone. Popular genres that grew out of African American song and dance forms of the early 20th century, like blues and jazz, influenced a worldwide renaissance of electric guitar playing in the late 20th century with rock and heavy metal.

Fiddles

The fiddle, with its horsehair bow, was an invention of the horsemen of the Central Asian steppes, from where it spread west through Arabic lands to Europe by 1000 CE and east to China around the same time. Unlike plucked chordophones, fiddles are capable of imitating the human voice because the bow can sustain a sound. The Chinese named the bowed fiddle *huqin*, literally "barbarian instrument" referring to its origin outside of China, and the most popular variety today is the *erhu* played with the bow threaded between the two strings (see Video 5–11). The Iranian *kamanche* has a spike attached to its lower end that supports the instrument on the player's knee. The violin family is a product of Renaissance Italy (early 16th century), where instrument families at that time were designed with a single basic form but of different sizes to match and support the full range of human singing voices. The **string quartet**—two violins, a viola, and a cello—has inspired some of the greatest European composers to write music for this ensemble. The violin (often called a "fiddle" when used to play folk or popular music) has spread throughout the world. It is the dominant instrument of the Western symphony orchestra, a leading instrument in Irish and Scottish dance music, and the most important accompanying instrument in **Karnatak** classical vocal music in South India. The violinist holds his instrument under the chin in the symphony orchestra; the fiddler holds the instrument in several ways, perhaps resting on the arm in an Irish session, or against the ribcage in a Louisiana **zydeco** band. The violinist in South India supports the scroll on her foot as she sits cross-legged on

Fig. 2.8 **Chinese *erhu* (L), and North Indian *sarangi* (R)**

the floor, and the Moroccan wedding musician holds the instrument (in this video a viola, known as *kamanja*) vertically by the neck. In the hands of each of these musicians, the violin tells a different story.

Also from India is a fiddle that uses a very different means for increasing resonance and volume. The *sarangi* (its name meaning "one hundred colors") is carved from a single piece of wood, the body covered by a skin or parchment membrane like a banjo. It has three thick melody strings that are bowed, and forty sympathetic strings positioned beneath the playing strings that enrich the overall sound when set in motion by the bowed strings above. The left hand stops the melody strings not with the fingertips but the cuticles, sliding the fingernails along the strings to produce nuances that imitate the human voice. The playing technique is extremely difficult to acquire and takes years to master.

Zithers

Zithers are chordophones whose strings are stretched across the top of the resonating chamber. They are found in various forms throughout the world. Box zithers originated in ancient Persia, spread east and west along trade routes, and today are widely distributed. They have been adopted into the art music of Iran (*santur*), and in folk traditions in Greece (*santouri*) and Hungary (*cimbalom*). During the Ming Dynasty (1368–1644) the instrument entered China, where it is called *yangqin* or "foreign instrument." One can frequently see street musicians playing these in Shanghai or Beijing. In Egypt and Turkey, the *qanun* is plucked with the fingers rather than being struck with hammers. The hammered dulcimer is a box zither popular in rural Appalachian regions of North America. In Europe, keyboard mechanisms were used by the late 1300s. During the Renaissance (ca. 1400–1600), the **harpsichord** became an important solo instrument played throughout the courts of Europe. It worked by means of a feather quill or leather pick plucking the string when a key was depressed. Bartolomeo Cristofiori (1655–1732), an instrument master for the Medici family in Florence, Italy, invented the piano (an abbreviation of "pianoforte") around 1700. His hammer mechanism resulted in a revolutionary instrument whose most innovative features were its ability to play both loud (*forte*) and soft (*piano*) sounds, depending on the force with which the keys were pressed, and its ability to sustain sounds by means of foot pedals.

Fig. 2.9   Iranian *santur* (L), and Vietnamese *dan tranh* (R)

The most common form in East Asia is the long board zither, which is not indigenous to any other world region. China had board zithers by at least 1500 BCE. The *guqin*, a board zither without bridges, was played by gentlemen scholars and government officials as a form of meditation and inner refinement—seldom for an audience. It was suppressed during the Chinese **Cultural Revolution** (1966–1976) because of this association with the feudal aristocracy, but is now making a comeback. A popular Chinese board zither, the *guzheng*, on which the strings are stretched over bridges, was associated with female entertainers, as was the Korean *kayagum* and Japanese *koto* (see Video 3–35). The Korean *ajaeng* is the only board zither played with a bow, and performs in numerous instrumental ensembles including those that accompany shamanic rituals (see Video 3–20). The Vietnamese *dan tranh,* played with finger picks, is used to accompany dramas and poetry recitals as well as in chamber groups and orchestras. Throughout East Asia, these instruments are associated with tradition and elegance; one often hears them today played in theaters and teahouses.

AEROPHONES

Free Aerophones

The simplest **aerophones** are those that produce sounds in air unconfined by a chamber, such as sirens and bullroarers. The bullroarer is a thin elliptical piece of wood attached to a string, swung around in the air and producing a distinct humming sound. Prehistoric cave paintings in Africa depict rituals involving the use of bullroarers; examples made of reindeer antlers, found in France, are believed to be more than 12,000 years old. The bullroarer is now most often associated with Australian Aborigines who use it in funerals and initiation ceremonies.

Flutes

Most other **aerophones** consist of a tube or vessel in which the air is excited by various means. Directing the flow of air against an edge of a surface, splitting the air current, produces a whistling sound. This is why the wind whistles as it blows against the corner of a building. Blowing on a soda bottle also produces sound in this manner. A **flute** works by directing the air current across an edge near the end of the tube; covering and uncovering the holes drilled into the tube changes the pitch of the instrument by changing the length of the vibrating air column. Archeological remains of flutes made of bone, tusk, and antler are among the oldest musical instruments. The fragment of what may be a flute made of the femur of a bear, dated at more than 40,000 years old, was found in a Neanderthal campsite in Slovenia. A 9000-year-old flute made of a bird bone found in a cave in China is fully playable, its pitches corresponding to the familiar "do-re-mi" of the Western major scale. Of course, the kind of music that musicians played on these instruments can only be imagined.

Worldwide, there are currently thousands of varieties of flutes. The Native peoples of North America have played wooden flutes for many generations. As with the Western concert flute, wooden and bamboo flutes in South Asia are held horizontally. The Hindu God Krishna is often depicted

Fig. 2.10   Krishna playing his flute under the sacred Kadamba tree. Illustrated page from Gita Govinda manuscript, India, 1790

playing a *bansuri*, surrounded by cows and dairymaids in a pastoral setting. The beauty of His flute music is symbolic of the spellbinding attraction He exerts upon His devotees. The side-blown *ney* of Turkey, Iran, and the Arabic world also has religious functions and associations; for the poet Rumi, its voice is that of the human soul longing to be reunited with the divine. The Japanese *shakuhachi* is an end-blown flute with a straight edge cut on the mouthpiece to split the air current. Buddhist monks have used the instrument to develop breath control and endurance while meditating upon its sound. The Irish pennywhistle and European recorder have a fipple (like a police whistle) at the mouth end that directs the air current against a sharp edge. There are also double and triple flutes, with one or more tubes producing a **drone** pitch, and even nose flutes from Hawaii held against the nostril. Like the lutes, flutes are found throughout the world; but unlike the lutes, their universal diffusion is due as much to independent invention as to cultural dissemination.

Panpipes and Ocarinas

Greek myth tells of the god Pan's love for the nymph Syrinx, who captivated him by the beauty of her singing. To avoid his advances, she sought protection from the river nymphs who transformed her into a hollow reed. Yet when the wind blew across the river, Pan could still hear her voice now emanating from the reeds. Distraught by his loss, Pan cut the reeds into descending lengths and tied them together to make an instrument that was thereafter associated with him: the **panpipes**, known as *syrinx* by the Greeks. The Quechua and Aymara people of the

Fig. 2.11 **North Indian side-blown** *bansuri* **(L); Japanese end-blown** *shakuhachi* **(C); and Lebanese oblique-blown** *ney* **(R)**

Andes Mountains developed ensembles of variously tuned panpipes (*zampoñas*). In Peru, "While modern panpipes...may offer a complete scale allowing solo performance, traditional models are played in pairs, as described by sixteenth-century chroniclers. The pipes share the melody, each with alternate notes of a whole scale so that two or more players are needed to pick out a single tune using a **hocket** technique. Usually one player leads and the other follows. While symbolically this demonstrates reciprocity within the community, practically it enables players to play for a long time without getting too 'high' from dizziness caused by over-breathing."[4] In Uganda, panpipes (*enkwanzi*) form part of instrumental ensembles, playing short repeating melodic-rhythmic phrases. In this video, we see the instrument being tuned by moving a wax plug up or down inside the tubes. Globular flutes, popularly known as ocarinas, are made of clay pottery or other materials, and have been in existence for at least twelve thousand years. They were found in the New World by Cortez during his conquest of Mexico and brought back to Europe. The Chinese **ocarina** (*xun*) was used in court rituals more than 2000 years ago. As stated above, these court rituals required the harmonious sounds of instruments made from a variety of materials, the *xun* representing the instrument category of earth or pottery. In 1998, Nintendo released its fifth video game in the *Legend of Zelda* series. According to a 1999 article in the *New York Times*,

> The new Nintendo video game, Legend of Zelda: Ocarina of Time, is on pace to become one of the best-selling video games ever. And its popularity seems to have spawned another craze—demand for real ocarinas, those flute-like musical instruments that look like sweet potatoes with finger holes.[5]

Oboes and Bagpipes

Many people are familiar with the sounds that can be made by blowing on a blade of grass or a leaf held between the thumbs and fingers. This demonstrates the basic principle of the type of aerophone that uses one or two thin pieces of reed mounted at the end of a tube to produce vibrations, as in the clarinet (single reed) or **oboe** (double reed). The English word "shawm" is often used to denote double-reed aerophones, and the term is related etymologically to the Turkish *zurna*, the Indian *shehnai*, and the Chinese *suona,* demonstrating how widely dispersed these instruments are. In Korea, the short wooden *taepyongso* has a flaring brass bell and a short double reed held in the mouth of the performer. It is the loudest of Korean instruments and was used in military processions in the absence of indigenous brass instruments other than simple tubes. The *nadaswaram* in South India is played by ritual musician-specialists at weddings and temple festivals, usually

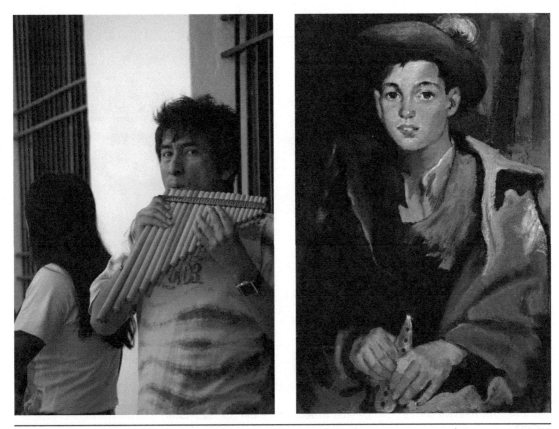

Fig. 2.12 Andean panpipes (L), and *Suonatore di ocarina* ("Ocarina player"), Attilio Polato, ca. 1930 (R)

Fig. 2.13 Turkish *zurna* with frame drum (L), and South Indian *nadaswaram* (R)

accompanied by drums (*tavil*). In this video, guest musicians from Chennai participate in the 5th Annual *Brahmothsavam*, a cleansing ceremony in honor of the Hindu God of Creation, Brahma, at the Venkateswaram Temple in Cary, North Carolina. In central and western China, where the long *suona* accompanies festive celebrations as well as funeral processions, the players use a technique called **circular breathing** to sustain the airflow through the instrument while taking in air, using the cheeks to store a constant air supply.

2-44

Fig. 2.14 *The Peasant Dance* (1567), Pieter Bruegel the Elder (ca.1525–1569), Kunsthistorisches Museum, Vienna

The sheepskin or pig's bladder of European bagpipes makes circular breathing unnecessary. Two methods developed in Europe to keep the bag filled with air; the Irish uilleann pipes employ a bellows system that the player pumps with the arm, and for most other bagpipes, the player blows into a mouthpiece to maintain sufficient air pressure while squeezing the bag to provide a constant airflow. At least two pipes emerge from the bag besides the mouthpiece. One is the chanter pipe that has finger holes for changing pitches and playing melodies. The other pipe (or pipes) provide a steady drone accompaniment that we will discuss in Lesson 3. In this video we see a replica of a medieval *cornamusa* (Italian bagpipe) with a single drone, played by its maker, Luca Paciaroni. Bagpipes were made in many regional styles during the Middle Ages, and were the party instruments of choice, as seen in this famous 16th-century painting by Pieter Bruegel the Elder. They were loud enough to keep a whole field full of revelers dancing.

Clarinets

Clarinets are aerophones with a single reed mounted in a mouthpiece. In Sardinia, triple-pipe clarinets (*launeddas*) have been played for more than 2000 years. The *pungi*, a double-pipe **clarinet** with gourd resonator, is used in India to captivate cobras and tourists alike. The reed in most ancient varieties of clarinet, including the *launeddas* and *pungi*, is made of the same material as the pipe, whether wood, bamboo, or river reed. For instance, the Lithuanian *birbynė* consists of a hollow reed with two or three finger holes and a strip cut into the top that vibrates when the reed is blown. Instruments of this kind were played by pre-Columbian indigenous peoples of both North and South America. Throughout northwest Africa, single-reed aerophones are made from a hollowed-out stalk of sorghum inserted into a gourd resonator. The hornpipe of the British Isles has a body of cowhorn to which a mouthpiece holding the reed is attached. The European clarinet was fitted with metal keys to increase the range and ease of playing during the 18th century, and this version of the family has had widespread adaptations.

Fig. 2.15 Sardinian *launeddas* (L); Indian *pungi* (C); Eastern European Roma (gypsy) clarinet (R)

Particularly in Eastern Europe and the Middle East, it often plays a predominant role in wedding and dance ensembles, as in the klezmer ensemble associated with the Jews of Southeastern Europe.

Free Reed

The **free reed**, or flexible metal tongue, was a musical technology developed more than three thousand years ago in China, and is used in "mouth organs" throughout the world. In East Asia, mouth organs

consist of a set of bamboo "pipes" of varying lengths each fitted with a metal reed and all secured together in a gourd or hardwood wind chest. The free reeds vibrate when a player inhales or exhales air through a mouth hole in the wind chest and simultaneously covers the finger hole of each pipe that the player wishes to sound. If a hole is left open, no sound is produced. In China, the *sheng* has a documented history dating back to 1100 BCE, and has been used both in instrumental ensembles and to accompany Chinese opera. In the highlands of Laos and northern Thailand, the *khaen* is used both for social functions and in religious rituals for inducing trance in spirit mediums. The video shows the legendary blind master musician Sombat Simlah in the Thai province of Maha Sarakham. The technology was brought to Europe in the 19th century and made possible the development of the accordion, the harmonium or reed organ, and the harmonica. In our current age of **globalization**, music unites the ancient and the modern in this concert of free-reed aerophones, the Chinese *sheng* and accordion.

Fig. 2.16 **Chinese *sheng***

Fig. 2.17   South Asian harmonium (L); Roma piano accordion player in Italy (C); Cajun button accordion (R)

Harmonium reed organs were once very popular in Europe and its colonies, and in North America. They were smaller and lighter than the piano and more durable in tropical weather. Two foot pedals activated the bellows that kept the air stream flowing. Before the development of the electronic organs of today, harmoniums were often used in small rural churches that couldn't afford a pipe organ. In India, missionaries introduced French hand-pumped harmoniums in the mid-19th century. There they became the most popular accompanying instrument for vocal music. We will meet them later on in Lesson 10.

The accordion was first patented by an Austrian instrument maker, Cyrill Demian, in 1829. Because it was loud and highly portable, the accordion spread throughout the world with European missionaries, colonizers, and immigrants. Soldiers of the Red Army brought the piano accordion to China where its association with the Working Class led to its use in Communist Party rallies and demonstrations. As the *bandoneon*, the button accordion is the instrument of choice for the Argentine tango (see Video 7–3, p. 98). In Irish sessions, musicians play the button accordion and the concertina, and the button accordion is also a favorite of Cajun musicians in Louisiana.

2-51

The modern church organ is perhaps the world's most complex form of aerophone, using electric bellows to force air though a variety of pipes, each set of pipes producing a characteristic and consistent timbre. Watch this video clip of the great American organist Virgil Fox playing the six ivory keyboards of the **Wanamaker Organ** in Philadelphia.

2-52

Trumpets and Horns

The Western orchestral category of "brass" instruments is included in the aerophone family because the buzzing of the performer's lips causes the air column enclosed in the brass tube to vibrate. The Australian didgeridoo is a natural wooden **trumpet** made of a trunk or limb of eucalyptus wood that has been hollowed out by termites. In many parts of the world, the end of a conch shell is cut off and the hole is placed against the lips to create a conch trumpet. In Tibet, far from the ocean in the center of the high Asian Plateau, conch shells (*dung-dkar*) have been used for both ritual purposes and signaling. Buddhist monks play conch shells in pairs from the tops of monasteries or nearby hillsides to invite the public to religious ceremonies, and the sound symbolizes the proclamation of Buddhist law to the world as the players face each of the four directions in turn. Ritual use of the *dung-dkar* in Tibet predates the introduction of Buddhism, for **shamans** in the Bon religion used conch shells to summon spirits "to help grow cattle or food and even banish evil spirits that caused illness and destruction."[6] The long telescopic metal trumpet *dung-chen* serves ritual purposes and accompanies ceremonial dances in Tibet and Ladakh (northern India) and in the Himalayan Kingdom of Bhutan.

2-53

The Ancient Romans developed brass tubes to use in military processions. These instruments produced only the pitches of the natural harmonics. In the Middle Ages, a slide was added to the tube so that pitches in addition to the harmonics could be played. This instrument, called the sackbut, is the predecessor of the modern trombone, and like the instruments of the violin family it was made in various sizes. In the 19th century, piston and rotary valves were fitted onto brass instruments such

Fig. 2.18   **Tibetan trumpets: conch** *dung-dkar* **(L) and metal** *dung-chen* **(R)**

as the French horn. These opened the airstream to additional lengths of tubing, further increasing the number of pitches the instruments could produce. The modern symphony orchestra has a full complement of trumpets, trombones, French horns, and a tuba. Other brass aerophones—cornet, baritone, flugelhorn, and euphonium—may be heard in this video of the North Carolina Brass Band. While the slide of the sackbut and, later, valves made brass instruments more versatile, the valveless bugle still serves important military functions as it has for centuries. Soldiers for generations have known the bugle calls from camp life, signaling "wake up," "chow time," etc. Bugle calls that could be heard above the fray on the battlefield announced "advance" and "retreat." At military funerals, the sound of the bugle honors the fallen. In this 1963 video that was broadcast around the world, U.S. Army bandsman Keith C. Clark plays the bugle at Arlington National Cemetery for the funeral of President John F. Kennedy, who had been assassinated three days earlier in Dallas, Texas.

Beginning in the 18th century, military units began to enlist and support ensembles of brass and percussion instruments to play for formation drills and ceremonial events. Napoleon believed that martial music was extremely important in maintaining the morale of his troops and he supported the Paris Conservatory in the training of young musicians for this reason. Governments around the world have since encouraged the establishment of wind bands, modeled after European military bands, to play for state occasions. In New Orleans, brass instruments from Navy bands were taken up by street entertainers and in the early 20th century became the instruments associated with Dixieland jazz. Louis Armstrong, the father of jazz improvisation, developed his signature style on the trumpet.

MEMBRANOPHONES

The term "**membranophone**" describes instruments on which musical sound is produced by striking or rubbing a stretched membrane. Generically called "drums," these instruments are distributed worldwide and are classified by the number of membranes (single- or double-headed) and by the shape of the resonating body (goblet, cylindrical, conical, barrel, hourglass, frame, etc.). Within these groups, some drums produce specific pitches and are tunable, like the timpani of the Western orchestra and the *tabla* and *mrdangam* of India. The timpani can be tuned two ways, by tightening or loosening the drum head with screws placed around its circumference, or manipulating a pedal device that does the same thing, but more quickly. An orchestra generally employs a set of two or three, which usually serve an accompanying role, supporting the bass of the harmony. However, this video shows Randy Max performing a rare timpani concerto. In Myanmar (Burma), the *pat waing* (literally "drum circle") is a set of twenty-one tuned barrel drums that hang inside a circular frame on which

Fig. 2.19   **Indian *tabla* drum pair (L); West African *djembe* (C); and Korean *changgo* (R)**

a performer can play melodic compositions. Drums are fine tuned with a tuning paste called *pat sa* (literally "drum food") that may be added or removed to raise or lower the drum's pitch for playing in different modes or scales. The *pat waing* is the lead instrument of the *hsaing waing* ensemble. On the "**talking drum**" in West Africa, players apply pressure to the strings that tie the drumheads to the body, stretching and loosening the membranes to obtain varying pitches. The drum's pitch inflections mimic the inflections of spoken language.

Most drums are not tuned to specific pitches and their role is primarily rhythmic. Goblet hand drums like the *derbake* are found throughout North Africa and the Near East, and are now played in many other parts of the world, due to the widespread interest in world music and dance. The performer in the video, Jussef Bichara, teaches at a dance school in Chile. The West African *djembe* is enjoying worldwide popularity. It is used as the lead drum in an ensemble that includes at least three cylindrical or barrel drums of varying size. These drums set up repeating rhythmic patterns while the lead *djembe* drummer plays intricate improvised variations, frequently responding to the movements of dancers.

Hourglass-shaped drums are found across Asia. In the Far East, they are associated with Buddhist ritual and theater. The large *changgo* hourglass drum of Korea is used in nearly every form of Korean musical performance. In court music, a delicate wand of bamboo strikes the right drumhead made of dog skin or horsehide while the open left hand taps the thicker left side made of cow skin. Many styles of folk song, like *chapka* (long narrative ballads about nature or the glories of the Buddha), use the *changgo* as rhythmic accompaniment, much as the guitar provides harmonic or chordal accompaniment in the West. In folk music, the *changgo* is often played standing up, with the bamboo wand in the right hand and a wooden mallet in the left. The instrument is tied to the body and the player dances gracefully while playing.

Cylindrical drums are played throughout the world and date back to prehistoric times. They were and are the most important instruments of the native peoples of North America. At **powwow** ceremonies, large double-headed cylindrical drums are set on the ground and played communally by groups of men, usually as accompaniment to dance. The Turkish *daul* or *davul* has two heads strung together with zigzag lacing, like similar bass drums in Greece, Albania, and several Middle Eastern countries. When played for outdoor dancing and in processions, the *daul* is almost always paired with the double-reed aerophone, the *zurna*. Cylindrical drums are particularly widespread in Western music, ranging from the bass drum of classical symphony orchestras and marching bands to the trap set in rock bands. Cylindrical in shape but classified separately by Sachs and Hornbostel, the single-headed frame drum is usually shallow and made of thin wood that provides little resonance when the membrane is struck. Frame drums are used in religious rituals by Shiite Muslims in Iran and Afghanistan, and by the Inuit of northern Alaska. Here the great percussionist **Glen Velez** demonstrates what is possible on this simple instrument. The tambourine, such as the Brazilian *pandeiro*, is a composite instrument: a frame drum combined with metal discs or jingles, which are **idiophones**.

Nowhere on earth is the variety of membranophones greater than in Africa, where they form an integral accompaniment to many forms of social and religious practice. Because the same or similar

Fig. 2. 20   Native American powwow drum (L), and Inuit frame drum (R)

drums can have different names in different tribal languages, classification can be quite bewildering. The world-renowned African ethnomusicologist Kwabena Nketia notes:

> There are bottle-shaped, cylindrical, conical, and goblet or hourglass drums. There are single- and double-headed drums; closed and open; tuned and untuned drums. There are those drums that are covered by ox hide and others covered by lizard, calf, or apron skins. Some are played with sticks and others with bare hands. There are drums with and without jingles and buzzers attached to the membrane. There are small, medium-sized, and very big drums. The diversity of tribes, languages, and musical systems is enormous; each tribe, each language group has a name for every instrument.[7]

In many parts of Sub-Saharan Africa, social and ritual occasions without drums are inconceivable. The African diaspora brought the richness of African percussion to the New World. While in most of North America, the drumming culture of the West African slaves was suppressed, in much of the Caribbean and South America, African percussion-based music was free to develop. Barrel drums called *congas*, derived from West African models, are the heart of Puerto Rican *salsa* and Cuban *rhumba* dance rhythms. In Africa barrel drums were fashioned out of logs, but in the New World they were made from barrel staves. Many forms of popular music that developed during the 20th century in the Americas and spread throughout the world are based on this rich rhythmic heritage.

2-64

IDIOPHONES

The fourth Sachs-Hornbostel instrument category is the most diverse. Idiophones are musical instruments whose materials themselves vibrate; the instrument's form contributes to its resonance and amplification. The word literally means "self-sounding." Ordinary tools, vessels, and weapons have been used to produce sounds and rhythms for festivals, rituals, and other occasions. In these special circumstances they become idiophones; however, producing musical sound is not their primary function. This category comprises instruments that produce a fixed pitch: bells, chimes, xylophones, thumb pianos, gongs, etc.; and instruments that produce indefinite pitch: woodblocks, scrapers, shakers (castanets, maracas, rattles), cymbals, etc.

Idiophones throughout the world are often used for signaling or other purposes on the borders of our concept of music. Consider the cowbells in Lesson 1, for example. Edgar Allan Poe's famous poem "The Bells" describes church bells pealing with joy for weddings or tolling the passing of a funeral procession, and alarm bells warning of fire or attack. In Buddhist temples throughout East Asia, large hanging bells are rung for ceremonial purposes, while small hand bells announce the end of meditation sessions. European bells were traditionally constructed with clappers on the inside, while those of East Asia were struck from the outside by external and separate strikers. In African and Latin American drum ensembles, single or double iron bells such as the *agogo* are often used to hold a steady pattern that serves as a sonic nucleus for complex and improvised drum patterns. Its high metallic pitch is always audible to drummers and dancers and so acts as the ensemble's timekeeper or conductor.

2-65

2-66

2-67

Like the iron bells of Africa and Latin America, a number of wooden and gourd instruments also serve the purpose of keeping time in percussion ensembles. The West African *sekere,* a bead net-covered gourd, and the seed-filled *hosho* gourd rattle of Zimbabwe fulfill this function. Joining the drums and cowbell in Cuban dance bands, the *guiro,* a notched gourd scraper, adds to the rhythmic accompaniment with its distinctive raspy sound. One of the most basic methods of producing rhythmic accompaniment is clapping together two similar objects. At the heart of Afro-Cuban music is the repeating pattern played on the *claves,* two short thick wooden sticks struck together. In Spain, flamenco dancers often accentuate their dance rhythms by playing wooden castanets.

Some idiophones are derived from common household objects or farming implements. In South India, a clay pot (*ghatam*) is struck and slapped by the bare hands of the performer producing an amazing variety of sounds. Brake drums are used as timekeepers in Trinidad's steel drum ensembles. **Indentured** laborers of India, transported to Trinidad and Suriname by British and Dutch plantation owners respectively following the end of the African slave trade, adapted a simple iron rod into a complex percussion instrument (*dhantal*). Players strike the

Fig. 2.21   **Cuban *guiro***

rod with an iron stirrup (formerly a metal horseshoe), and provide rhythmic accompaniment in classical music performances. In this video of *baithak gana* (literally, "seated singing") in Suriname, the *dhantal* and double-headed barrel drum (*dholak*) accompany the vocalist who plays a harmonium. African American slaves who were not allowed to play drums on plantations became experts in playing washboards, spoons, and other household implements. The washboard became a popular rhythm instrument in zydeco and other folk and popular genres. The musical saw was often incorporated into vaudeville as a novelty act, and is now sometimes heard in popular music bands, television commercials, and movie soundtracks.

Fig. 2.22   **South Indian *ghatam* (L), and Indian *jaltarang* (R)**

The word "xylophone" derives from the Greek words *xylon* for wood and *phone* for sound. Instruments made from tuned wooden bars or keys are found in many parts of the world. Known as the marimba, it is the national instrument of Guatemala. Xylophones are also featured in a number of Southeast Asian ensembles. In Thailand and Cambodia, the *ranat ek* is an important member of the *pi phat* ensemble. In Java, Indonesia, the *gambang kayu* is the only wooden-keyed instrument in the **gamelan** ensemble, which almost entirely comprises idiophones made of bronze. Wooden xylophones are popular throughout equatorial Africa. In Uganda, the xylophone has many names (*amadinda, akadinda, embaire,* etc.), sizes, numbers of keys, and tuning systems, differing according to ethnic group. All are constructed from hardwood logs that are carefully selected and shaped into slabs. The performance technique for the *embaire* requires two or more musicians to sit on opposite sides of the instrument, and by alternating mallet strokes they create rapid interlocking patterns. The *balafon* of West Africa has gourds suspended below the wooden keys that serve to increase resonance.

The Indian *jaltarang* consists of a set of ceramic or metal bowls filled with water and struck with beaters. The differing bowl sizes and water levels produce the instrument's range of pitches. The vibraphone was popularized in American jazz by Lionel Hampton. It has tuned metal keys suspended over tubes, which enclose internal baffles spun by an electric motor that produces the sound effect for which the instrument is named.

Metal tongues of different lengths attached to a lateral bar and placed over a wooden board or box resonator constitute the lamellaphone or "thumb piano," so called because the tongues are plucked primarily with the thumbs. Often these instruments are placed inside large gourds or cut-off plastic jugs to give further resonance for outdoor performances. **Lamellaphones** are found primarily in Africa, where they occur in many sizes and shapes, and go by many names such as *sanza, kalimba,* and *mbira*. Among the Busoga people of Uganda, it is called the *endongo* and is often played in pairs, as seen in this video clip. The *mbira dzavadzimu* is the national instrument of Zimbabwe and is one of the largest and most developed lamellaphones in Africa. Its name means "instrument of the ancestors" both because it is of ancient origin and because it is used by the Shona people to connect the living with the spirit world (see Video 11–3).

Cymbals, thin round concave discs of metal, are either crashed together or suspended and struck. In Turkey, dancers use small brass finger cymbals (*zil*) to perform an especially energetic style of belly dancing. As belly dance (known as **raqs sharqi** in Egypt) spread throughout the world, particularly in the late 20th century, finger cymbals spread also. In this video from New York, note how the dancer uses *zil* to accentuate her dance rhythms. Buddhist monks throughout Asia have used cymbals such as the Tibetan *rolmo* to accompany chanting and ceremonial events. The Zildjian Company of Istanbul has been manufacturing cymbals for over four hundred years, and it continues to be the global center of the cymbals industry. Soultone cymbals are made in Turkey also, as are most of the cymbals used in Western orchestras and popular music ensembles.

Fig. 2.23 Zimbabwean *mbira* (L), and West African *balafon* (R)

While the word **gong** comes from the Javanese language, gongs of all sizes are used throughout East and Southeast Asia. In China and Korea, gongs do not have knobs like the Javanese ones. In "Beijing opera" (*jingju*) two small gongs are used to accompany singing and punctuate action. One has a pitch that ascends when struck; the pitch of the other descends. In this video, two folk singers accompany themselves with these two **hand-held gongs**. In the Philippines, ensembles of **tuned gongs** accompany dances and celebrations. The players perform alternating strokes that create melodies, much like hand-bell ensembles in America. These interlocking patterns reinforce community cohesion and interdependence. Large gongs are typically hung from a frame, as is the Chinese *tam tam* that has been incorporated into the Western symphony orchestra. Percussionist David Skidmore demonstrates in this video clip two techniques on the **Chinese tam tam**: the strike and the roll. In China, the *tam tam* is used for ceremonial purposes.

Two music ensembles made up primarily of idiophones are the Javanese *gamelan* and the Trinidadian steel band. The **Javanese gamelan** is composed of tuned, knobbed gongs (*bonang, kenong, kethuk, kempyang*), metallophones (metal-keyed instruments: *gender, slenthem*), wooden-keyed xylophones (*gambang*), and suspended gongs of various sizes (*kempul, gong ageng*) that punctuate the melody with time-keeping patterns. In the video, a Javanese ensemble plays music for a wedding party. Similar ensembles are also used throughout the Indonesian islands of Java and Bali to accompany dance and theatrical performances. In Trinidad, the steel band consists of various sizes of steel drums or pans, each made from the hammered-out bottom of a 55-gallon oil drum. The steel pan was invented in the 1930s in Trinidad and Tobago to replace the drums that had been outlawed by the colonial British authorities during Carnival. Its development as an ensemble instrument played in **steel bands** throughout the Caribbean and elsewhere is a marvel of human ingenuity.

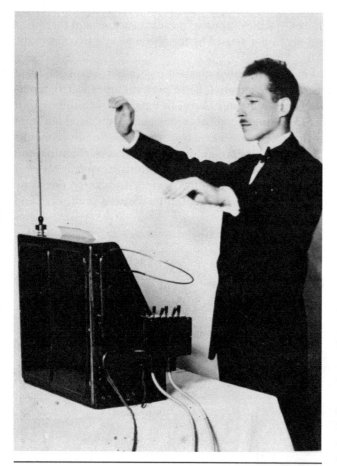

Fig. 2.24 **Leon Theremin (1896–1993) playing his theremin**

ELECTROPHONES

In 1940, Curt Sachs added the **Electrophone** category to the Sachs-Hornbostel classification system to describe instruments whose sound is produced using electricity. The first completely electronic musical instrument was the theremin, invented in 1919 by Russian physicist Leon Theremin. Here is a short documentary on the theremin by world-renowned performer and teacher, **Carolina Eyck.** What gives the theremin its unearthly sound quality is its relatively pure sound wave with no overtones. The first synthesizer was demonstrated by Dr. Robert Moog in 1964. In 1981, the film score of the British movie *Chariots of Fire* was composed primarily on synthesizer by Vangelis, sending shockwaves through the entire music industry. While traditional musical ensembles continue to record most Hollywood **film scores**, a great deal of contemporary popular music is put together entirely through digital means, with sampling technologies mixing prerecorded music and electronically-generated sounds.

ENSEMBLES

People play musical instruments alone, or to accompany their own or others' singing. Sometimes two or more instruments of the same kind play together, blending their sound to enhance and reinforce the overall volume. Often in ensembles, individual instruments or groups of instruments perform a different function. In a Scottish Highland Bagpipe band, for example, marching pipers play the melody and drone while drummers provide the rhythmic accompaniment. In other cases, instruments of different timbres play together creating an enriched sound because of the contrast in sound "colors." In this video clip of a **traditional Korean ensemble**, bowed board zithers (*ajaeng*), fiddle (*haegum*), bamboo flute (*taegum*), and oboe (*piri*) all play the same melody, each instrument adding its own unique timbre. The kind of complex sound produced by an ensemble like this is called "**heterophony**," which we discuss in Lesson 3. The Korean hourglass drum (*changgo*) plays rhythmic patterns known as *changdan*. Frequently, a chordophone and/or aerophone provide a melodic line while a membranophone and/or idiophone provide a rhythmic substructure. Much of the traditional music of the Middle East and South Asia is organized this way. In this example from the **South Indian Karnatak tradition**, violinist Aishu Venkataraman performs the lead melodic line, accompanied by a double-headed barrel drum (*mrdangam*) and a small tambourine (*kanjira*). In music cultures that utilize a system of harmony, lutes, accordions, or keyboard instruments often provide that function. Some societies have developed large ensembles, such as the military brass band; in others, small groups are favored. Like music, dance is also a human universal, and in dance music, combinations of membranophones and idiophones are common. Consider the trap set of the swing band with its cylindrical drums and suspended cymbals.

CONCLUSION

Some musical instruments are simple and require little time and practice to gain proficiency. Others require years of intense labor and observation of elders, or formal study under a master teacher. The videos that you have watched and the instruments you have observed are testaments to the extraordinary ingenuity and craftsmanship of the designers and makers of these instruments. They are also testaments to the men and women who have given so much pleasure to so many by devoting their lives to the mastery of them. In these videos, you have watched some of the world's great vocalists and instrumentalists, including Jimmie Rodgers, Umm Kulthum, Mohammad Reza Shahjarian, Wu Man, Sergio and Odair Assad, Jimi Hendrix, Virgil Fox, and Glen Velez. You have also seen amateur and folk musicians who are continuing traditions that extend back for generations and who serve their communities by providing music for dancing, worship, celebrating, and lamenting. The world would be so much the duller without them and their music.

KEY CONCEPTS

Anatomy of the human voice
Human vocal differentiation: biological
Human vocal differentiation: cultural

Enculturation
Vocal timbre
Instrument classification systems
Sachs-Hornbostel system
Chordophone

Aerophone
Membranophone
Idiophone
Electrophone

Q THINKING ABOUT MUSIC QUESTIONS

1. Is there such a thing as a "natural" human singing voice? Or are all voice types conditioned by cultural inheritance and social expectations?
2. Listen to the video recording of Jimmie Rodgers again. What, in the quality of his voice, made it so emblematic of rural America in the early 20th century?
3. Do you consider yourself a "singer"? If not, do you know others who consider themselves singers? What factors contributed to this self-identification? The sheer enjoyment of singing? Success in a school or church choral program? Peer or family recognition of a particular talent?
4. How would you describe a familiar instrument in terms of the concerns Jan Mrázek expresses and the things this writer finds most important?
5. What does Jan Mrázek find limiting about the ways that instruments are described and classified by scholars?
6. Consider the violin, the guitar, and the accordion. These instruments are found throughout the world and have been adapted to many different cultural situations. Discuss how each of these instruments has been adapted to suit different musical and cultural contexts.

NOTES

1 Frank Tenaille, *Music is the Weapon of the Future: Fifty Years of African Popular Music* (Chicago: Lawrence Hill Books, 2002), 13.

2 Jan Mrázek, "Xylophones in Thailand and Java: A Comparative Phenomenology of Musical Instruments," *Asian Music* 39/2 (2008): 59.

3 The Sachs-Hornbostel classification system places the lyre in the "Lute" category (SVH #321), but we place it with the "Harps" (SVH #322) because of a closer physical resemblance. Erich M. von Hornbostel and Curt Sachs, "Systematik der Musikinstrumente: Ein Versuch," *Zeitschrift für Ethnologie* 46 (1914): 553–90; trans. Anthony Baines and Klaus Wachsmann, "Classification of Musical Instruments," *Galpin Society Journal* 14 (1961): 3–29. Source consulted: "SVH Classification," http://www.wesleyan.edu/vim/svh.html.

4 "Peruvian Traditional Music," Peru Gateway Travel, Edition 2014, http://www.peru-explorer.com/traditional_music.htm.

5 Sharon R. King, "Compressed Data; Can You Play 'Feelings' on the Ocarina?" *New York Times*, February 15, 1999, http://www.nytimes.com/1999/02/15/business/compressed-data-can-you-play-feelings-on-the-ocarina.html.

6 Clay Irving, "Eight Auspicious Symbols of Bhutan," last updated January 17, 2010, http://www.panix.com/~clay/currency/Bhutan-8-symbols.html.

7 J. H. Kwabena Nketia, "The Musical Languages of Subsaharan Africa," report prepared at the request of UNESCO for presentation to the Meeting on Musical Traditions in Africa, held in Yaounde, Cameroon, February 23–27, 1970. Quoted in Ashenafi Kebede, "*The* Music of Ethiopia: Its Development and Cultural Setting" (PhD diss., Wesleyan University, 1971), 158.

Lesson 3
What is Music Made of?
The Elements of Music

When most of us listen to music on our smartphone or computer, or experience it in the context of a concert, movie, or religious ritual, we usually do not concern ourselves with the ways musical sound is organized. Often the music moves in and out of the center of our attention, serving as a stimulus for physical movement, mood, or a succession of memories, associations, and fantasies. Music is frequently connected with other forms of expression such as song and dance, and the lyrics or the dance movements might be at the forefront of our attention. However, music can be contemplated as the coordinated interaction of a number of elements such as rhythm, melody, and harmony, each of which contributes to an overall expressive purpose. We could compare this to a wristwatch that contains hidden inner workings directing moment by moment the digital numbers or position of the hands. We normally look at a watch to tell the time, not to ponder its electronic or mechanical movements, but people who design, market, repair, or write books about watches are very much concerned with these internal parts and functions. Similarly, professional musicians—performers, composers, teachers, and scholars—consider music in terms of its elements in order to understand how music is created, remembered, taught, incorporated into wider social contexts, and connected to socially held meanings and values. Understanding music analytically can focus our attention on musical sound and help us to engage more fully with its richness and diversity throughout the world. Musical systems along with the purposes they serve vary widely, yet by paying attention to their inner structural workings we may observe among them broad areas of convergence.

One such area of convergence relates to the ways music is generated, by means of a contrast or tension between fixed, pre-composed elements and those that are produced spontaneously in performance. The terms "composition" and "improvisation" refer to these complementary tendencies. Many performances present existing compositions—musical structures that have been prepared and preserved either through memory, notation, or sound recording technology. Others are generated at the time of performance through processes of spontaneous musical creativity, based upon pre-existing patterns and norms. Most common, however, is a combination of the two. In traditional Irish music, for example, performers memorize a large corpus of tunes (reels, jigs, hornpipes, polkas, etc.) that are passed on orally from one generation to the next, and they play this repertoire in group sessions, dances, and concerts. Yet performance is not simply the precise repetition of tunes; musicians embellish the melodies using learned techniques of **ornamentation,** they string together melodies in new tune medleys, and they vary the numbers and types of tunes they play depending on the social context. In addition, sometimes they compose new tunes that add to the ever-growing corpus that constitutes the tradition.

Another area of convergence that we might find particularly useful when examining music across a wide cultural and historical spectrum is *periodicity* and *contrast.* "Periodicity" is a word that composer and theorist Michael Tenzer borrows from physics referring to the regular recurrence of phenomena like wave forms, life-cycle stages, and lunar phases; the turning of the seasons and the alternation of day and night. We experience our world as ordered and predictable by the cycles we experience in time. As with periodicity in our physical world, the repetition of melodic and rhythmic patterns in music creates a sense of stability "through return or constancy, and such stability will always be in dynamic dialog with change."[1] From the verse-refrain structures of songs to the one-two one-two drumbeats of a march, patterns of recurrence and their potential for near infinite variation underpin much of the world's music. Yet with the exception of certain styles of religious chant or modern "electronica" dance beat patterns, repetition and return is only half the story. In a march, while the drumbeats are the same throughout the event, melodies above the drumbeats change and provide contrast. In the verse-refrain form, the melody remains constant and the song lyrics change from verse to verse. Musical structures such as these often provide a balance between stability and novelty.

RHYTHM

Music is fundamentally an expression of our experience of time, as the visual arts and architecture are expressions of our experience of space. Much of our understanding of time is based on patterns of motion, many of which are rooted in our biological make-up. From our heartbeat, our respiratory cycle of breathing in and out, and our two-legged means of locomotion, to the alternation of our sleeping and waking, the rhythms of our sexuality, birth, aging, and death—these regularities structure the shape of our lives. Repeating patterns—periodicities—we also experience in the natural world with the rolling of surf, the tides, the changing of the seasons, and the phases of the moon that provide a sense of time passing and its continuous renewal. Perhaps the most basic element of music, the one that is most dynamically felt at the level of our bodies, is rhythm, the organization or grouping of musical sounds in time. Music may have a heavy rhythmic emphasis as in dance music, or little rhythmic stress as in soft ballads and lullabies. Different musical cultures have different ways of organizing musical time, and worldwide there is great variety. The following examples illustrate some of the ways in which musical time may be structured and experienced in different parts of the world.

REGULAR AND FREE RHYTHM

Much of the world's music is organized around more or less regular time units, like the duration separated by two successive handclaps or beats on a drum. These in turn are organized into repeating groups of two, three, or more beats with an emphasis on the first beat of each group. Like footsteps and heartbeats, rhythmic patterns may range from very slow and languid to very fast and peppy, with all gradations in between. Consider the "Stars and Stripes Forever" march by John Philip Sousa, written to coordinate the movements of a parade of soldiers. In this video clip of a **football marching band,** the drums and cymbals mark the steady "left right, left right" two-beat pattern that drives the marchers into the formation of the American flag, as the drill team interweaves red, white, and blue banners to complete the effect. If the drummers were to speed up the pattern, the marchers would move around the field faster. The word "meter" is used to describe the beat pattern (one-two, one-two, for example), and "tempo" describes the speed. In contrast, some genres of music, such as jazz and swing, derive their vitality and energy from rhythmic irregularity and syncopation (accenting offbeat rhythms). Listen to this recording of the jazz standard, **"It Don't Mean a Thing (If It Ain't Got That Swing),"** sung by the great jazz diva Ella Fitzgerald. She sings "doo wop doo wop doo wop" against the regular beats of the piano, bass, and drums (called the "rhythm section" in a jazz combo). This kind of exchange between the steady beat of the rhythm section and the "off the beat" syncopation of the melody is what is meant by the word "swing."

Many non-Western musical systems organize rhythm into longer periods, with greater numbers of beats, such as the Arabic *iqa'*, the Korean *changdan*, and the Indian *tala*. These patterns, referred to as **rhythmic modes**, are sometimes defined by the alternation of different sounds that are produced on a drum. Smaller, faster-moving divisions often fill in the time between the larger temporal units. The goblet-shaped hand drum of Egypt, *dumbek*, produces two basic sounds: a deep resonant one when the hand hits the drum head in the center (referred to by the onomatopoeic syllable *dumm*), and a high-pitched crisp one (*takk*) when the head is struck on the rim. In this video clip, the great Leba- nese percussionist **Souhail Kaspar** demonstrates the ten-beat cycle *sama'i thaqil*. The video shows how the drummer improvises complex and varied "fills" based on the underlying structure of the ten-beat cycle, relating this Middle Eastern practice to both the composed/improvised relationship and the periodicity of the repeating pattern offset by the ever-changing variations. Indeed, these basic recurrent phrases are subject to near-infinite elaboration and embellishment. When used to accom- pany belly dance (*raqs sharqi*), the two tones correspond to movements made by the feet and hips of the dancer, who skillfully responds to the drummer's spontaneous creativity.

In the case of the Korean *changdan*, the *puk* barrel drum is used to provide a rhythmic underpin- ning or framework during performances of **pansori**, a storytelling tradition we discuss in Lesson 13. A scene from the 1992 feature film *Sopyonjae* shows a storyteller (**kwangdae**) teaching his stepson the basic strokes of the pattern *choongmoli* (*chungmori*) so he can accompany his sister, who is learning to be a *kwangdae*, in storytelling performances. As with the *dumbek* strokes, each stroke is designated by an onomatopoeic syllable. The *puk* produces three separate sounds that are arranged in time to con- struct the *changdan*. As shown in the movie scene, the boy hits the double-headed drum either with his flat left hand (*kung*), a stick held in the right hand on the wooden frame (*tak*), or both together on the two drum heads (*hap* or *doong*). A pause is *ut*. The boy plays the 12-beat rhythmic pattern, calling out the stroke names as he goes. Note the sharp accent on the ninth beat (*tàk*) of the cycle:

Hap kung-tak kung-tak-tak/ Ut kung-tàk doong.... doong
1 ___ 2 ___ 3 ___ 4 ___ 5 _ 6 / 7 _ 8 ___ 9 ___ 10 _ 11 _12

Likewise in North India, each *tabla* drum stroke has its own drum syllable, and *tabla* players learn to play drum patterns by reciting the drum syllables. The 16-beat rhythmic cycle *tin tala* is recited as follows:

dha dhin dhin dha / dha dhin dhin dha / dha tin tin ta / ta dhin dhin dha //

Music without a regular pulse is said to be in free rhythm. In various parts of the world, religious texts are recited to melodic contours that follow the natural flow of speech patterns, or incorporate poetic meters. Forms of instrumental music also emphasize melodic invention unstructured by a strong pulse or meter. Japanese *shakuhachi* flute players shape melodic phrases that coincide with the natural outflow of breath. Thus the music seems to float freely and spontaneously, unbound by metrical control. This style of music lends itself to contemplation because it does not stimulate the kind of bodily involvement that strong rhythmic pulse and pattern do.

POLYRHYTHM

When two or more rhythms are played simultaneously, the resulting sound is known as **polyrhythm** or rhythmic **polyphony** (from the Greek for "many sounds"). In West African drumming, individual drummers within a group each play a different rhythmic pattern that interlocks with the others to create a dense and complex polyrhythmic texture. Often an idiophone such as a metal bell or shaker is used to keep time and orient the various parts to a common framework. Watch this video clip of a *djembe* ensemble from Guinea demonstrating **polyrhythm** and its relationship to spoken lan- guage. The video begins with the building of the *djembe* drum and ends with its use in performance, accompanying dance. Notice that each drummer performs a characteristic phrase that interlocks with the others. The whole is held together by the metallic clicks of the metal bell (*agogo*). In Rio de Janeiro, percussion bands called **bateria** drive the rhythms of the famous Carnival street parades. This video, taken at a neighborhood **samba school**, shows the *bateria*'s last rehearsal before Carnival. On drums, metal bells, and shakers (idiophones) of different sizes, musicians play patterns that interlock to produce a loud, dense, complex sonic tapestry, which in turn compels the dancers to move their feet and bodies in sync. In these traditions, music and dance are inseparably linked; the two are understood as a single category, with one inconceivable without the other.

WORK RHYTHM

People around the world have long used music as a way of providing rhythmic accompaniment for repetitive work as well as a pleasant distraction from the drudgery of physical labor. In the past, **prison work gangs** in the United States sang songs to regulate their work rhythms, as in this 1966 video clip of inmates from the Ellis unit of Huntsville prison in Texas singing as they swing their axes to fell large trees. In this video from Ghana, West Africa, women are **hoeing garden rows**, the motions of their labor coordinated by the rhythm of their singing. Also notice in these clips the alternating call-and-response pattern typical of much African and African American music.

GROOVES AND DANCE RHYTHMS

Dance forms throughout the world are defined by short, repeating rhythmic phrases, referred to as "**grooves**" by ethnomusicologist Charles Keil and others. Rhythmic patterns and the footwork that they motivate in dancers define the various forms of Western ballroom dance: the foxtrot, cha-cha-cha, and waltz, for example. Using digital and sampling technologies, DJs collect beats from many sources that they process into groove tracks to use at dance parties and raves, and to accompany rappers. In West African traditions, drumming is typically based on three dynamic relationships: (1) short interlocking phrases often played by the bass drums, shakers, and bells; which (2) support and contrast with free improvisations by the lead drummer; who (3) interacts with the movements of the dancers. In this video from a **wedding party in Mali**, dancers and members of the percussion ensemble connect and freely improvise in a dynamic and exciting rhythmic give-and-take.

RHYTHMIC VIRTUOSITY

"**Virtuosity**" is a term used to describe a high level of skill; a virtuoso is a musician who demonstrates great technical and artistic ability. In many cultures rhythmic virtuosity is highly valued as a source of aesthetic pleasure, apart from its role in coordinating the movements of marchers, laborers, and dancers. Consider these three examples from cultures that prize rhythmic complexity. In the first video we see the great West African drummer Nana Kimati Dinizulu performing on the "**hand and foot drum**" of the Ga people of Ghana. Note the relationship between the complex and dense improvised "riffs" of Dinizulu and the steady and continuous pattern of the bell, played in the background, which serves as a timekeeper holding the performance together. The term *clave* (Spanish for "key" or "code") in Afro-Cuban music similarly refers to a core rhythmic pattern that repeats throughout a piece and is clearly audible because of the different timbre of the timekeeping instrument. The West African performance exemplifies the creative tension between fixed and free elements found in many forms of music worldwide. In the second example, we see a fusion band from Sweden that includes guest performer Vikku Vinayakram, a virtuoso *ghatam* player from South India, demonstrating the technical aspects of his highly cultivated art. The third example shows the incomparable "King of Latin Music," Tito Puente (1923–2000) playing *timbales* in a recording studio. He was born in New York City's Spanish Harlem to Puerto Rican immigrant parents. After serving in the U.S. Navy during World War II, he attended the Juilliard School on the G.I. Bill. As a composer, arranger, and band leader, Tito Puente was one of the most important figures in American popular culture during the 1950s and 60s, bringing to the mainstream such Latin and Caribbean dance rhythms as the cha-cha-cha, mambo, merengue, and salsa.

MELODY

Melody is a sequence or succession of pitches—sounds of a single, measurable frequency—arranged in musical time. A melody or tune is often what we remember after listening to music, and what we are able to sing ourselves. A melody has an identity for us, and often carries meanings, feelings, and associations. According to Palestinian musician Simon Shaheen, a melody is "a group of notes that are in love with each other."[2] This is the element of music that is attached to words in a song. Imagine a shepherd on a hill tending the sheep and playing idly on a wooden flute. He improvises, selecting pitches at will from those available on his instrument. It may be that a particularly serendipitous combination strikes his fancy and he plays it over and over, working with it, getting it "just right." It becomes *a melody* that he can then play for, and teach to, his friends. The shepherd's melodic improvisations here are the raw material for his musical invention: his melody or tune. By listening to a few examples, we can sample the diversity of melody in our world from the perspective of pitch vocabulary, **melodic contour**, and ornamentation.

PITCH VOCABULARY

From all possible pitches or tones, cultures employ particular ones from which their melodies are derived. The arrangement of a particular set of pitches in ascending or descending order we call a scale or mode, and the distance between one pitch and another, an **interval**. It is the difference between these scales that gives melodies from different parts of the world their distinctive character. Much Western music uses the pitches of major or minor scales, which are based on whole and half-tone intervals. Each of these scales carries an association for listeners familiar with the tradition, the major scale often suggesting happier feelings than the minor scale. Whether these associations are based on inherent acoustical properties, or are learned through early childhood enculturation, is not well understood. Javanese *gamelan* orchestras play music based on a five-tone scale (*slendro*) or a seven-tone scale (*pelog*), each having a different interval structure. Since most *gamelan* instruments are made of bronze or other metal and have fixed pitches that cannot be tuned in performance, *gamelan* orchestras often consist of two sets of instruments, one for each scale system. Pairs of instruments are placed at right angles to each other so that the musicians all face one direction when performing music in the *pelog* scale, and then all turn ninety degrees to play their *slendro* instruments. In theatrical performances where the *gamelan* plays an accompanying role, *pelog* instruments are played during the daytime and the *slendro* set is played at night.

 Maqam is an Arabic term, originally meaning "place" or "location," that refers to a system of melodic modes and scales central to musical practices from North Africa through Central Asia into China. Each *maqam* consists of both a group of pitches arranged in ascending or descending order, and melodies traditionally generated from those notes that convey a mood or feeling. In Azerbaijan, a derivation of the term, *mugam*, refers to the entire system of classical music from that culture. In this short video, two of the greatest modern practitioners of the art, father and daughter Alim and Fargana Qasimov, demonstrate the deeply expressive and spiritual qualities of *mugam*. In Xinjiang, an autonomous region of northwestern China, the predominant melodic system of the Uighur people consists of twelve modes called *muqam*. This video taken at a busy restaurant in Kashgar, the westernmost city in China, shows three Uighur musicians performing and improvising traditional *muqam* melodies on *tambur* (five-string long-necked lute), *ghichak* (spike fiddle), and *dutar* (two-string long-necked lute). In North India, the classical *raga* system encompasses hundreds of different scales—of five, six, or seven tones—that musicians use to compose and improvise melodies. "In its broadest sense," writes Indian music scholar and performer George Ruckert, "the word [*raga*] refers to the 'color,' and more specifically the emotion or mood produced by a particular combination or sequence of pitches."[3] *Ragas* not only carry associations of feeling (related to the Sanskrit concept of *rasa*, "juice, sap") but also are associated with times of day and seasons of the year. Watch this brief video clip of two of the greatest 20th-century masters of **Hindustani** classical music, Ravi Shankar (1920–2012) on *sitar* (long-necked fretted lute) and Ali Akbar Khan (1922–2009) on *sarod* (short-necked fretless lute), recorded at the Concert for Bangladesh at Madison Square Garden in 1978. They are accompanied by master drummer Alla Rakha (1919–2000) playing the *tabla* drum pair, and Lakshmi Shankar

3-14

3-15

3-16

3-17

on the drone lute (*tambura*). The soloists demonstrate their remarkable skill and technique with lightning fast, virtuosic playing.

Five-tone (**pentatonic**) scales characterize Chinese and other East Asian as well as Sub-Saharan African traditional melodies. In this video clip, a blind performer in Suide, central China, plays "**Moon Reflected in the Second Spring**," a pentatonic piece for solo *erhu* (two-string fiddle) composed by a blind musician of the past, the famous Abing, aka Hua Yanjun (1893–1950).

MELODIC CONTOUR

As we use contour lines to mark elevation levels on a geographical map, we can also describe the rise and fall of pitches in a melody in terms of contour. Australian aboriginal peoples have long used the melodic contours of ancestral songs to affirm territorial boundaries. "Aboriginal Creation myths tell of the legendary totemic beings who had wandered over the continent in the Dreamtime [distant past], singing out the name of everything that crossed their path—birds, animals, plants, rocks, waterholes—and so singing the world into existence." As author Bruce Chatwin explains in his book *The Songlines*, these songs constitute a "labyrinth of invisible pathways which meander all over Australia and are known to Europeans as 'Dreaming-tracks' or 'Songlines'; to the Aboriginals as the 'Footprints of the Ancestors'."[4] Each Aboriginal inherits a stretch of the Ancestor's song and the land over which the song passes; the verses are title deeds to the territory, which can be lent to or borrowed from others via song swaps, extending each individual's song maps and granting to others "rights of way."[5] While the song words can be changed, the melody always remains the same; "the melodic contour of the song described the nature of the land over which the song passes. So, if the Lizard Man were dragging his heels across the salt-pans of Lake Eyre, you could expect a succession of long flats, like Chopin's 'Funeral March'. If he were skipping up and down the MacDonnell escarpments, you'd have a series of arpeggios and glissandos, like Liszt's 'Hungarian Rhapsodies'.... [Melody] is a memory bank for finding one's way about the world."[6]

Melodies often follow the contours of natural speech, particularly when they are associated with texts. They are often divided into logical structural units called phrases, which correspond to the grammatical structures of language. Consider the popular hymn "Amazing Grace". Each verse consists of two sentences separated by a period: "Amazing Grace how sweet the sound, that saved a wretch like me. I once was lost but now am found, was blind but I now I see." The melody, in two phrases, mirrors this structure with a pause at the end of the first sentence where the singer takes a breath.

3-2

Melodic contours not only distinguish one melody from another but can characterize entire musical genres. **Native American Plains Indian songs** begin high in the falsetto range and descend through a terraced contour to a low ending pitch. In contrast to this long pulsating, descending line, **Tibetan Buddhist chant** moves slowly around a few extremely low pitches. Melodic contours seem to be as recognizable as human faces. Compare the national anthems of the United Kingdom and the United States. "God Save the Queen" has a melody in which the notes move mostly in step (**conjunct motion**), up and down the scale encompassing a narrow range. The "Star-Spangled Banner," on the other hand, has large skips (**disjunct motion**) and covers a much wider range. Periodically, bills have been introduced in Congress to change the national anthem to "America the Beautiful" because it is so much easier to sing.

3-3

3-4

ORNAMENTATION

Ornamentation refers to the embellishing of melodic pitches. Techniques for embellishing melody such as vibrato, trills, shakes, and other gestures of inflection vary widely and are important in establishing the identity of a musical style. In many world cultures where melody is the primary vehicle for musical expression, ornamentation plays an important role. The Korean genre of sung poetry known as *sijo* is characterized by the use of a deep pitch fluctuation. *Sijo* melodies have few pitches and move very slowly, yet they still hold a fascination for the listener because of the complexity of the singer's ornamentation. Similarly Korean instruments, like the bowed zither *ajaeng*, are constructed to produce ornaments that replicate vocal pitch fluctuations. The seven- or eight-stringed instrument is bowed with the right hand; the left hand presses down on the flexible silk strings to the

3-19

3-20

left of the bridges to produce the characteristic ornaments. Another highly ornate style comes from South India, in which ornaments inflecting pitches are called *gamak*. An interesting feature of this classical musical system is that the scale pitches themselves are sounded only with the ornaments. A proverb among musicians in this part of the world is: "a note without a *gamak* is like a night without stars." In this style of music, known as Karnatak, short devotional songs called *kriti* are expanded through repetitions, non-verbal elaborations, and improvised sections to produce highly developed performances. In this video, Dr. Vijayalakshmi Subramaniam performs the *kriti*, *"Shadanane"* ("The Six-Headed God").

In Middle Eastern music, elaboration of the Arabic *maqam* scale pitches is integral to the performance of both vocal and instrumental melodies. In this video clip, Lebanese musician Naji Hilal demonstrates on the *ud* (Arabic lute) an unadorned melody and then fully realizes it in the style of Arabic improvisation known as *taqsim*. Ornamentation is also an important feature of instrumental music composed for keyboard in 18th-century France, Italy, and Spain. In this video clip, the musician plays a composition by François Couperin (1668–1733) on the harpsichord. Since the harpsichord had no means of sustaining pitches, unlike the piano that was developed later and had that capability, players used ornamentation to fill in the gaps between pitches.

HARMONY

The term "harmony" is used to account for a number of features of musical sound. It refers to relationships between pitches that sound either in succession or simultaneously. It also refers to the combining of notes to produce chords, and the way in which chords relate to each other to produce progressions that can propel musical motion. Because musical situations are often social and participatory, it is not surprising that many traditions developed with music composed of multiple parts. In many parts of the world, depth is added to a melodic line by means of a drone: a single pitch or combination of pitches that runs through the entire performance. Bagpipes, for instance, are often fitted with reed pipes that sound a constant drone pitch to accompany the chanter pipe with finger holes for sounding the melody pitches. The Bulgarian *gaida* has a blowpipe for filling the bag with air, a chanter pipe on which the melody is played, and a single long drone pipe. The musical experience is based on the contrast between the stability of the drone pitch and the decorative complexity of a highly ornamented melody. In this video clip, master *gaida* player Dafo Trendafilov (1919–2010) welcomes guests to his village in the Rhodope Mountains for an evening celebration. In Indian classical music, the *tambura* (long-necked lute) serves no other function than to provide an ambient drone underpinning melodic lines. In this video, *dhrupad* singer Shanti Shivani performs the North Indian *raga bhairavi*. *Dhrupad* is a form of contemplative vocal music with a five-hundred-year history.

The ancient Greeks and others described how pitches produced by vibrating strings, which are related in length by simple ratios (1:2, 2:3, 3:4, 4:5), are consonant or harmonious when sounded together. These relationships are called intervals, and the intervals of the octave, fifth, fourth, and third are described respectively by the ratios listed above. The discoveries of the Greeks became the basis for harmony as it developed in Europe. Triadic harmony based on thirds, and chord progressions were in use by the time of the early Renaissance. Some famous works from the European tradition (like Beethoven's "Moonlight Sonata" in C♯ Minor") draw their primary source of inspiration and expression from **harmonic progressions**. Many genres of popular music are defined by a basic chord progression, like the twelve-bar blues heard in Muddy Waters' 1951 song "Honey Bee." A single bass line played on the guitar can also provide a strong harmonic accompaniment to a vocal melody, as illustrated in Johnny Cash's song "I Walk the Line." Christian missionaries brought the practice of hymn singing, with its emphasis on congregational participation and **four-part harmony**, to many areas of the globe. Here is an example from **Malawi** in southeastern Africa. Notice how local musicians have created a style that is unique to that regional culture by blending the music lessons provided by the missionaries with their own local customs and tastes. The worldwide popularity of instruments like the guitar, accordion, and piano, which are capable of producing more than one pitch at the same time, suggests how the harmonic system based on chords has come to be accepted globally as an important, even indispensable musical ingredient.

TEXTURE

Texture describes how various simultaneous parts fit together to create the whole musical sound, and is therefore related to harmony. We use four terms to define the different kinds of musical texture. The combination of simultaneous parts is a characteristic of all these musical textures except monophony.

MONOPHONY

Monophony refers to a single melody line performed by one or more voices or instruments. A solo voice singing an unaccompanied melody, such as the folk ballad "Lady Margaret and Sweet William" or this highly ornamented song from **Mongolia**, provides a clear example of monophonic singing. A choir of voices singing the same melody line is also monophonic, as heard in this example of Benedictine nuns from France singing a **Gregorian** chant, as might have been sung in a Christian convent a thousand years ago. Solo, monophonic instrumental music is found in musical traditions around the world. Here are three examples played by musicians who are renowned in their own societies: Ivan Kovachev on the Bulgarian bowed *gadulka*; Ustad Rahim Khushnawaz of Herat in Afghanistan playing the *rabab* plucked lute; and Jalal Ahmad of Bangladesh playing the **bamboo flute**. Note that toward the end of the *rabab* video, Ustad Rahim is joined by Ustad Karim Herawi on the *tabla* drums, adding a rhythmic structure to what began as a melodic improvisation in free rhythm. Another example of monophony is the combination of contrasting melodic timbres often with rhythmic accompaniment. Consider this example, "*Samai Nahawand*," played by Simon Shaheen on *ud*, Maya Beiser on cello, and Glen Velez on frame drum. Although consisting primarily of a single melody, the difference in timbre between the plucked and bowed instruments in addition to the rhythmic underpinning of the drum gives the music depth, interest, and forward motion.

POLYPHONY

A polyphonic texture consists of two or more independent melodies performed simultaneously. In Zimbabwe, the Shona people play the *mbira* (thumb piano) in pairs, the two instrumental lines woven together to create a dense and complex texture. Listen to "*Nhemamusasa*" played by two of the great Shona *mbira* musicians of the 20th century, Cosmas Magaya and the late Ambuya Beauler Dyoko. The leading part (*kushaura*), played by Dyoko, introduces the basic melodic pattern. After approximately twenty seconds, Magaya joins in with the intertwining part (*kutsinhira*). Both rhythmically and melodically, the two parts interlock creating a dense polyphonic weave of sound. The singing of the **Baka** people in the central African rainforest provides another example of polyphonic music. Here each singer repeats a melodic phrase that interlocks with the phrases others sing. In this highly social practice, each part becomes meaningful only when joined with others, and the pleasure comes from being part of something larger than oneself. Likewise, the simultaneous singing of different lines arranged for the four voice parts—soprano, alto, tenor, and bass—was the standard musical practice at the time of Shakespeare, when **Thomas Morley** (1557–1602) composed madrigals, setting to music the poems of the Bard and his contemporaries. More recently, the simultaneous sounding of The Mamas and the Papas' male and female vocal lines creates a polyphonic texture in their 1965 hit single "California Dreaming."

HOMOPHONY

A homophonic texture is one in which a single melody is accompanied by supporting harmony. Listen to the homophonic texture in the song "Paper Airplane" by bluegrass-country artist Alison Krauss and her band Union Station. In this title track of the 2011 bluegrass album that won Krauss her 27th Grammy Award, the singer's vocal melody is prominent above the accompanying instruments of mandolin, guitars, and string bass. Now listen to the opening of the second movement of Beethoven's 5th Symphony, which provides an example of orchestral **homophony**. The music begins slowly with the cellos and violas playing a melody line and the double bass providing a simple *pizzicato* (plucked) accompaniment. When the woodwinds take over in a descending melodic response, other orchestral instruments join to provide a fuller, more complex accompaniment. Another example is the four-part vocal harmony of the barbershop quartet, an unaccompanied male vocal group made popular in the early 1930s by the Mills Brothers. Interest in this genre reached the level of a national fad with a song from the musical *The Music Man*, "Lida Rose," and to this day there are over 30,000 barbershop quartets in the U.S. While the leader sings the words to the main melody, three singers harmonize with a textless "oooo."

Music may remain in one texture throughout a song or instrumental piece, or may move from one texture to another, as in the call-and-response form of South African *isicathamiya* singing. In this style a solo lead singer alternates with group vocal harmony creating an unaccompanied choral music that moves back and forth between monophony (single melody line) and homophony (accompanied melody). The group in the video, Ladysmith Black Mambazo, led by the group's founder Joseph Shabalala (b. 1941), has been one of the world's leading *a cappella* groups for more than fifty years.

HETEROPHONY

A single melody performed slightly differently yet simultaneously by two or more musicians creates a heterophonic texture. In a number of music cultures, heterophony is the dominant form of musical organization. Japanese *sankyoku* ("music for three") played by the *koto* (long zither), *shamisen* (three-stringed lute), and *shakuhachi* (bamboo flute) exemplifies heterophony, as heard in this performance of "*Shojo No Tsuru*" ("A Crane in the Pines"). Each instrument more or less follows the contour of the melody, as does the voice. The deviations from the basic line as well as the contrast in timbre provide the kind of depth to the listening experience that other cultures satisfy with harmony or polyphony.

From Dublin to Tokyo, musicians often gather to play at "sessions" in Irish pubs and bars. They bring their instruments such as fiddles, flutes, whistles, button accordions, and guitars, and play together from memory a shared repertoire of Celtic dance tunes. Melody players typically join together three tunes (such as jigs, reels, or hornpipes) in a medley and play each of them three times. They ornament and vary the tunes slightly according to the traditions and capabilities of their individual instruments as well as their level of skill and inspiration. This mode of performance maximizes group participation without minimizing individuality. In Shanghai teahouses, a similar tradition called *jiangnan sizhu* is practiced. The name refers to the Jiangsu region south of the Yangtse River (*jiangnan*) and the wind and stringed instruments, traditionally made of bamboo and silk (*sizhu*), that comprise the ensemble. Unlike with the Irish session, the instruments are sometimes owned by the teahouse and musicians come and go taking turns playing them, novices in the early afternoon and the most experienced closing the session.[7] Also unlike in the Irish session, the repertoire of *jiangnan sizhu* pieces is relatively small and musicians typically play many repetitions of each melody, gradually moving from slow, heavily ornamented variations to quick versions of the basic melodies. The musicians each vary the melody with ornamentation based on the idiomatic techniques and conventions of their instruments, creating the characteristic heterophonic texture. After playing a few pieces, they may also exchange instruments since the musicians can often play several.

FORM

Form refers to the structure or internal organization of a musical composition or improvisation. Form identifies repetitions, contrasts, and variations of musical ideas or events, and defines music in terms of sections characterized by particular themes, melodies, rhythm patterns, etc. Consider the example of the **Albanian funeral ritual** that you listened to in Lesson 1. The form is the juxta-position and repetition of the various elements (unison cries and divergent clamoring) that make up the performance. Note here that periodicity and improvisation both play important roles; in the continuous repetition of the long descending cries by the mourners, and in the spontaneity of their combined vocal outpourings. In the Albanian funeral lament we also hear a solo-group contrast, as one or a few voices begin each descending cry and others then join in. A similar "call-and-response" pattern with a vocal leader and chorus is common in much Sub-Saharan African music, as well as in African American R&B and gospel. Songs in many parts of the world consist of an alternating verse and refrain form, with the music mirroring the structure of the lyrics, as in Bob Dylan's song "Knockin on Heaven's Door." Listen to this rendition of **"Knockin on Heaven's Door"** by country superstar Dolly Parton and the South African *isicathamiya* group Ladysmith Black Mambazo. After a brief instrumental introduction, singer Dolly Parton performs the first verse, "Lord, take this badge off of me, I can't use it any more..." This is followed by the refrain, "Knock knock knocking on heaven's door," in which she is joined by Ladysmith Black Mambazo in a call-and-response pattern. Then Parton sings the second verse, "Lord, take these guns away from me, I can't shoot them any more..." What makes this performance so compelling is its combination of the verse and refrain song form with call-and-response as well as the mixing of genres and styles, the two elements discussed below.

The term "form" applies to music on both a micro and macro level. It can describe a short tune like "Twinkle, Twinkle, Little Star" in terms of the relationship between its three phrases:

> Twinkle twinkle little star, How I wonder what you are.
> Up above the world so high, Like a diamond in the sky,
> Twinkle twinkle little star, How I wonder what you are.

The first and last lines, which are identical, share the same melodic contour, whereas the middle, contrasting line has its own contour. This form can be described as A-B-A or ternary form. Form also describes much longer and more complex musical constructs. In the South Indian Karnatak tradition, for example, the three-part *kriti* form has a refrain-like *pallavi* section alternating with a secondary refrain section, *anupallavi*, and with verses (*charanam*) producing a complex performance that encompasses both pre-composed music and improvisation. Hip-hop producers create groove tracks, combinations of pre-recorded beats, that they loop to provide a repetitive structure over which rappers, beatboxers, and breakdancers can perform for indefinite and flexible periods of time.

GENRE

The term "genre" derives from the Latin *genus*, a word familiar to students of biology as a type or category within a system of classification. Categories of music are often grouped together according to stylistic, contextual, and historical similarities. Recording companies, for example, will use familiarity with a particular tradition to market new artists by placing them within a pre-existing category. Rock, hip-hop, country, soul, jazz, classical, etc. are all genres. Wedding and funeral songs are genres defined by occasion. Salsa, **cumbia**, and **reggae** are genres based upon characteristic dance beats and place of origin: Puerto Rico, Colombia, and Jamaica respectively. Often identification with a particular genre is related to and marks class or regional divisions within a society: in America, bluegrass is associated with the rural Appalachian Mountains region while hip-hop is considered an urban genre. In Trinidad, among the descendants of East Indian indentured laborers, two types of wedding songs are performed by women at weddings: *byah ke git* are old songs with deep roots in the ancestral home of North India, while *lachari* are contemporary songs, often comical and with sexual innuendos. Pop songs in China are called **tongsu**. These popular entertainments are composed and recorded by government-employed artists and receive government support and approval. In contrast, Chinese rock songs (*yaogun yinyue*) often have subversive lyrics and express individualistic and anti-establishment sentiments. Rock musicians in China are not supported by the state and are marginalized by the lack of radio play and popular venues in which to perform.

STYLE

The term "style" refers to the sum total of the ways musicians combine the elements described above to create music that has coherence and identity. The term can be used broadly to speak of national styles, as in French as opposed to Russian style, historical "stylistic periods" such as the Renaissance or Contemporary, and regional styles like traditional New Orleans or **San Francisco** Jazz. It can also be used to identify individual styles—Elvis Presley and Norah Jones having "a style of their own." Genres like hip-hop, country, classical, etc., are defined by expectations for a particular "sound" and style that audiences recognize and respond to. Musicians make stylistic decisions based upon the contextual demands of a particular occasion. Encountering the electric guitars and dance rhythms of Christian rock in the high Anglican Church of England would be strange indeed, whereas in many American evangelical churches this style of music is normal.

Musicians often work within traditions, following conventional ways of making music that meets and responds to the expectations of their audiences. Music often follows teacher–pupil lines of transmission across generations. In the classical Hindustani tradition of North India, the term *gharana* refers to such a lineage, often maintained within extended families, preserving a consistent style of performance by which musicians identify themselves. *Pansori*, a genre of Korean musical storytelling, is practiced in two styles: a Western style (*Sopyonjae*) and an Eastern style (*Dongpyonjae*). These styles are described by practitioners and audiences in contrasting terms—stories in *Dongpyonjae* are told in a heavy and vigorous manner, while *Sopyonjae* is "sorrowful and tender" (from the 1993 movie *Sopyonjae* by Im Kwon Taek). In the Western symphony orchestra, the conductor imposes stylistic decisions relating to speed, volume, and balance on a large group of instrumentalists. However, the conductor's decisions are highly determined by the musical score of the composer, who often is not present or even alive at the time of the performance. A conductor will often impose a personal style on a performance that contrasts with that of other conductors, who may interpret the same score quite differently.

Some musicians work against traditional expectations, finding inspiration in new digital technologies, performance venues, and ever-evolving social circumstances. Many contemporary composers are using electronic instruments and pre-recorded tape to dispense with the symphony orchestra, conductor, and/or musical score entirely. Acoustic instrumentalists "go electric" to reach new audiences by developing more commercial, pop-oriented styles. Irish rock bands like the Cranberries, using electric guitars, African-based rhythms, and ear-splitting amplification, have created a hybrid style based on traditional Irish music. Their performances may make listeners with more traditional tastes cover their ears, while audiences accustomed to the high decibel level of rock, punk, and heavy-metal are enthusiastic about the contemporary performance style.

3-39

3-17

CONCLUSION

As we hope you have observed from the first three lessons, "sounds organized by humans for musical purposes" constitute a complex and diverse realm of human engagement, expression, and creativity. Music integrates the individual and social dimensions of our experience in ways that are difficult to define, but may nonetheless be indispensable. It is a universal form of human expression whose roots reach back into the dim recesses of pre-history. In our next lesson we consider the question "Where does music come from?" The simple answer is "no one knows," as no one knows where language or religion or visual representation of the observable world—what we call "art"—originated. But it is precisely these complex codes of communion, engagement, and relationship that made our distant ancestors distinctly and recognizably human.

KEY CONCEPTS

Composition and improvisation	Grooves and dance rhythms	Harmonic progression
Periodicity and contrast	Rhythmic virtuosity	Texture
Elements of music	Melody	Monophony
Rhythm	Scale	Polyphony
Rhythmic mode	Mode	Homophony
Free rhythm	Melodic contour	Heterophony
Polyrhythm	Ornamentation	Form
Work rhythm	Harmony	Genre
		Style

Q THINKING ABOUT MUSIC QUESTIONS

1. Choose a recording of music that you are familiar with. As you listen to it, can you recognize the two "areas of convergence" discussed at the beginning of this lesson: Composition vs Improvisation, and Periodicity vs Contrast? Describe them in your own words. Now listen again to the selections in this lesson: "*Shadanane*," "Moonlight Sonata," and "I Walk the Line." Try to do the same.
2. Explain in your own words the concepts of "rhythmic mode" and "**melodic mode**."
3. Listen to the following four selections (from Lesson 3 "Texture"): Benedictine nuns, "California Dreaming," *isicathamiya*, "*Shojo No Tsuru*." In each case, describe the texture and how that affects your listening experience.
4. Choose two music videos linked to Lesson 3 and describe their musical styles in terms of at least three musical elements discussed in the lesson. In what ways are the videos similar and different?
5. Think about the relationship between musical sound and context, and consider how the way music is used shapes the way it sounds. Choose two of the videos in Lesson 3 and explain the music in terms of its elements (rhythm, melody, harmony, etc.). Then suggest how the elements relate to the specific context in each case.

NOTES

1   Michael Tenzer, ed., *Analytical Studies in World Music* (Oxford and New York: Oxford University Press, 2006), 22.
2   Interview with Simon Shaheen in the documentary film series, *Exploring the World of Music, VI: Melody,* Pacific Street Films and the Educational Film Center, 1999.
3   George Ruckert, "Hindustani Raga," in *The Garland Encyclopedia of World Music, Vol. 5: South Asia*, ed. Alison Arnold (New York: Garland Publishing, 2000), 64.
4   Bruce Chatwin, *The Songlines* (London: Pan Books, 1988), 2.
5   Chatwin, *The Songlines*, 64.
6   Chatwin, *The Songlines,* 119–120.
7   Isabel Wong, "The Music of China," in Bruno Nettl et al., ed, *Excursions in World Music*, 5th ed., (Upper Saddle River, NJ: Pearson Education, 2008), 104.

Lesson 4
Where Does Music Come From?
The Origins of Music

The image of Shiva Nataraja, Lord of the Dance, is found in many temples in South India and reached its present form more than a thousand years ago. The image depicts the god Shiva, one of the three great divinities of the Hindu trinity, dancing on the back of a dwarf who represents ignorance. In his upper right hand he holds a drum whose beat accompanies the god's ecstatic movements, through

Fig. 4.1 Shiva Nataraja (L), and Shiva's *damaru* drum (detail) (R)

which the universe comes into being. In one of his left hands he holds fire, symbol of the destructive forces that will bring the universe to an end. Thus the image encompasses the entire span of time, and the god's music becomes not merely the symbol of creation but the creative power itself, which sustains the cosmos.

With no definitive evidence on where music came from or when it began, humans over the centuries have created numerous myths and stories to explain its origins. In this lesson we discuss some of these myths, as well as several more recent evolutionary theories relating to the origins of music to see what light they shed on our understanding of music's universality and the multiple functions it serves in human life.

ORIGIN MYTHS

The ancient Greeks, like the Hindus, believed that music preexisted humanity and was part of the very order of the cosmos. The "Music of the Spheres," whose perfect harmonies were believed to permeate the universe, was inaudible because humans would have heard it continuously from birth, and so were insensitive to the sound. However, harmonious *human* music, based on mathematical proportions, mirrored the perfect music of the heavens and allowed humans to participate in that perfection. In an early Christian context, the 4th-century bishop St. Basil attributed the invention of music directly to God, saying: "When, indeed, the Holy Spirit saw that the human race was guided only with difficulty toward virtue…what did He do? The delight of melody He mingled with the doctrines so that by the pleasantness and softness of the sound heard, we might receive without perceiving it the benefit of the words."[1] Visual artists from diverse religious traditions represent heavenly realms as places filled with divine music. This painting by the Italian Renaissance artist Raphael (1483–1520) depicts the Patroness of Music, St. Cecilia, renouncing the pleasures of earthly music, represented by the scattered instruments at her feet, in exchange for the heavenly choirs above. As she contemplates eternity, she rejects even human-made sacred music, represented by the organ slipping out of her grasp.

Fig. 4.2 *St. Cecilia with Saints* (ca. 1514–1516), Raphael (1483–1520)

Some myths are based in religious beliefs and teachings—as with Shiva Nataraja—in which the beginnings of sound and music are integrally linked to the creation of the world. Others place the origin of music in the realm of human ancestors or the spirit world. Yet others ascribe music's origin to human invention. All origin myths and narratives serve to satisfy our basic human curiosity and desire to find an answer to the as yet unanswered and perhaps unanswerable question, "Where did music come from?" and also to account for its mysterious attractiveness.

The first two origin myths we present below, from West Africa and the Hopi Nation of the southwestern United States, place the origin of music with the creation of the cosmos. As in the Shiva Nataraja example at the beginning of Lesson 4, music in these myths is the very force of creation.

Fig. 4.3 **African *sanza* (lamellaphone)**

"THE WORLD WAS CREATED TO THE NOTES OF A SANZA"
(BANTU, WEST AFRICA)

In the beginning, there was nothing.
Neither light, nor darkness.
Nothing but boredom.
And Nyambé, creator of the Bantu, was bored to death.
One day, he asked Imagination:
"What's there to do?"
Imagination answered:
"Make a *sanza*! As soon as you start playing it,
your boredom will go away."
So Nyambé made himself a *sanza*, plucked a reed
and the first sound of music was heard,
from which emerged the sun.
Another note of the *sanza* created man,
soon joined by a wife and many children who very
soon populated the earth. And so it is that all men,
white and black, yellow and red, were born of the *sanza*.
And even now as I speak, I am making a child…
another child…many children, of all colors…This
is why the Bantu love all men without distinction.[2]

THE MYTH OF SPIDER WOMAN (HOPI NATION)

The Spider Woman myth of the Hopi people of the southwestern United States is also a story of the cosmos-creating power of music. Spider Woman, one of the co-creators of our world, in the beginning made twin boys from earth and saliva. She brought them to life by singing the Creation Song over them. To the first twin she gave the duty of keeping the world in order. The second she instructed to "go about all the world and send out sound so that it may be heard throughout all the land." This twin would then be known as Echo, "for all sound echoes the Creator." When he did this, "all the vibratory centers along the earth's axis from pole to pole resounded his call; the whole earth trembled; the universe quivered in tune. Thus he made the whole world an instrument of sound, and sound an instrument for carrying messages, resounding praise to the Creator of all."[3]

Some myths link the origin of music with the creation of human beings, as in this **Sufi** narrative from Kashmir.

THE ANGELS' SONG (SUFIS IN KASHMIR)

Sufis (Islamic mystics) in the North Indian state of Kashmir relate that Allah, the Creator and Protector, gave life to Adam by blowing the fire of the soul into the human body of clay, chanting the words "to be." The Lord commanded the soul into Adam's body but from fear the soul would not enter. "The angels then 'sang in' the melody: 'Into the body, into the body, get into the body'."[4] The singing of the angels was thus the original act of creation, and their divine sound filled the human world. This sound was then ordered into eight musical pitches, and human music was born.

Music in some narratives is considered a gift from divine beings, as in the early Christian view of St. Basil referred to above, and in this story from ancient India.

A GIFT FROM THE GODS (ANCIENT INDIA)

According to the *Natya Shastra*, a 2000-year old Indian treatise on music, dance, and drama, music was originally a divine gift from the gods to mankind. In ancient times, the god Indra together with other gods asked Brahma, the Creator, to give something to humans so that they would turn away from their evil ways, from their greed, lust, and anger. Brahma decided to give to humans the celestial art of music as a plaything and distraction. The Hindu heaven was filled with divine beings (*gandharvas* and *apsaras*) who were well versed in the musical arts. The gods sought a suitable human who was wise enough to receive from them this sacred gift. Music was thus conveyed to the world through a single sage known as Narada,[5] who had been a *gandharva* in a previous birth. Narada, in turn, taught this divine art to humanity.

Fig. 4.4 Sage Narada playing the *vina*

Several myths place music in an ongoing relationship or connection between humans and spirit beings. In the following two examples, humans receive songs in dreams and visions as manifestations of sacred power.

OLD MAN TULH (AUSTRALIAN ABORIGINAL MYTH)

In Aboriginal mythology, songs come from ancestors and are transmitted to the world of the living through dreams. One of the myths of the Mari-ammu people of northwestern Australia involves the song-giving ancestor Old Man Tulh. He is one of many world-creating ancestors who were active at the beginning of time. Old Man Tulh appears in dreams to certain individuals called songmen and gives them *wangga* songs and dances that they must then perform in ceremonies. The success of a ritual depends on mingling songs of the living with these songs that the long-ago dead bring to the dreaming songmen. The songmen must replicate not only the melody, rhythm, and words of the received song, but also must exactly imitate the voice of Old Man Tulh. It is the timbre of the ghostly voice that gives the singers their power, and it is through the living singers that the dead can participate in the ritual life of the people.[6]

VISION QUEST (NATIVE AMERICAN SALISH AND SIOUX NATIONS)

In the rite of passage known as the "Vision Quest," practiced in a number of Native American societies, songs were the primary evidence of divine contact and empowerment. Anthropologist Alan Merriam writes of the Native American Flathead people of western Montana: "The most important single fact about music and its relationship to the total world is its origin in the supernatural sphere. While it is clearly recognized that some songs are individually composed by human beings, and that some other songs are borrowed from neighboring peoples, all true and proper songs…owe their origin to a variety of contacts experienced by humans with beings which, though a part of the world, are superhuman and the source of both individual and tribal powers and skills."[7]

In the following story, the great Oglala Sioux prophet Black Elk (1863–1950) describes his encounter with supernatural beings from whom he learns a song:

> The grass was young and I was on horseback. A thunder storm was coming from where the sun goes down, and just as I was riding into the woods along a creek, there was a kingbird sitting on a limb. This was not a dream, it happened. And I was going to shoot at the kingbird with the bow my Grandfather made, when the bird spoke and said: "The clouds all over are one-sided." Perhaps it meant that all the clouds were looking at me. And then it said: "Listen! A voice is calling you!" Then I looked up at the clouds, and two men were coming there, headfirst like arrows slanting down; and as they came, they sang a sacred song and the thunder was like drumming. I will sing it for you. The song and the drumming were like this:
>
> Behold, a sacred voice is calling you;
> All over the sky a sacred voice is calling.
>
> I sat there gazing at them, and they were coming from the place where the giant lives (north). But when they were very close to me, they wheeled about toward where the sun goes down, and suddenly they were geese. Then they were gone, and the rain came with a big wind and a roaring.[8]

Several myths give musical instruments a divine origin—in some cases from a "trickster deity"—like the next three from ancient Greece, West Africa, and the Near East.

INVENTION OF THE LYRE (ANCIENT GREECE)

Greek mythology attributes the invention of several musical instruments—the lyre, panpipes, and flute—to Hermes, the messenger of the gods and the son of Zeus and the nymph Maia.

A Homeric Hymn from between the 7th and 6th centuries BCE tells the story of Hermes who invented the lyre on the day he was born, as well as the flute and panpipes.[9] Son of Zeus and the nymph Maia, Hermes was the youngest and most cunning of the Olympian gods. On the morning of his birth, he escaped the swaddling bands his mother had wrapped him in, as she slept in their cave on Mt. Cyllene, and went out seeking food and adventure. As soon as he stepped

Fig. 4.5 Ancient Greek jar (580–500 BCE) depicting Apollo playing the lyre

over the threshold he was distracted by the sight of a tortoise waddling across his path, and had a grand idea.

> He took up the tortoise in both hands and went back into the house carrying his charming toy. Then he cut off its limbs and scooped out the marrow of the mountain-tortoise with a scoop of grey iron…He cut stalks of reed to measure and fixed them, fastening their ends across the back and through the shell of the tortoise, and then stretched ox hide all over it by his skill. Also he put in the horns and fitted a cross-piece upon the two of them, and stretched seven strings of sheep-gut. [39–40, 43–48]

He plucked the strings one by one and each sounded marvelous. Accompanying himself on his new invention, he sang a glorious song about himself and his divine parentage. Then he hid the lyre in his cradle and went in search of his brother Apollo's sacred cows grazing on the mountains of Pieria. Finding them, he hastily invented fire, rubbing dry sticks together, and butchered and roasted two. He herded fifty more back to Mt. Cyllene and hid them in a grotto. Then the infant god huddled back into his swaddling bands beside his mother and pretended to sleep. It wasn't long before Apollo, the sun god who sees all, tracked the stolen cows to the cave and accused Hermes of the theft. "Child, lying in the cradle, make haste and tell me of my cattle, or we two will soon fall out angrily." [254–255] Hermes denied everything, asking how he, an infant, could steal cattle. "This is no task for me: rather I care for other things: I care for sleep, and milk of my mother's breast, and wrappings round my shoulders, and warm baths…. Neither am I guilty myself, neither have I seen any other who stole your cows—whatever cows may be; for I know them only by hearsay." [266–268, 275–277]

The argument was interrupted by the arrival of Zeus, their father, who brought the two brothers before the council of the gods on Mt. Olympus to settle the dispute. When Hermes could no longer deny the theft, he took out the lyre he had fashioned and began to play. Hearing the beautiful notes,

> Phoebus Apollo laughed for joy; for the sweet throb of the marvellous music went to his heart, and a soft longing took hold on his soul as he listened. Then the son of Maia, harping sweetly upon his lyre, took courage and stood at the left hand of Phoebus Apollo; and soon, while he played shrilly on his lyre, he lifted up his voice and sang, and lovely was the sound of his voice that followed. He sang the story of the deathless gods and of the dark earth, how at the first they came to be, and how each one received his portion. [420–429]

And Apollo cried, "Slayer of oxen, trickster, busy one, comrade of the feast, this song of yours is worth fifty cows, and I believe that presently we shall settle our quarrel peacefully." [436–438] Thus the lyre became Apollo's own instrument, exchanged for the cattle, and thereafter he was known as the god of music. Hermes, for his part, invented the panpipes and flute, to play while looking after the cattle he had purchased with the lyre.

"HOW THE DAN GOT THE BAA DRUM" (WEST AFRICA)

This myth from the Dan people of Liberia also attributes the invention of a musical instrument to a trickster deity.

A woman was sent by her husband to the forest to gather leaves for a sauce. She hears a strange and enchanting voice. Following the sound, she finds a genie sitting atop a termite mound in the middle of an empty field, beating a thing that people would later call the Baa Drum. The Genie spoke:

> "With us, we dance to this thing. If I beat it, you'll dance to its voice from here all the way down there…" The genie beat the drum and the woman began dancing.[10]

When she did not return home, the husband sent their son, who also became entranced by the new sound and started to dance. The husband, looking for his family, followed them to the field. He too could not resist; first his neck began to shake, then his arms, then his whole body. The people of the village, missing the man and the woman, went looking for them in the forest. Before they heard the sound, the villagers saw them from afar. "Why are you moving about like that?" they shouted, for they had never seen dancing. But as they approached, the villagers heard the sound and they too were caught in the drum's spell. After a time, an elephant hunter, who had been following the trail of an elephant for seven days, came upon this scene. He saw men and women, children and old people all dancing in the field. He told the genie to stop the dance. And the genie stopped. "Where does this drum come from?" he asked.

> The genie said, "It comes from our village. It's to this rhythm that we dance in the evening. When there's a party, everyone without exception…they all come and line up and dance together."[11]

The hunter asked, "How do you make the thing speak?" And the genie instructed him on the drum's construction from a hollow log and the skin of a dead animal.

Fig. 4.6 West African cylindrical drum, Accra, Ghana

> "When the skin dries, its voice becomes beautiful. Then you beat on it."[12]

"We will take this beautiful thing with us back to our village," said the hunter. The genie refused. So the hunter pointed his loaded rifle at the genie and fired. The drum rolled to the ground.

> Then the hunter said, "Pick up the drum and take it to the village. Instead of dancing here in the field, take this beautiful thing to the village so we can dance down there." They picked up the drum and they all went back to the village. Once they reached the village, they gave everyone this advice: "Anyone who wants to have a good party, let him do it with the drum. And we'll dance."

So it was that we [humans] got the drum. Then we learned to make more. At festivals, we pick them up and dance.[13]

JUBAL AND LAMECH (JEWISH AND ISLAMIC MYTH)

According to the Old Testament book of Genesis, the invention of music in Jewish tradition is ascribed to Jubal: "the father of all who play the harp and flute" (Genesis 4:21, New International Version). Later Jewish sources attributed to Jubal the origin of all musical instruments as well as singing. With the beginning of Islam in the 7th century, Muslim writers claimed music originated not with Jubal but his father Lamech, and not with the harp and flute but with the Arabic *ud*. A 9th-century Muslim text associates the origin of the *ud* with the human body, in the form of Lamech's son.[14]

Lamech had no children until old age, then finally having a son, the boy died at the age of five. Lamech grieved and hung his son's body on a tree until the flesh fell off the bones. Eventually only the

Fig. 4.7 Egyptian *ud* player

thigh, leg, and foot remained. Lamech then made an instrument of wood to represent the thigh, leg, foot, and toes, with strings for the sinews, and he played on it and wept, becoming the first person to sing a lament. The instrument was called an *ud* because it was made of wood.

In this Islamic tale from Kashmir in South Asia, it is the musical notes themselves, not instruments, that have a divine origin.

MOSES STRIKES THE STONE (SUFIS IN KASHMIR)

A Kashmiri Sufi tale attributes the origin of Persian melody to Moses as he led the Israelites out of Egypt.

> On seeing a stone in the middle of the Nile River, Moses wanted to return to pick it up but did not do so. Angel Gabriel appeared to Moses and told him to pick it up, saying some day he would find a use for the stone. Tired and thirsty after spending forty days in the desert with his tribe, Moses prayed to God. Angel Gabriel appeared again and told Moses to strike the stone with his staff. The stone cracked into twelve pieces and from each burst a spring, and the echoes of the springs blended together. As his tribe drank the water, Moses "departed into a flight of fancy in these sounds"…In his own tongue he read some verses in those melodies and gave them the name of the twelve *maqams* (melodic modes).[15]

Two final myths explain music as inherent in the very nature of existence. Like the ancient Greeks, the Chinese believed that through music, humans could participate in the perfection of the cosmos.

FRICTION BETWEEN HEAVEN AND EARTH (ANCIENT CHINA)

In ancient Chinese thought, musical sound was believed to originate in the friction between heaven and earth, and between the *yin* (the passive female principle) and the *yang* (the active male principle). According to ancient Chinese thinkers, music was conceived as a natural force resulting from the dynamic interactions between the elements. The *Record of Ritual Music and Dance* from the late Zhou period of Chinese history (ca. 6th–3rd centuries BCE) documents this concept:

> The *chhi* [vital force] of earth ascends above: the *chhi* of heaven descends from the height. The *yang* and the *yin* come into contact; heaven and earth shake together. Their drumming is in the shock and rumble of thunder; their excited beating of wings is in wind and rain; their shifting round is in the four seasons; their warming is in the sun and moon. Thus the hundred species procreate and flourish. Thus it is that music is a bringing together of heaven and earth.[16]

LEGEND OF THE YELLOW BELL (ANCIENT CHINA)

Perhaps the most famous Chinese legend on the origin of music places it ca. 2700 BCE when the Chinese Emperor Huang Di sent his mathematician Ling Lun to the far western mountains of China to cut a set of twelve tuned bamboo pipes. These would be used to provide pitches for a set of bronze bells. The largest was named the Yellow Bell, yellow being the imperial color. From this measurement, all the other pitches were derived, and the pitches became the tonal system for Chinese music. When the bells were played in rituals of state, the sound was so perfect that it united and harmonized the human realm with nature and the divine under the beneficent rule of the Chinese Emperor, the Son of Heaven.[17]

These myths and others like them do more than provide an explanation of music's origins. They also underscore music's importance to the living, and serve as a basis and justification for the ways people use music within their societies. Thus, in the case of the two West African myths, music is integral to socialization and group cohesion. In the story of Jubal, music's central role in funerals and mourning is legitimized. The ancient Chinese legend of the Yellow Bell points out the ways ritual music establishes the prestige of the emperor; with the Australian Aborigines, song unites the living with the dead and the first ancestors in shared community. In every case, music is seen as a source of connection between people, and between the human and trans-human worlds: nature, the ancestors, and the gods.

ORIGIN THEORIES

Associations with dreams, the supernatural, and myth suggest human involvement with music at deep levels of consciousness. Many musicians have spoken of the mysterious sources of musical inspiration. Bassist Ed King of the southern rock band Lynyrd Skynyrd claims that the chord progression and guitar riffs of "Sweet Home Alabama" came to him, note for note, in a dream. Joseph Shabalala, founder of the popular South African *isicathamiya* group Ladysmith Black Mambazo, launched his career following a series of dreams. American composer Aaron Copland writes in his book *What to Listen for in Music*: "The composer starts with a theme; and the theme is a gift from Heaven. He doesn't know where it comes from—has no control over it. It comes almost like automatic handwriting."[18] Modern neuroscience has reached the same conclusion. Oliver Sacks, Professor of Clinical Neurology and Psychiatry at Columbia University, writes:

> We humans are a musical species no less than a linguistic one. This takes many different forms. All of us (with very few exceptions) can perceive music, perceive tones, timbre, pitch intervals, melodic contours, harmony, and (perhaps most elementally of all) rhythm. We integrate all of these and "construct" music in our minds using many parts of the brain. And to this largely unconscious structural appreciation of music is added an often intense and profound emotional reaction to music.[19]

The involvement of multiple designated sites in the brain suggests that humans have musical perception and skill "hard-wired" into our neurophysiology as a genetic inheritance. Why this is so remains a mystery. The phenomenon has nevertheless been studied by those whose research is involved with humans at the very dawn of our evolutionary history.

From a scientific point of view, the question "Where did music come from?" has lately become a subject of intense interest and debate. Recent discoveries in neurophysiology, human paleontology, and infant psychology, among other fields, have brought music to the forefront of the study of human mind/ brain relationships, evolution, and social integration. The simple answer to the above question is "No one knows," although there has been much speculation. As with many basic human behaviors such as tool use, upright locomotion, and language, music's origins may never be discovered or fully understood. Moreover, unlike tool use, music itself leaves little trace in the fossil record upon which to base or support an origin theory.

The capacities to make and respond to music are universal and biologically supported by our genetic makeup. From a Darwinian, evolutionary perspective, this suggests that musical "instincts" were selected and passed on to offspring because they gave some survival, adaptive, and/or reproductive advantage to our distant hominid ancestors. Relevant archeological findings, though small, are tantalizing in their implications. What may be a bear femur flute, a fragment of which was found in a Neanderthal burial site in Slovenia and dated at 50,000 years old, has raised considerable controversy. If it is indeed a flute, and not (as some assert) an oddly chewed bone, it would be the oldest musical instrument yet discovered. Of course, humans could have been producing intentional sounds with their voices, bodies, and natural objects in the environment for millennia before constructing instruments out of non-perishable materials. These sounds would have accompanied dance movements and would have been incorporated into rituals and daily activities. Therefore while evidence is scant, it suggests that humans have been making music for a very long time, and a number of theories propose that music, along with language, developed at that time when our earliest ancestors became recognizably "us;" that is, human.

A 40,000-year-old flute made of vulture bone found in a cave in southwestern Germany, reported in *National Geographic News* in 2009, is the world's oldest artifact that is without doubt a musical instrument. The article states: "The ancient flutes are evidence for an early musical tradition that likely helped biologically modern humans communicate and form tighter social bonds...Music may therefore have been important to maintaining and strengthening Stone Age social networks...allowing for greater societal organization and strategizing." Quoting archeologist Nicholas Conard of the University of Tübingen in Germany who studied these flutes, the article continues:

> Think how important music is for us. Whether it's at church, a party, or just for fun, you can see how powerful music can be. People often hear a song and cry, or feel great joy or sorrow. All of those kinds of emotions help bond people together.[20]

Why did humans evolve innate capacities for making and responding to music? An inherited trait, according to evolutionary theory, promotes either survival or reproductive advantage. Scholars and researchers disagree on what advantages our ancestors gained from their musical capacities. Unlike tool making, language, and our upright posture and bipedal locomotion, it is not obvious what music did to promote survival and reproductive success. Even now, it seems to some like "mere entertainment" or a useless behavioral extravagance, despite the fact that all societies have music and that billions of dollars are spent on it annually. Below we introduce five theories that scholars have put forward to explain or shed light on why humans are born with these innate capacities.[21]

IMITATION OF SOUNDS OF THE NATURAL WORLD

For our purposes we are not considering sounds produced by animals and natural forces like wind and water to be music, but many researchers have considered these to be important in several ways when thinking about music in human evolution. There are certainly sounds in the natural world that resemble human music making, and the imitation of these sounds by our ancestors could plausibly have influenced its development. Birdsong in particular is often cited as a source for human musical inspiration. It has also been noted that two of the primary reasons birds "sing"—to mark territory and attract mates—are important in human music making as well, as evidenced by the sheer number and universality of national anthems, fight songs, and love ballads. Yet despite the similarities between human music and birdsong, they evolved separately and have only coincidental resemblance.

SOCIAL BONDING BEHAVIORS AMONG HIGHER MAMMALS

Certain higher mammals exhibit behaviors that resemble human music making in more subtle and sophisticated ways. Researchers have observed **humpback whales** "composing" their songs; that is, adding on new phrases to melodic contours "sung" in previous mating seasons, and repeating and altering musical units in highly creative ways. In other words, their songs are not simply instinctual, but are subject to creative processes. Some primates use vocalizations to acknowledge or strengthen social bonds. **Gibbons**, who are monogamous unlike most mammals, sing morning duets with their mates in one of the animal kingdom's most impressive sonic displays. The **gelada baboons** of Ethiopia use coordinated group vocalizations to resolve conflicts and re-establish group harmony. Perhaps geladas experience "temporary physiological synchrony"—a state of mutual metabolic and emotional coordination—through group vocalizing, much the way humans experience a feeling of solidarity and social cohesion from choral singing and at concerts and festivals. Primatologist Bruce Richman, who spent years studying the geladas, suggests that during the course of human evolution, the use of melody and rhythm developed as a specialized language of group emotional and physiological bonding, "a kind of vocal grooming." Indeed, Richman was struck by how human-like these vocalizations are both in sound and apparent function.[22]

Anthropologist John Blacking suggested that singing and dancing preceded by several hundred thousand years the development of spoken language, in which words are linked to meanings. "There is so much music in the world that it is reasonable to suppose that music, like language and possibly religion, is a species-specific trait of man."[23] Singing and dancing, like the grooming behaviors of the gelada baboons, contributed to the bonding of social groups upon which early human survival depended and continues to depend.

MUSIC AS A FORM OF COURTSHIP DISPLAY IN THE ATTRACTION OF MATES

Charles Darwin, in his study *The Descent of Man, and Selection in Relation to Sex,* wrote, "[I]t appears probable that the progenitors of man, either the males or females or both sexes, before acquiring the power of expressing their mutual love in articulate language, endeavored to charm each other with musical notes and rhythm."[24] Darwin argued that music preceded speech in human evolution and was connected with courtship behaviors between the sexes. He had observed that birds, particularly males, sing much more often during the mating season to attract mates, defend territory, and repel rivals. These sounds, which convey emotion and intention, are describable in the terms we use for musical analysis such as pitch, rhythm, and timbre.

Darwin's position that music evolved in humans as a complex biological adaptation related to male courtship display has been defended recently by evolutionary biologist Geoffrey Miller. Along with artistic creativity, language, and fitness indicators like dance, Miller claims that musical competence in males signaled to perspective mates such desirable traits as endurance, intelligence, resourcefulness, coordination, and general health. According to Miller, musical creativity and complexity in humans may have been the result of a kind of "endless arms race" in which "our ancestral hominid-Hendrixes could never say, 'OK, our music's good enough, we can stop now," because they were competing with all the hominid-Eric Claptons, hominid-Jerry Garcias, and hominid-John Lennons."[25] The process that he calls the "runaway" theory of evolution led peacock males, for instance, to grow ever larger and more elaborate tail feathers, since the one with the largest had the best chance of attracting a mate and passing along the long-tail trait to the next generation. So human musicians would have developed ever more flashy and complex musical displays for the benefit of their prospective mates, and those who competed most successfully would have passed on their musical talent to the most offspring.

EVOLUTIONARY MODELS OF MUSIC AND LANGUAGE

Several origin theories underscore the fact that human communication by means of spoken language, as opposed to written language, conveys meaning not only through the grammatical sense of words, but in the *sounds* and inflections of speech. These elements include those that most resemble the qualities of musical sound: volume, pitch, speed, timbre, etc. Consider the sentence "I love you." The range of possible meanings based on the stress used in *spoken* language render the sentence quite ambiguous in print. If, in spoken language, the first word is stressed: "*I* love you," the sentence implies that *I*, as opposed to the person over there, love you. If the third word is emphasized: "I love *you*," the meaning changes. I love *you* instead of the other person over there. If the emphasis is placed upon the verb: "I *love* you," the meaning emphasizes love as opposed to hate or indifference. And if the sentence is spoken ironically and as a question: "*I...* love *you*?" with a rise in pitch at the end, it can mean the exact opposite of its dictionary meaning as in, "you gotta be kidding!" If music developed in relationship to language, as many scholars believe, it is the *intonational* aspects of spoken language—its tone, pitch, speed, accentuation pattern—that it most resembles, rather than the *grammatical* elements (sentence structure and literal meaning).

Neuroscientist Steven Brown believes the faculties of music and speech may have emerged from a stage of human development he calls "Musilanguage."[26] This combination of sounds and gestures (the rudiments of dance and theater), by which our ancestors communicated, would have contained elements of what would become language and music. Through vocalized sound, humans convey two kinds of information, "referential meaning" and "emotive meaning." Language and music are each able to express both, to varying degrees. The verbal sound-structure T-R-E-E for example, *refers to* that big leafy thing growing in the yard (referential meaning). Excited speech, such as "HEY! THAT TREE IS ABOUT TO FALL ON YOUR HEAD!" *conveys emotion* (emotive meaning). Here we have words with dictionary meanings, and a vocal delivery—loud and urgent—that conveys the emotional charge. To use a musical example, the Wedding March has referential meaning in conveying associations relevant to the occasion, as in "Here Comes the Bride," everyone stand! It also has emotive meaning, conveying powerful feelings appropriate to the solemnity and joy of the occasion through its stately rhythm and simple, memorable melodic contour. Brown sees the various functions of language and music existing along a spectrum, rather than occupying mutually exclusive communication domains. According to this view, music and language differ mainly in their emphasis rather than in their fundamental nature. As the two ends of the spectrum became more specialized, they diverged into the two communicative modes of music and language, although each retained vestiges of the other. East Asian tonal languages such as Cantonese, and "sing-song" speech that characterizes spoken Welsh and Norwegian, contain vestiges of music in spoken language. African drum languages work the opposite way, containing vestiges of spoken language in a system that is fundamentally musical.

MUSIC'S EVOLUTION IN MOTHER–INFANT BONDING BEHAVIORS

One of the most compelling theories of music's origins is that proposed by Ellen Dissanayake. She argues persuasively that music began with the interactive sound sequences and give-and-take behaviors that characterize the bonding of mothers and their infants. These behaviors, in turn, were adaptations necessitated four million years ago by "the collision course between two incompatible anatomical trends": bipedal (two-legged) locomotion and greatly increased brain size and capacity. According to Dissanayake, for humans to gain the various survival advantages that standing and walking upright on two legs brought, a number of profound adaptations had to occur. Of course, these adaptations took place incrementally over many generations. "Over four million years, hominid brains more than doubled in size.... Obviously there was a conflict at the time of childbirth between a large-brained infant and the narrow pelvis shape necessary to support an upright walker, requiring several other adaptations that would ease the risk to both mother and infant."[27] One of the important adaptations that accommodated this change was human infants being born prematurely so that the head would fit through the narrow birth canal before it grew too large. "If human infants were as mature at birth as infant apes are, [pregnancy] would last for twenty-one months and result in a twenty-five-pound baby.... A human infant's brain continues to grow and mature outside the womb: between birth and age four, its size triples."[28] The result of these adaptations is a long period of infant helplessness. "Because human infants were helpless for a far longer time after birth than any other species, they required prolonged attention and care. Mothers and infants who found ways to develop and sustain intense affective bonds would have been at an advantage over mothers and infants who did not."[29]

The vocalizations of the mother, imitated by the infant with coos and squeals within a few months of birth, are "composed of elements that are literally, not metaphorically, musical."[30] These **mother–infant interactions** are remarkably similar around the world, with infants responding to the pitch, contours, and rhythms of the mother's voice in addition to facial expressions, gestures, touching, and patting, and a whole repertoire of dynamic, interactive engagements. "Imitation and matching each other's vocalizations and facial expressions, both involuntary and deliberate, contribute to mutual enjoyment and attunement."[31]

Fig. 4.8   **Ellen Dissanayake, March 2008**

Dissanayake maintains that these behaviors are innate; infants respond instinctively to these "motherese" sounds and gestures, and parents instinctively perform them for their babies. However, as with other innate behaviors like learning to speak or to swim, for which we are also genetically prepared, mother-infant bonding behavior requires post-natal fostering to be activated and developed. "A child who never hears language will not learn to speak; someone who lives in the desert will not learn to swim; women who have never been around babies will not instinctively know how to care for them [despite having the predisposition]."[32] It is this interaction between innate, inborn capacities and living "out in the world" that produces the nature/nurture dynamic that characterizes human experience. Through interactions with parents and other caregivers, infants learn to respond to and produce musical sounds that have pitch, rhythm, and melodic contour. They learn these behaviors from the very beginning of life in the context of intensely pleasurable social interactions, and they learn to experience human connectedness through these sounds. Humans maintain this capacity into adulthood, which enables them to replicate the behaviors with their own offspring.

CONCLUSION

Each of the developmental theories presented above presupposes that music served important functions in aiding the survival of our hominid ancestors. These include group cohesion, communication, reproductive advantage, and mother-infant intimacy. For whatever reason or reasons, the capacity to make and respond to music is part of our genetic makeup. Human biology changes extremely slowly over many generations, but human technologies and expressive forms and behaviors—those aspects that constitute "culture"—can change dramatically within a single generation. While we share fundamentally the same genetic code with our ancestors who hunted, gathered, and presumably "musicked" on the African Savannah 100,000 years ago, the music we now respond to is quite different. The world we inhabit, of MP3s, shopping malls, and digital superhighways, is far removed from the world for which our bodies were adapted. The fact that so much of our brain development occurs after birth, means that while humans have few useful instincts they have an enormous capacity for learning. We fiddle and strum our musical instruments with hands whose digits and opposable thumbs originally evolved to hold tree branches and then to make and use tools. Our ancestors built upon a repertoire of innate and inherited capacities and taught their innovations to their children. Just as weapons over the millennia have evolved from chipped flint arrowheads to missiles and "smart" bombs, and storage technologies have evolved from woven baskets to computer hard drives, so the proto-musical activities of our distant ancestors have developed over generations of cultural transmission into the spectacular range of sounds and instruments and music technologies we have today.

KEY CONCEPTS

Origin myth	Reproductive advantage	Intonational aspects of
Ancestor or spirit realms	Evolutionary theories	speech
Origin theory	Social bonding	Mother–infant interaction
Darwinian evolutionary	Courtship display	Referential and emotive
perspective	"Musilanguage"	meaning
Promotion of survival		

(Q) THINKING ABOUT MUSIC QUESTIONS

1. Choose three of the myths presented in this lesson, and explain what each tells us about attitudes, beliefs, and values.
2. Explain in your own words the relationship between the grammatical and intonational aspects of spoken language. How do the intonational components of spoken language resemble music?
3. In what ways do *you* think music has contributed to the survival of our species?
4. Make up your own origin of music myth that has relevance to the way music functions in your own life. Does your myth relate to music's promotion of survival and reproductive advantage, and if so, how?
5. Lesson 4 proposes four scientific theories that suggest a deep relationship between music and human codes of communication. Theorists have emphasized music's possible origins in the following human relationships: a) the bonding of social groups, b) courtship, c) the grammatical and intonational aspects of speech, and d) interactions between mother and child. Discuss each of these four relationships both in terms of the origin of music theories and your own observations of music in human life today.

NOTES

1 Piero Weiss and Richard Taruskin, "The Church Fathers on Psalmody and on the Dangers of Unholy Music," in *Music in the Western World: A History in Documents* (New York: Schirmer, 1984), 25.
2 Francis Bebey, "The World Was Created to the Notes of a Sanza," in Leonardo D'Amico and Francesco Mizzau, ed., *Africa Folk Music Atlas* (Florence, Italy: Amharsi Edizioni Multimediali, 1997), 4.
3 Frank Waters, *Book of the Hopi* (New York: Penguin Books, 1977), 4–5.
4 Gordon Arnold, trans. "The Angels' Song," from Daya Ram Kachroo "Khushdil," *Taraana-e Saroor* [On Music in Kashmir] (Srinagar: Jammu and Kashmir Government, Research and Publication Dept., 1962), 1.
5 David Courtney, "Mythological Origins of Sangeet" (1988), last updated February 5, 2012, http://chandrakantha.com/articles/indian_music/myth_origin.html.
6 Allan Marett, *Songs, Dreamings, and Ghosts: The Wangga of North Australia* (Middletown, CT: Wesleyan University Press, 2005), 16–17.
7 Alan P. Merriam, "The Importance of Song in the Flathead Indian Vision Quest," *Ethnomusicology* 9/2 (1965), 91.
8 John G. Neihardt, *Black Elk Speaks* (New York: Washington Square Press, 1972), 14–15.
9 Citations in this origin myth from "Hymn 4 to Hermes," *The Homeric Hymns and Homerica with Eng. Trans. by Hugh G. Evelyn-White* (Cambridge, MA: Harvard University Press; London, William Heinemann Ltd, 1914), public domain, http://www.perseus.tufts.edu/hopper/text?doc=Perseus%3Atext%3A1999.01.0138%3Ahymn%3D4
10 Hugo Zemp, "The Origin of the Baa Drum," in Leonardo D'Amico and Francesco Mizzau, ed. *Africa Folk Music* Atlas (Florence, Italy: Amharsi Edizioni Multimediali, 1997), 58.
11 Hugo Zemp, "The Origin," 62.
12 Hugo Zemp, "The Origin," 62.

13 Hugo Zemp, "The Origin," 62.

14 From al-Mufaddal ibn Salama, *Kitab al-malahi* ("The Book of Musical Instruments"), in Amnon Shiloah, *Music in the World of Islam* (Detroit: Wayne State University Press, 1995), 36–37.

15 Gordon Arnold, trans., from "Khushdil," *Taraana-e Saroor*, 16–17.

16 Joseph Needham, *Science and Civilisation in China*, Vol. 4, Pt. 1, Sec. 26 (Cambridge: Cambridge University Press, 1961), cited in Lewis Rowell, *Music and Musical Thought in Early India* (Chicago: Chicago University Press, 1992), 54–55.

17 The Legend of the Yellow Bell is documented in many sources. See Jenny So, ed. *Music in the Age of Confucius* (Seattle, Washington: University of Washington Press, 2000), 29.

18 Aaron Copland, *What to Listen for in Music* (New York: McGraw Hill, 1957), 18.

19 Oliver W. Sacks, *Musicophilia: Tales of Music and the Brain* (New York: Alfred A. Knopf, 2007), xi.

20 James Owen, "Bone Flute is Oldest Instrument, Study Says," *National Geographic News*, June 24, 2009, http://news.nationalgeographic.com/news/2009/06/090624-bone-flute-oldest-instrument.html.

21 Anthony Storr, "Origins and Collective Functions," in *Music and the Mind* (New York: Ballantine Books, 1992), 1–23.

22 Nils L. Wallin et al., ed. 2000. *The Origins of Music* (Cambridge, MA: MIT Press, 2000), 301.

23 John Blacking, *How Musical Is Man?* (Seattle: University of Washington Press, 1973), 7.

24 Charles Darwin, *The Descent of Man, and Selection in Relation to Sex* (London: John Murray, 1871), 880.

25 Geoffrey Miller, "Evolution of Human Music through Sexual Selection," in Nils L. Wallin et al., ed., *Origins of Music*, 343.

26 Steven Brown, "The 'Musilanguage' Model of Music Evolution," in Nils L. Wallin et al., ed. *Origins of Music*, 272.

27 Ellen Dissanayake, *Art and Intimacy: How the Arts Began* (Seattle: University of Washington Press, 2000), 13.

28 Ellen Dissanayake, *Art and Intimacy*, 14.

29 Ellen Dissanayake, *Art and Intimacy*, 14.

30 Ellen Dissanayake," Antecedents of the Temporal Arts in Early Mother–Infant Interaction," in Nils L. Wallin et al., ed. *Origins of Music*, 34.

31 Ellen Dissanayake, "Antecedents," 393.

32 Ellen Dissanayake, *Art and Intimacy*, 12.

Lesson 5
What is Music For?
The Functions of Music

CULTURAL EVOLUTION

In Lesson 4, we noted that all humans have inherited a genetic aptitude for making and responding to music and we presented explanatory theories for why this is so. In Lesson 5 we discuss the functions that music has served over millennia. Having developed the aptitude for what today we call music, our distant ancestors began the dynamic processes that now present us with an infinitely rich and complex expressive inheritance. We can imagine them responding to the rhythms of biology—bipedal locomotion, the respiratory cycle, the pumping heart—and imitating natural sounds from insects and birds to wind and water, and also the sounds of their natural emotional expressions like laughing, weeping, panting, sighing, and shouting. They may have become fascinated by echo phenomena and special timbres produced by vocalizing in caves and other resonant acoustical spaces. These became intentional and replicable musical utterances and contributed to rhythmic and tonal vocabularies and singing styles. Over thousands of generations, music has changed in myriad ways along with all the other shared attitudes, values, goals, technologies, and practices that characterize human societies or groups that we call, in sum, "culture." Humans create music out of the sounds around them, and as the sounds change, music likewise changes. As new technologies and modes of livelihood developed, the social soundscape of people's daily lives became filled with the sounds of pounding grain, churning butter, chipping flint, galloping horses; and, more recently, trains and factories. Technological advances, from agriculture to the forging of metals, silk production, the electric turbine, audio recording and the MP3 file, all contributed new possibilities for sound production and creativity. For millennia, each successive generation inherited from the previous generation a musical "language," a set of melodic and rhythmic patterns and ways of organizing them into songs, dances, and rituals. Either gradually or suddenly these changed, as new sounds and technologies were developed, new musical styles were encountered, new purposes for music were found. Differences in environment, modes of livelihood, social structure, language, religion, and many other factors account for the enormous diversity of musical styles and preferences among groups and individuals in the world today.

Each of the origin theories presented in the previous lesson presupposes that music was of some important use in aiding the survival of our hominid ancestors. These uses include group cohesion, communication, sexual advantage, and mother-infant intimacy. Yet a number of cognitive psychologists and other scientists, most famously Steven Pinker of Harvard University, suggest that music really served no adaptive function. Pinker has called music "auditory cheesecake".... It just happens to tickle several important parts of the brain in a highly pleasurable way, as cheesecake tickles the palate." His controversial view is that *spoken language* did indeed evolve as an advantage-giving adaptation; and music developed as an accidental by-product, an "evolutionary parasite." Pinker states, "Compared with language, vision, social reasoning, and physical know-how, music could vanish from our species and the rest of our lifestyle would be virtually unchanged."[1] In this lesson we consider some of the ways in which music functions today. Here we provide evidence, we believe, that Pinker is wrong. For whatever reason or reasons music became part of our world and our humanity, it has come to serve a number of unique functions beyond the merely hedonistic upon which the viability of our social structures, hence our survival as a species, may in fact rest.

MERRIAM'S FUNCTIONS OF MUSIC

In his classic study *The Anthropology of Music*, Alan P. Merriam (1923–1980) presented ten functions that music serves among nearly all peoples of the world. In this lesson we examine these ten functions as evidence against Pinker's claim that music is a superfluous indulgence. Placed together, they suggest that there are many aspects of personal and social life that could not be performed as well, or at all, without music. Based on his study of the Basongye people of the Republic of Congo, Merriam describes how essential music is for many aspects of their society, and, he believed, for all societies. Merriam writes:

> More specifically, a major funeral cannot take place among the Basongye without the presence of a professional musician and his music.... The professional musician makes his appearance after the body has been interred and performs a number of functions which he alone can contribute.... It is also the musician's role [among others] to help the mourners begin to forget the tragedy of death. Upon his appearance [during the fourth day of the funeral]...people begin to smile and joke for the first time since the death.... The musician is a key figure in the funeral. He is similarly a key figure in other kinds of activities, including dancing, hunting, certain religious behavior, and other aspects of Basongye life as well. Indeed, without the musician, whose numerous roles have been barely touched upon here, the structure of much of Basongye behavior would be markedly changed.[2]

Merriam concludes, "There is probably no other human cultural activity which is so all-pervasive and which reaches into, shapes, and often controls so much of human behavior."[3] While music is not a "universal language"—its meanings do not cross cultural boundaries as readily as some have suggested—it is universally used within a great variety of social contexts. Although music does not convey meaning in the same way as spoken language, it does seem to convey something, and to express aspects of our experience that language cannot. You will recall that our definition of music placed a great emphasis on "purpose": it was the *purposes* sounds were used for that made them music. Here we attempt to delineate what some of these musical purposes, or functions, are. Merriam provides a useful set of categories by which we can organize the great diversity of human musical expressions. Of course, any given musical example may serve multiple functions, and the categories do overlap. Nevertheless, when taken together, these "generalizations which are equally applicable to all societies"[4] validate the enormous importance of music in the healthy functioning of humans both individually and in their societies, a claim that cannot be made of Pinker's "Cheesecake."

1. THE FUNCTION OF EMOTIONAL EXPRESSION

The expression of emotion is clearly one of music's most basic functions in human life. But how is emotion translated into musical sounds, or stated another way, how do musical sounds embody and convey human emotions? The precise nature of the relationship is not well understood. Nevertheless, the function of Emotional Expression is first on Merriam's list. He quotes anthropologist Edwin G. Burrows' description of the South Sea Tuamotu people (in French Polynesia), among whom music is for "stimulating and expressing emotion in the performers, and imparting it to the listeners. The emotion may be religious exaltation, as in the creation chant and song of the sacred red bird; grief, as in the laments; longing or passion, as in the love-songs; joy in motion; sexual excitement, and a variety of other emotions.... Underlying all of these in greater or less degree is the general function of stimulating, expressing, and sharing emotion."[5] Ethnomusicologist David McAllester writes:

> With us a principal function of music seems to be as an aid in inducing attitude. We have songs to evoke moods of tranquility, nostalgia, sentiment, group rapport, religious feeling, party solidarity, and patriotism, to name a few. Thus we sing to put babies to sleep, to make work seem lighter, to make people buy certain kinds of breakfast foods, or to ridicule our enemies.[6]

In India, a theory of correspondence between melodic systems (*ragas*) and emotions was presented in a treatise on stagecraft, the *Natya Shastra,* nearly two thousand years ago. Because the music described in the ancient treatise was used to accompany a drama, it was essential that the mood (**bhava**) conveyed by the music was appropriate to the situation it accompanied. A musical scale or melodic gesture is said to contain an emotional essence (*rasa*) that allows all present, performers as well as listeners, to experience the same emotion at the same time. The treatise recognized eight basic emotions: love, joy, anger, compassion, disgust, fear, courage, and wonder; to which a ninth was later added, peace.

John Lennon's song lyrics in **"Mother"** describe the singer's one-sided relationship with his mother and father. As the song progresses, the emotional anguish expressed in his singing builds in intensity until the ending with its impassioned cry: "Mama don't go! Daddy come home!" After leaving the famous band The Beatles, John Lennon entered an intensive period of self-examination under the care of psychotherapists Arthur and Vivian Janov. Arthur Janov had written an influential book on the subject of a new form of therapy he had developed called "Primal Scream," based on the assumption that pent-up childhood trauma causes psychological pain in adults. Patients were encouraged to re-live vividly and express viscerally their suppressed childhood anguish. This technique inspired Lennon's writing of several songs in the early 1970s with his wife, artist Yoko Ono, including "Mother." Whether as performers or listeners, many find in music a cathartic outlet for relieving pain or suffering, for releasing otherwise inexpressible feelings, and for regaining psychological balance.

Also, Portuguese *fado* ("destiny, fate") is a vocal genre whose lyrics and music embody deep feelings of longing and nostalgia (*saudade*). The genre arose in 19th-century Lisbon, although the style originated much earlier and is considered one of the world's oldest folk musics. For more than a century, its lyrics and moods have expressed the cares and sorrows of the poor and working-class patrons of the taverns where the *fadista* sings deep into the night, accompanied by the *guitarra* (12-string

Fig. 5.1 **Portuguese *fado* singer, Ana Moura (1979–)**

Portuguese guitar) and the *viola* (Portuguese bass guitar). In her song *"Fado Loucura,"* internationally renowned *fado* singer Ana Moura pours out her feelings of sadness, wearing the traditional long black dress and shawl of the female *fado* singer.

Watch this video of **Tito Puente's salsa band**, playing in the South Bronx. What do you think a seventy-year-old man with a pair of *timbales* can do for a downtrodden neighborhood? What feelings can he and his band inspire? How are feelings transmitted from the band to the audience?

An announcement for an International Conference on Music and Emotion in the United Kingdom (2009) states that: "Emotion's crucial role in musical experience has long been the object of philosophical reflection.... Contemporary work on music and emotion is happening in fields as diverse as aesthetics, psychology, sonic arts, evolutionary biology, anthropology, and neuroscience. Ironically, the subject is relatively neglected by music theory itself."[7] Australian neuroscientist Manfred Clynes carried out research into music's emotional language, as featured in a 1988 PBS Nova film titled, *What Is Music?* His research explored the relationship between physical gestures, such as those pianists use at the keyboard, and the resulting sonic "gestures" that emerge from the piano as music. On the basis of sophisticated psychological experiments on both American and Australian Aboriginal subjects, Clynes concluded that composers and musicians consciously or unconsciously use archetypal sound gestures—drooping ones for grief, bouncing ones for joy—to convert emotion into musical sound. These emotions are then transmitted through the music to the audience. Clynes' research suggests the existence of a universal emotional language that is found everywhere in music.

However, there is evidence that unlike facial expressions such as smiles and frowns that *are* universal, much of the expressive power of music is culturally determined. In 1903, when the first European record company opened in China to produce recordings for local consumption, the foreign businessmen were baffled: the differences between the songs were too slight to detect. On one occasion, a local musician was singing and a company representative asked the Chinese go-between if it wasn't a love song. The reply was "No. He is singing about his grandmother."[8] Now in the 21st century, forms of popular music circulating globally through **mass media** like radio, cinema, and the internet, have weakened barriers between civilizations that rendered the expressive power of some music opaque. Even without understanding the language of lyrics, people can often find in songs deep forms of emotional expression. One does not need to understand Portuguese to weep over a *fado*.

2. THE FUNCTION OF AESTHETIC ENJOYMENT

Merriam's second function, Aesthetic Enjoyment, refers to music when it is the central focus of our attention, not part of some entertainment or ritual event beyond itself. We often associate music fulfilling this function with classical traditions and concert situations, and the experience of this music is one elevated above the everyday. In many parts of the world, some types of music have a status equivalent to art treasures found in museums or great literary texts, and these are often considered among the highest expressions of a civilization. In Japan and Korea, renowned musicians are given the status of "Living Cultural Treasures," and the music they perform, "Intangible Cultural Assets." Whether the aesthetic dimension lies in the quality of the music itself or in the quality of listeners' receptivity to it is unclear. John Cage suggests, with his *4′33″* we discussed in Lesson 1, that a taxi horn or the unwrapping of a hard candy can trigger an aesthetic experience for the deep listener. While aesthetic listening may occur in many settings, a concert auditorium epitomizes this function by providing a space set apart from other social concerns where people gather specifically for the purpose of making and listening to music.

The following examples demonstrate a range of aesthetic musical experiences from a variety of cultures. In each case, the term "aesthetic" is applied because the music is meant to be savored like a fine wine, and enjoyed for its expressive beauty.

1) The first example is from a documentary film about French musician **Nadia Boulanger** (1887–1979), the greatest composition teacher of the 20th century. In the first segment she comments on the mystery of musical "masterpieces," which have the uncanny power to move a listener to tears or raptures, or to provide the experience of beauty that is usually associated with the natural world: sunrises and seascapes, for instance. But exactly where that power resides, she cannot say. Then, we see her and her students listening with rapt attention to just such a masterpiece: an art song by the

19th-century German composer Johannes Brahms. It is precisely this kind of deep listening that characterizes the aesthetic experience.

2) Internationally renowned Iranian vocalist, **Mohammad Reza Shahjarian**, performs Persian classical vocal music (*avaz*), accompanied by master musicians Kayhan Kalhor on *kamanche* (spike fiddle) and Hossein Alizadeh on *tar* (long-necked lute). Listen especially to the characteristic vocal ornamentation (*tahrir*) at 0'36" that we also noted in Lesson 2, describing the voice of Persian singer Afsâne Ziâ'i. In these first two examples, the music is a vehicle for the artful presentation of poetry, and the two art forms are intricately linked. Classical singing in Iran is often performed in private homes at social gatherings that include the enjoyment of food, tea, conversation, poetry, and music (see Map 5–1, p.74).

3) The Japanese art song "*Kyo no shiki*" ("Four Seasons of Kyoto") is sung and played on the *shamisen* (three-string plucked lute) by **Satoyuki**, as accompaniment to the graceful dance performance of Naosuzu. Both artists are geishas (professional female entertainers) of the Kamishichiken district in northern Kyoto. In this performance, music and dance together constitute the aesthetic experience, rather than music alone. Note the flexible rhythm of the vocal part in relation to the more steady beat of the *shamisen*, and the heterophonic texture between these two melodic lines. Geishas have traditionally performed such songs and dances for a clientele of wealthy businessmen, merchants, and government officials at exclusive tea houses in which men enjoy the company of these highly educated and artistically trained professional female companions.

4) **Bi Kidude** (ca. 1910–2013) of Zanzibar was perhaps the oldest performer in the world when this video was taken in June 2004 (see Map 10–1, p.160). She is accompanied by the "Culture Musical Club" *taarab* orchestra, founded in 1958. Since at least the 1920s, Bi Kidude had been the leading exponent of Zanzibari *taarab,* a genre whose name means "ecstasy" in Arabic (see *tarab*). The term highlights the belief, held throughout the Middle East and East Africa, that this music is a source of intense delight bordering on intoxication. Here she is performing at the annual Les Orientales Festival in France. Performances at music festivals are important venues for experiencing music aesthetically.

In each of these videos, music is intended to serve as the center of attention for the listeners. The performers are all highly trained professionals whose artistry is prized by their respective societies. Where the Aesthetic function ends and the next function, Entertainment, begins is unclear. We can certainly attend a symphony concert for entertainment, and pay attention to music at a religious ritual or political rally for its aesthetic appeal.

3. THE FUNCTION OF ENTERTAINMENT

Music has an entertainment function in all societies. Almost as soon as children learn to talk and walk, they learn to sing and dance "for the fun of it." Many people engage in music making and listening as a way of passing the time: girl scouts singing around a campfire, herders yodeling to their cattle, and the prisoner in the cell block blowing on a harmonica. Songwriter Jimmy Buffet might feel embarrassed if his "Cheeseburgers in Paradise" were categorized as "art" or "aesthetic expression." He might simply say that his music is supposed to give pleasure. The Louisiana Cajun band **Steve Riley and the Mamou Playboys**, which we will meet again in Lesson 8, is both entertaining the crowd and motivating the dance (see #6, The Function of Physical Response). In Tibet, yak herders spend long hours alone on the high plateau tending their animals and singing their songs to alleviate boredom and solitude. Children sing as they skip rope, commuters tap out rhythms on the steering wheels of their cars, and friends get together for evenings of communal music making in string bands, drum circles, *a cappella* doo-wop quartets, etc. Ethnomusicologist Ter Ellingson writes: "Music enhances, intensifies, and . . . transforms almost any experience into something felt not only as different but also as somehow better."[9]

Music as entertainment has become a multi-billion-dollar global industry supported by transnational corporations, and electronic and digital media systems. Particularly with the development of sound recording and broadcast technologies, music has become a commodity to be bought, sold, and passively consumed. Many people now, through the sharing of digital sound files, radio and television broadcasts, and public speaker systems, spend their entire days accompanied by a musical soundtrack while they drive, walk, exercise, work, shop, eat, and ride in elevators. Many people say that they simply cannot live without music.

4. THE FUNCTION OF COMMUNICATION

"Music is not a universal language,"[10] Merriam notes. Although music is used universally as a mode of communication, it is within shared social contexts that performers and listeners shape and interpret its meanings. Music is often used by lovers to convey their intimate messages of courtship. Music provides a specialized format for worshipers to offer up their prayers and devotions. In a more practical vein, advertising jingles communicate the messages of the marketplace. West African drumming has been used for many generations as a way of conveying messages over long distances. Drum languages imitate the sounds and intonations of spoken language using special drumming techniques. Among this gathering of Yoruba master drummers in Nigeria, tradition meets modernity as the royal drummer tries out an American-produced **Remo talking drum**, made not of traditional wood but of state-of-the-art "advanced acousticon" material. In syncretic religions of the New World that blend West African beliefs and Roman Catholicism, such as **Vodun** in Haiti and **Candomblé** in Brazil, worshipers play drum rhythms through which they communicate directly with African deities, inviting them to participate in rituals of celebration and healing. In this video clip, Surinamese playwright Henk Tjon demonstrates the talking drum *apenti*, which "speaks" in the ceremonial Kumanti language, a ritual language of the Akan people of Ghana brought to the New World on slave ships more than four hundred years ago. At the end of the video, we see a Saramaccan drummer using the same drum to invite the African deities of his ancestors to participate in a ritual. The Saramaccan Maroons are descendants of slaves who escaped colonial plantation labor in the 17th and 18th centuries and re-established African village life deep in the Amazon rainforest of South America.

In some cases, music itself, without text or gesture, functions as a kind of language with specific, linguistic meanings. Among the Hmong in Laos, when a young man hopes to arrange a tryst with a young woman, he plays a bamboo jaw harp outside the walls of her bedroom. She knows immediately what the sound signifies! The soldier called to charge or retreat by a particular bugle melody relies similarly on its communicative function. While the lover and the soldier count on the power of music to communicate important information, these codes of communication must be learned.

Music often provides a kind of envelope for lyrics, which communicate directly through words. When the melodies are played without the lyrics, the listeners can often recall them and understand the meaning by association. Yet, music functions as more than simply an envelope or delivery system. It adds a significant dimension, whereby a trite message like "a kiss is just a kiss, a sigh is just a sigh," when sung, becomes a sincere, heartfelt communication. **5-1**

5. THE FUNCTION OF SYMBOLIC REPRESENTATION

Music functions in all societies as a symbolic representation of objects, ideas, beliefs, and behaviors. Musical instruments represent nations, like the Irish harp and the Russian balalaika. Music symbolizes time periods and locales, as movie producers well know when they use bagpipes to accompany the title credits for a film set in Scotland, for example. One way that music symbolizes is through imitation or suggestion. Trumpet fanfares and drum cadences symbolically represent military life because their sounds are drawn directly *from* military life. In Western symphonic **"program" music**, composers attempt to depict non-musical situations, objects, or states of being, as in Debussy's *La Mer*, a musical portrait of the sea. "*Sai Ma*" (**Horse Race**) by Huang Haihuai is a popular piece for the Chinese two-stringed fiddle *erhu* that evokes the excitement of a galloping stallion. Many cases of this kind of overt representation could be cited, yet there is some doubt whether one could correctly identify what was being symbolized without the descriptive titles.

Another way that music symbolizes is through learned association. Musical instruments, genres, melodies, and other elements may be used to symbolize non-musical referents by juxtaposition or intentional pairing. The relationship between music and what it represents, however, is often arbitrary and has to be learned. For instance, a scrap of melody may symbolize a commercial product like a brand of coffee when television viewers repeatedly hear the two joined in advertisements. In ancient China, "the five [pentatonic] scale tones were linked with the five virtues—benevolence, righteousness, propriety, knowledge, faith";[11] in Rwanda, the drum is the symbol of political power, since ceremonial drummers always accompanied the king whenever he appeared before his people. Writing

Fig 5.2   **Men playing *balalaikas* of two sizes at a "City Day" parade in Staraja, Russia**

in the 1940s about music used in radio dramas, George Davis noted that, "serialized Radio-drama [composers] create musical themes by which characters will be identified. The appearance of these themes will announce the characters, suggest their influence, etc."[12] From the 1930s through the 50s, a march from Gioachino Rossini's *William Tell Overture* (1829) was used as the theme music for the popular North American radio series and television show *The Lone Ranger*. For those who listened to and watched the program, Rossini's music was forever associated with the masked Texas ranger and his Native American friend, Tonto.

Music symbolizes more complex and intangible aspects of human experience and social organization. "All societies, for example, make distinctions between the social roles of children and adults, which are reflected in music...Game songs, counting songs, language songs, and many others are specific to children." Merriam continues, as children grow older, they give up these songs and move, "either abruptly or gradually into the sphere of adult music."[13] For many adults, nursery rhymes symbolize days of childhood just as songs of bygone years featured on "oldies" radio stations symbolize youth and the days of courtship. For the immigrant, music from the mother country serves as a powerful symbol of a distant homeland. The Caribbean island of Trinidad has a large population of East Indian descent whose ancestors were brought to the island as indentured servants by the British to work in the sugar cane fields. For **Indo-Trinidadians**, *tassa* drumming represents India, the ancestral home and place where this form of drumming originated. It is also a popular form of cultural expression that is associated with weddings and other festive occasions. This cultural expression is symbolic both of the occasion and of the participants' roots in the traditions of their ancestors. Calendrical and important life-cycle events, festival days, and seasons are symbolized throughout the world by special musical styles and repertoires.

Christopher Small, in his 1998 study *Musicking*, writes that music is fundamentally a symbolic activity wherein "the act of musicking establishes in the place where it is happening a set of relationships, and it is in those relationships that the meaning of the act lies...relationships between person and person, between individual and society, between humanity and the natural world and even perhaps the supernatural world. These are important matters, perhaps the most important in human life, and...we learn about [and celebrate these relationships] through musicking."[14]

6. THE FUNCTION OF PHYSICAL RESPONSE

Music can have a profound effect on human physiology. The pace of music and its other features and associations may have a sedative or stimulative effect on the listener. Soft, gentle music relaxes patients in dentist chairs and lulls babies to sleep, while pep bands rouse the fans at basketball games. During the Second World War, music piped into weapons plants was controlled for speed and intensity to keep workers going at a steady pace throughout the day, using a technique called "stimulus progression." Music is used to pump up athletes before the big game, or whip warriors into an adrenaline frenzy before battle. American GIs on patrol in Iraq listened to heavy metal with its double-pedal bass drums and tremolo-style guitars. Musicologist Jonathan Pieslak notes that this is a good way to prepare mentally for a mission because it "sounds considerably like the consistent discharge of bullets fired from an automatic gun."[15] Rhythm patterns coordinate the steps of social dancing, from the chaste minuet to the highly erotic tango. Courtly dances in 17th-century France, like the gavotte and bourée, were defined by and inextricably linked to patterns of choreography performed by Lords and Ladies under the watchful eye of Louis XIV, The Sun King.

The massed bagpipes and drums of the **Royal Military Tattoo** at Edinburgh Castle in Scotland provide the driving rhythms that enable the band to march in perfect formation. Bagpipers have marched with military regiments in Scotland at least since the Battle of the North Inch of Perth in 1396, and they now march at Highland games, military tattoos, and other ceremonial events. At a **New Orleans jazz funeral parade**, on the other hand, the slow somber cadence accompanying the mourners to the gravesite changes at a certain point to lively jazz rhythms. Mourners now become dancers, joyfully celebrating the life of the deceased and their faith in salvation. For Charles Keil, the human response to rhythm is a mystery worth investigating. He proposed a "joyous science of groovology" with the central research question: "What do we [musicians] have to do with our bodies playing these instruments and singing in order to get their bodies [the folks in the crowd] moving, bobbing their heads, snapping their fingers, up from their tables and dancing?"[16] This mystery raises two further questions: How do musicians get the music inside the people and the people inside the music? How does musicking bring people together and inspire feelings of transcendence and community?

As we will note in Lesson 11, music is used in many religious traditions to inspire moods of tranquility or ecstasy, and in extreme cases produces altered states of consciousness that include **trance**, seizures, or deep meditation. Music is widely used in medicine and therapeutic situations. Traditional healers of the Laotian Hmong work with a *qeej* (mouth organ) player "to guide a dead person's soul back through the twelve heavens with his hauntingly resonant cluster of six steamed bamboo tubes."

Fig. 5.3   **The Minuet**

Within the Hmong refugee community in Merced, California, "where bamboo is hard to come by, *qeejs* are sometimes made of PVC plumbing pipe. It is said that if the *qeej* player is good, the soul will have no trouble following directions from the plastic."[17] The Louis Armstrong Center for Music and Medicine at Mount Sinai Beth Israel Hospital in New York City does pioneering work in the therapeutic implications of music and physical response. Through both research and clinical practice, physicians and music therapists work together developing effective healing strategies. In this video, Dr. Joanne Loewy discusses the history of **music therapy** as a branch of medicine and shows some recent applications in a modern hospital setting.

The final four functions are collective and relate to the use of expressive culture to form cohesive and integrated social networks and institutions.

7. THE FUNCTION OF ENFORCING CONFORMITY TO SOCIAL NORMS

Merriam writes, "Songs of social control play an important part in a substantial number of cultures, both through direct warning to erring members of the society and through indirect establishment of what is considered to be proper behavior."[18] He includes in this function school songs and songs of initiation whereby children and adolescents learn proper modes of conduct. Among the Mbuti pygmies of the Democratic Republic of the Congo, for example, adolescent girls celebrate puberty with the Elima ceremony in which older women teach songs that instruct them in the responsibilities and privileges of womanhood. Each girl learns a short phrase that, when sung together with the interlocking phrases of the other girls in her cohort, contributes to a dense polyphonic and harmonious texture. Their song is not complete unless each part is sung, and each part only has meaning when joined to the whole. Thus the act of singing both represents and activates the social bonds that assure the cohesion of the group. In the Judaic tradition, young adolescent boys celebrate their **Bar Mitzvah** at the age of thirteen, after which they are held accountable for their actions and are considered full members of their faith community. During the **Bar Mitzvah** ceremony, the young boy reads verses from the Torah (the first five books of the Jewish Bible), often using the traditional chant that he has learned from a rabbi or cantor over many months or even years of preparation. Since the late 19th and early 20th centuries, many Jewish communities also celebrate a girl's coming-of-age with the Bat Mitzvah ceremony.

When conformity to officially sanctioned norms becomes odious or repressive, songs of protest provide a means of publicly expressing opposition. Collective singing of "We Shall Overcome," for example, solidified the group cohesiveness of civil rights activists during the Selma to Montgomery, Alabama, march for voting rights in March 1965. In situations of strict repression and censorship, song is often the only form of protest allowed. Indeed, musicians are often on the front lines of civil strife and silenced by empowered and armed authorities. From "Yankee Doodle" during the American Revolution to "The Patriot Game" during Ireland's struggle against British rule in the mid-20th century, these songs inspire people with the courage to act in the interests of their side in the conflict. The song "**The Patriot Game**," sung here by Liam Clancy, tells the story of Fergal O'Hanlon, an Irish Republican Army volunteer who was killed at the age of twenty while taking part in a raid on British police barracks on January 1, 1957. The composer of the song, Dominic Behan, imagines the thoughts of the young revolutionary as he lies dying of bullet wounds.

8. THE FUNCTION OF VALIDATION OF RELIGIOUS RITUALS AND SOCIAL INSTITUTIONS

Through the collective singing of sacred hymns and patriotic songs, people validate their belief systems, rituals, and social institutions. By "validation" we mean the act of affirming our allegiance to the groups to which we belong. The mere presence of appropriate music in a social event makes that event special by separating it from ordinary time. When people at such an event participate together in music making—singing, dancing, clapping, or simply listening attentively—they are mutually affirming their shared beliefs and values. We encountered this function in Lesson 4 with the theory that, like gelada baboons, humans evolved as social animals who use group singing as a vehicle for achieving social harmony. Worship services in many religious traditions include congregational singing that accompanies rituals, promoting group cohesion by creating a shared atmosphere of devotion, reverence, and sanctity. In this video from Kimissis Tis Theotokou Greek Orthodox Church in Brooklyn, New York, the **male choir** performs at the altar a hymn composed in the 9th century by Saint Kassia (ca. 805–ca. 865). She is one of only two Byzantine women whose literary and liturgical works are known to have survived to the present. Note that some of the singers participate by intoning a drone on the first note of the scale. This is one of the earliest surviving forms of Christian chant, with roots in the Eastern Roman Empire. Being present at this traditional performance reaffirms for the congregation the reality of their faith, in which they experience the performance together as "an entering into the reality of the Kingdom of God, an ascent to an invisible reality."[19] Often rituals that foster group solidarity involve music with deep roots in the past, like the Byzantine chant described above; for shared history, tradition, and custom, expressed through music, catalyze feelings of unity and belonging. Singing patriotic songs before athletic events and at political rallies accomplishes the same function.

9. THE FUNCTION OF CONTRIBUTION TO THE CONTINUITY AND STABILITY OF CULTURE

"If music allows for emotional expression, gives aesthetic pleasure, entertains, communicates, elicits physical response, enforces conformity to social norms, and validates social institutions and religious rituals, it is clear that it contributes to the continuity and stability of culture."[20] While all aspects of culture—language, diet, forms of tool making and architecture, etc.—play roles in ensuring continuity and stability, "not many elements of culture afford the opportunity for emotional expression, entertain, communicate, and so forth, to the extent allowed in music." Merriam cites examples from a variety of cultures that concur with Nietzsche's famous dictum, "Without music, life would be a mistake." A Sia Indian once remarked to anthropologist Leslie White, "My friend, without songs, you cannot do anything."[21] In 1956, anthropologist Richard A. Waterman "summarized the contribution of music to the continuity and stability of Yirkalla culture in Australia in pointing out that as an enculturative mechanism (that is, a mechanism for the transmission and maintenance of culture), music reaches into almost every aspect of life:

> Throughout his life, the Aboriginal is surrounded by musical events that instruct him about his natural environment and its utilization by man, that teach him his world-view and shape his system of values, and that reinforce his understanding of Aboriginal concepts of status and of his own role. More specifically, songs function as emblems of membership in his moiety [clan subdivision] and lineage, as validation of his system of religious belief, and as symbols of status in the age-grading continuum. They serve on some occasions the purpose of releasing tensions, while other types are used for heightening the emotionalism of a ritual climax. They provide a method of controlling, by supernatural means, sequences of natural events otherwise uncontrollable. Further, some types of songs provide an outlet for individual creativity while many may be used simply to conquer personal dysphoria [unhappiness]. In every case, the enculturative function of the music in helping to shape the social personality of the Aboriginal in the Yirkalla pattern rather than in some other, is apparent.[22]

In West Africa, the hereditary *jali* (praise singer) records and passes on the history and genealogy of his patrons and his community through his narrative songs. This oral tradition has continued since the founding of the Malian empire in the 13th century. In non-literate cultures, narrative songs have served not only to document the past but to teach children about their culture, society, and history. In this short documentary on a **music school in Kirina, Mali**, we see how these hereditary music and dance traditions are now being passed on to children in the 21st century.

Alim Qasimov, one of Azerbaijan's foremost singers of traditional *mugam* music, taught this vocal art to his daughter Fargana, and she now joins him on the international concert stage. Together, they pass on their songs to Fargana's daughter Fatima, continuing this family tradition. Realizing the importance of children learning songs by heart and of developing their talent at a young age, Alim gives his granddaughter the opportunity to perform, preparing her for a music career of her own one day. In this video, we see Fatima in a **house concert** accompanied by Qasimov's own musicians.

Map 5-1 Azerbaijan, Iran, and Turkey in West Asia

Source: *Garland Encyclopedia of World Music*, Volume 6: The Middle East

The oil painting *The Banjo Lesson* (1893), by African American artist Henry O. Tanner, vividly captures the passing on of music and musical skills from one generation to the next; and by extension, a way of life and an inherited sense of self.

Music also plays a role as a catalyst for social change, contributing to dis-continuity and in-stability. Because musical styles are so flexible and able to generate new meanings and associations rapidly, music frequently serves as harbinger for new and revolutionary value systems, fashions, and changes in social mores. For instance, the 1960s in North America and Europe was a period in which young people sought to distinguish themselves from their parents' generation by growing their hair long, rejecting the materialistic values they attributed to their society, and taking part in massive street protests against war and social injustice. The popular musicians of the time—The Beatles, Bob Dylan, the Grateful Dead—were leaders of this social revolution. In many parts of the world, modern communication technologies are carrying popular musical forms from urban centers to formerly isolated rural areas, enticing the children of farmers and herders

Fig. 5.4 *The Banjo Lesson* (1893), Henry O. Tanner (1859-1937)

off the land in what is perhaps the greatest mass migration in the history of the world: that from the agrarian countryside to the slums and shantytowns surrounding great megacities like Mumbai, Nairobi, and Rio de Janeiro.

10. THE FUNCTION OF CONTRIBUTION TO THE INTEGRATION OF SOCIETY

After the terrorist attacks of September 11th, 2001, songs like "God Bless America" became anthems that brought Americans together in an unprecedented expression of unity. "Music...provides a rallying point around which the members of society gather to engage in activities which require the cooperation and coordination of the group,"[23] thus integrating society. Kwabena Nketia writes, "For the Yoruba in Accra, performances of Yoruba music...bring both the satisfaction of participating in something familiar and the assurance of belonging to a group sharing similar values, similar ways of life, a group maintaining similar art forms. Music thus brings a renewal of tribal solidarity."[24] Cultural anthropologist Victor Turner (1920–1983) coined the term "*communitas*" to describe the intense experience of merging one's individual identity with a group's identity during festivals, religious meetings, political rallies, and rock concerts. A live performance by the Madagascan *a cappella* trio Salala provides a vivid example of music contributing to *communitas*. The three male singers were all members of the Antandroy ethnic group from Madagascar's dry and impoverished south (see Map 9–2, p. 137). The Antandroy faced prejudice from the peoples of the more developed north, and when they moved to the cities to escape the poverty of their region, they took jobs at the very bottom of the economic ladder, like night watchman and rickshaw driver. The vocal trio Salala, including their bass vocalist Sengemanana who died in 2001, became spokespersons for their ethnic group, drawing on traditional Antandroy songs for their material. In 1998 they released a CD titled *Salala*, from which the song "*Lanitra Manga Manga*" (Blue, Blue Sky) became a national hit broadcast frequently over the radio. A video of their 2005 live performance in a huge outdoor soccer stadium in the capital Antananarivo reveals the extraordinary power of a song to unite people in a shared experience of deep emotion. The group begins to sing the song "*Lanitra Manga Manga*" to enormous applause, and the entire audience then spontaneously unites in singing the lyrics, at which point the trio drops out. The song continues in a remarkable call and response between Salala and their audience, joining everyone present in this intense, joyful music making.

5-3 🔊

5-22 🎞

CASE STUDY: "THE INTERNATIONALE"

"The Internationale" is possibly the most famous socialist song ever written, and some musicologists believe that it was sung by more people around the world than any other song in the 20th century. Eugène Pottier composed the original French words as a revolutionary poem in 1871, and after Pierre Degeyter set the words to music in 1888 the song spread rapidly through Europe and beyond. The song lyrics have been translated into nearly a hundred different languages. Since the late 19th century the song has been sung by socialists, anarchists, communists, trade unionists, and many others around the world. The words express an idealistic hope that some day we will all live in a world without wars, exploitation, oppression, and repression, a world in which there is justice and freedom for all people. The original song has six stanzas in French; the following is an English translation of the first two together with the refrain:

> Arise, you prisoners of starvation
> Arise, you wretched of the earth
> For justice thunders condemnation
> There's a better world in birth
> No more tradition's chains shall bind us
> Arise you slaves, no more in thrall
> The earth shall rise on new foundations:
> We have been nought, we shall be all
> > Tis the final conflict
> > Let each stand in his place

The international working class
Shall be the human race
We want no condescending saviors
To rule us from their judgment hall
We workers ask not for their favors
Let us consult for all
To make the thief disgorge his booty
To free the spirit from its cell
We must ourselves decide our duty
We must decide and do it well
Tis the final conflict
Let each stand in his place
The international working class
Shall be the human race[25]

Pottier wrote the poem after the fall of the Paris Commune in 1871. The Paris Commune was an uprising against the French government by workers who supported socialism and feared a restoration of the monarchy after France's defeat in the Franco-Prussian War of 1870–1871 and the collapse of Napoleon III's Second Empire. The song was a call to the ordinary, hardworking men and women of the world to stand up against those who deny them freedom and who wield power unfairly. It called on all those suffering any kind of injustice to unite as one voice, to find strength in a common belief that injustice won't succeed and that truth and freedom will prevail. The message resonated so strongly with so many people that it became an international rallying cry. However, following the Russian Revolution of 1917 the song was adapted as an anthem of the Soviet Union, and later by the Maoist regime in China. In the West it took on a very different connotation during the Cold War, when it could no longer be used as a labor union or progressive anthem without seeming unpatriotic. It came to symbolize the totalitarian regimes of the Communist Bloc. The change in context from a working class rallying song to the official anthem of a totalitarian state transformed the meaning of the song and also the ways in which it was sung.

Peter Miller, in his 2000 documentary *The Internationale,* tells the story of this song from its origins in late 19th-century France through its journey around the world to its survival and revival in the 21st century. In the many contexts in which it took root—several of which appear in the linked film excerpt of *The Internationale*—this song fulfilled each of the functions enumerated above. The power of this historically important song lay precisely in its capacity to express, symbolize, and communicate meanings and feelings across time and space, and to serve as a repository for the aspirations of millions.

CONCLUSION

In this first unit, we have discussed four questions that are central to musical understanding: What is music? What is it made of? Where did it come from? What is it for? The answer to each of these is complex, open-ended, and suggestive of music's significant place in human experience. Music is involved in the most important circumstances in the lives of individuals and communities. It is integral to the personal realms of courtship and mating, childrearing, work and leisure, celebration and mourning; it marks holidays and can be heard publicly in coronations and inaugurations, sporting events, wartime muster, protest and rebellion. In the three units that follow, we examine the near universal roles music plays in three human domains: in the expression of identity, in the observation of religious traditions, and in aspects of social life. Music has the power to express emotion; to enthrall us with beautiful sounds, rhythmic grooves, and sonic forms; to entertain us and communicate in ways that words cannot; to symbolize abstract concepts; to move us physically and affect us neurologically; to bind us together into cohesive social groups; to validate our public institutions and rituals; and to contribute to the continuity, transformation, and integration of societies. Therefore it is not surprising that it should figure importantly in how we as individuals and groups project our identity, celebrate our beliefs, and shape our everyday experiences.

KEY CONCEPTS

Biological evolution vs cultural and social evolution

Pinker's "Cheesecake"

Music as evolutionary parasite

Function of Emotional Expression

Function of Aesthetic Enjoyment

Function of Entertainment

Function of Communication

Function of Symbolic Representation

Function of Physical Response

Function of Enforcing Conformity to Social Norms

Function of Validation of Religious Rituals and Social Institutions

Function of Contribution to the Continuity and Stability of Culture

Function of Contribution to the Integration of Society

Communitas

Q THINKING ABOUT MUSIC QUESTIONS

1. How would you explain the difference between the Function of Aesthetic Enjoyment and the Function of Entertainment? Think of a musical selection that you enjoy. Is there a difference in the way you experience it, if you allow it to serve one or the other function?

2. Consider four situations in which music symbolizes something: in advertising, in education, in sports, and in video games. Can you think of a specific example of each?

3. In what ways does music affect *you* physically? Pump you up? Chill you out? Get your toes tapping?

4. Watch again the Madagascan band Salala performing in front of the crowds in the Antanarivo soccer stadium. What functions of music is the song "*Lanitra Manga Manga*" serving?

5. Watch again the video of the granddaughter of the great Azeri singer Alim Qasimov performing at a house party in Azerbaijan. In what ways is music functioning in this social gathering?

NOTES

1 Steven Pinker, *How the Mind Works* (New York: W. W. Norton, 1997), 528.

2 Alan P. Merriam, *The Anthropology of Music* (Evanston, IL: Northwestern University Press, 1964), 215–216.

3 Merriam, *Anthropology of Music,* 218.

4 Merriam, *Anthropology of Music,* 218.

5 David P. McAllester, "The Role of Music in Apache Culture" (1960), quoted in Merriam, *Anthropology of Music,* 220.

6 David P. McAllester, "The Role of Music in Apache Culture" (1960), quoted in Merriam, *Anthropology of Music,* 220.

7 International Conference on Music and Emotion, August 31–September 3, 2009, Durham University Music Department, UK, https://www.dur.ac.uk/ias/events/events_listings/?eventno=5756.

8 Richard C. Kraus, *Pianos and Politics in China* (Oxford and New York: Oxford University Press, 1989), 35.

9 Ter Ellingson, "Music and Religion," in *The Encyclopedia of Religion*, ed. Mircea Eliade (New York: Macmillan, 1987), 168.

10 Merriam, *Anthropology of Music,* 223.

11 Merriam, *Anthropology of Music*, 245.

12   George Davis, "Music-Cueing for Radio-Drama" (1947), quoted in Merriam, *Anthropology of Music*, 240.

13   Merriam, *Anthropology of Music*, 247.

14   Christopher Small, *Musicking: The Meanings of Performing and Listening* (Middletown, CN: Wesleyan University Press, 1998), 13.

15   Jonathan Pieslak, *Sound Targets: American Soldiers and Music in the Iraq War* (Bloomington: Indiana University Press, 2009), 150

16   Charles Keil, "Groovology and the Magic of Other People's Music," (2010), 1, www.musicgrooves.org/articles/GroovologyAndMagic.pdf.

17   Anne Fadiman, *The Spirit Catches You and You Fall Down: A Hmong Child, Her American Doctors, and the Collision of Two Cultures* (New York: Farrar, Straus and Giroux, 1997), 227–228.

18   Merriam, *Anthropology of Music*, 224.

19   "Byzantine Chant," accessed March 28, 2014, http://www.liturgica.com/html/Byzantine_Chant.jsp.

20   Merriam, *Anthropology of Music*, 225.

21   Leslie A. White, *The Pueblo of Sia, New Mexico*, Washington: Bureau of American Ethnology Bulletin 184 (1962): 115, quoted in Merriam, *Anthropology of Music*, 225.

22   Richard A. Waterman, "Music in Australian Aboriginal Culture—Some Sociological and Psychological Implications," in *Music Therapy* V (1956): 41, quoted in Merriam, *Anthropology of Music*, 225–226.

23   Merriam, *Anthropology of Music*, 227.

24   J. H. Kwabena Nketia, "Yoruba Musicians in Accra," *Odu* 6 (1958): 43, quoted in Merriam, *Anthropology of Music*, 226.

25   "The Internationale" song lyrics, English translation by Charles Kerr, in the *Little Red Songbook* of the International Workers of the World (IWW), first published by a group in Spokane, Washington in 1909.

UNIT 2
MUSIC AND IDENTITY

INTRODUCTION

In this unit, we examine how music operates in shaping, exploring, and expressing identity. We might define "identity" as the sum of those inherited and acquired factors that make up who we are at a given point in our lives. These factors include homeland, age and gender, profession, beliefs, and values. It is also those distinguishing characteristics by which we know others, both as individuals and groups. Between the poles of our experience as autonomous and unique individuals and as members of groups that temper our individuality, we make choices that form and represent our identity. We also identify ourselves and our groups on the basis of difference from those we are not. Music serves as a powerful vehicle for projecting our individuality while also connecting us with communities to which we feel a sense of belonging. Furthermore, music conveys to us auditory images of other individuals and groups.

Music's intimate ties with place and time serve to illustrate the richness of its associations with identity. Bagpipes of Scotland, harps of Ireland, opera in Italy are powerful symbols of place and, by association, history and value. The songs of the cattle herders in the Swiss Alps have marked the region with the sonic association of yodeling. Many places are identified by dances that originated there: the samba of Brazil, the tango of Argentina, highlife of Nigeria, and the polka of Central Europe. In the United States, regions are deeply connected with genres of song and dance: bluegrass in Kentucky, *tejana* along the Rio Grande, and jazz in urban centers like New York, Chicago, Kansas City, and of course, New Orleans.

Music also has the power to evoke the past along with associated feelings and memories. Music inspires nostalgia for times gone by and places we have known. In the documentary *The Internationale*, the Russian musicologist Vladimir Zak describes his ambivalent feelings toward the song by stating that it brought to mind the hypocrisy, lies, and broken promises of the Soviet state, and yet singing it also recalled strong feelings associated with his childhood and playing "revolution" in his backyard. As noted in Lesson 5, oldies channels on the radio capitalize on music's evocative power to bring back the memories of youth and romance to middle-aged listeners; and immigrants gather in social clubs to listen to the music of the old country to which they may never return.

In Lessons 6 to 9 we examine in detail four manifestations of identity that powerfully illuminate how music functions in human life: 6. Music and Individual Identity; 7. Music and Group Identity; 8. Music and Hybrid Identity; and 9. Music and Oppositional Identity.

Lesson 6
Music and Individual Identity

When you consider your own identity—how you understand yourself and project yourself to the world—imagine your reflection in many differently angled mirrors. In your family you are a brother or sister to your siblings, son or daughter to your parents, grandson or granddaughter to your grandparents. Each of these relationships defines different aspects of your personality. In different situations you may consider a primary aspect of your identity your gender, your nationality, your religion, your ethnicity or race, your generation or age group. In relationship to the wider world, you are an American or member of another nationality, in which case you are, perhaps, an immigrant. You are marked by the region you grew up in: a Northerner, a Southerner, etc. You hold affiliations to political parties, to educational institutions, social, civic, and religious organizations. Some aspects of your identity are yours by birth and are unchangeable; others you choose and can change at will. We are all enmeshed in a web of relationships that gives our lives the structure, meaning, and sense of belonging that constitute our identities. Many aspects of your identity you express by making or listening to the music that is associated with your region, religion, nationality, generation, etc. Like the clothes you wear, your playlist and the songs you sing present to others a sense of who you are. Music often serves as a rallying point and marker for subcultures to which you may belong. Popular music genres such as hip-hop, metal, emo, **techno**, alternative, and country bring together people who share common values. Through music, each of us projects and receives impressions of identity at the level of feelings.

At a dinner party following a music conference in Central China, scholars, students, and local officials share a final meal at a hotel restaurant. After the toasts and the speeches, the singing begins, as is the custom. One by one, in no particular order, each participant comes up to a microphone in the front of the banquet hall and shares a song of his or her choosing. Because the conference has included participants from many parts of the world, there is quite a variety of singing styles, languages, and levels of confidence and competence. The Chinese participants, used to this custom, are ready to belt out a folk song at the drop of a hat. The Americans seem a bit more self-conscious, although Sam, a university student from New York, has no trouble finding his voice with an old Elvis Presley ballad that everyone enjoys. Strangers become friends, as each in turn takes the microphone and performs a song that serves as an introduction, an auditory calling card. One of the members of the party, Wangmo, is a nineteen-year-old Tibetan researcher from the Plateau Music Project, about which you will read

Fig. 6.1 **Yak herd on the Tibetan Plateau**

more in Lesson 9. She grew up in a nomadic family that followed a herd of sheep, yak, and horses across the Central Asian Plateau, one of the highest, coldest, and most isolated regions of the world. At the hotel party, she sings a song addressed to the "Sky Mother," and later explains that in her early life she had spent many hours alone with the herds, and singing was both a way to pass the time and to communicate with other herders, out with their own animals a long distance away. Wangmo's song carries to the dinner guests something of the thin air, wide vistas, loneliness and emptiness of her childhood world. The New York singer of Elvis also communicates something of who he is and what his life and his world are like. Because the singing voice is so much a part of who we all are as individuals, both Wangmo and Sam were able to convey in a few moments an intensely felt impression of their identities.

At the banquet described above, the hosts assume that everyone can sing. There are no exceptions. As noted in Lesson 2, "The ability to sing is as universal as the ability to speak." However, like athletic ability, musical ability is unevenly distributed throughout the general population, with some people possessing superior musical ability, as measured by a standard appropriate to their society and its musical expressions. Also like athletic ability, superior musical skill may be developed through specialized training. Some individuals come from "musical families," raising the question of whether specialized aptitude rests on genetic inheritance or on musical training in early childhood, or both. In the social and ritual life of the Venda of southern Africa, for example, it is expected that everyone will participate in dancing, while the more accomplished musicians, by a combination of natural ability and applied effort, become drummers. Ethnomusicologist John Blacking writes, "The Venda may not consider the possibility of unmusical human beings, but they recognize that some people perform better than others." Why some people and not others become "musicians" is a combination of factors:

The Venda may suggest that exceptional musical ability is biologically inherited, but in practice they recognize that social factors play the most important part in realizing or suppressing

Fig. 6.2   Everyone dances; the music specialist becomes the drummer

it. For instance, a boy of noble birth might show great talent, but as he grows up he will be expected to abandon regular musical performance for the more serious (for him) business of governing.... Conversely, a girl of noble birth has every encouragement to develop her musical capacities, so that as a woman she can play an active role in supervising the girls' initiation schools which are held in the homes of rulers.[1]

Many people find in music an outlet for creativity and self-expression. They feel that the music they listen to and enjoy in some sense defines who they are, both as individuals and members of groups. To a degree, every individual human being is unique, different from every other both by genetic inheritance and particular life experiences. Some people, however, due to unusual physical or mental aptitudes and extraordinary life events, opportunities, or challenges, are exceptional. When such individuals become musicians, they can have a lasting impact on the musical development of their societies. In this lesson we discuss five individuals whose unparalleled musical skill and creativity distinguished them as innovators. They each mastered a musical style, then built upon the foundation of that inherited tradition to create a highly individual form of musical expression.

LUDWIG VAN BEETHOVEN (GERMANY/AUSTRIA)

It may seem obvious that music and art in general serve as vehicles for self-expression. From early childhood, we are taught that crayons and clay are tools for developing creativity, and singing or playing an instrument provides an outlet for our feelings. We expect artists to reveal aspects of their individual lives and experiences through their work and we study their biographies to understand more fully the nature of their artistic expression. Yet at least for the professional artist in the Western world, self-expression is a fairly recent expectation. When Michelangelo painted the ceiling of the Sistine Chapel in the early 16th century, for instance, he was expressing the values and beliefs of the church, and those of his patron Pope Julius II who commissioned the work. Artists worked primarily within churches and aristocratic courts that provided secure employment and financial support in return for control of their artistic output. The great Viennese composer, Wolfgang Amadeus Mozart (1756–1791), struggled his whole life to please the aristocracy on whom his livelihood depended. In the opening of Mozart's *Eine Kleine Nacht-musik*, composed in 1787, we hear no trace of the anguish the composer felt at the death of his controlling father in the same year, despite the fact that we know of this anguish from surviving letters written around the same time. Instead, we hear expressed the aristocratic power and gentility of the nobles for whom Mozart composed this after-dinner entertainment. Mozart is masterful at juxtaposing complementary gestures of strength and elegance, mirroring and legitimizing an idealized musical portrait of his patrons.

6-1

Fig. 6.3 **Beethoven (1770–1827) at age 49, when he was completely deaf**

It was not until the late 18th century in Europe that artists began moving outside this **patronage system**. Ludwig van Beethoven (1770–1827), working a generation after Mozart, was among the first successful independent artist-entrepreneurs. He made his living first from public concerts as a performing pianist, often playing his own compositions, and then from his publishing royalties and commissions. He is known for the highly personal style of composition he developed, and is one of the first musicians to use music self-consciously to express the unique idiosyncrasies of his individual identity.

By 1804, when Ludwig van Beethoven composed his Fifth Symphony, much had happened in the world to change the status and expectations of the artist. The position of the aristocracy in Europe had been weakened by the American and French Revolutions and the rise of Napoleon. New economic opportunities for a rising urban middle class created audiences for public concerts and published music scores. Beethoven was able to survive outside the patronage of court and church, and found an audience for his music among the middle class whose wealth derived not from title and inheritance but from struggle and risk-taking. Beethoven was afflicted by growing deafness while writing his Fifth Symphony; and in his famous Heiligenstadt Testament, a letter from 1802 addressed to his brothers, he reveals profound hopelessness: "What a humiliation for me when someone standing next to me heard a flute in the distance and I heard nothing, or someone standing next to me heard a shepherd singing and again I heard nothing. Such incidents drove me almost to despair; a little more of that and I would have ended my life. It was only my art that held me back. Oh, it seemed to me impossible to leave the world until I had brought forth all that I felt was within me. So I endured this wretched existence."[2] Thus he overcomes his suicidal inclinations, strengthened by his belief in the transformative power of the music that he feels is his unique purpose to bring into the world.

The first movements of both Mozart's *Eine Kleine Nachtmusik* and Beethoven's Fifth Symphony utilize a musical template popular from the mid-1700s in Central Europe called (by later analysts) "sonata form." Composers developed such structures to give coherence to large-scale compositions based upon repetition, contrast, and development of musical materials. Beethoven, however, distorts the existing conventions of the sonata form in a variety of ways in order to serve his subjective expressive purposes. The sonata form movement typically consists of an opening "exposition" presenting two or more contrasting musical themes, a middle section developing these ideas, a final section repeating the initial themes, and a short concluding "coda." Listen to the first movement of Beethoven's Fifth Symphony. Following the dramatic development section and just after Beethoven returns explosively to the opening four-note motif that serves as the seed for the entire movement (indeed, the entire symphony), he interrupts what should have been a restatement of the movement's opening music. The entire orchestra stops playing; the conductor stops conducting. In the audio track at 4'27", a lone oboe plays

6-2

a wandering, downward-moving phrase. The brief interruption of the music's momentum seems to heighten rather than relieve the built-up tension, and recalls the soliloquies of Shakespeare in which a lone actor separates himself from the action and addresses the audience. Indeed, the oboe seems to be asking the question of Hamlet in Shakespeare's most famous soliloquy, the question implicit in Beethoven's Heiligenstadt Testament: "To be or not to be?" Is a life so compromised, a life of unending struggle, worth living? As the symphony resumes and re-gathers its energies, Beethoven seems to answer with a resounding "Yes!" The final coda is the longest section of the first movement and seems to go on and on; the rest of the symphony, ending with its triumphal C Major fourth movement, seems to answer the fateful question in the affirmative. Thus, Beethoven's Fifth Symphony may be heard as a musical revelation of the composer's inner psychological state.

His influence on Western art music was profound; he created a new musical language of self-expression. Ever since the ancient Greek philosopher Pythagoras put forward his ideas on the "music of the spheres," "most Western musicians had agreed that musical beauty was based on a mysterious connection between sound and mathematics, and that this provided music with an objective goal, something that transcended the individual composer's idiosyncrasies and aspired to the universal," writes British author Dylan Evans. "Beethoven turn[ed] away from an other-directed music to an inward-directed...focus on the composer himself."[3]

Building on the conventions of his predecessors like Mozart to express new, intensely personal sentiments for new concert audiences, Beethoven bridged the old feudal order and the modern world of the urban middle class. His music still speaks to millions, one of history's most durable musical voices.

RAVI SHANKAR (INDIA)

Our next case study involves a musician of a classical tradition in North India, far from the Western world, whose connections with the West nevertheless afforded him a unique position as musical and cultural mediator and ambassador. Ravi Shankar, who was born in 1920 in Benares

Fig 6.4   Ravi Shankar (1920–2012) performing in New Delhi, 2009, at the age of 88

and died December 11th, 2012 in San Diego, California, was one of the greatest performers of Indian classical music of the 20th century (see Map 8–3, p. 123). He began his performing career as a dancer and musician in his brother Uday Shankar's "Hindu Ballet" troupe, and spent many of his teenage years touring Europe and North America. This experience allowed him at an early age to see his brother as a star performer on the international stage, and also as an emissary spreading Indian culture abroad. Furthermore, learning of Western musicians' ignorance of Indian classical music, Ravi Shankar fostered an ambition to change this. At the age of eighteen, he entered into a traditional master-disciple (*guru-shishya*) relationship with esteemed musician Ustad Allaud-din Khan. Within the North Indian classical tradition, this relationship is both quite formal and extremely demanding, requiring a commitment of utter devotion akin to taking religious orders. Shankar moved to the small Central Indian village of Maihar where his guru lived, and for seven years remained there as a member of Allauddin Khan's household, practicing *sitar* and mastering the ancient and intricate art of melody (*raga*) and rhythm (*tala*). Finally, with the blessing of his guru, he began his career as a solo artist, playing concert performances, radio recitals, and after India's Independence in 1947 becoming Director of Music at India's national broadcast service, All India Radio.

An opportunity to play for the renowned American-born violinist Yehudi Menuhin came for Shankar in 1952 in New Delhi. This event began a long relationship of mutual respect and collaboration between the two artists. Shankar composed chamber music for violin and *sitar*, and Menuhin's deep passion for Indian music led to several joint concert performances and recordings. Composition for Shankar became an avenue for experimentation as well as for collaboration with non-Indian musicians. He wrote works for French flute player Jean-Pierre Rampal, Japanese *shakuhachi* master Hosan Yamamoto, and Japanese *koto* virtuoso Musumi Miyashita. He created film scores for Indian and Western films, including *Gandhi, The Apu Trilogy*, and *Mirabai*. In 1971, Shankar composed and performed the first ever *Concerto for Sitar and Western Orchestra* with conductor André Previn and the London Symphony Orchestra, blending Indian and Western instruments and musical styles.

In the mid-1960s, Ravi Shankar's relationship with British singer and guitarist George Harrison brought enormous and unprecedented exposure to Indian music in the West. George Harrison took *sitar* lessons, and not only immersed himself in Indian classical music and philosophy but introduced Indian musical elements into several of his songs for his band The Beatles. The effect was explosive. The *sitar* and Indian music entered the soundscape of Western popular culture, and other rock bands including The Kinks, The Yardbirds, and The Rolling Stones incorporated Indian sounds as well. Ravi Shankar unexpectedly became a rock idol. He initially welcomed this role, performing on stage at the **Monterey Pop Festival** in California in 1967 and at Woodstock in New York two years later, although the subsequent link between India and the hippie generation's drug-taking led him to end his performances at pop festivals. His celebrity status earned him a Visiting Professorship at City University in New York, and enabled him to continue his mission of exposing Western audiences to Indian music and musicians. He was one of the first to bring other solo Indian artists to the West, starting with the Festival of India concerts in 1968.

Ravi Shankar has played a unique role as cultural ambassador for Indian music around the world. As the first Indian classical instrumentalist to gain an international reputation, he pioneered the role of musical mediator and advocate. In concert performances, his fluency in English enabled him to explain the complex melodic and rhythmic systems of North Indian music to new audiences with clarity and charm. Many Indian artists have since followed in Ravi Shankar's footsteps, nurturing global audiences for Indian classical music. His own daughter Anoushka Shankar is now carrying on the mantle, having studied *sitar* exclusively with her father. Anoushka performs as a virtuoso sitarist, recording albums and composing and collaborating with Western artists, including her sister, jazz and pop diva Norah Jones. Until the end of his life, Pandit Ravi Shankar continued to perform concerts around the world and serve as India's preeminent musical ambassador. Just as Beethoven served as a bridge between two historical epochs, the feudal and the modern, Shankar brought the music of India to the West and created an audience for it. He was one of the first "World Music" artists whose vast musical personality and unique experience redefined the role of the musician in the age of mass media and globalization.

Fig. 6.5 Maria Stoyanova (1953–) playing the *gaida* bagpipe

MARIA STOYANOVA (BULGARIA)

Maria Stoyanova (b. 1953) is a professional performer and teacher of the Bulgarian *gaida* or bagpipe. Bulgaria is a small country in Eastern Europe that, during the time of Maria Stoyanova's childhood, was isolated, agrarian, and part of the Soviet bloc of communist countries. What makes her story unusual is that in the traditional Bulgarian rural society she grew up in, only men played musical instruments in public.

Ethnomusicologist Timothy Rice writes that in this society,

Men and women had, and to a certain extent still have, their distinct spheres of activity, including musical activity. Men, for example, had primary responsibility for taking care of animals, plowing fields, building houses, making wine and spirits, and representing the family in the public arena. Women had primary responsibility for cooking food, cleaning the house and yard, making clothes, and caring for children. Music making was linked to these patterns of work. Men and boys spent long hours alone in pastures and forests with their animals; they made musical instruments from animal skins and wood; and played them as a way to while away the long hours of solitude. Women's and girls' hands, in contrast, were always busy with housework, and thus not free to play instruments. Thus they learned to sing songs as they learned to embroider, knit, and cook in the social environment of the home among their grandmothers, mothers, aunts, older sisters, and cousins...[but] with the rarest exceptions, never learned to play musical instruments. With all their domestic responsibilities, when would they have had time to practice?

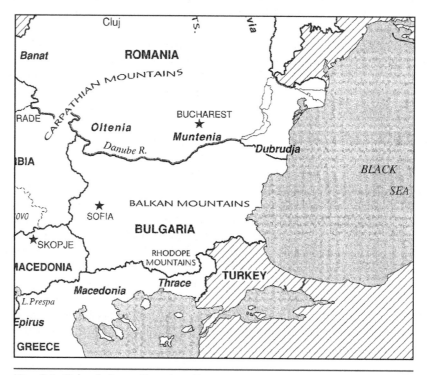

Map 6-1 Bulgaria in southeastern Europe

Source: *Garland Encyclopedia of World Music,* Volume 8: Europe

As a child, Maria was fascinated by the sound of the *gaida* that her father and uncles played. When no one was home, she would take her father's out from under the bed where it was stored and try to play it. When her family discovered this, she was forbidden to continue, but persisted anyway. When she heard that the government was inviting students her age to audition for a newly formed high school for traditional Bulgarian music, she appeared before the admissions panel with her father's *gaida* and caused an uproar. In the first place, a girl playing the *gaida* went against the traditions the school was trying to preserve; and in the second, the jury found the thought of a girl blowing into the instrument unseemly and suggestive. However, the communist ideology of the 1960s called for equal opportunity of the sexes, and the constitution put into law "the full emancipation of women."[4]

Maria went on to study *gaida* at a conservatory for traditional music and later became the principal teacher there, as well as a distinguished performer and leader of one of the country's most prestigious wedding ensembles. She came of age after the Second World War, at a time when traditional gender roles were being redefined and renegotiated. The unusual tenacity she exhibited as a girl learning to play the forbidden instrument met with ultimate success because of shifts in her society at that time, expanding the possible roles a woman could play, and allowing the identities of woman and instrumental musician to co-exist.

Watch this video clip of **Maria Stoyanova** playing at a Rom wedding in 1998. The Rom people, pejoratively known as "Gypsies," have contributed greatly to the musical life of Eastern Europe despite their relatively low social standing. As in many cultures, weddings in Bulgaria constitute one of the most important venues for musical performance. They are also occasions for the enactment of a society's most traditional forms of communal expression. Although the accordion, electric keyboard, and drum set are fairly recent additions to the wedding band, replacing more traditional instruments, the *gaida* is so ancient and expressive of Bulgarian core values that a proverb states, "a wedding without a *gaida* is impossible." When Stoyanova performs, as she often does with the famous wedding band Kanarite ("The Canaries"; not shown in this video), her presence "always cause[s] quite a stir and provoke[s] lots of audience comments.... Her *gaida* playing helped Kanarite make a memorable

impression and contributed to their reputation."[5] In the video, she begins with a highly ornamented piece in free rhythm, accompanied by changing chordal harmonies on the accordion and guitar. Around a minute into the performance, she turns and signals to the drummer, and the band launches into a fast dance called the *ruchenitsa* that has a driving 7-beat rhythmic pattern of 1–2, 1–2, 1–2–3. With the entrance of the drum set outlining the beat structure, the dancing begins. The irony that the *gaida,* most traditional of all wedding band instruments in her community, is most un-traditionally played here by a woman, is not lost on the audience.

SALIF KEITA (MALI)

Salif Keita (b. 1949) is one of West Africa's most famous and influential singers, songwriters, and producers. He was born in the former colony of French Sudan, now the Republic of Mali, and is a direct descendant of Sunjata Keita, who founded the Malian Empire in the 13th century. Among the Mande-speaking peoples of Mali, occupations are hereditary and are identified by family names. The surname Keita indicates the ruling aristocracy. In traditional Mande society, musicians (*jalolu* singular *jali*; also known by the French term *griots*) had

Fig. 6.6 Salif Keita (1949–) performing at the Festival del Millenni in Barcelona, Spain, 2013

Heroes died with their anxiety.
Scholars died in their tears,
From that moment,
This snowy land
Became the battlefield of brothers,
Nephews and nieces left as orphans.
Ah ha ha ha [*sound of grieving*]
That's why we Tibetans
Had to change our own way of living and admire others,
Abandoned our own warmth and slowly welcomed the cold.[6]

(English translation by Tsering Samdrup and Dawa Torbert)

The song, with lyrics by Choedrag himself, suggests that the greatness of the Tibetan people lay in past glories and now lies in the preservation of traditional ways. The contemporary musical idiom speaks to a generation familiar with the popular styles they hear on the state-sponsored radio stations. In this next video taken on a very cold night in December 2007, **Choedrag** sings a newly composed song in a traditional folk idiom, accompanying himself on the *dranyin* with author Jonathan Kramer recording a cello track. Here you can see the interior of his cell and his recording equipment. From this small room, Choedrag composed, recorded, and produced music that, while modern in its use of technology and popular idioms, expressed the traditional values that he believes Tibetans need to affirm if they are to resist **assimilation**.

BEDŘICH SMETANA (BOHEMIA/CZECH REPUBLIC)

Bedřich Smetana (1824–1884), "the father of Czech national music," was a composer and pianist born in Bohemia, then part of the Austrian Empire.

Using the expanded harmonic and orchestral resources pioneered by Beethoven and other early 19th-century Romantic composers, Smetana and many of his contemporaries later in the century wrote richly evocative music incorporating folk elements to convey a sense of national identity, solidarity, and pride to middle class urban audiences. The ideal of the nation-state swept Europe in the second half of the 19th century, inspired by the democratic principles put forth in the American and French Revolutions and intensified by the failed uprisings of 1848 against the Austrian Empire. At this time, program music became a potent symbol of national identity, and Poland, Norway, Finland, Russia, Hungary, and Bohemia all produced composers of nationalist music who attained international reputations. In each country, musicians found that by evoking heroes and legends of the mythic past, folk tales and dances, scenes of the countryside and peasant life, they could produce symphonic music that carried audible markers of a region and way of life. Smetana used all of these nationalistic themes in the six short symphonic pieces with descriptive titles (**tone poems**) that comprise *Ma Vlast* (My Fatherland, 1874–79), one of the greatest works to come out of the 19th-century Nationalist Movement. The six tone poems are as follows:

Vyšehrad the castle in Prague that was the home of the original Czech kings
Vltava one of the main rivers that flows through Bohemia
Šárka a female warrior who is the main character in a folk legend
Zkeských luhu a háju "From Bohemia's meadows and forests"
Tábor a city in southern Bohemia that was the site of a famous 15th-century battle
Blaník a mountain in which a mythological army sleeps, waiting to awake and defend the country in a time of crisis.

Fig. 7.10 **Bedřich Smetana (1824-1884)**

Map 6-2   **West Africa showing Mali and Côte d'Ivoire**

Source: *Garland Encyclopedia of World Music,* Volume 1: Africa

important roles as oral historians, orators, genealogists, and praise singers. (We study this tradition in more detail in Lesson 13.) For a member of the aristocratic Keita family to become a musician was unheard of. Being born an albino, however, and consequently ostracized by both his family and community, Salif Keita turned to performing music in Bamako, the capital city, after poor eyesight eliminated teaching as a career option. He said in a 1992 interview with Banning Eyre of *Afropop Worldwide* Radio, "There were two ways I could go. I could become a delinquent and practice banditry or I could play music. There was no other way. Because I was a noble, it seemed better to play music than become a crook. So I chose music."[6] He was soon recognized for having an unusually powerful and expressive singing voice, and at the age of nineteen he joined first the Rail Band and then *Les Ambassadeurs,* the two most popular bands of the day. Political repression led him to emigrate first to neighboring Côte d'Ivoire and then to Paris where he became an international celebrity.

In the 1980s, worldwide interest in African-based popular music (known in the recording and broadcasting industries as "**Afropop**") reached its peak. From Mali and other countries of the region—Senegal, Guinea, Gambia—came a number of prominent musicians, mostly from *jali* families, who pursued highly successful careers in Europe and North America. Salif Keita, with his fusion of Islamic/*jali*-inspired roots singing in his native language Wolof, and electronic and synthesizer-backed accompaniments, became known as "The Golden Voice of Africa." Yet by the 1990s he was frequently criticized for pandering to the tastes of the primarily European public with overly-produced, slickly-packaged recordings. From 1995 comes his song "Africa" on the Paris-produced album *Folon* for Mango Records. In this song, African traditional instruments—the "talking drum," *kora* (large harp-lute), and *djembe* (goblet-shaped hand drum)—combine with electric guitars, bass, synthesizer, and keyboards to produce African-flavored music with a techno beat. Keita sings this song in French, the language of Mali's European colonizers.

6-3 🔊

In a 1996 interview, Salif Keita spoke with Opiyo Oloya of CIUT FM Radio in Toronto:

O.O: Your music is slowly gaining attention around the world. I have met some of your fans from the former Yugoslavia. They say, Salif is a great singer. What is it in your music that makes someone from Yugoslavia listen to it?

S.K.:   You know, if you wanna call everybody, one thing you have to do is to call them with music. To tell you the truth, music is everybody's name (laughs). You understand what I mean.

O.O: Yes I understand.

S.K.:   With music, you don't have to say, Hey Philippe, Suzanne or Pierre. No, music is the name for everybody. If it comes from your heart, people will love it because everyone has a heart too. It's from one heart to another heart...You know the life of a musician is like an egg. You start from egg and grow into the chicken (laughs very heartily). You understand what I mean, don't you?[7]

At the age of fifty in 1999, Salif Keita began writing songs in a simpler, more personal and direct musical idiom. His song *"Ananamin"* ("It's Been So Long") from his album *Papa* reveals a different side of

Keita's musical identity. In this recording, he uses only acoustic instruments and sings in Wolof. Around the year 2000, Salif Keita returned to Africa to live. In a later interview with Banning Eyre, following the release of *Moffou* (2002) and its sequel *M'Bemba* (2005), Keita reflects on his musical life:

B.E: You know, Salif, looking back over all of your records, I notice that most of them are different. Most of the time, we hear a new Salif record, and we don't know what we are in for. But now, you have done two records in a row using more or less the same approach, and the same band. Does this mean you have finally found your true road? Or can we expect other revolutions in your sound in the future?

S.K.: No, I think I found the road that I must follow. I must try to combine my experience and my sensibility. Me, I always wanted to do acoustic music with a lot of heart, a lot of soul, without a lot of electronics. This is what I have been wanting to research. I think I've found my road.

B.E: That's fascinating. We could say that the history of all those other records was a voyage that led to this sound, right?

S.K.: In a sense, that is true. I would say that all the records I have made are good. But I think that now, with these two records, this is really what I want to do, more close to my heart. To my reality, in fact. Because I had not been to school, I had to work with other people, engineers, musicians, producers. I had to meet other cultures. This gave me a lot of experience in order to find my road.[8]

It took Salif Keita more than thirty years composing and performing music to find his authentic voice, "to find his road." Perhaps he had lost himself trying to write music that would appeal to every "Philippe, Suzanne or Pierre." Perhaps he had to, in the words of playwright Edward Albee, "go a long way out of his way in order to come back a short distance correctly."[9] Keita built a studio in Bamako, the capital of Mali, where he produced acoustic music rooted in the traditions of his native land, collaborating with musicians he had played with for decades. His later style is exemplified by the song "Dery" from the album *M'Bemba* (2005). He came home to himself. Having once sought to compose pop songs that everyone sings, he returned to his own authentic voice. Through this voice, he could express aspects of his identity that he had moved to the background—a West African man, a Wolof-speaking Mande, a Muslim, a blind albino and thus from a group that has historically been outcast in his native land. He himself chose early in life to take on the identity of a musician while rejecting his aristocratic family status and identity. Yet, despite his continuing success in his homeland, some members of Keita's own family have never forgiven his betrayal of his ancestry.

6-4 🔊

CUI JIAN (CHINA)

While Beethoven and Ravi Shankar are associated with the classical music traditions of Europe and India respectively, Cui Jian (b. 1961) is a popular artist who made historic contributions to modern Chinese culture. He performed his own unique style of rock music and thereby challenged the authority of the Chinese government. The Communist Party, which came to power in 1949 led by Mao Zedong, took over all channels of public media and placed them at the service of the government's various agendas. In his book *China's New Voices*, author Nimrod Baranovitch writes:

For close to three decades in China after 1949, one could hear in public a single voice, that of the party-state. The government dictated much of culture and imposed unity in almost every domain. The new revolutionary trend extended from suppression of political views that did not agree with those of Chairman Mao Zedong as far as the attempt to eliminate regional, ethnic, class, and even gender differences.... During the decade of the Cultural Revolution (1966–76) in particular, only militant revolutionary songs that praised the leadership and a handful of revolutionary operas and ballets were allowed to be performed in public.[10]

Fig. 6.7 Cui Jian (1961–) performing at the Capital Gymnasium, Beijing, 2005 in his first fully approved concert in twelve years

Following the death of Mao in 1976 and the rise of his successor, Deng Xiaoping, there was a decided liberalization of state control in areas of public culture. Previously forbidden forms of popular entertainment from outside the country provided an appropriate soundtrack to new forms of free-market economic activity and cultural expression. Popular songs, called *tongsu*, were gradually introduced to the airwaves, with styles influenced by such Western forms as jazz and disco, and yet the government still exerted tight control. Songwriters and performers had to belong to separate government work units, and any "sexual songs, nihilistic songs, morbid songs, violent songs" or songs critical of state policies were censored.[11] Typical *tongsu* songs had strongly patriotic themes. Particularly following the **Pro-Democracy Movement's Tiananmen Square** protests in 1989 and their violent suppression by the military, the government tried to calm political tensions and replace frustrated desires for further social liberalization by promoting patriotic fervor through song titles such as "China, China I love you" and "The Communist Party Brings Good Times."

Cui Jian, of Korean ancestry, had been a child-prodigy trumpeter who joined the Beijing Symphony Orchestra at the age of fourteen. However, he was captivated by American pop singers like Simon and Garfunkel, whose recordings were just making their way into newly opened China, and in his spare time took up the electric guitar and song writing. He burst onto the public stage at a government-sanctioned *tongsu* pop concert in Beijing in 1986. At this televised event, he was one of a hundred invited singers. His standout performance challenged the status quo in a number of ways: his dress was casual in the manner associated with Western rock musicians, and the strong insistent beat and his rough vocal style had a "direct, unrestrained, and liberating quality." The song he sang, "Nothing to My Name," was "a celebration of lack of control. It was the antithesis of both the traditional Confucian aesthetics of moderation and restraint...as well as the antithesis of the official communist aesthetic of polished and disciplined professionalism."[12] What was perhaps most radical about the song was that Cui Jian had written it himself—it was unheard of for a singer to publicly sing his or her own song—and the song was about Cui Jian's own subjective experience and identity. The personal pronoun in the lyrics is "I," not "we." The song introduced to a generation of Chinese youth the free and nonconformist values associated in the West with rock and roll.

6-5

"Nothing to My Name"

I've asked tirelessly, when will you go with me?
But you just always laugh at my having nothing
I've given you my dreams, given you my freedom
But you always just laugh at my having nothing

Oh! When will you go with me?
Oh! When will you go with me?

The earth under my feet is on the move,
The water by my side is flowing on,
But you always just laugh at my having nothing
Why haven't you laughed your fill
Why will I always search?

Could it be that before you I will always have nothing?
Oh! When will you go with me?
Oh! When will you go with me?

The earth under my feet is on the move
The water by my side is flowing on
I'm telling you I've waited a long time
I'm telling you my very last demand
I need to grab both your hands
Only then will you go with me
That's when your hands will tremble,
That's when your tears will flow
Can it be that you're telling me you love my having nothing?[13]

(English translation by Andrew Jones)

Of course, the song's implication that after forty years of Communist Party control one should find oneself "having nothing" was seen as a strong indictment of failed policies. "Nothing to My Name" became the anthem of the Pro-Democracy students during the period leading up to the events in Tiananmen Square (1989), although Cui Jian himself was banned from public stage performances following his notorious premier. In early 1990, Cui Jian was surprisingly allowed to give a concert tour as a fundraiser for the Asian Games. However after the first few concerts when he chose to sing his song "A Piece of Red Cloth," its thinly veiled condemnation of the Chinese Communist Party led to the tour's early termination.

6-6

That day you tied my eyes with red cloth
You covered up the sky
You asked what I was looking at
I said I saw happiness.
This feeling comforts me
It lets me forget that I have nowhere to go.[14]

(English translation by Nimrod Baranovitch)

His situation today is quite different. He has performed throughout the world, appearing on stage with top rock bands such as The Rolling Stones and Deep Purple. In recent years he has headlined at major festivals in China; indeed, he hired the Beijing Symphony Orchestra, which he officially left in 1987, to back his own band for two concerts on New Year's Eve 2010 and New Year's Day 2011.[15] No other popular musician from China has had such an impact on the international stage.

CONCLUSION

Each of the artists discussed above, while conveying through music a distinctive and extraordinary individual identity, also expresses aspects of collective identity that are discussed in the next three lessons: Group Identity, Hybrid Identity, and Oppositional Identity. Ludwig van Beethoven profoundly influenced musical styles in Central Europe and elsewhere for more than a hundred years after his death, and more than any other composer he came to represent the core values of European classical music. The individuality and triumph over adversity he expressed through his revolutionary symphonies came to be associated with liberation movements and the democratic aspirations of millions. A melody from his 9th Symphony, the "Ode to Joy," is now the official anthem of nearly five hundred million members of the European Union. On July 1, 2013 at the stroke of midnight—the very moment Croatia joined the European Union—Beethoven's 9th Symphony with its famous anthem was played at a celebratory outdoor concert in Zagreb, that nation's capital. Ravi Shankar, throughout his long and distinguished career, also served as a powerful icon of group identity. He was a living embodiment of traditional North India. Through his music he communicated Indian culture to the Western world, which he was uniquely prepared to reach as cultural mediator. Maria Stoyanova's

6-4

gender made her performances at weddings distinctive challenges to long-held ideas about music and social relationships. Nevertheless her *gaida* and the dance tunes she plays upon it evoke to Bulgarians and Rom alike traditional values. Salif Keita's success as an Afropop artist derived from his ability to package the songs and rhythms of his native Mali in the high-tech recording and performance club styles that his European and American audiences enjoyed. It was the "hybridizing" of his musical identity—traditional Malian with international pop—that he came to regret and pull back from late in his career. Cui Jian's musical identity is oppositional. As a Chinese rock musician, his music and persona embodied a set of values—individualistic, self-expressing, discontented with the status quo—that contradicted the Chinese authorities who, since the Communist Revolution of 1949, had tightly controlled media outlets and all forms of cultural practice.

KEY CONCEPTS

Individual identity	Wedding ensemble	Techno music
Patronage system	Gender roles	Authentic voice
Sonata form	Hereditary occupations	Tiananmen Square
Musical mediator	*Jali* (pl. *Jalolu*)	Pro-Democracy
Musical ambassador	*Griot*	Movement
"World Music"	Afropop	

(Q) THINKING ABOUT MUSIC QUESTIONS

1. Consider the five individual musicians whose personal and particular early life experiences contributed to innovative forms of musical expression that in turn affected the music of their society. Can you think of three more such innovators? How did each use music to express the uniqueness of his or her identity?

2. According to the lesson, Salif Keita found his authentic style and "voice" at age 50. What does it mean to *you* to be "authentic?" If you were a professional musician, what would *your* authentic style be like?

3. In your own experience, are there particular gender divisions in your society such as Maria Stoyanova encountered in hers? Are there particular gender roles and expectations in the musical life of your community?

4. If you had been at the hotel party in China described at the beginning of the lesson, what song would *you* sing, and why? (Remember, in that context, you *have* to sing *something*.)

5. In the United States, individuals have many choices of music to listen to, of concerts to attend, of CDs and MP3s to purchase and download. How might these musical choices be understood as a projection of an individual's identity? How do you use music to "express yourself" either as a performer or a listener?

6. Based on the case study of Ludwig van Beethoven in this lesson, consider what was going on in Beethoven's life at the time he was writing his 5th Symphony, and also the social and political situation at the turn of the 19th century in Europe. How do *you* think Beethoven expresses his individual identity in this symphony?

NOTES

1   John Blacking, *How Musical is Man* (Seattle and London: University of Washington, 1973), 46.

2   Ludwig van Beethoven, "Heiligenstadt Testament," accessed July 23, 2014, http://home.swipnet.se/zabonk/cultur/ludwig/beeheil.htm.

3   Dylan Evans, "Beethoven was a Narcissistic Hooligan," *Guardian*, June 7, 2005, http://www.theguardian.com/music/2005/jun/07/classicalmusicandopera.television.

4   Timothy Rice, *Music in Bulgaria: Experiencing Music, Expressing Culture* (New York and Oxford: Oxford University Press, 2004), 14–15.

5   Timothy Rice, *Music in Bulgaria,* 4.

6   Banning Eyre, *In Griot Time* (Philadelphia: Temple University Press, 2000), 91.

7   "Opiyo Oloya Interviews Salif Keita," April 23, 1996, in Toronto, Canada, *RootsWorld*, http://www.rootsworld.com/rw/feature/keita2.html.

8   "Salif Keita: 2006," interview with Banning Eyre, New York—Paris, 2006. *Afropop Worldwide*, accessed July 23, 2014, http://archive.today/gXZuC.

9   From Edward Albee's one-act play *The Zoo Story* (1958).

10 Nimrod Baranovitch, *China's New Voices: Popular Music, Ethnicity, Gender, and Politics, 1978–1997* (Los Angeles: University of California Press, 2003), 1.

11 Andrew Jones, *Like a Knife: Ideology and Genre in Contemporary Chinese Popular Music* (Ithaca, NY: Cornell University East Asian Program, 1992), 48.

12 Nimrod Baranovitch, *China's New Voices,* 33.

13 English translation of Cui Jian's song lyrics, "Nothing to My Name," by Andrew Jones, in *Like a Knife*.

14 English translation of Cui Jian's song lyrics, "A Piece of Red Cloth," by Nimrod Baranovitch, in *China's New Voices*, 237.

15 Private correspondence with Jonathan Campbell, December 20, 2013; author of *Red Rock: The Long, Strange March of Chinese Rock and Roll* (Hong Kong: Earnshaw Books Ltd., 2011).

Lesson 7
Music and Group Identity

From school fight songs to national anthems, music is one of the fundamental ways in which people express their solidarity with other people as members of groups. At social rituals like sporting events, civic holidays, coronations, and state funerals, special music marks the occasion and establishes the proper mood: festive, celebratory, dignified, or solemn. Participatory group singing of anthems and patriotic songs encourages feelings of unity and public acknowledgment of shared history, values, and allegiances. Through music we celebrate our collective identities and project them to others; by their music, we know something of the feelings and values of others. Entering the airport in Fiji, for example, the traveler's first encounter with Fijian culture is a traditional song performed by two musicians playing ukuleles. Fijian music—friendly, laid-back, "Island Music"—establishes a sense of locale, a mood, a sonic threshold to the pleasures that the tourist is there to enjoy. Anthropologist Tony Seeger states, "Music and food are two features of human culture that circulate most widely in the world today while maintaining elements of their origins."[1] Music conveys features that are familiar to most travelers—harmonies, rhythms, instruments—while at the same time conveying, through sound, markers of a particular locale, time, and history. In this lesson, we explore various aspects of the roles that musical instruments, dances, performers, composers, and traditions play in celebrating and projecting a group's identity.

MUSICAL INSTRUMENTS (IRELAND, ARGENTINA)

Musical instruments often serve as emblems or icons for groups. The commemorative quarters of both Tennessee and Louisiana states are engraved with musical instruments, proclaiming to all Americans the importance of music to the identity (and tourist industry) of Nashville, Memphis, and New Orleans.

Tourists leaving from Seoul-Inchon International Airport in South Korea can pick up souvenir key chains attached to tiny *changgo* hourglass drums. Because this drum plays such an important role in most forms of traditional music in Korea, the chances are good that a tourist has heard one at a restaurant or cultural event and would therefore treasure the keepsake. Indian restaurants bearing the name and logo "*Sitar*" can be found in Philadelphia, Albany, San Diego, Knoxville, Pasadena,

Fig. 7.1   The U.S. Mint's State Quarters for Tennessee and Louisiana

Vancouver, and elsewhere. In the restaurant as you are eating, you hear the piped-in strains of the instrument. Its unique timbre and the style of music it plays suggest that here is an authentic experience of Indian culture. Often, an instrument takes on the iconic status of a nation or ethnic group because it is indigenous or unique to that place or people. The steel drums were invented in Trinidad but now project a pan-Caribbean identity. The *bandura* of Ukraine, the *cimbalom* of Hungary, and the *dan tranh* of Vietnam all remain tied to, and serve as, icons of their original home.

The Celtic harp has been an emblem of Irish identity since at least the 10th century. Traditionally, Irish harpers were highly skilled storytellers and **minstrels** who performed for the nobility and thus enjoyed prestige and royal protection. At the end of the 16th century, during Tyrone's Rebellion (1594–1603), a popular uprising against English rule, Elizabeth I banned the playing of the harp as an act of sedition against the crown. The English accused the Irish harpers of being spies, since they traveled freely between the courts of the rebellious chieftains. Harpers were hung and their instruments destroyed despite the fact that the English liked harp music. While traditional Irish music is played more often today on instruments such as the fiddle, the pennywhistle, the concertina, and the guitar, it is the harp that decorates the official Irish coat of arms. The Irish harp is also the trademark of Guinness beer, which, when combined with Harp lager, makes a drink called a "Black and Tan" in Dublin.

The violin, invented in the late 16th century in Italy, played a prominent role in Western classical music throughout its history, but as the "fiddle" it has been adopted into various traditional music contexts around the world. In Cape Breton in northeastern Canada, the fiddle is ubiquitous in music sessions, performances, and dances, where musicians play and adapt Scottish and Irish tunes that their ancestors brought to the New World. A statue of the instrument stands sixty feet high on the Sydney waterfront, proclaiming to cruise ship passengers and island visitors alike the fiddle's singular importance as an expression of Cape Breton identity. Accordions of all sorts took root in many parts of the world following the invention of the first "squeezebox" in early 19th-century Germany. Their presence in contexts as diverse as Argentina and Madagascar demonstrates the phenomenon known to ethnomusicologists as "**glocalization**": the adaptation of globally diffused technologies to particular local customs and purposes. The *bandoneon*, a type of button accordion invented in Germany around 1860, is the national instrument of Argentina. It was originally intended by its German manufacturers to be used by missionaries to play at services in churches without organs. However, when it arrived in the port of Buenos Aires at the end of the 19th century among the few possessions of German and Italian immigrants, it was found to be the perfect accompaniment to an urban dance form that was gaining popularity there: the tango. Through their association with place, each of these instruments visually and aurally projects group identity. Furthermore, these associations are deepened by the contexts in which they

Fig. 7.2   Ukrainian *bandura* (L), and Hungarian *cimbalom* (R)

Fig. 7.3   The *bandoneon* (L), and monuments to the *bandoneon* in Buenos Aires (C) and the fiddle in Sydney, Cape Breton (R)

are used: parties, festivals, holidays, concerts. It is at events like these that people come together to express solidarity with each other and with the traditions they share.

DANCES (ARGENTINA)

In many parts of the world, national and ethnic identity and pride are also expressed through dance forms that carry strong associations with the history and traditions of a group. The "steps" of a dance are physical expressions of a rhythmic pattern that, like dress and food, mark the day-to-day realities that constitute a way of life. In the context of the dance, important aspects of social organization are publicly performed. Gender roles, courtship patterns, generational obligations, and rites of passage are both ritualized and actualized through the dance. In the Caribbean and Latin America, many islands and nations are so closely identified with dances that it is difficult to think of the one without the other. Columbia has *cumbia*, Brazil has samba, Jamaica has reggae, Dominican Republic has merengue, Puerto Rico has *bomba* and *plena*, and more recently a pan-Latino dance form, salsa, that is now performed throughout the world.

   The **tango**, called "the vertical expression of a horizontal desire," has been associated worldwide with Uruguay, Argentina, and especially the city of Buenos Aires at least since the 1920s. In 1926, Hollywood actor and matinee idol Rudolph Valentino danced the tango in *The Four Horsemen of the Apocalypse*, launching the dance to international popularity as the new media of the time—film, radio, and the phonograph—spread local styles around the globe.

Map 7-1   Argentina, Uruguay, and Chile in southern South America

Source: *Garland Encyclopedia of World Music*, Volume 2: South America, Mexico, Central America, and the Caribbean

Of the tango, Teddy Peiro and Jan Fairley write in *The Rough Guide to World Music*:

> Nobody can exactly pinpoint tango's birthplace, but it certainly developed amongst the *porteños*—the people of the port area of Buenos Aires—and its bordellos [houses of prostitution] and bars. It was a definitively urban music: a product of the melting pot of European immigrants, Criollos [people of mixed European and African ancestry], blacks and natives, drawn together when the city became the capital of Argentina in 1880. Tango was thus forged from a range of musical influences that included Andalucian flamenco, southern Italian melodies, Cuban habanera, African *candombé* and percussion, European polkas and mazurkas, Spanish contradanse, and, closer to home, the *milónga*—the rural song of the Argentine *gaucho* [cowboy]. It was a music imbued with immigrant history.
>
> In this early form, tango became associated with the bohemian life of bordello brawls and *compadrítos*—knife-wielding, womanizing thugs. By 1914, there were over 100,000 more men than women in Buenos Aires, thus the high incidence of prostitution and the strong culture of bar-brothels. Machismo and violence were part of the culture and men would dance together in the low-life cafés and corner bars practicing new steps and keeping in shape while waiting for their women, the *minas* of the bordellos. Their dances tended to have a showy yet threatening, predatory quality, often revolving around a possessive relationship between two men and one woman. In such a culture, the *compadríto* danced the tango into existence.[2]

 In this video clip of Argentine dance orchestras, you can see the prominent role of the *bandoneon*. Because the instrument was so difficult to play, yet had the mournful, sentimental sound that fit the mood early pioneers of the genre were seeking, the tempo of the dance slowed to accommodate the *bandoneonistos,* allowing thereby more intimate and sensual moves by the dancers.

Fig. 7.4 **Argentine tango**

VOICES (ARGENTINA, PORTUGAL, USA, EGYPT)

Carlos Gardel (1887–1935) was the most influential tango singer of his day, and in Argentina he continues to be revered. More than any other figure, he raised the music and dance of tango from the slums and bars of the Buenos Aires waterfront to the popular entertainments of the middle class and the glamorous nightclubs of the wealthy. Gardel's career entered a new phase with the advent of radio broadcasts and films. In more than a dozen movies, he sang of the loves, the losses, the loneliness, and the tragedy of a nation of immigrants. His death in a plane crash at the height of his career only solidified his position as the voice of his country.

7-1

Fig. 7.5 Carlos Gardel (1887–1935)

The electronic recording and broadcast technologies and industries of the early 20th century created the mass media that revolutionized the ways people worldwide experienced and consumed music. This technological revolution, which began with Thomas Edison's "talking machine," allowed musicians like Gardel to gain iconic status both within their home region and abroad. By 1930 a musical personality could reach not just hundreds or thousands in auditoriums and clubs, but millions. As the impact of the mass media became more and more all-pervasive, certain highly gifted and charismatic singer-performers became symbols of their country, their ethnic group, their region, and their generation.

Portuguese *fado* singer Amália Rodrigues (1920–1999) began her singing career as a child on the streets of Lisbon, and from the age of fifteen sang professionally in nightclubs. Immediately following World War II a career in commercial recordings and films made her an international celebrity. Her remarkable voice, deeply expressing the melancholy and longing of so many *fado* songs, earned her the title "*Rainha do Fado*" (Queen of *Fado*) over her fifty-year stage and recording career. When she died on October 6, 1999, tens of thousands attended her State Funeral, and the BBC announced: "Portugal mourns the 'voice of its soul'." Listen to this 1955 recording of Amália Rodrigues singing "*Tudo isto é fado*" (All of this is *fado*).

7-2

Chorus:

Vanquished souls
Lost nights
Bizarre shadows
In the Mouraria
A pimp sings
Guitars cry
Jealous love
Ashes and fire
Pain and sin
All of this exists
All of this is sorrowful
All of this is fado

(English translation by Fernando Reis)

Louis Armstrong and Duke Ellington became icons of American jazz both in the U.S. itself and abroad. A generation later, singers Elvis Presley and John Lennon were symbols of post-World War II youth culture. Each projected an image that was controversial: reviled by parents who had lived though the Great Depression and the War, and emulated by their offspring who longed for the freedom and rebellion that these artists represented. In the 1960s, **Otis Redding** (1941–1967) and **Janis Joplin** (1943–1970) each cultivated a unique singing style that came to represent for their audiences a number of values related to race, class, and region. Both died before the age of thirty, so their short but brilliant careers are linked to a moment in history when the music industry was at the forefront of a social and political revolution.

Umm Kulthum (1904–1975) was known as "The Voice of Egypt." Her rise to iconic status coincided with the development of mass media in Egypt. Her career exemplified the unifying power of a popular artist in the new technological era, and her voice, like that of Carlos Gardel in Argentina and Amália Rodrigues in Portugal, came to represent an entire nation. But her career to an exceptional degree was shaped by, and to an extent shaped, the turbulent times in which she lived. Ethnomusicologist Scott Marcus writes:

> With her ever-rising fame and the growth of the new radio medium, Umm Kulthum was given an unprecedented honor: on January 7, 1937, she began giving live-radio-broadcast concerts on the first Thursday of each month from November or December to June, a practice that continued throughout the rest of her life and, with recordings, even after her death. When Gamal Abdel Nasser came to power in Egypt after the 1952 revolution against the Egyptian monarchy, he understood the potential of the voice and persona of Umm Kulthum for promoting Egyptian and indeed pan-Arab unity. Thus, one of his first acts was to dramatically strengthen the broadcasting power of the Egyptian national radio so that the signal could be received throughout the Arab world, as far north as Lebanon and Syria. There are countless stories of how the streets would empty as the time for her Thursday concerts approached and people took their seats in front of a radio. I have heard such stories from Israelis, Lebanese, and Moroccans. In the 1960s, Nasser created the "Umm Kulthum" radio station, an all-music station that still features broadcasts of Umm Kulthum songs twice a day...Umm Kulthum not only became "The Voice of Egypt" to the people of the Arab world, but they also embraced her as their own. Thus she became a part of Arab individual and collective identity.[3]

We might wonder, "Why her?" Of the millions of Egyptians and thousands of Egyptian singers, why did Umm Kulthum attain the unique status of culture bearer? We have already mentioned that she came of age with the rise of the recording and broadcast technologies that made possible the phenomenon of the national or international "superstar." Through these technologies, her voice and image were projected upon the national and pan-Arab consciousness, and millions saw in the image and heard in the voice something utterly authentic, something of their deepest sense of self and the lives they were living.

She was raised in a small village in the Nile Delta where her father was the *imam* (prayer leader) and a singer of traditional wedding songs. Because the practice of Islam rests upon the recitation of the Qur'an in classical Arabic, correct enunciation of the language is highly prized in Egyptian culture. Her career began by joining her father at wedding performances dressed as a boy to avoid the social censure of women singing in public. As a singer, her exquisite pronunciation that she learned from her father along with her melodic art was the first attribute of her performance style to be praised. Her singing became more renowned and her travels with her father extended to the large cities of Cairo and Alexandria.

Fig. 7.6 Umm Kulthum (1904–1975) She became a master of *maqam*, the melodic system of classical

Map 7-2 **Egypt and the Near East**

Source: *Garland Encyclopedia of World Music*, Volume 6: The Middle East

Arabic modes that form the basis of both composition and improvisation. Like her, much of the Egyptian population had moved from the countryside to the cities in the great 20th-century urban migrations, marking the end of traditional agrarian ways that had lasted for millennia. Thus her life embodied both the humble roots of the millions in her audience as well as the highest values of their artistic traditions and faith. In **Umm Kulthum's** *concerts,* her songs went on for hours as audiences demanded that she repeat certain lines over and over, each time with different melodic improvisation and emphasis. She understood the media and music industry, and managed her career impeccably. But beyond any power of analysis, she conveyed a sense of authenticity, of genuine "Egypt-ness"; and could generate through her singing an environment of *tarab*, enchantment.

In the Lebanese novel, *The Hakawati* (2008), by Rabih Alameddine, a young boy recalls drinking tea in a Beirut cafe while listening to the Thursday evening Umm Kulthum radio broadcast with his uncle and friends:

> Applause could be heard on the radio. "She's onstage," Uncle Jihad whispered. "She has arrived." Silence...Her voice came on, clear, strong, powerful. The room sighed in unison at her first utterance, then quieted again. A man wearing dark eyeglasses held together with a gray piece of tape leaned back in his chair as if he were about to be showered with rose petals. Another man conducted an imaginary orchestra with both hands...Umm Kulthoum carried the melody, sang of love in Egyptian dialect, and the words of longing made sense...She repeated each line, once, twice, three times, more, until it vibrated within me...When she finished the melody, the room shook. Men applauded, stood up, yelled at the radio. "Long may you live!"..."May God keep you!"
>
> "It didn't happen," one man said to the radio. "You have to do it again."
>
> She did...When she finished the melody the second time, the audience erupted...A short man stood on a table and shouted "Allah-u-akbar [God is great]."...She began the same melody again. I was in ecstasy. The room shook in delight...By the time she was done, a full hour into the song, the room was utterly exhausted and hoarse..."Umm Kulthoum is the quintessential Arab," Uncle Jihad said [as we drove home together]. "She's probably the one person whom all Arabs agree to love."[4]

Four million people attended Umm Kulthum's funeral in Cairo in 1975, one of the largest gatherings in human history.

7-3 🔊

Fig. 7.7 Statue of Umm Kulthum in a square named after her, on the site where her home once stood in Cairo

COMPOSERS

Following the tragic and shocking events of September 11, 2001, Americans found a renewed sense of solidarity through the song "God Bless America." This popular anthem of American renewal, first featured in the Hollywood film *This is the Army* (1942), was composed by Irving Berlin (1888–1989), a Russian Jewish immigrant and son of a cantor (Jewish liturgical singer). During his extraordinary career that spanned more than six decades, Berlin wrote more than fifteen hundred songs, many of them iconic of the American experience. About him, composer Jerome Kern once said, "Irving Berlin has no place in American music. He *is* American music. Emotionally, he honestly absorbs the vibrations emanating from the people, manners, and life of his time and, in turn, gives these impressions back to the world—simplified, clarified, and glorified."[5]

ACKO CHOEDRAG (CHINA/TIBET)

Acko Choedrag (b. 1976), a Tibetan Buddhist monk in China's western province of Qinghai, formerly the Tibetan province of Amdo, presents a more recent example of an artist expressing through music the aspirations of a group. Choedrag is also a media producer and something of a regional pop star. In his monk's cell he has set up a sound and editing studio to produce the video compact disks (VCDs) on which his reputation and fame rest. A member of the self-enclosed monastic community of Kumbum, originally built in 1436, Choedrag lives in this traditional world of meditation and ritual as well as the modern world of cell phones, jeans, shades, and digital media production. His VCDs, available throughout the Tibetan cultural region, combine original songs based on religious and folk materials with video images of the regional landscape and ritual life, both monastic and popular. This artist has managed to walk an incredibly thin line between religion and celebrity, representing traditional Tibetan identity through modern technology. Choedrag produces songs that affirm Tibetan unity for a society encroached upon by the modern world. His biography reveals the life of a musician from one of the world's most remote regions.

The Tibetan people are the indigenous inhabitants of the high plateau of Central Asia, the so-called "Roof of the World." Under King Songtsän Gampo in the 7th century CE, Buddhism became the state religion. Throughout its subsequent history, Tibet's political borders fluctuated greatly; at times the Tibetans enjoyed peace and stability, at times the empire fragmented due to internal feuds among the rulers or invasions by the Mongols or Chinese. From the mid-17th century, Tibet was ruled by a succession of monastic kings who held the title of Dalai Lama. Although isolated for much of their history yet living at the crossroads of the great Indian and Chinese civilizations, the Tibetans developed profound, complex, and unique artistic, architectural, musical, literary, and philosophical traditions. In 1724, China absorbed the two eastern provinces of Tibet, Amdo and Kham. In 1950, the army of the People's Republic of China took the western province of U-Tsan, traditional heartland of the Tibetan region and site of its capital Lhasa and the Dalai Lama's palace, the Potala. The

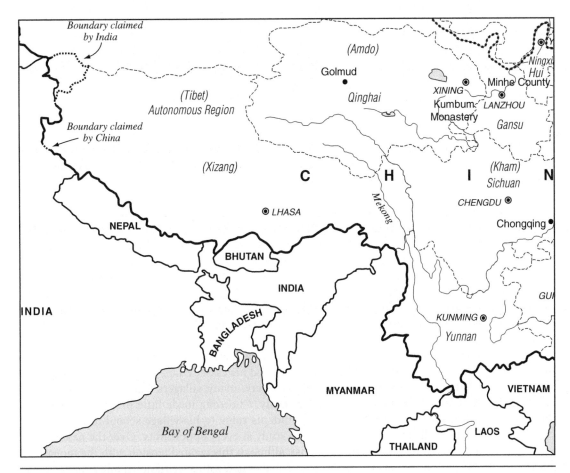

Map 7-3   The Tibetan region in western China

Source: *Garland Encyclopedia of World Music*, Volume 7: East Asia: China, Japan, and Korea

Fig. 7.8   Labrang Monastery, Gansu Province, People's Republic of China

14th Dalai Lama, along with thousands of refugees, fled across the Himalayas into India in 1959, following the Chinese military's brutal suppression of a popular uprising. There in the Himalayan town of Dharamsala he formed a government-in-exile.

Choedrag was born on January 9th, 1976, in an isolated farming village called Yaru. As the ninth child in his family, he was free from the obligations of herding and farming when he was young. His mother, a well-known singer in the community, taught him how to sing from the time he was able to speak. She was often invited to perform at wedding parties and would take Choedrag along with her. There he learned the musical traditions of the villagers. At the age of eight he attended a primary school for two years where he learned to read and count. He had a special feeling towards the Buddhist monks, who were a ubiquitous presence in his world. When monks were invited by the villagers to recite long passages of scripture at household gatherings, he would sit with them. At the age of ten his parents sent him to live with his uncle, who was a monk in a local monastery, and there he learned the monastic traditions of chanting.

When he was eighteen he went to Labrang Monastery, a great center of Tibetan Buddhist learning, to further his education. While at Labrang, he traded his cassette tape recorder for a guitar with another monk. When he returned to his local monastery, many villagers from this remote corner of the highland plateau came to see this musical rarity. Choedrag made little progress on learning the instrument, however, until some university students came to his village school to teach. Some could play the guitar well, and he went to them to study at every opportunity. Over the next several years, he developed a reputation as a fine guitarist, although this created tension with the monastery authorities. In 1999, at the age of twenty-three, he collaborated with a well-known folk singer, Gonpo Donrup, on his first album titled *Go*. It was distributed throughout the Tibetan cultural region and was played frequently on government-run, Tibetan-language radio stations. His financial success, which enriched the monastic community as a whole, changed the way the monastery administrators thought of Choedrag's career, and he was now free to compose and record from his monastery cell.

Fig. 7.9 **Choedrag playing his *dranyin* (Tibetan lute) (L), and recording on his computer (R)**

Choedrag undertook a serious study of Tibetan traditional music and Buddhist texts that influenced his developing compositional style. With money he had earned from his early projects, he purchased digital audio and video recording equipment, and in 2006 his VCD *Tibetans* was released and broadcast throughout the region. The music combines traditional folk melodies, religious chanting, and pop rhythms; and is mixed with video imagery of life in the monastery and the Tibetan countryside. In the Summer of 2008, prior to the Beijing Olympics, there was rioting in the region against what many Tibetans saw as Chinese suppression of Tibetan language, culture, religion, and autonomy. Choedrag's recording equipment was confiscated and for a short time he was placed under house arrest.

In this video clip of two selections from Acko Choedrag's *Tibetans*, the first song, "Praying," is an unaccompanied invocation based on religious chant. The highly ornamented style of singing would be recognized immediately by a Tibetan listener as deeply traditional. The video imagery shows the artist in his monk's robe meditating by one of the important natural landmarks of the region, Qinghai Lake, which is the largest inland body of water in China and considered sacred by the Tibetans. The first two lines of the text come from a meditation treatise by a famous lama (Buddhist high priest); the second two were added by the singer.

> Never leaving the side of true gurus [teachers]
> And benefiting from the glory of the Dharma [Buddha's Teaching] in all the lifetimes.
> After finishing "the good qualities of the levels and paths"
> Achieve Buddha-hood quickly!
>
> *(English translation by Tsering Samdrup and Dawa Torbert)*

The second song, "Tibetans," from which the album takes its name, is in a contemporary musical idiom with synthesizer accompaniment. It also carries traces of traditional Tibetan identity in the language as well as in the ornamented vocal style. The recording juxtaposes contradictory impressions of a contemporary musical style with images important to Tibetan identity such as the Potala palace (the Dalai Lama's former residence in Lhasa), pilgrims practicing forms of walking meditation, other forms of ritual worship, prayer flags, prayer wheels, religious paintings that decorate the landscape, and the Tibetan people themselves.

> **Nephews! Nieces!** [*as background singing*]
>
> Endless time is forever passing,
> The glorious stories are still told,
> In a radiant age,

Map 7-4   The Czech Republic and the Vltava River in central Europe

Source: *Garland Encyclopedia of World Music*, Volume 8: Europe

The second tone poem of the set, *Vltava* (more commonly known by its German name, 7-1
Moldau), is a musical depiction of a journey along the Vltava river as it flows from the mountains
of southern Bohemia, first southeastward then north through Prague and merging into the Elbe
river. Smetana wrote the following paragraph explaining this composition, to be included in a
concert program:

> The composition depicts the course of the river, beginning from its two small sources, one
> cold the other warm, the joining of both streams into one, then the flow of the Moldau through
> forests and across meadows, through the countryside where merry feasts are celebrated; water
> nymphs dance in the moonlight; on nearby rocks can be seen the outline of ruined castles,
> proudly soaring into the sky. The Moldau swirls through the St. John Rapids and flows in a
> broad stream toward Prague. It passes Vyšehrad [where an ancient royal castle once stood],
> and finally the river disappears in the distance as it flows majestically into the Elbe.

As you listen to the recording, you will hear each phrase in the composer's description tied to an
episode in the music: two flutes evoke the streams flowing out of the mountain, horns evoke forest
hunts, folk dance tunes represent the peasant weddings performed on the banks of the great river.
Muted strings create a dreamy, mystical sound for the water nymphs dancing in the moonlight. A
great surge of orchestral excitement represents the St. John Rapids, and finally the main theme of the
previous tone poem *Vyšehrad* is repeated to represent the river's arrival in the capital, Prague.

AARON COPLAND (USA)

American composer Aaron Copland (1900–1990) sought to use the European conventions of the
symphony orchestra and the genres associated with high art concert music—the symphony, opera,
and ballet—to convey an American identity that draws from, but ultimately transcends, its European

7-5 🔊

7-6 🔊

Fig. 7.11 Aaron Copland (1900–1990)

roots. Copland was born in Brooklyn to Russian-Jewish immigrant parents, and studied composition in France with Nadia Boulanger before returning to New York to pursue a career as a freelance composer. Like many artists of the 1920s, he was inspired to express through music the ideals and aspirations of American Democracy. Although his education had grounded him in the techniques of European modernism, he used this training to transform the music of America's people—jazz, folk songs, hymns, fiddle tunes, and spirituals—and bring it to the concert hall. In the early 1940s, Copland composed several ballet scores depicting the American Wild West (*Rodeo* and *Billy the Kid*) and early 19th-century rural Pennsylvania (*Appalachian Spring*). In these works he created a nationalist music that portrayed the lives of ordinary working Americans. In "Hoedown," the final scene from his 1942 ballet *Rodeo*, Copland captures the exuberance of frontier social life: the square dance, the reel, the rip-snortin' buckaroo a-courtin'. He evokes the spirit of the West through quotations and re-workings of folk dance melodies: "Bonaparte's Retreat" and "Miss McLeod's Reel." His instrumental *Fanfare for the Common Man* has also come to evoke "the spirit of the American pioneer," symbolizing in its wide intervals and strong brass harmonies the ambitious explorers of the American nation across land, sea, and space. Here, the kind of brass fanfare that had traditionally announced the arrival of a monarch receives a populist treatment: it is the ordinary citizen who is accorded this recognition and honor. Copland is remembered as the Dean of American Composers, whose influence would shape the history of American symphonic music, Broadway musicals, and Hollywood film scores.

MULTICULTURAL SOCIETIES (SURINAME)

In a multicultural society in which people of diverse ethnic and cultural backgrounds live together and interact, music and dance are important ways the various groups celebrate and perpetuate allegiance to their ethnic community, shared ancestry, a distant homeland, or to a way of life that is no longer viable in the modern world. Suriname, formerly called Dutch Guyana, is a country on the northern coast of South America that has a distinctly multicultural society. It is approximately the size of the state of Wisconsin and has a population of around 520,000 people. Most of its population lives in a narrow strip of low-lying grassland along the Caribbean Coast, and in the capital Paramaribo situated on the west bank of the Suriname River. This and several other rivers have headwaters deep in the rainforest of the Amazon Basin that covers around eighty percent of the land, extending south to the Brazilian border.

Because of a unique pattern of colonization, conquest, resistance, slavery, indentured servitude, and post-modern environmental plunder, the country has one of the most diverse populations in the world. Carib, Trio, Waraka, and Arawak Amerindians—descendants of the region's original inhabitants—live in villages along the coast and deep in the interior, and as an assimilated population in the multicultural capital, Paramaribo. The first European settlers were English farmers who moved down from the Caribbean island of Barbados, and Portuguese Jews who moved up from Brazil. This community was escaping religious persecution, and built there the first synagogue in the New World. The English traded Suriname to the Dutch in 1667 in exchange for New Amsterdam, the modern site of New York City. The Dutch created a plantation economy, growing sugar cane and coffee, with imported African slaves providing the backbreaking labor. Suriname is home to the world's largest **Maroon** population, the descendants of 17th- and 18th-century slaves who escaped from the

Map 7-5   Suriname in northern South America

Source: *Garland Encyclopedia of World Music*, Volume 2: South America, Mexico, Central America, and the Caribbean

plantations and fled down river into the nearly impenetrable rainforest. From there, for a hundred years, they led daring raids against the planters and fought wars of resistance against the Dutch colonial army until treaties were finally signed in the 1760s, granting them territorial homelands in the interior. To this day their descendants maintain the forms of social organization and cultural practice of their West African ancestors in villages deep in the rainforest. When slavery ended in 1863, the Dutch plantation owners began importing Chinese, East Indian, and Javanese indentured workers to replace the emancipated slaves. Unlike the permanence of slavery, indentured laborers were given freedom following a period of servitude. The Asian workers were given the option of returning to their homelands or remaining in the colony. Creoles (the descendants of slaves who remained on the coastal plantations) and newly, often illegally arrived Brazilian gold miners complete the complex picture.

Most Surinamese speak the local **Creole** language, Sranan Tonga (Suriname tongue), made up of elements from Portuguese, English, Dutch, and several African languages. However, Dutch, a holdover from the colonial period, remains the official language that all school children learn. Many Surinamese also speak the language of their ethnic communities: Hindi, Javanese, Hakka (a Chinese dialect), and Saramaccan (the language of the largest group of Maroons). In such an ethnically and linguistically complex society, music is an important expression and symbol of the identity that each individual shares with others of a common ancestry, as well as with all fellow Surinamese.

All children learn the Surinamese national anthem in school, and sing it with their parents at sporting events and civic ceremonies. In a performance the words are sung twice, in Dutch and in Sranan Tonga. With the line "Wherever our ancestors came from," the song celebrates collective allegiance to their shared country despite the diversity of their ancestral origins.

Opo kondreman oen opo
Rise countrymen, rise
Sranan gron e kari oen
The soil of Suriname is calling you
Wans ope tata komopo
Wherever our ancestors came from
Wi moes seti kondre boen
We should take care of our country
Stre de fstre wi no sa freed
We are not afraid to fight
Gado de wi fesi man
God is our leader
Heri libi te na dede
Our whole life until our death
Wi sa feti gi Sranan
We will fight for Suriname[7]

Beyond this expression of shared identity, some children study the traditional songs and dances of their ancestral homelands. Deep in the forest, a group of Maroon boys practice the drumming patterns

Fig. 7.12   **Maroon village scene (L); Maroon drummer (C); and Suro-Javanese *gamelan* musician (R)**

that their fathers perform at rituals and festivals. A few will eventually travel upriver to the capital and become leaders in the popular music industry. This popular music is driven by the vital African "**roots rhythms**" that have been preserved for hundreds of years in the forest. In Paramaribo, a Carib Indian culture society, Paramuru, holds classes for children in dances that will be performed at annual **Native American** celebrations. The girls in this video are taught to imitate the eagle and the panther even though they live in town and never see the animals that populated their ancestors' forest home. In another part of town, the Afro-Surinamese Culture Society (*Na Afrikan Kulturu fu Sranan* or NAKS, founded in 1947) holds this class where **teenage Creole** girls practice songs and dances that derive from the African-based religion called **Winti**. Dancers invoke deities of the sky and earth through special drum patterns and dance steps. The call-and-response singing invokes Mama Issa (Mother Earth) and Legba, the guardian of the doorway. As these Creole girls practice their African-derived arts, girls from the East Indian community rehearse **dances** based on the **Bollywood** movies that keep them connected culturally to their ancestral home.

7-10
7-11
7-12

The Javanese of Suriname celebrate their "Arrival Day" on August 9th. On that date in 1900, the first contract laborers from the Dutch East Indies, as Indonesia was then called, disembarked to replace the British East Indian indentured laborers who themselves replaced the freed slaves. To celebrate this anniversary, the Javanese community in Paramaribo and the surrounding farming towns gather at the Indonesian Cultural Center for a day of soccer, music, and food. The highlight of the afternoon is a performance of the *jaran kapang* ("hobby horse dance"). Teams of teenage dancers

7-13

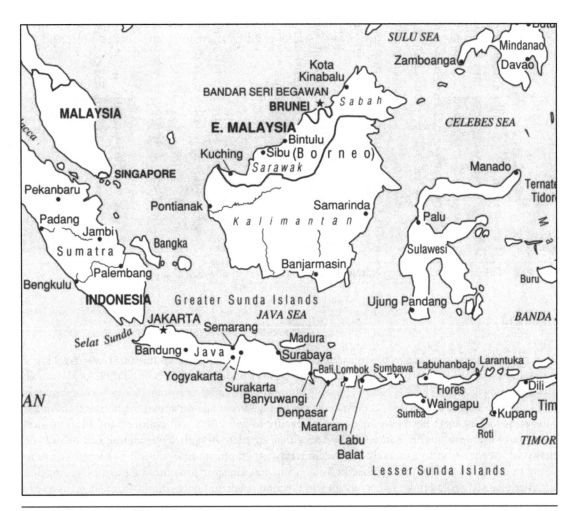

Map 7-6   **Java and Bali in Indonesia, Southeast Asia**

Source: *Garland Encyclopedia of World Music*, Volume 4: Southeast Asia

7-14 compete for the honor of performing at the year's most important cultural event for the Javanese community. The dance is accompanied by the *gamelan*, an ensemble of iron-keyed instruments led by the player of the barrel drum *kendang*. As the original laborers did not bring musical instruments with them from Java, they had to forge them from scrap iron and melted-down farming implements, and they meticulously tuned them by ear based on their memory of an Old World tuning system—an extraordinary accomplishment. The dancers on hobbyhorses, along with "clown" sidekicks, move in unison to an orderly choreography imitating stylized horse movements. At a certain point in the dance-ritual, specially chosen adult dancers take over the hobbyhorses and become entranced by the horse spirits. In trance for more than an hour, they buck and tumble, eat grass and unhulled rice, and drink enormous quantities of water. Suddenly one or two drop the hobbyhorses and become possessed by the spirits of birds, then lions, then monkeys, then snakes, in acts of controlled mayhem, overseen by the elders who carefully watch over the dancers. The dance provides a link with relatives and ancestors from the home country, where it also performed, as well as to a spirit world with which the Javanese readily commune. Part religious ritual, part entertainment, the *jaran kapang* is a powerful and durable expression of Javanese identity.

Young Surinamese learn the values and beliefs of their parents and ancestors through cultural forms like songs and dances. Through music and dance they also learn about the histories and cultures of the other groups that constitute Surinamese society. In school music and social studies classes, for instance, children learn about the instruments associated with each group through kits that are assembled by the cultural ministry and made available to teachers. The photographs below show instruments associated with Native American, East Indian, and Javanese cultures for school children in Suriname: drums and maracas (rattles) are used in Native American rituals and are associated with their identity, as are the ankle bells of Hindustani dance and the *gamelan* instruments of the Javanese. By learning about the instruments, school children learn about their own culture and the others that make up Surinamese society.

Fig. 7.13   **Surinamese school kits: Native American (L); East Indian (C); and Javanese (R)**

CONCLUSION

As we have noted elsewhere, while music itself is universal, music is not a universal language. Local musical expressions convey meanings that may not be fully understandable beyond their local context. However, now in the early 21st century, people not only communicate instantaneously via computers and smartphones but can share and even make music together while separated by thousands of miles. Musicians and listeners have easy access and exposure to many different cultures, and local musical forms have been profoundly influenced by styles that circulate broadly over satellite and broadband networks. Music is no longer exclusively defined by geographical and political borders. We are as likely to see and hear Beyoncé's music in Tokyo, Buenos Aires, or Johannesburg as in Los Angeles. International styles of popular music like rap and techno reach audiences worldwide. These styles are able to carry local meanings within communities while at the same time giving listeners a sense that they share a cosmopolitan identity. Visionary music producers see the possibility of music serving as an expressive medium that could truly unite the world. Consider "Playing for Change," a multimedia music project started in 2004 by producers Mark Johnson and Whitney Kroenke. Their goal was to "inspire, connect, and bring peace to the world through music." Their pilot project was to record a local street musician, Roger Ridley in Santa Monica, California, playing a single song, "Stand By Me," (1961) by Ben E. King, and then travel around the world to such places as India, South Africa, the Middle East, and Ireland to record musicians playing the same song each in her or his own style. Returning to the U.S. they mixed many different versions to create an edited performance that gave the illusion of a world of musicians playing together and, symbolically, "standing by" each other.

7-15

Fig. 7.14   **Bob Marley (1945–1981) ca. 1970**

If the sound technologies of the early 20th century—motion pictures and radio broadcasts—made possible the spectacular reach and influence of Carlos Gardel and Umm Kulthum, it was the international recording industry of the late 20th century—Billboard Charts, Grammy Awards, *Rolling Stone* magazine, disc jockies, gold and platinum albums—that made Bob Marley (1945–1981) a worldwide celebrity artist. The style he performed called reggae, a derivative of Jamaican dancehall music, was one of the first popular styles with a truly global reach. Born in a small village, Rhoden Hall, on the island of Jamaica to a nineteen-year old Afro-Caribbean mother and an absentee fifty-year old English father, Marley came to represent a number of group identities: those associated with a song and dance form (reggae), a hair style (dreadlocks), a religion (Rastafarianism), a nation (Jamaica), a region (the Caribbean), a historically-dispersed population (the African diaspora), and indeed, the poor and powerless everywhere. Bob Marley is one of the most influential musicians of the 20th century, for while rooted in the particulars of his individual identity—a Jamaican, a Rastafarian, a mixed-race musician who championed the cause of the oppressed—he aspired to universality. The worldwide web and digital technology of the 21st century provide Marley's "One Love", as produced by "Playing for Change," a format through which this song symbolically unites the world.

7-16

KEY CONCEPTS

Group identity	Thomas Edison's "talking machine"	Tone poem
Glocalization		Ethnic community
National and ethnic identity	Superstar	Slavery/indentureship
	Culture bearer	"Roots Rhythms"
Urban music	"Egypt-ness"	
Mass media	19th-century Nationalist Movement	

Q THINKING ABOUT MUSIC QUESTIONS

1. In this lesson, we encountered several singers who seemed to express through their voices different collective identities: Carlos Gardel, "The Voice of Argentina"; Umm Kulthum, "The Voice of Egypt"; Janice Joplin and Otis Redding, "Voices of the 60s," etc. Can you think of a singer who shares and expresses an aspect of *your* identity? If one of your parents or grandparents was asked the same question, how do you think they would answer?

2. Listen again to the two songs from Acko Choedrag's *Tibetans* recording. They are in very different styles. How do they *both* express aspects of contemporary Tibetan identity as you understand it from the case study.

3. Is Surinamese society and musical life like America's in miniature? If so, how? If not, how is it different?

4. Think of a group of people you are connected with that shares a common bond (cultural, ethnic, geographic, racial, social, etc.) and describe what music expresses the identity of that group. How does the music express this identity? Through lyrics? Musical instruments? Elements of music (e.g. melody, harmony, rhythm)? What are the markers that put the "identity" into the music?

5. You read about a Madagascan vocal trio, Salala, at the end of Lesson 5, and watched the band's 2005 concert in a soccer stadium in Antananarivo. Which "group" identities is the vocal trio expressing in its performance, and in what ways do these singers and their song mobilize, inspire, and celebrate group identity?

NOTES

1 Anthony Seeger, "Foreword," in Laurent Albert, *The Music of the Other: New Challenges for Ethnomusicology in a Global Age*, trans. Carla Ribeiro (Aldershot, England: Ashgate, 2007), vii.

2 Teddy Peiro and Jan Fairley, "Tango," *The Rough Guide to World Music*, Vol. 2, in Simon Broughton and Mark Ellingham, ed., (London: Rough Guides Ltd., 2000), 304.

3 Scott L. Marcus, *Music in Egypt: Experiencing Music, Expressing Culture* (Oxford and New York: Oxford University Press, 2006), 118–119.

4 Rabih Alameddine, *The Hakawati* (New York: Anchor Books, 2009), 166–167.

5 Marilyn Berger, "Irving Berlin, Nation's Songwriter, Dies," *New York Times*, September 23, 1989, accessed July 25, 2014, http://www.nytimes.com/1989/09/23/obituaries/irving-berlin-nation-s-songwriter-dies.html.

6 English translations of Acko Choedrag's Tibetan song lyrics by Tsering Samdrup, who also assisted in the biographical writing on Acko Choedrag, and Dawa Torbert.

7 Surinamese National Anthem lyrics, in Sranan Tonga and English translation, are in the public domain, http://www.nationalanthems.info/sr/htm.

Lesson 8
Music and Hybrid Identity

The term "hybrid" refers generally to a blending of two or more different components, such as a hybrid plant bred from two diverse species, a mythological creature that is part human and part animal or bird, or a hybrid car powered by electric batteries and a gasoline engine. In this lesson we explore the concept of "**hybridity**" as it applies to cultural and musical identity. Hybrid music refers to the blending of two or more different musical styles or traditions. Individuals or groups perform music that contains markers of multiple identities to project their own mixed cultural heritage or some other fusion of cultural backgrounds as expressions of hybrid identity. Today, creative artists on all continents blend musical styles and compositions in novel ways. Consider this imaginative arrangement of Johann Pachelbel's *Canon in D* (original version, ca. 1680) performed on Korean *kayagums* (long zithers) with beatboxing, DJ scratching, and break dancing. The layers of identities here include the expression of traditional Korean culture (through the sound of the *kayagums*), Western classical and cosmopolitan culture (Pachelbel's *Canon*), hip-hop and urban youth culture (beatboxing and scratching), and international pop culture (break dancing).

Another form of modern hybrid musical expression comes from the collaboration of musicians from different parts of the world. American singer-songwriter Paul Simon worked together with the South African *a cappella* vocal group Ladysmith Black Mambazo on "Diamonds on the Soles of Her **8-1** Shoes" (*Graceland* album, 1986). Paul Simon's venture was controversial at the time, since there was an international boycott against South Africa in the 1980s due to its **Apartheid** system of racial separation and institutional discrimination. Yet, *Graceland*'s popularity created a fashion throughout the global music industry for this kind of hybrid joint venture. More recently, American country, pop, and bluegrass band "Bela Fleck and the Flecktones" collaborated with Tuvan throat singer Ondar and Indian *tabla* drummer Sandip Burman on "A Moment So Close" (*Outbound* album, 2000). The stylistic juxtapositions in this video are striking. The variety of dress, hair, and nationality seen on the stage is in contrast to the surprising level of coherence expressed between vastly divergent musical styles. As with the "Playing for Change" example in the previous lesson, fusion and hybridity of musical styles present a powerful symbol of the possibilities for global harmony among people.

Long before digital technologies and international travel routes facilitated these contemporary **musical fusions**, the primary reasons for cross-cultural contact and interaction were conquest, trade, and migration. As populations move from one geographical location to another, whether by choice or by force, they take with them not only material possessions but cultural traits and traditions. Their retention of culture, language, religion, and music varies widely depending on the circumstances of their migration and on the social and political situation in their new homeland. Africans brought to North America as slaves were forbidden to use the drums that were so important in African social and religious life. Yet from their field hollers and spirituals, new forms of African American musical expression developed such as the blues and gospel. The nomadic Roma, known variously as Tzigane or Gypsies, spread throughout Europe and northern Africa in their long migration from northwest India beginning over a thousand years ago. In each country they passed through or settled in, they integrated local musical styles and instruments with their own traditions. Deprived of land for farming and excluded from many other occupations, they found work as professional musicians, mastering the genres and styles of the dominant society.

In a new homeland, immigrants negotiate their identity by expressing complex and shifting allegiances, often to both their ancestral culture and the new social situation. In this lesson, we look at three case studies of music and migration: Cajun people in Louisiana, **Montagnards** in North Carolina, and East Indians in Trinidad. A final case study explores the adoption and adaptation of Western symphonic music in the creation of a hybrid form of national music in early 20th-century China.

CAJUNS AND CREOLES IN RURAL LOUISIANA (USA)

The term "Cajun" derives from the word Acadian, the original name for the French settlers of Acadia, a region of modern-day eastern Canada. The early settlers in this part of the French colonial empire were builders, soldiers, sailors, and farmworkers who came from Poitou and surrounding regions in west-central France. They thrived in their new Acadian homeland from their arrival in 1604 until the British took control in 1713 and renamed the colony Nova Scotia. The French-speaking Roman Catholic Acadians refused to swear allegiance to the British Crown and were deported in 1755. Several thousand eventually made their way down to colonial Louisiana where they were welcomed by the French and Spanish inhabitants, also Catholics. They settled in the bayous and prairies of the region, reestablished their communities, and retained their language and culture. Over time, the surrounding ethnic groups—Creoles (people of mixed French and African descent), Afro-Caribbeans, Anglo-Americans, Spanish, Germans, and Native Americans—began to adopt the cultural traditions and language of the Acadians, who in turn absorbed cultural traits of their neighbors. From this cross-cultural exchange, brought about by proximity and to a lesser extent intermarriage, there emerged a new Louisiana "Cajun" society.

The first generation of Acadians in Louisiana preserved their French musical heritage by singing long unaccompanied narrative songs (*complaintes*). Families entertained themselves in the evenings with both old and new songs reflecting their migrant experience. To this day, Cajun farming communities celebrate **Mardi Gras** with old French traditions that include begging songs, which are part of neighborhood dress-up parties like that shown in Video 8-5. The revelers, in costumes similar to those worn in rural France, travel from farmhouse to farmhouse acting out skits and requesting food and drink from each family.

Musical instruments among the first settlers were rare, but by the end of the 18th century the Acadian exiles had the means to acquire violins, common to their lives in Acadia as well as those of their ancestors in France. Fiddlers and singers accompanied traditional house dances (*bals de maison*), playing waltzes, mazurkas, polkas, and contredanses as well as Virginia reels, jigs, and hoedowns learned from their Anglo-American neighbors. A twin fiddling style also developed that has continued to this day, with the second fiddle playing a percussive bass or harmony beneath the melody line. By the mid-19th century, Cajun dance bands had adopted the button accordion, brought into Louisiana by German settlers in Texas. The button accordion could easily be heard in noisy dance parties and was a much sturdier instrument than the fiddle. The accordion, cheap and readily available, was also picked up by recently freed African slaves who played such a dominant and

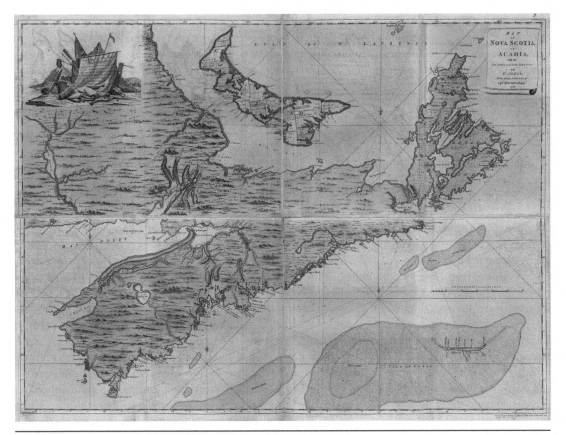

Fig. 8.1 **Map of Acadia, Nova Scotia, 1754**

creative role in shaping the musical life of the region. At the turn of the 20th century, black Creole accordion player Amédé Ardoin, together with white Cajun fiddler Dennis McGee, introduced a new hybrid form of expression. As folklorist and musicologist Alan Lomax demonstrates in his documentary film *Cajun Country*, Ardoin's new "active, pulsing" accompaniments contained elements of traditional African rhythms creating "a hot, syncopated accordion style [that] put the heat into" earlier Cajun dance forms and harmonies.[1] Creole and Cajun musicians continued through the 20th century to combine musical resources.

In the 1950s, a new Creole popular genre emerged called zydeco. Its characteristic sound derived from the combination of Cajun dance music with African American jazz, blues, and R&B. A local Louisiana flavor was retained by adding triangle, washboard, and spoons—implements of the rural life of Creole sharecroppers—to the traditional fiddle and accordion. Listen to the driving percussive sounds on piano accordionist Clifton Chenier's recording of "Zydeco Sont Pas Sale," the term "zydeco" coming from a colloquial pronunciation of the song's original French title, "Les Haricots Sont Pas Sale" ("The Snap Beans aren't Salty"). The first female accordionist to lead a zydeco band was Ida Lewis ("Queen Ida") Guillory, a Creole button accordion player from Lake Charles, Louisiana. She formed Queen Ida and the Bon Temps ("Good Times") Zydeco Band in the 1970s, and sang English, French (her mother tongue), and bilingual songs. Louisiana state and local school boards had made English-language education compulsory in 1916. The French language became stigmatized, and Cajun culture became associated with poverty and ignorance. While Cajuns and Creoles had continued to sing in French, they also began singing and recording English-language and bilingual songs. Not until the late 1960s did state laws reestablish French-language education and officially endorse a Louisiana French renaissance movement. Listen to Queen Ida Guillory singing the song "C'est Moi" from her album *Cookin' with Queen Ida and her Zydeco Band* (1989), with verses in English and chorus in French. From its origins as dancehall music of southwestern Louisiana, zydeco has become an internationally celebrated musical form, performed from Scandinavia to Japan. In 2007, a separate category for zydeco and Cajun music was created for the Grammy Music Awards.

The traditional Cajun fiddle and accordion sound declined from the 1930s to 1950s as many Cajun dance bands introduced electric guitars, drum sets, and amplification. The end of isolation for many rural Cajuns brought a dilution of Cajun identity, blending into the sameness of Middle America. Several factors had hastened the Cajun march from isolation into participation in the mainstream: the discovery of Mexican Gulf oil in 1901, the participation of Cajuns and Creoles in World War I, the development of highways and transportation, and the advent of mass media and national broadcasting.[2] As Cajun musicians imitated national musical styles such as country, bluegrass, western swing, and rock and roll, commercial Cajun recordings began sounding unmistakably Americanized.

A **revitalization** movement began, however, with the success of Iry Lejeune and his recording of "La Valse du Pont d'Amour" in 1948. A blind Cajun accordionist and singer, Iry Lejeune played in the old style of Amédé Ardoin. He drew crowds wherever he performed. Lejeune's success revived interest in the traditional Cajun sound, especially among Cajuns returning from the battlefields of World War II. Other button accordion players such as Joe Falcon and Nathan Abshire picked up their instruments again, and local music stores and recording companies once again supported regional Cajun music. Further impetus to the revitalization of Cajun music came in 1964 when a Cajun band consisting of Gladius Thibodeaux, Louis Lejeune (Iry's cousin), and Dewey Balfa was invited to perform at the Newport Folk Festival in Rhode Island, and unexpectedly received thunderous applause. Such huge success brought national attention to traditional Cajun music and spawned many efforts to preserve and promote this musical culture, including the establishment of the Louisiana Folk Foundation, the Council for the Development of French in Louisiana (CODO-FIL), the Center for Acadian and Creole Folklore, and Cajun music festivals around the state. In the following decades, this resurgence of Cajun music has continued; musicians play in dance halls and at festivals, and popular dance bands such as **Steve Riley and the Mamou Playboys**, featuring the washboard and driving rhythms of zydeco, carry Cajun music forward into the 21st century. This hybrid roots music continues to thrive and remains an important way in which Cajuns express and celebrate their mixed cultural heritage.

Fig. 8.2 **Clifton Chenier (1925–1987) on piano accordion, with his brother Cleveland and John Hart, 1975 (L), and album cover of** *Queen Ida and the Bon Temps Zydeco Band: On Tour* **(1982) (R)**

Fig. 8.3   Steve Riley and the Mamou Playboys at the 2012 Rhythm and Roots Festival in Charlestown, Rhode Island

MONTAGNARDS IN NORTH CAROLINA (USA/VIETNAM)

The Montagnards are indigenous tribal peoples of the Central Highlands of Vietnam who arrived in the United States as political refugees beginning in the mid 1980s. The time period and circumstances of their migration and settlement differ significantly from those of the Cajuns, yet like the Cajuns they retain native cultural and musical traditions while adapting to and adopting aspects of American culture. The Montagnards refer to themselves as *Anak Cu Chiang* (Mountain People)—some use the Rhade term *Dega* (Original People)—and are largely Bahnar, **Jarai**, Rhade, M'Nong and Koho peoples. Their ethnicity, culture, and languages clearly set them apart from the lowland Vietnamese in their former Southeast Asian homeland. Until the mid-19th century, these tribal peoples lived in isolation as farmers and hunter-gatherers. In the mid 1800s, French Catholic missionaries arrived in the highlands; and from 1885 France ruled Vietnam until the end of the French Indochina War (1945–1954). The French colonial government granted autonomy to the Montagnards in 1946, enacting a Federal Ordinance. However the new President of South Vietnam, Ngo-Dinh Diem, struck down the ordinance in 1956 and Montagnards lost autonomy over their territory. President Diem resettled half a million Vietnamese on Montagnard lands and abolished Montagnard courts and property rights. In the war between North and South Vietnam (1959–1975), United States Special Forces recruited Montagnards to fight alongside them against the North Vietnamese Communists. With the defeat of the American military in 1975, thousands of Montagnards fled their villages and many others were imprisoned, executed, or eventually died in re-education camps, because of their allegiance to the American military and their connection with the South Vietnamese government. The first group of 212 Montagnard soldiers turned in their weapons near the Thai-Cambodian border in 1986 and sought political asylum in the United States. They were resettled as refugees in North Carolina, a state that offered

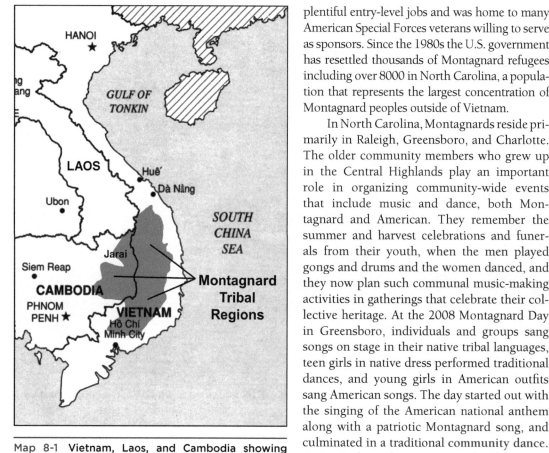

Map 8-1 **Vietnam, Laos, and Cambodia showing Montagnard Tribal Regions**

Source: *Garland Encyclopedia of World Music*, Volume 4: Southeast Asia

plentiful entry-level jobs and was home to many American Special Forces veterans willing to serve as sponsors. Since the 1980s the U.S. government has resettled thousands of Montagnard refugees including over 8000 in North Carolina, a population that represents the largest concentration of Montagnard peoples outside of Vietnam.

In North Carolina, Montagnards reside primarily in Raleigh, Greensboro, and Charlotte. The older community members who grew up in the Central Highlands play an important role in organizing community-wide events that include music and dance, both Montagnard and American. They remember the summer and harvest celebrations and funerals from their youth, when the men played gongs and drums and the women danced, and they now plan such communal music-making activities in gatherings that celebrate their collective heritage. At the 2008 Montagnard Day in Greensboro, individuals and groups sang songs on stage in their native tribal languages, teen girls in native dress performed traditional dances, and young girls in American outfits sang American songs. The day started out with the singing of the American national anthem along with a patriotic Montagnard song, and culminated in a traditional community dance. Some weeks earlier, musicians had rehearsed the dance accompaniment on hanging gongs and barrel drum in the driveway of a Raleigh residence. The performance of both Montagnard and American music, like the mixture of language and dress, clearly expresses their dual allegiance to their old and new homelands and their resulting hybrid identity in America.

In the privacy of their homes, Montagnards listen to both American music and Southeast Asian music. Some play native Montagnard musical instruments such as the *trung* (bamboo xylophone) and *goong* (tube zither), played in the videos by Dock Rmah, and the *ding nam* (mouth organ) played by Y Dha Eban; others have taken up the guitar and drum set. American-born Montagnard children and youth are learning Montagnard songs as well as American ones, and some musically talented individuals are composing their own songs either in their native tongue or in English, or both. In Raleigh, community leader and musician Hip Ksor writes his own songs in Jarai, his mother tongue, and plays them on guitar adding chordal harmony. His song lyrics often refer to the separation of his people, including his own family, divided between North Carolina and the Vietnamese Central Highlands. Hip spent over ten years in Vietnamese jails, persecuted under the Communist government for his political beliefs, before gaining freedom and sanctuary in the U.S. as a refugee. His song "*Char Dega*" (Dega Country) reveals his hopes and dreams, now remote, of one day returning to Vietnam and reuniting with his relatives. Watch this video clip of Hip Ksor singing the first verse and chorus of his song "*Char Dega*" (lyrics below translated by Hip Ksor).

> This year, the star is divided in many parts,
> This year, the moon is blooming like a flower,
> This year, look over the country, it is green,
> This year, all the streams gather together

Chorus:

Stand up, we go together, (repeat)
O look over there, the Dega country,
There are flowers blooming everywhere in the jungle
This year, the water plant in the stone is blooming,
This year, the leaf comes up at the wrong season,
Everywhere on the road the bird with the red beak (*pak k'tra*) flies around to ask for something,
In every river valley the bird is looking for something

Chorus:

Stand up, we have to reach, (also: we have to dream)
O look over there, the Dega country,
The mountain is green and the water is good.

An aspiring musician in the Raleigh Montagnard community is Bom Siu, a.k.a. Mondega, who fled Vietnam in 1996 at the age of nine with his father, a freedom fighter, and other family members. After surviving his troubled teenage years living in a refugee housing complex in Raleigh, Bom Siu was introduced to music by his older brother, and soon after he discovered hip-hop artists Tupac Shakur and the Wu Tang Clan. Both the art form and these artists became his inspiration. Mondega began singing and composing his own rap songs in both English and his mother tongue of Jarai, as in "Mondega for the People" (Jarai at 2'21"). He has now become a respected Asian American hip-hop artist and producer performing locally and regionally. For Mondega, rapping and hip-hop culture are his way of speaking out for the rights of his people, of reaching out to and empowering Montagnard youth, and of expressing his own hybrid Montagnard American identity, as in his song "Transition" (2011).

Upon arrival from Vietnam, members of this community encountered American music all around them in the larger cultural environment of their adopted home. Hip and Mondega represent two approaches to the refugee experience, characteristic of the generation to which each belongs. For Hip, America represents freedom and safety, but also separation and alienation from the life, language, land, and people he once knew. In his musical creativity, he gives expression to his nostalgia for the lost homeland, while also serving his community as a link to Montagnard music and cultural forms now transplanted in North Carolina. Mondega adopts an identity of American urban youth and "uses hip-hop as a tool to speak on behalf of the Asian youths living in America, and for his people suffering back home in South East Asia."[3] While Hip is suspended between two worlds, Mondega is in many ways as American as his neighbors, in dress, dialect, and musical taste. Yet Mondega too reveals his Montagnard heritage by rapping in his mother tongue of Jarai and in the stories he communicates to other Montagnard youth. His hip-hop name itself comes from "Mon" ("Montagnard") and "Dega" ("Sons of the Mountains," a term they use to refer to themselves). Thus, as a rapper, he speaks for his people.

Fig. 8.4 **Raleigh musician and Montagnard community leader, Hip Ksor**

Will the teenage girls who swap tank tops and jeans for the long traditional wrap-arounds of their parents and grandparents at Montagnard celebrations learn and perpetuate the gongs, tube zithers, and dances taught by Hip and the members of his generation? Will they teach the traditional songs and dances to *their* children? Or will third-generation Montagnards totally assimilate?

INDO-TRINIDADIAN MUSIC (TRINIDAD/INDIA)

Trinidad is the southern-most island in the West Indies.

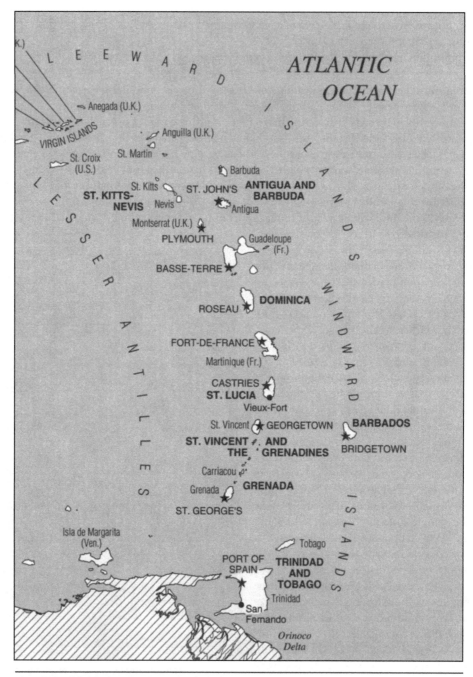

Map 8-2   Trinidad and Tobago in the West Indies

Source: *Garland Encyclopedia of World Music*, Volume 2: South America, Mexico, Central America, and the Caribbean

This former British colony has a population of approximately 1.3 million. The largest ethnic group is now the Trinidadian population of Asian Indian descent, which numbers slightly more than Trinidadians of African heritage, known as Creoles. (The term "Creole" in Trinidad refers generally to peoples of African and mixed Afro-European descent.) Indians were brought from India to Trinidad by its British colonial rulers between 1845 and 1917, after the emancipation of slaves on the island in 1838, to work as indentured laborers on the sugar cane plantations. Most came from the Indian states of Bihar and Uttar Pradesh, and over 75% chose not to return to India after 1917.

Over centuries, Trinidad Creoles created a distinct and dynamic music culture from which steel drums, calypso, and the limbo dance originated. The calypso song form in particular, with roots going back to West Africa, was closely connected to Trinidadian Creole identity. Prior to independence from the British in 1962, calypso lyrics often provided the most reliable source of local news, with clever calypsonians using word play to get around the colonial censors. Until the 1970s, the music and dance styles of the Creoles and East Indian communities had little influence on each other. Then,

Map 8-3   **North India showing the states of Bihar, Uttar Pradesh, and Rajasthan**

Source: *Garland Encyclopedia of World Music*, Volume 5: South Asia: The Indian Subcontinent

a popular modern genre emerged from the East Indian population called "**chutney**," aptly named after a spicy Indian condiment. Chutney's origins lie in songs and dances that women performed at weddings and other life-cycle events in India. These wedding songs had lewd lyrics and erotic dance movements. The fast tempo, often spicy love lyrics sung in Hindi, and the sensuous dancing and "wining" (pelvic rotation) of modern chutney reflect its Indian heritage. In the past in both India and Trinidad, Indian men and women typically did not dance together on public occasions such as weddings. "A man who danced with women," writes ethnomusicologist Peter Manuel, "would have been considered effeminate, while a woman who danced with men...would be assumed to be of loose morals."[4] Gradually, however, there was relaxation of social inhibitions in the East Indian community due to the influence of West Indian Creole culture, in which intimate male–female dancing was the norm. As chutney became more popular and more influenced by Creole dance music, its performers added electric guitars, drum sets, and amplified voices to the traditional *tabla* drums and *dhantal* to give it a more modern sound. The electric keyboard often replaced the harmonium. The hip swiveling of young chutney dancers provoked public outcry from conservative and ultra-religious members of the Indo-Trinidadian community, denouncing chutney wining as vulgar and obscene. Yet as is evident in this video of an Indo-Trinidadian wedding celebration in 2008, chutney and chutney wining remain as popular as ever.

In the mid 1980s another new crossover style emerged from the Indo-Trinidadian community. In 1987, Drupatee Ramgoonai released her first album titled *Chatnee Soca*. The term "**soca**," from soul and calypso, had already been applied to a Creole blend of the earlier calypso beat and topical lyrics with soul, R&B, and funk introduced from North America. **Chutney soca** is a combination blending chutney melodies, soca rhythms, and songs sung in both Hindi and English language versions. By the mid-1990s, both Indo-Trinidadian and Creole artists were singing English language chutney socas and performing them in the enormously popular calypso/soca competitions held annually during Carnival time. These events are hugely popular in Trinidad, attracting hundreds of singers and thousands of listeners, and earning large cash prizes and star status for

Fig. 8.5 **Sally Sagram performs at the Chutney Soca Monarch finals in San Fernando, Trinidad, 2011**

Fig. 8.6 Mungal Patasar and his band Pantar perform at Lincoln Center's Caribbean Roots Festival, New York City, July 2000

the winning Monarchs. One of the most successful modern chutney soca performers is Sharlene Boodram, whose cover of a French hit song "Joe Le Taxi" became an international hit. She begins her multilingual song "Chutney Time" (1994) by counting off in Hindi, "*ek, do, tin, char*" ("one, two, three, four"). One can hear hip-hop and rap, Hindi film songs, techno, and Afro-Caribbean beats layered beneath the clever wordplay of the calypsonian. Chutney has indeed come a long way from its original context in Hindu weddings. Since the late 1990s, chutney and its offshoot chutney soca have become internationally popular music and dance genres. Songs by Indo-Trinidadian and Creole singers circulate around the world via the internet and satellite radio, and chutney singers perform live concerts in New York, Toronto, and other major cities with sizeable Caribbean immigrant populations.

Another expression of musical hybridity in the Indo-Trinidadian community may be heard in the fusion band Pantar led by sitarist and composer Mungal Patasar. Mungal was born in Trinidad in 1948, of parents who emigrated from India, and learned to play a number of musical instruments in his youth including the Indian harmonium and *dholak* drum, the Western clarinet and mandolin, and the Indo-Trinidadian *dhantal*. In his early twenties he took Indian *sitar* lessons with Professor H.S. Adesh in Trinidad and later traveled to India to study *sitar* at Banaras Hindu University. In addition to this interest in Indian classical music, Mungal began experimenting with musical fusion, mixing Indian music with calypso and jazz. He formed his band Pantar in 1994, naming it after the two lead instruments, the steelpan ("pan") and the *sitar* ("tar" meaning string). His vision was to embrace the diverse cultures of the Caribbean in his band, and the result was a collaboration of Indo- and Afro-Trinidadian musicians and a fusion of musical styles. Pantar's band members play electric guitar, electric bass, Western drum set, Indian *tabla* drums, tenor steel pan, second pan, keyboards, flute, saxophone, wind synthesizer, and *sitar*. The band released its first album *Nirvana* in 1997, followed by *Dreadlocks* in 2000. Mungal continued his creative collaborations on his third album, *Calabasse Cafe* (2006), described in the disc notes as "the place where all the beautiful streams of the different cultures of the Caribbean meet...the convergence of Europe, Africa, the Americas and the Orient." Watch this excerpt from a rehearsal of "Awake" (*Dreadlocks*, track 4) at Mungal Patasar's home in 2008. The band creatively adapts the original version of "Awake" adding new harmonies, solos on guitar and wind synthesizer (including a quote from The Beatles' "Norwegian Wood"!), and North Indian classical music patterns such as the rapid alternation of *sitar* and drumset (standing in for the Indian *tabla* drums) at 1'28". Mungal Patasar and Pantar have gained international recognition at performances in the U.S. and Europe. In reviewing the 2006 Womex World Music festival in Seville, Spain, Banning Eyre writes, "For Sean Barlow and I, the standouts this year were Afel Bocoum of Mali, X Alfonso of Cuba, El Tanbura of Egypt,...and—a surprise—an eclectic band from Trinidad and Tobago, Mungal Patasar and Pantar, who combine steel pans and Caribbean pop beats with Mungal's own Indian sitar."[5]

These examples of chutney and indo-jazz fusion show how this Indo-Trinidadian community has maintained links with its cultural homeland of India. As an immigrant population it continues to face choices on the degree to which it assimilates with the Creole population and simultaneously fosters the culture of its ancestral roots. What emerges is a vigorous hybrid culture in which Indo-Trinidadians preserve, adapt, and negotiate an identity that expresses complex and shifting allegiances to both the distant homeland and their New World home.[6] At the same time they share an island with the Creole population, whose diet, language, music, dance, and customs have enriched Indo-Trinidadian life, and who in turn have been enriched by the proximity of their Asiatic neighbors.

MAY 4TH MOVEMENT (CHINA)

Another interesting example of hybridity deals with musical reforms proposed by Chinese intellectuals following the First World War. During the 19th century, China suffered a number of defeats at the hands of Western armies with their superior weapons technologies. The industrial powers of the West and Japan had by coercion opened foreign-ruled districts within Chinese port cities or had taken areas of the Chinese coast under colonial rule: Hong Kong for Britain, Macau for Portugal, Taiwan for Japan, and Qingdao on the Shandong Peninsula for Germany. The Qing Dynasty emperors (1644–1911) and the populace at large considered these conquests deeply humiliating but were powerless to reclaim these territories.

In 1911, the Chinese Revolution overthrew the Qing Dynasty and established a republican form of government for the first time in China's 4000-year history. The new Republic of China supported the Allied Powers against Germany in the First World War, sending more than 100,000 laborers to France for the war effort. When Germany was defeated in 1918, the Chinese assumed that the Shandong Peninsula would revert to Chinese control, since the Treaty of Versailles divested Germany of all overseas colonial holdings. Yet Japan, now the most powerful industrialized nation in Asia, pressured and won over the Allied negotiators and took control of the Shandong Peninsula. On May 4th, 1919, more than 5000 university students took to the streets of Beijing to protest the weak response by their government to what became known as the "Shandong Problem." There followed a period of social unrest marked by intense cultural re-evaluation as urban intellectuals sought to account for China's weakness and technological backwardness, and to find a way forward that would lead to the building of a strong and united country. The **May 4th Movement** was a call for reform of all aspects of Chinese culture and society: art, literature, education, language, and music. The music of the old feudal order was deemed "unscientific," backward, and regressive. It was distinct, the reformers complained, for what it lacked relative to Western music. An American-educated Chinese journalist wrote in 1919: "So, in one word, Chinese music lacks a standard in every respect. It has no standard scale, no standard pitch, no standard instruments, no standard music compositions."[7] Western instruments like the piano and violin became extremely popular among the urban elites. Western notation was adapted for use in music education, and Chinese instruments were modified to produce timbres and intonation more like Western instruments. Traditional pentatonic folk songs were provided with chordal harmonies and Western-style accompaniments. A number of European

Map 8-4 **Eastern and central China showing Shandong Peninsula, Shanghai, Wuxi, and northern Shaanxi Province (Shaanbei)**

Source: *Garland Encyclopedia of World Music*, Volume 7: East Asia: China, Japan, and Korea

Fig. 8.7 Ma Sicong (1912–1987) on Chinese stamp, ca. 2012

composers and educators taught in China and encouraged local composers. Russian musicians in particular, fleeing the chaos in their own country following the 1917 Bolshevik Revolution, took active roles in bringing symphonic music to China. Young musicians, eager to take part in the modern world that Europe represented, embraced these innovations. A number furthered their education with study in Europe, and many became highly accomplished artists. A new kind of Chinese national music emerged.

Among the most important of these accomplished Chinese musicians was violinist Ma Sicong. Born of a family of scholars, Ma showed great early talent and was sent to Paris for musical study twice: at the age of eleven for the violin, and again at twenty for composition. He was known as "China's King of the Violin," and his compositions for orchestra and violin were extremely popular. Following the Communist victory in 1949, Ma became the Founding President of the Central Music Conservatory in Beijing. Among his compositions for Western instruments are symphonies, concertos, operas, and ballets: genres associated with the European classical tradition. Yet most are based upon Chinese folk melodies, pentatonic scales, and recognizable gestures associated with Chinese performance practices, like frequent sliding between pitches. To these, he adds chordal accompaniment and structural principles developed from his studies in the West. Among his most popular compositions is "Nostalgia," a movement (section) of a larger work, *The Inner Mongolian Suite* (1937), which was heard all over China in the 1950s. Its popularity was based on the familiarity of the folk tune on which it is based, the sentimental mood that inspired a longing for a distant home and a simpler time, as well as the harmony and instrumental timbres that by the 1950s had been completely absorbed and accepted as the musical language of the "new" China. Listen to this performance of "Nostalgia" by Hsiao-mei Ku and Benjamin Ward of Duke University. Professor Ku performed for Ma Sicong as a child prodigy in China when she was nine years old.

CONCLUSION

The power of music often lies in its ability to project multiple identities simultaneously, expressing various cultural strands through audible markers. The listener can hear these markers and, while recognizing each as a component of hybrid identity, experiences the expressive whole as greater than the sum of its parts. In Cajun music we hear the sounds of the cumulative history of its people, a history that includes migration, encounters with others, and with new technologies and ways of life. The result is music that is meaningful, enjoyable, and danceable in the present, and at the same time rooted in the combined expressions of past generations. Among the Montagnards, music is a way for an immigrant community to express feelings about both a distant and lost homeland and an adopted country that offers freedom and protection. Music is also a contested area for cultural negotiations across generational lines, as grandparents watch their grandchildren born in America seek an identity that more closely resembles American youth than their family members back in the Central Highlands. In Trinidad, an island nation shared almost equally by two ethnic groups of quite distinct heritage, the Indo-Trinidadian population negotiates between identification with the rich cultural expressions of India, and the hip and contemporary styles of their Creole neighbors. Finally, Chinese intellectuals intentionally hybridized traditional music with Western compositional techniques in order to express to themselves and the world China's entry into the modern age.

In the previous Lesson 7, we discussed the multicultural society of Suriname. Members of this society must negotiate a sense of self between a number of possible allegiances: as citizens of the former Dutch colony; as descendants of people who came from a distant ancestral home; or, in the case of the Caribs and Arawaks, as people indigenous to the region. And, together with all their fellow citizens, people of Suriname can celebrate among themselves and for the rest of the world a uniquely Surinamese identity, shaped by the particular environment of the Caribbean Sea, the rainforest, and the rivers that connect them. In the capital city of Paramaribo, a multiethnic dance troupe performs dances that showcase Surinamese hybrid culture and identity at regional and international cultural events. In this video clip, the amateur dancers of **The Folkloristisch Ensemble** express the various ethnic identities of Suriname through characteristic dance movements. Each member had to learn all the dance styles in preparation for a performance at an international dance festival. A musical score was prepared, based on a Surinamese folk song, with each section in a style that reflected a different ethnicity. For the choreography to communicate the hybrid nature of Surinamese identity—whereby each member embodies through social proximity a bit of all the other identities—the dance roles were mixed up. The Javanese dancer performs with the maraca rattle of the Carib, the Chinese woman dances to polyrhythmic drumming of the Maroons, while the Maroon dancer twirls a Chinese paper parasol. At the end the dancers huddle together in a circle to represent that the various communities together make up a unified society. The leading spokesperson and creative visionary of Suriname's multicultural identity was the playwright Henk Tjon, who wrote more than eighty stage plays built upon the unique complexities of his native Suriname. For the pan-Caribbean festival Carifesta, which celebrates the diverse artistic and cultural traditions of Caribbean and Latin American nations, Henk Tjon organized the percussion ensemble, Ala Kondre ("All Colors"), consisting of performers from each of Suriname's ethnic groups. At **Tjon's funeral** in September 2009, Ala Kondre performed in a state ceremony honoring his enormous contributions to the cultural life of his country. Those present witnessed an expression of hybridity in which each strand was honored, no strand dominated, and the overall impact was that of unity in diversity.

8-20

KEY CONCEPTS

Hybrid identity	Indigenous	Hybrid culture
Musical fusion	Refugee	Old Feudal Order
Ancestral culture	Collective heritage	Chinese national music
Revitalization	Assimilation	

Ⓠ THINKING ABOUT MUSIC QUESTIONS

1. The music reforms in China that began with the May 4th Movement created a fusion of Western harmonies and Chinese melodies. How did this hybridized form of expression contribute to creating a "modern" Chinese identity? When you listen to the performance of "Nostalgia," played on the piano and violin, what makes it sound "Chinese" to you?

2. Watch again the video of the funeral of Henk Tjon. How does his percussion ensemble "Ala Kondre" express both Group and Hybrid Identities? In the case of Group Identity, *which* groups? And how is each expressed? Consider instruments, dances, costumes, rhythms, etc

3. Think of a genre of popular music in America (rock, hip-hop, country, etc.). How could you think of it as a hybrid genre? What musical elements contributed to its defining sound?

4. Many Americans have a "hyphenated" identity—Chinese-American, African-American, Latin-American, for example. Talk to a member of your family, a classmate, or a neighbor for whom this applies. How do they use music to express the different parts of their identity? How do the different generations of their family relate to music of the ancestral homeland in contrast to mainstream American music?

5. Why did Cajun music in Louisiana nearly disappear in the mid 20th century, and why did it make a comeback? Think about how people in America (the land of immigrants) negotiate their identities between the local and the mainstream: America as "melting pot" vs. America as "colorful mosaic."

6. The video of traditional Korean zithers (*kayagum*) playing Pachelbel's *Canon in D* accompanied by beatboxing, DJ scratching, and break dancing (Lesson 8 Introduction) is an advertisement for an apartment complex in Seoul, South Korea (ROK). Considering the various identities expressed in the performance, what kind of tenants do you think this advertisement was meant to attract?

NOTES

1   Alan Lomax, producer and narrator, *Cajun Country: Don't Drop the Potato*, American Patchwork film series, 1990.

2   Barry J. Ancelet, *Cajun and Creole Music Makers: Musiciens cadiens et créoles* (Jackson, MS: University Press of Mississippi, 1999).

3   "Mondega—I Have a Dream," notes on YouTube page, video uploaded by mylifeandrhymes, 2010, https://www.youtube.com/watch?v=3as1kIMJ5gw.

4   Peter Manuel, *East Indian Music in the West Indies: Tan-singing, Chutney, and the Making of Indo-Caribbean Culture* (Philadelphia: Temple University Press, 2000), 172.

5   Banning Eyre, "WOMAD 2006: Report and Photo Essay" (photos by Banning Eyre and Sean Barlow), *Afropop Worldwide,* no longer available online, formerly at, http://www.afropop.org/multi/feature/ID/660/ WOMEX 2006: Report and Photo Essay.

6   Helen Myers, "Indian, East Indian, and West Indian Music in Felicity, Trinidad," in Stephen Blum, et al. *Ethnomusicology and Modern Music History*, (Champaign, IL: University of Indiana Press, 1991), 231–241.

7   Lieu Da-kun, "Chinese Music," in *Peking Leader Special Anniversary Supplement—China in 1918,* Peking [Beijing], February 12, 1919, cited in Kuo-huang Han and Lindy Li Mark, "Evolution and Revolution in Chinese Music," in Elizabeth May, ed. *Musics of Many Cultures: An Introduction* (Berkeley: University of California Press, 1980), 22.

Lesson 9
Music and Oppositional Identity

In the previous three lessons we have seen how music serves as a symbol of individual, collective, and hybrid identities, and as a vehicle through which felt and shared emotions, experiences, and values are expressed. Music is involved in the projection of these identities through advertising, tourism, popular media, and collective rituals like sporting events, festivals, and religious ceremonies. Aspects of our identity may derive not from what we belong to but what we oppose. One can describe oneself as anti-Communist, anti-corporate, anti-monarchy. Our athletic teams and their fight songs exemplify the concept of oppositional identity. The home team's identity is constructed in opposition to the visiting team without whom markers of identity like mascots and fight songs become unnecessary. Oppositional relationships are power relationships, and music is often involved in the expression of power. Some power is institutional and some is subversive of institutions. Throughout history, music has served as a potent marker of institutional power and prestige. For more than three thousand years, Chinese emperors sponsored elaborate rituals of state that validated the legitimacy of the rulers, rituals that featured music and dance. Emperor Akbar the Great (1542–1605) of the Indian **Mughal Empire** invited the finest musicians of the realm to perform at court as a display of his magnificence. Among them was the legendary Mian Tansen (ca. 1493–ca. 1586), an important composer and singer in the development of the classical tradition whose continuing influence may be heard in the artistry of Pandit Ravi Shankar. Akbar named this master musician one of his *Navaratnas* ("nine jewels," nine great courtiers), so great was his esteem. Musicians of the court ensemble, called the *naubat*, performed a variety of functions and were frequently depicted in Mughal paintings of court life, as seen in the illustration overleaf.

> They played when the emperor made his daily presence before his subjects, they heralded processions, were used for signaling in battle, provided accompaniment for female dancers in the harem and were an indispensable part of celebrations which marked the birth of an heir, marriages, the new year and other festivals.[1]

Like the royal robes, the lavish furnishings of the palace, the royal insignias, and uniformed palace guards, the *naubat* and its music were continuous reminders of the emperor's authority and power.

Fig. 9.1 *Naubat* drummers, and lute and frame drum players accompanying dancers at the court of Emperor Akbar the Great, 16th-century Persian miniature

The modern symphony orchestra, which often serves as the crowning jewel of the arts establishment in major cosmopolitan cities, had its origins in the aristocratic courts of Europe. For several centuries the kings of Buganda maintained the largest and most powerful state in central Africa, and their palaces resounded throughout each day with music. The musical richness at court featured xylophone ensembles, the royal flute band, the songs of the king's harpist and lyre players, as well as praise drumming and dancing.

Not only political power but also military power has for millennia been symbolized and projected through music. In the Old Testament book of Joshua, the armed men of Israel went forth "led by the priests who blew trumpets" and brought down the walls of Jericho. Roman legions marched across Europe to the sound of brass trumpets and horns. These instruments signaled instructions such as "advance" or "retreat" to soldiers in battle. They also signified the authority of the general and were blown when an action was carried out under his command, as when a soldier was executed for treason or cowardice. The **Janissary** bands of the Ottoman Empire (1299–1922) proclaimed the military superiority of the ruling Sultan with double-reed pipes (*zurna*), trumpets (*boru*), bass drums (*davul*), small kettledrums (*nakkara*), large kettledrums (*kos*), cymbals, triangles, and the jingling bells of the Turkish crescent. By the 16th century, the Janissaries became a model for military marching bands throughout Europe. Napoleon Bonaparte, rising to power in the aftermath of the French Revolution (1789–1799), placed enormous importance on military bands, both for ceremonial occasions such as the review of the troops, and for coordinating his army's marching and drill. In the 19th century, with European powers colonizing much of the world, the military band became a standard presence in colonial territories. Now in the post-colonial era virtually every military establishment around the globe has adopted and adapted the military band.

Music has also frequently served as an expression of oppositional identity, as we saw in *The Internationale* in Lesson 5. During the 1950s and 1960s, in both the Civil Rights and anti-war movements in the United States, musicians were on the front line of resistance. Singers such as Bob Dylan, Harry Belafonte, Pete Seeger, Odetta, and Joan Baez were public voices articulating the anger and frustration of millions seeking social justice and peace. Members of the Irish Republican Army, trade unionists in Korea, and Chinese students in Tiananmen Square similarly used songs, drums, and guitars as weapons against the power of the state. Aware of the subversive power of music to unite people for collective action, governments have frequently resorted to censorship, suppression, and even murder to silence the musical voices of protest. It should be noted that the powerful have many ways to express their power; the powerless have few. Therefore music becomes one of the most potent weapons to wield for those who oppose institutional power.

In this lesson we present four case studies in which people use music to express an oppositional identity. First, in Latin America from the 1950s through the 1970s, members of the *Nueva Canción*

Fig. 9.2 Turkish Janissary band playing (L to R) *çevgan* (bells on a pole), *kaba zurna* (bass double-reed pipe), and trumpets in Bucharest, Romania, 2007 (L), and Roman horns on Trajan's Column in Rome (R)

("The New Song Movement") championed the rights of the oppressed and the values of democracy against the brutal oppression of military dictatorships and powerful oligarchies. Second, in South Africa during the struggles against white supremacist rule and its policies of separation and subjugation of the majority non-white population, musicians served a variety of subversive functions. For the past four decades, hip-hop has spread from New York City around the world as the primary popular music genre of youth. In this third case study we explore how music provides an outlet for the expression of discontent felt by young people with limited opportunities to find a more constructive role for themselves in their society. Finally we take up a case study in far western China in which university students collect traditional songs on digital recorders as a means of preserving their vanishing culture from the onslaught of modernity.

NUEVA CANCIÓN (CHILE/LATIN AMERICA)

In his acceptance speech for the 1982 Nobel Prize for Literature, the Colombian writer Gabriel García Márquez enumerated for his European audience the collective woes and violent crimes that Latin Americans had endured over the previous several decades.

> We have not had a moment's rest. A promethean president [Salvadoré Allende of Chile], entrenched in his burning palace, died fighting an entire army, alone...There have been five wars and seventeen military coups...twenty million Latin American children died before the age of one—more than have been born in Europe since 1970. Those missing because of repression number nearly one hundred and twenty thousand. Numerous women arrested while pregnant have given birth in Argentine prisons, yet nobody knows the whereabouts and identity of their children who were furtively adopted or sent to an orphanage by order of the military authorities. Because they tried to change this state of things, nearly two hundred thousand men and women have died throughout the continent, and over one hundred thousand have lost their lives in three small and ill-fated countries of Central America: Nicaragua, El Salvador and Guatemala.... One million people have fled Chile, a country with a tradition of hospitality—that is, ten per cent of its population. Uruguay, a tiny nation of two and a half million inhabitants which considered itself the continent's most civilized country, has lost to exile one out of every five citizens. Since 1979, the civil war in El Salvador has produced almost one refugee every twenty minutes. The country that could be formed of all the exiles and forced emigrants of Latin America would have a population larger than that of Norway.
>
> © The Nobel Foundation 1982[2]

Yet he concludes by stating, "In spite of this, to oppression, plundering and abandonment, we respond with life. Neither floods nor plagues, famines nor cataclysms, nor even the eternal wars of century upon century, have been able to subdue the persistent advantage of life over death. An advantage that grows and quickens."

To the guns and batons of military repression, musicians throughout the continent responded with song. From Nicaragua to Argentina and Chile, singers took up the cause of the poor, the imprisoned, and the oppressed rural *camposinos* in the "New Song Movement" or *Nueva Canción*. "The groups Quilapayún, Inti Illimani and singers such as Victor Jara, Patricio Manns, and Ángel and Isabel Parra epitomise a generation of musicians across the continent and beyond whose formative years in the 1950s and 60s were rooted in ideals of social justice and equality."[3] Although most of the singers in this movement were college-educated members of the urban middle class, they drew their musical inspiration from the traditions of the poor farmers and indigenous peoples of the Andes, traditions dating back to the pre-Columbian period and the early Spanish settlement. Their songs and recordings established an internationally recognized Latin American style marked by evocative poetry and often the sounds of the small armadillo-backed, plucked lute called the *charango*, and the flutes and panpipes of the Andes. As Márquez explained, most of the songs of Violetta Parra (1917–1967) of Argentina and Victor Jara (1932–1973) of Chile, two of the most famous members of the Movement, were not overtly political but rather were profoundly life affirming.

Map 9-1 Latin America

Source: *Garland Encyclopedia of World Music*, Volume 2: South America, Mexico, Central America, and Caribbean

In 1970, a popular election in Chile brought to power the socialist Salvadore Allende. Under Allende's leftist coalition government, Jara and other songwriters and singers enjoyed widespread popularity, performing regularly at a small nightclub in the capital Santiago. Jara had been politically active in the period leading up to Allende's election, singing frequently at political rallies. On September 11, 1973, a US-backed military coup brought down the government. Allende was killed and

9-1

9-2

Fig. 9.3   Victor Jara (1932–1973)

thousands of his supporters, including Victor Jara, were rounded up and imprisoned in a downtown soccer stadium. There, his captors broke his wrists so that he could not play his guitar and taunted him with requests, according to eyewitness accounts, as he lay on the ground. Defiantly, he sang part of the song of Allende's political party, after which he was executed by machine gun.

Victor Jara has become a symbol throughout the world of the oppositional musician martyred for the cause he lived for. The great American folk musician and activist Pete Seeger, whom we met before as narrator of "The Internationale" in Lesson 5, created a performance piece around Jara's final poem, *Estadio Chile*, written on a scrap of paper and smuggled out of the soccer stadium after his murder. Seeger's moving narration memorializes Jara as a symbol of the oppositional musician's struggle for the cause of human freedom and dignity.

His most famous song, *Te Recuerdo Amanda*, has no shaking fist, but the memory of a lovely young woman going to meet her boyfriend at the factory where he works: a simple acknowledgment of life's surprising beauty.

> I remember you, Amanda,
> the wet street,
> running to the factory where Manuel worked
>
> The wide smile, rain in your hair,
> nothing mattered,
> you were going to meet with him
> with him, with him, with him, with him
>
> Five minutes,
> life is eternal
> in five minutes
>
> The alarm sounds
> for returning to work
> and you, walking, light up everything,
> the five minutes make you blossom.

(English translation by Susan Navey-Davis)

The soccer stadium in Santiago where Victor Jara died now bears his name.

MUSIC DURING SOUTH AFRICAN APARTHEID (SOUTH AFRICA)

South Africa is the southernmost country on the continent of Africa, with a population of approximately 49 million of which almost eighty percent are black African (Zulu, Xhosa, Venda, etc.), nine percent are white, nine percent "colored" (of mixed race), and 2.5 percent Indian (South Asian). The strategic location of South Africa, coupled with a temperate climate more like Europe than anywhere else in Africa, led to wide-scale settlement of this region by successive waves of European immigrants over more than three hundred years. Beginning in 1652, Dutch settlers (called **Trek Boers**, meaning "white farmers") spread north and east into the interior, despite frequent violent encounters with native African populations. They were guided by a pioneering myth similar to the "manifest destiny" of the American West. The British landed at Cape Town in 1795 and likewise moved north and east,

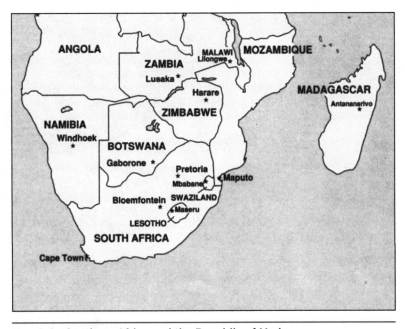

Map 9-2 Southern Africa and the Republic of Madagascar

Source: *Garland Encyclopedia of World Music,* Volume 1: Africa

annexing land for the crown. Throughout the next two hundred years, thousands of settlers from Great Britain, The Netherlands, and elsewhere arrived and spread through the hinterlands waging wars against each other and the native populations. Europeans controlled nearly the entire region that is today's South Africa by the middle of the 19th century. Only the far northeast remained out of their control. The last holdouts were the descendants of Shaka's great Zulu empire, who resisted the European invasion until 1887 when they finally gave in to superior British firepower. The British army then took on the descendants of the original Dutch settlers in the Boer War of 1899–1902.

The Union of South Africa came into being on May 31, 1910, with the incorporation of all the lands claimed by the **Afrikaners** (South Africans of Dutch, German, and French descent). Immediately the white population instituted harsh segregationist policies that isolated most black South Africans. In 1948 after winning the whites-only general election, the National Party institutionalized its racial policies in a system known as **Apartheid**, the legal and systematic separation of the races. All inhabitants were classified into racial groups—black, white, colored or mixed race, and South Asian—and each group was assigned separate and segregated areas and facilities. Black South Africans were denied citizenship and forced to live either in "homelands," economically unproductive regions of the country, or in "townships," urban living areas on the edge of "white-only" cities and towns. Only blacks with approved jobs were allowed into white areas, and then only if they carried an identification pass. Transportation, education, civil facilities such as hospitals, and public facilities such as swimming pools and beaches were all segregated. Such harsh racial discrimination sparked popular uprisings, protests, and in some cases armed insurrection, but the police met all opposition with suppression and brutality. The period of Late Apartheid (1960–1994) was marked by worldwide pressure for its dismantling in the form of economic boycotts and censure. A particularly brutal incident occurred in 1960 that brought international attention to this racial strife. A crowd of several thousand black South Africans staged a peaceful demonstration in the town of Sharpeville against new passbook laws, requiring all non-whites to show an internal passport to any white person who requested to see it. Police opened fire on the unarmed group, leaving sixty protesters, including women and children, dead in the street. Photographs of the dead appeared in newspapers around the world.

A number of South African musicians went into political exile during this period and used the status they acquired abroad as internationally famous artists to rally support for the economic boycott in Europe and North America. Singer Miriam Makeba, pianist Abdullah Ibrahim (born Adolph Johannes Brand), and jazz trumpet virtuoso Hugh Masekela all spread the message of racial oppression in their homeland, and used their music and celebrity to keep the plight of black South Africans before the

Fig. 9.4 **Hugh Masekela performing at the 35th Anniversary Playboy Jazz Festival, Hollywood Bowl, June 2013**

9-3 international public. One of Masekela's most famous compositions, "*Stimela* (Coal Train)," dramatically describes the tragic conditions under which the miners of Johannesburg lived out their lives. Hugh Masekela grew up in the mining camps of Johannesburg in the 1940s and 50s where his grandmother owned a *shebeen* (tavern) catering to the mineworkers. He was not a miner himself, but as a boy he worked in the tavern. An anti-Apartheid Anglican chaplain gave him his first trumpet when he was fourteen. By the age of twenty, he was performing with the premier South African band, the Jazz Epistles. Following the **Sharpeville Massacre**, he left the country to live in political exile for the next thirty years, enjoying a brilliant musical career in Europe and North America.

During the chaotic decades of the 1970s and 80s, music became a central site for public negotiations in the complex multicultural, multilingual, and multiracial society of South Africa. Musical developments and interactions came to play a significant role in the long and painful process of resistance, conflict, and resolution. Interaction and understanding among the various groups were severely impeded by government repression and censorship. One critical role that music played during the last two decades of Apartheid was to provide opportunities for interracial and intercultural collaborations that symbolized opposition to the government's racist and segregationist policies. The first racially mixed band in South Africa was formed in 1969 when Johnny Clegg, a sixteen-year old white, middle-class student in Johannesburg, met Sipho Mchunu, an eighteen-year old Zulu gardener, and the two began playing music together. They found few locations where a bi-racial group could perform, which forced Johnny and Sipho to play either on the streets or in a few select, unofficial venues.[4] The duo blended Zulu music and dance styles with rock and Celtic music. They sang in both English and Zulu, and their song lyrics were frequently political in nature. 9-4 In "*Akanaki Nokunaka*," for example, Johnny and Sipho sang about the government's removal and destruction of a traditional rural community under its forced relocation program. Their first album, *Universal Men* (1979), received critical acclaim in the press as the wave of the future, yet received no radio airplay in South Africa because of the segregationist laws. In 1981, South African radio 9-5 banned their song "*Impi*" (from their second album *African Litany*) about a Zulu defeat of the colonial British army. The song nevertheless became an underground hit and brought the duo, then named "Juluka," both national and international recognition leading to tours of Europe and North America in 1982 and 1983. As the first multiracial band in South Africa, Juluka used music making

Fig. 9.5 Multiracial band Juluka, with Johnny Clegg (rear left) and Sipho Mchunu (next to Clegg), London, 1983

as a means to transcend social, cultural, and racial differences. They sang of the social realities of life in South Africa, while simultaneously exploring musical fusions that drew together modern and traditional styles and urban and rural genres. Johnny and Sipho opened the door for other interracial and intercultural musical collaborations in the 1970s and 1980s.

One particularly powerful collaborative strategy was the juxtaposition of the two national anthems: "*Die Stem Van Suid-Afrika*" (The Call of South Africa), the South African national anthem before the end of Apartheid, and "*Nkosi Sikelel' iAfrika*", the anthem of the African National Congress outlawed during Apartheid. Some composers blended the two anthems to suggest and symbolize social fusion and ideological harmony, as in the popular radio announcer Dan Moyane's superimposition of the words to "*Nkosi Sikelel' iAfrica*" over the tune of "*Die Stem*." Others employed the anthems' melodies and/or lyrics to present cynical, satirical, or subversive commentaries on the political and social situations. The group Bright Blue used the banned South African anthem as an inconspicuous theme in the bass of its song "Weeping" on the album *Bright Blue* (1984). To astute listeners the theme was obvious, and the song circulated widely in the underground world of clubs and bars. "It was a long time before the message was received by the authorities," writes anthropologist Ingrid Byerly, "and the song was banned immediately when the subversive content was recognized."[5] Songwriter and band member Dan Heymann's website includes a link to the original "Weeping" video, directed by Nick Hofmeyr. These fusions allowed individuals to express not only their opposition to the repressive and racist governmental policies, but their vision for a new, democratic South Africa in which all members of society would have full and equal rights and opportunities.

As with the American Labor movement of the late 19th century, the Civil Rights movement in the 1950s and 60s, and the anti-Vietnam War movement of the 1970s, musicians in late Apartheid South Africa were on the front lines. Ordinary people faced police truncheons and fire hoses with singing for group solidarity and to maintain courage. Of the protest musicians, Ingrid Byerly writes:

[They] deserve recognition—not necessarily for the lasting value of their musical aesthetics, but for mobilizing change in a moment when their art could be instrumental in that change. The tendency for protest artists' work to become clichéd or passé in retrospect is great, and this is all the more the pity, for they served their purpose when their purpose was most needed."[6]

In 1990, a newly elected president, F.W. de Klerk, under intense pressure both from within the country and abroad, dismantled the policies of Apartheid and held elections with universal suffrage in 1994. Victory was finally achieved for the long disenfranchised black South Africans. The transition to democracy had taken place over many decades, with the participation of millions of average South Africans of all races, and without the bloody civil war that many at the time thought was inevitable.

GLOBAL HIP-HOP (TUNISIA, USA, GREENLAND, UGANDA)

A headline on the English language website of the international news network Al Jazeera from January 7, 2011 reads: "Tunisia arrests bloggers and rapper." The article, from the North African country Tunisia, tells of 22-year-old rapper Hamada Ben-Amor, known to his fans as El Général, who had just posted on the internet a song called, "Mr. President, Your People Are Dying." The lyrics focused on the absence of employment opportunities for urban youth in the country. His brother was quoted in the article, saying:

> Some 30 plainclothes policemen came to our house to arrest Hamada and took him away without ever telling us where to. When we asked why they were arresting him, they said "he knows why."[7]

The arrest of the El Général came in the wake of several weeks of violent public protest following the suicide by fire of a young fruit seller whose cart had been confiscated by the police. In an already volatile situation, the arrest of Ben-Amor sparked days of intense rioting that ultimately contributed to the overthrow of President Zine al-Abidine Ben Ali. This was the beginning of the so-called Arab Spring that swept across North Africa from Libya to Egypt to Syria. With the internet providing an easy and instantaneous outlet for rappers and hip-hop artists and their political messages, government crackdowns through censorship and arrests became increasingly common.

Fig. 9.6 Hamada Ben-Amor performs at a Tunisian opposition party meeting in Tunis, 2011, following the ousting of President Zine al-Abidine Ben Ali

Hip-hop has become a global phenomenon that includes rap music, break dancing, graffiti art, dress, tattoos, and other forms of identity expression. It began in the Bronx, New York City, during the early 1970s. One of the first hip-hop artists was an immigrant Jamaican disc jockey, DJ Kool Herc (real name, Clive Campbell, b. 1955). Using two turntables, he developed a technique for extending instrumental breaks in popular music genres like funk, soul, and R&B, and talking over those extended breaks. This technique developed into a new genre called "rap" that became especially important to young people in the Bronx who had no specific musical training. Through vocal wordsmithing and rhythmically spoken rhyming poetry, rappers could vent their frustrations against poverty, unemployment, crime, and interracial violence, while at the same time participating in a new art form that had its own virtuosic skill set. However, the roots of rap as an oppositional genre go much deeper than a single individual and a single locale.

Fig. 9.7　DJ Kool Herc performing in Grand Army Plaza, New York City, 2008

Rap's forebears stretch back through disco, street funk, radio DJs, Bo Diddley, the bebop singers, Cab Calloway, Pigmeat Markham, the tap dancers and comics, the Last Poets, Gil Scott-Heron, Muhammed Ali, acappella and doo-wop groups, ring games, skip-rope rhymes, prison and army songs, toasts, signifying and the dozens, all the way to the griots of Nigeria and the Gambia. No matter how far it penetrates into the twilight maze of Japanese video games and cool European electronics, its roots are still the deepest in all contemporary Afro-American music.[8]

What started out as local street party music became a national media phenomenon in the 1980s, with competing East Coast and West Coast styles. In 1988, after years of neglect by mainstream media, the first hip-hop show appeared on MTV. Images of African American hip-hop culture, including break dancing and inner city fashion—expensive sneakers, gold jewelry ("bling") and low-slung pants—were circulated on a national scale as the reach of American popular culture became more and more pervasive. Hip-hop also came to be associated with various forms of criminality including drug dealing and violence aimed at the police and women. It was the subject of governmental investigations, with campaigns to clean it up and to restrict adolescents' access to it. By the late 1990s, hip-hop had become the dominant artistic expression of opposition to the white middle-class status quo. As the reach of American popular culture grew ever more pervasive, it became a global phenomenon.

In his introduction to *Global Noise: Rap and Hip-Hop Outside the USA*, ethnomusicologist Tony Mitchell writes:

In the pages that follow, we will encounter Japanese b-boys [breakdancers] struggling with the hyperconsumerism of Tokyo youth culture, Italian posses promoting hardcore Marxist politics and alternative youth culture circuits, and Basque rappers using a punk rock—hip-hop syncretic to espouse their nationalist cause and promote the rights of ethnic minorities globally. Rappers in war-torn Bosnia declare their allegiance with the violent lives of gangsta rappers in South Central Los Angeles, and a rap group in Greenland protests that country's domination by the Danish language. Rap and hip-hop culture's incorporation into dance music culture in Korea and Bulgaria is examined, as are its Islamic and African manifestations in France and the United Kingdom, and its indigenization in Australia and Aotearoa-New Zealand. Its adaptations in both Francophone and Anglophone Canada contrast with its growth as a commercial force in Holland's music scene.[9]

The global hip-hop phenomenon is an interesting example of a cultural pattern called "glocalization," first introduced in Lesson 7, referring to the adaptation of global processes to local circumstances. Because of mass media and worldwide trade and communications, local communities are now infused with goods, services, images, and cultural artifacts from the rest of the world, particularly from the technologically most advanced societies. In Greenland, a protectorate of Denmark, the Inuit ride across the frozen landscape on Japanese skidoos (snowmobiles) wearing sneakers manufactured by American companies in Vietnamese sweatshops. While this is an example of globalization, in Greenland these goods from the outside world are adapted to the local situation, and to them local meanings are attached. So too the sounds and images of hip-hop culture traverse the world via the internet and other communication media, and become adapted to local use. In the case of hip-hop, a music genre and a fashion that carries general oppositional connotations, local media producers use it to challenge perceived local injustices. In this YouTube video by the Greenland Inuit hip-hop group Nuuk Posse, the rapper is challenging the imposition of the Danish language on his native culture. This issue is only of local concern, but the band adopts images that have become associated worldwide with oppositional identity, like skateboarding and graffiti.

Ironically, politicians occasionally co-opt the hip-hop style to reach younger constituencies. On the same day in 2011 that the BBC and Public Radio International posted the rap video that landed the Tunisian artist in jail, they posted a video produced by the president of the East African country of Uganda asking an imagined public, "Do you want another rap?" The president delivered two verses of traditional African political speech loaded with proverbs and metaphor over a breakbeat. This is a powerful example of glocalization. The elder statesman in Western formal attire mixes the traditional imagery of African discourse with the visual cues of the rap music video to make himself, the establishment figure, appear oppositional and therefore on the side of those who oppose the establishment.

PLATEAU MUSIC PROJECT (CHINA/TIBET)

In Lesson 7, we met the Tibetan Buddhist monk, Acko Choedrag, and his songs and videos that feature images of traditional Tibetan religious life. These songs and images are both symbols and celebrations of Tibetan ethnic and cultural identity. On the high plateau of Central Asia, as in many parts of the world, traditional life, sacred and secular, is rapidly changing beyond recognition. Like endangered species under threat from changes in habitat, cultural forms are also disappearing because of transformations in the human environment. Industrialization, economic development, modernization, and globalization are all responsible for eroding lifeways that form the basis of traditional music, much of it intimately tied to such day-to-day activities as herding and farming and other forms of labor. In western China and Tibet, the highest inhabited region of the world with an average altitude of 16,000 feet, these pressures are exacerbated by an influx of Han Chinese, the majority ethnic group. The central government has relocated millions into the rural territories of minority groups like the Tibetans, seeking to alleviate overcrowded cities and to exploit the mineral wealth of the sparsely inhabited hinterland. With this new population comes Chinese-language mass media: radio, videos, CDs, and DVDs, while the internet provides quick access to popular music from distant urban centers.

Tibet was incorporated into modern China in 1950 through military invasion. During the Cultural Revolution (1966–1976) there was a state-sponsored campaign against "local nationalism," that is, allegiance by minority groups to their ethnic identities rather than to the Chinese Communist State. Students from the large cities of eastern China traveled throughout the country destroying markers of ethnic identity, and in the Tibetan region closing monasteries and defacing buildings and works of art. By government decree, languages other than Mandarin were forbidden in radio and TV broadcasts and education. Since the end of the Cultural Revolution, government policies against minorities have been somewhat relaxed. However, on the Central Plateau, the modern world itself threatens to engulf the region's fragile rural ways of life (see Map 7–3, p. 103). Mass media and recording devices have a homogenizing effect, eroding regional differences within the Tibetan areas. With electrification, tape recorders, radios, and TVs became available. Tibetans began losing interest in older forms of expression that had been passed down orally in families and communities. Now they are more likely to sing songs learned from CDs and the internet than from family members or local villagers. Wedding songs, for instance, have been particularly affected in this way.

Changes in farming and herding through modern techniques have made many music genres obsolete. For example, families for generations have transmitted songs to sing to ewes (female sheep) when they have difficulty letting down their milk. Because herders now use electric milking machines, the songs have lost their context and function. Modernization has brought other fundamental changes in traditional life.

With a shift to a consumer culture, people are more likely to consume culture than to produce it. As highways, power lines, and satellite dishes bring to the Plateau more and more music from inner China, Hong Kong, Taiwan, India, and the West, people have become creatively less self-sufficient and more dependent on external sources of music. One example of significant impact is in the singing of lullabies.... [Hearing recorded music] influences people's perception of their own musical talent.[10]

Within a generation, thousands of songs may vanish.

Fig. 9.8 Plateau Music Project student song collector, Tserang Tso (second from left), with (left to right) her mother, grandmother, brother, and sister

   The Plateau Music Project (formerly known as the Tibetan Endangered Music Project) was founded in 2005 by Australian anthropologist, Gerald Roche, and his students at Qinghai Normal University. With digital tape recorders in hand, the students have collected traditional songs in opposition to the encroachment of time and inevitable cultural change. In 2007, the students posted an "**infomercial**" on YouTube describing their project and soliciting contributions. At the same time their emphasis expanded to include a number of other ethnic minorities from the region, as reflected in the name change to "Plateau Music Project." Students received training from more experienced collectors both in the use of digital technologies and in soliciting songs from older, skeptical villagers and relatives. More than seven hundred songs have been archived, and some have been posted on YouTube, such as this **love song** and **nomadic song**. On return trips to the villages, the students presented the elders with CDs. Hearing these songs that have seemed old fashioned, obsolete, and worthless, validated for students and elders alike their shared cultural heritage, creating a link across generations that stood in opposition to cultural extinction. In April 2014 the Plateau Music Project, along with a number of other NGOs (Non Governmental Organizations) operating in Qinghai province, was shut down for reasons unknown.

CONCLUSION

Musicians have worked on both sides of oppositional divides, lending their talents and charisma to entrenched power structures as well as those of reform and revolution. The Czech novelist Milan Kundera, in his historical novel *The Book of Laughter and Forgetting*, describes the paranoia of a tyrant when a pop star goes abroad:

> When Karel Gott, the Czech pop singer, went abroad in 1972, Husak got scared. He sat right down and wrote him a personal letter.... The following is a verbatim quote from it. I have invented nothing.
>
> *Dear Karel, We are not angry with you. Please come back. We will do everything you ask. We will help you if you help us...*
>
> Think it over. Without batting an eyelid, Husak let doctors, scholars, astronomers, athletes, directors, cameramen, workers, engineers, architects, historians, journalists, writers, and painters go into emigration, but he could not stand the thought of Karel Gott leaving the country.[11]

Some musicians attempt to survive in dangerous regimes, pursuing their careers while still attempting to resist tyranny from within. In the Soviet Union, composers lived in fear of writing music that Stalin and his bureaucrats would find insufficiently "**proletarian**." The composer Dmitri Shostakovich (1906–1975) relates how in 1948, after being officially denounced by the government, he waited at night in the corridor by the elevator for the police to come take him away—as they had many other artists and musicians—so that his family would not be disturbed. In South Africa under the Apartheid regime, musicians worked in constant danger of censorship, imprisonment, or banishment. The

Fig. 9.9   Pau Casals (1876–1973) (L), and Dmitri Shostakovich (1906–1975) (R)

Spanish cellist Pau Casals (1876–1973) famously denounced the Fascist dictator Francisco Franco and went into exile following the Spanish Civil War in 1936, never to return to his home. He had been warned that he would be murdered if he ever came back. Casals spent the rest of his life campaigning for various anti-fascist and humanitarian causes. In 1971, at the age of 96, he was presented with the United Nations Peace Medal.

At the conclusion of Lesson 7, we noted how music can serve as a unifying force in human experience, and in this lesson we note how music can act as a marker of divisions between human groups. In each of the case studies above, we examine a context in which power is distributed unequally between opposing factions. What we see in *Nueva Canción* is musicians serving as the spokespersons for those who oppose a regime and seek to redress injustices. The same is true in the Apartheid struggle, where control of the government, the economy, the media, and the police was held by the Apartheid regime, while on the other side is the creative ingenuity of musicians to use expressive culture to mobilize, to inspire acts of resistance, and to catalyze a vision of a more just reality. How *can* music serve both to unify as well as to challenge and oppose vested power? We might think back once again to Merriam's functions of music. Music can stimulate emotions associated with harmony and unity as well as those associated with defiance and rage. Music can symbolize groups, ideas, and values, and then communicate those ideas and values in ways that are both overt and subtle. Music can also give aesthetic pleasure and provide entertainment, and at the same time contribute to the solidarity and cohesiveness of groups, which can be mobilized in common cause.

In its power to both unite and divide human groups, music resembles religion, which is also a commonality of human social experience. Like music, religion is a dominant factor in individual and group identity, and as we shall see in Unit 3, the beliefs, motivations, ways of life, and ethical systems that religions embody are often expressed and enacted through music.

KEY CONCEPTS

Oppositional identity	Economic boycott	Eroding lifeways
Power relationships	Interracial/Intercultural	Cultural Revolution
Subversion	collaboration	Local nationalism
Military band	Protest artists	Consumer culture
Political exile	Rap/Rapper	

(Q) THINKING ABOUT MUSIC QUESTIONS

1. Read again the quote from Gabriel García Márquez' 1982 Nobel Prize acceptance speech describing the plight of Latin America's poor. In the face of so much oppression and sorrow, what roles can music and musicians serve? Correlate your response with some of Merriam's ten functions.

2. Why do you think the *Nueva Canción* musicians chose to use simple folk and indigenous instruments and styles to express their opposition to totalitarian regimes?

3. In South Africa, Johnny and Sipho created a hybrid musical style, blending Johnny's Rock and Celtic styles with Sipho's traditional Zulu style. Why was their music a potent sonic weapon against the assumptions of racial separation?

4. Describe a case of music supporting a power structure or status quo, and a case in which music is used to oppose a power structure or status quo. In what ways does the music communicate support in the first case, and opposition and resistance in the second?

5. The song "The Internationale" is a classic oppositional song. Think of two others from the past or present. What do the songs oppose, and how effective have they been in uniting voices for a cause?

6. In his song "*Stimela* (Coal Train)," South African jazz trumpeter Hugh Masekela sang of the hardships suffered by his fellow black South Africans during Apartheid. How did Hugh Masekela use music and lyrics in this song to express his oppositional identity?

NOTES

1 Shalini Saran, "Agra's Musical Past," *The Hindu*, December 3, 2000, reprinted in *Music* (The Hindu eBooks: Kasturi and Sons Ltd., 2003), 20, http://www.ocf.berkeley.edu/~aathavan/libraire/carnatic/carnaticmusic.pdf.

2 Gabriel García Márquez, "The Solitude of Latin America" (Eng. trans.), Nobel Lecture, December 8, 1982, Nobel Prize for Literature 1982, cited with permission, © The Nobel Foundation 1982. http://www.nobel prize.org/nobel_prizes/literature/laureates/1982/marquez-lecture.html

3 Jan Fairley, "*Nueva Canción*," *Grove Music Online* (Oxford University Press, 2010).

4 *Rhythm of Resistance* (Harcourt Films, 1979), Beats of the Heart series, directed and written by Jeremy Marre.

5 Ingrid Byerly, "'Mirror, Mediator, and Prophet': The Music Indaba of Late-Apartheid South Africa," *Ethnomusicology* 42/1 (1998): 33–34.

6 Ingrid Byerly, "Mirror, Mediator, and Prophet," 36.

7 Yasmine Ryan, "Tunisia Arrests Bloggers and Rapper," in *Al Jazeera*, English-language news website, January 7, 2011, accessed January 13, 2011, http://english.aljazeera.net/news/africa/2011/01/20111718360234492.html. See also, joshasen, "The Rap That Sparked a Revolution: El General (Tunisia)," in *Hip-Hop Diplomacy*, January 21, 2011, http://hiphopdiplomacy.org/2011/01/31/the-rap-that-sparked-a-revolution-el-general-tunisia/.

8 David Toop, *Rap Attack 2: African Rap to Global Hip-Hop* (London: Serpent's Tail, 1991), 19, cited in Tony Mitchell, ed. *Global Noise: Rap and Hip-Hop Outside the USA* (Middletown, CT: Wesleyan University Press, 2001), 4.

9 Tony Mitchell, ed. *Global Noise: Rap and Hip-Hop Outside the USA* (Middletown, CT: Wesleyan University Press, 2001), 1.

10 Tsering Bum and Gerald Roche, "The Plateau Music Project: Grass-roots Cultural Preservation on the Tibetan Plateau" (2010), accessed July 24, 2014, http://people.audrn.net/profiles/blogs/the-plateau-music-project

11 Milan Kundera, *The Book of Laughter and Forgetting* (New York, NY: Penguin Books, 1980), 181.

UNIT 3
MUSIC AND THE SACRED

INTRODUCTION

It is a near-universal phenomenon that music has deep and complex relationships with religions throughout the world. In virtually every society some forms of religious expression are encoded in musical sound. Trying to understand why this is so and what it tells us of the nature of music, is the goal of this unit. However, just as music was difficult to define, the word "religion" is also highly problematic, especially when using a term that derives from the Judeo-Christian/Greco-Roman worldview as a global concept. Indeed, finding a single defining essence shared by all of the world's religions is probably impossible; it is certainly beyond the scope of this course. Nevertheless, throughout the world, systems of belief, moral codes, explanatory narratives, sacred texts, communication and communion with unseen powers and beings, calendrical and life-cycle rituals together constitute powerful frameworks by which people find order, meaning, and control over their lives. Collectively held, they bind families, communities, and societies together with shared values and emotional connections.

The near-universality of music in religion can perhaps be explained by the range of functions it serves. Each of the functions of music enumerated by Alan Merriam (as discussed in Lesson 5) can be applied to religious contexts. Music provides a vehicle for the *expression* of religious emotions of awe, joy, and wonder. Worshipers respond *aesthetically* to its beauty as being akin or analogous to the beauties of celestial realms. Music's *entertainment* function has served as a tool for attracting converts, for drawing people to religious rituals and sustaining their interest once there. Through music, humans *communicate* with ancestor spirits, supernatural beings, and divine powers as well as with each other. Through music, adults communicate religious teachings to their children. Music is often used as a powerful *symbol* of the other realms and beings that religions hold sacred. The church bells and the organ in traditional Christian communities and the **adhan** or "Call to Prayer" of the Islamic world symbolize community worship and represent shared values, beliefs, and practices. Throughout Africa and the African diaspora in the New World, drums provide a sonic connection to gods and ancestors and represent their continued and abiding presence in the community. Musical instruments are symbolic of sacred beings: Lord Krishna's flute, King David's harp, and Gabriel's trumpet. Music is used throughout the world to stimulate *physical* states of repose and contemplation as well as ecstasy and trance. In many religious communities, dance is an appropriate response to divine presence and is an expression of embodied joy and devotion. Beyond these relationships with the religious experiences of individuals, music in religious contexts *reinforces social norms, validates rituals,* and *contributes to the continuity and integration of society.* Religious music, like religion itself, serves to *stabilize* and *perpetuate* social practices and institutions. Most religious music is heard and performed in groups and often serves as a public expression of a faith community.

While music is almost universally incorporated in religious ritual, the *kind* of music considered appropriate has been the subject of intense debate. In Western Christianity as practiced in America, even within a single congregation there is often a lack of consensus as to what music to use for a given ritual or context. Divisions may run along sectarian lines: some people feeling, for instance, that only the most gifted musicians within the community should perform—their gifts considered of divine origins. Others believe that musical participation should be egalitarian and communal—fervor of faith and not quality of voice makes one worthy to participate. Communities become divided along generational lines, with older congregants wanting to maintain traditions while younger members of the community seek contemporary musical expressions that more closely match their experience and taste. Elsewhere, the very inclusion of music in worship is subject to highly ambivalent attitudes. In early Christianity, the Church Fathers sermonized on both sides of the music debate. The 4th-century Christian theologian St. Basil praised congregational **psalm** singing in the highest terms, but he condemned all forms of instrumental music. He and other early evangelists sought to eradicate the use of instruments because they were held to be sacred to the Pagan gods like Apollo and Dionysus, and their efforts were successful. Only vocal music was performed in Christian practice until around 1000 CE when the organ made its way into the church. In one of the most eloquent and influential passages on music from the early Christian period, St. Augustine (354–430) states his belief that he is lost in sin when he finds himself paying more attention to the melody of the song than the sacred text to which it is set. "Yet," he writes in his *Confessions* (ca. 398), "when I find the singing itself more moving than the truth which it conveys, I confess that this is a grievous sin, and at those times I would prefer not to hear the singer." Indeed, at those times he felt inclined, as bishop, to "exclude from my ears, and from those of the Church as well... those lovely chants to which the Psalms of David are habitually sung." Yet in the end he is "inclined to approve of the custom of singing in church, in order that by indulging the ears weaker spirits may be inspired with feelings of devotion."[1] He recounts in the same passage how it was the beautiful singing of his teacher St. Ambrose, Bishop of Milan, that first turned his heart toward the teachings of the church.

Fig. 10.1 *Saint Augustine in his Study,* Sandro Botticelli, 1494, Uffizi Gallery, Florence

Within Christianity today, there is enormous diversity of religious musical practices. The United House of Prayer employs gospel brass "shout bands" consisting primarily of trombones, bass drum, and cymbals as the central component of religious worship. In contrast, many **Primitive Baptist** congregations in the United States use vocal music in worship but exclude all musical instruments. Both denominations find support for their positions regarding musical practices in scripture, but come to opposite conclusions. Psalm 150, for instance, clearly validates and supports the use of instruments in worship: "Praise him with the sound of the trumpet; praise him with the psaltery and harp." Primitive Baptists, however, cite the absence of any mention of musical instruments in the New Testament as evidence that, like animal sacrifice, musical instruments are no longer warranted following the coming of Christ. In the religion of Islam, music has also held a contentious position. Musicologist Amnon Shiloah describes the "interminable debate" surrounding the practice of listening to music (*sama*) as a religious act.[2] The controversy derives from the lack of a position one way or another taken in the Qur'an, the holy book of Islam. "Both those in favour of music and those opposed had recourse to it, which is perplexing because nothing in the *Qur'an* concerns music explicitly." Those in favor of music often cite the saying of Muhammad, "Allah has not sent a prophet except with a beautiful voice, and Allah listens more intently to a man with a beautiful voice reading the *Qur'an* than does the master of a singing-girl to her singing." Those against music will tell the myth of how Satan, jealous of King David's beautiful voice singing divine praise, "summoned his hordes and ordered them to devise something equally powerful. They then invented the reed-pipes and lutes...."[3] This of course supports the suspicion of musical instruments shared by early Christian theologians.

Pagan, Judeo-Christian, and Islamic believers all recognize

the overwhelming power of music, which exerts an irresistibly strong influence on the listener's soul. Acting as a kind of charm, music produces either sensual pleasure or extreme excitement, and its maximal effect can send the listener into an emotional, even violent paroxysm. As a result of this untamed power, or spontaneous effect, the listener loses control over his reason and behaviour and is consequently governed by his passions.[4]

This passage from Shiloah is especially relevant to the religious experience of trance, discussed in Lesson 11. The unresolved question and source of controversy concerns whether these heightened experiences are divinely inspired or whether they are distractions from the spiritual life.

Many religions of Africa and the Indian subcontinent hold music in unequivocal, high regard. In Sub-Saharan Africa, drumming is used to evoke deities and ancestor spirits, and dancing provides evidence of their spiritual presence in human bodies. Descendants of African slaves brought many of these practices to the New World. In parts of the Caribbean and South America, religious/drumming traditions continued more or less unmolested by the slave-owning society, and these became the roots for a wealth of dance rhythms and forms. In North America, the drumming was suppressed to a greater degree, but not entirely eliminated. Today, African American Christianity has been invigorated with these African rhythms, now re-contextualized as gospel music. In Hinduism, singing, dancing, drumming, and playing musical instruments are experienced as powerful expressions of the sacred. Indeed, musical sound itself is revered as a manifestation of the Divine: *Nad Brahman* ("God as sound"). In most forms of Buddhism, music is more subdued, but nevertheless present as the setting for the recitation of holy texts (*sutras*), or to accompany rituals celebrating Buddha's life and teachings. In Korea, a genre of song called *chapka* has survived in which Buddhist teachings were performed by missionaries seeking converts, using indigenous folk melodies. Similarly, as Islam spread through the Hindu heartland of northern India in the 15th century, a musical form called *qawwali* developed through which a population accustomed to experiencing and celebrating the divine through music could continue the singing and dancing, but now in the name of Allah.

In this unit, we examine religious music from a variety of perspectives. In Lesson 10, we explore the use of music in liturgical chant and devotional singing. Lesson 11 focuses on ways in which religious feelings, states, and narratives are embodied and enacted through music. These include musically-inspired states of heightened emotion, ecstasy, and trance; and sacred narratives presented through dance and theater. Lesson 12 deals with the power of music to separate sacred spaces and times from secular, everyday experience; and to shape the structure of religious rituals.

NOTES

1   St. Augustine's *Confessions* (398 CE), cited in Pierro Weiss and Richard Taruskin, *Music in the Western World: A History in Documents* (New York: Schirmer, 1984), 32.
2   Amnon Shiloah, *Music in the World of Islam: A Socio-cultural Study* (Detroit: Wayne State University Press, 1995), 31.
3   Amnon Shiloah, *Music in the World of Islam,* 33.
4   Amnon Shiloah, *Music in the World of Islam,* 34.

Lesson 10
Sacred Chant and Devotional Singing

SACRED CHANT

Ethnomusicologist Ter Ellingson, writing on the relationship between music and religion, makes the point that most religious traditions put special emphasis on vocal music. "This is usually because of its capacity to communicate meanings through the words of song texts, because the human body seems more a part of divine creation than instruments created by human artifice, or because of negative associations of instruments and their music."[1] While in some religious traditions, voices perform alone, there is no known case of the opposite—the complete exclusion of the voice. In this lesson, we examine the roles music plays as a vehicle for the performance of sacred texts. The Vedas of India, the Psalms of the Old Testament, the Buddhist *sutras* (scriptures), the Qur'an, and the creation stories of the Navaho are all performed aloud to melodic contours and metrical patterns. This widespread practice suggests that music is a form of heightened speech—a special mode worthy of the words it carries—in a way that ordinary speech is not. The terms "chant" and **"cantillation"** refer generally to the recitation of religious narratives, beliefs, and texts on melodic tones. Sacred chant has served as a vehicle for the expression of faith for millennia. In the history of Western music, for example, the singing or chanting of psalms "is surely the oldest continuous musical tradition,"[2] stretching from early Judaic times (1000 BCE and earlier) to psalm singing in Jewish and Christian worship today. Sacred chant encompasses many different musical forms and styles: from Buddhist chants of Tibet and Japan to Hindu chants of India; from ancient Vedic recitation to the chanting of Islamic mystical (Sufi) brotherhoods; from early Christian Gregorian chant to Byzantine chant of the Greek Orthodox Church.

In many cases, the chanted *words* are the primary focus of the musical expression; the melody, rhythm, and instrumental accompaniment, if any, play a supportive and secondary role. Watch this video clip of a **Korean Buddhist monk** reciting sacred text based on the teachings of the Buddha, punctuating his own chanting with gong strokes. Each syllable of the text gets just one or two notes of the chant. The rhythm follows the natural flow of the text, and is supported by a simple melodic contour. This kind of syllabic chanting used in many religious traditions may be understood as an

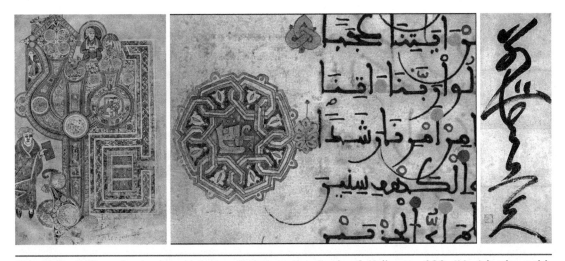

Fig. 10.2 **Calligraphy in sacred texts: Christian—the Book of Kells, ca. 800 (L); Islamic—gold-illuminated Qur'an from Morocco, 17th century (C); and Buddhist—Japanese Zen, by Muso Kokushi, 14th century (R)**

equivalent to the beautiful calligraphy in illuminated manuscripts, in which both music and writing serve to enhance and embellish sacred words. However, in other traditions of cantillation, *musical* aspects are paramount. Another form of Korean Buddhist chant called *pompae* takes a single line of text from one of the scriptures (*sutras*) and greatly expands it by sustaining a single syllable over many notes. A scriptural verse that can be spoken in a few seconds is stretched out in this manner for twenty minutes or more, thus rendering the text difficult to understand, if not incomprehensible. A similar practice, called melisma, was used by medieval European monks. The differing emphasis of the chant styles on words or melody may represent a more general distinction in the way the chants are used: syllabic chant may be a form of communication among humans by which religious narratives or sermons are conveyed; **melismatic** chant may be an aesthetically beautiful musical offering for unseen divine listeners.[3] In some cultures, the sounds of religious chant are as different from the secular music of the region as the musics of foreign countries. Perhaps this is because strong, conservative monastic traditions preserve musical practices over generations. Isolation in monasteries and strict adherence to tradition prevent the kinds of fluid adaptations to changing social and technological factors and outside influences that shape secular music.

VEDIC CHANT (INDIA)

Arguably the oldest unbroken tradition of chant in existence is that of Vedic chant in India. **Veda** literally means "knowledge" and the Vedas are the sacred hymns and prayers that were revealed to seers (*rishis*) in ancient India at least 3500 years ago. The Vedas have been passed down orally since that time by members of a hereditary priestly caste, called Brahmins, from father to son and from teacher to student. The recitation of appropriate verses accompanied virtually every aspect of ritual life, from the lighting of sacred fires and pouring of sacrificial oils to weddings, funerals, and other rites of passage. The musical elements—melody and meter—were inseparable from the texts and were thus considered sacred and immutable. The Vedas are organized into four collections based on their ritual purpose. The oldest collection, the *Rigveda*, consists of 1028 hymns grouped according to the deity they invoke, some five hundred addressed to Agni, the god of fire, and to Indra, the god of storms, thunder, and war. The *Samaveda* contains chants to be sung by the priest at the Soma sacrifice (*soma*, an intoxicating drink from the soma plant). This ritual is seldom performed today. The *Yajurveda* comprises sacrificial prayers, and the fourth Veda, the *Atharvaveda*, differs from the other three in containing spells, incantations, and magical formulas. **Brahmin** priests chanted the ancient Sanskrit verses unaccompanied and with great precision. "Particular care had to be taken to preserve

Fig. 10.3 Nambudiri Brahmin priests performing *Athirathram*, a 12-day-long Vedic ritual to Agni, God of Fire, in Trissur, Kerala, 2011

these," writes ethnomusicologist Charles Capwell, "because their very sounds were considered to be the necessary means for coercing the gods to provide for the needs of the people."[4] As seen in this video clip, young students of **Vedic Chant** learn the correct chant pitches and rhythms orally, their learning supplemented by hand and head movements to ensure that no recitation is incorrect or lost. Notice that the students learn the melodic formulas, consisting of only three pitches, accompanied by head motions up, down, and to the side.

PLAINCHANT (MEDIEVAL EUROPE)

The oldest continuous musical tradition of the Western world is the singing of psalms, as documented in Judaic tradition. Psalm verses exhorted the faithful to praise the Lord with voices, instruments, and dance in the temple at Jerusalem: "Sing unto the Lord with the harp...and the voice of a psalm. With trumpets and the sound of the cornet" (Psalm 98). Worship in the synagogues (study houses for prayer) employed simpler, purely vocal music. The early Christian church drew on this latter tradition for its rituals and music. Jesus had proclaimed "For where two or three are gathered together in my name, I am in the midst of them" (Matthew 18:20). Thus, early Christians gathered together for the singing of psalms and prayers. These were incorporated into the central ritual of the early Church—the Mass. St. Basil the Great, a 4th-century Bishop in Asia Minor (modern day western Turkey), wrote of the important benefits of chanting for these congregations: "Psalmody, bringing about choral singing, a bond, as it were, toward unity, and joining the people into a harmonious union of one choir, produces also the greatest blessings, charity"; and "a psalm calls forth a tear even from a heart of stone. A psalm is the work of angels...a spiritual incense."[5] Melodic formulas from earlier Jewish practices, and newly composed melodies were gradually collected and standardized during the first millennium of Christianity. The composition of these melodies was attributed to Pope Gregory I (ca. 540–604) under the influence of the Holy

Spirit, giving them authority and stature as "Gregorian Chant," a term used interchangeably with **plainchant**. Preserving and standardizing ritual melodies across Western Europe that began during the reign of Charlemagne (742–814) led to the development of music notation. This body of notated melodies, numbering in the thousands, accompanied all the rituals of the Church Year. In monasteries, convents, and parishes, choirs sang the sacred texts and teachings of the early Roman Church to these simple, unaccompanied plainchant melodies, transmitting Christian teachings in a simple yet appealing manner. This recitation at a **Benedictine convent** in France demonstrates the continuity of the practice into the present.

Notation and the rise of music "literacy" not only aided preservation and standardization, but notation also encouraged a new form of musical creativity in the adding of multiple parts to the chant melodies. From the unison singing to two then three then four and more vocal parts, the development of polyphony mirrored the developments in architecture and church organization of the late Middle Ages. As church music became increasingly complex, emphasis shifted from the clarity of the words to the glorious sound of musical harmony. By the beginning of the 17th century, music for worship had become quite elaborate, with the addition of multiple choirs, soloists, and instruments. While composers still used the ancient Gregorian melodies, they became increasingly hidden within multi-part textures. Music notation was continuously refined over the next thousand years, and had a profound impact on the development of music in the Western world. Ultimately, with a global reach, this was the most important development in sound preservation technology until the invention of sound recording at the end of the 19th century.

BUDDHIST CHANT (LAOS, CHINA, TIBET)

The sacred texts of the Buddhist traditions consist primarily of sermons that the historic Buddha, Siddhartha Gautama (563–485 BCE), delivered orally to his disciples. These provided instructions for how to live in the world free from pain and suffering, how to establish monastic communities for mutual support, and how to realize the ultimate goal of life: *nirvana* (enlightenment). Generations of his followers repeated these teachings from memory and codified them by topic into the *Tripitaka* ("Three Baskets"). Around four hundred and fifty years after the Buddha's death, they were finally written down. The most orthodox branch of Buddhism, **Theravada** ("the Ancient Teaching"), which continues to flourish in Sri Lanka, Myanmar (Burma), Thailand, and Laos, utilizes these teachings in Pali, their original language. Within Theravada Buddhist monasteries and temples, monks recite the sacred texts in simple melodic patterns in preparation for long hours of meditation.

As Buddhism traveled from its original home in India north and northeast into Central Asia and China, it combined with indigenous religions like Daoism and became more eclectic, devotional, and ritualistic. The historic Buddha came to be seen as an earthly manifestation of a celestial emanation, having many non-material forms and powers. The Buddhist traditions that developed from this later interpretation became known as **Mahayana** ("Great Vehicle"). In this video from Shanxi Province in the People's Republic of China, monks have gathered in the *gompa* (prayer hall) to honor the Enlightened One with collective chanting and processing—a form of **"walking meditation."** The monks chant a repeating mantra or sacred phrase beginning "*Namo Amitabha*," invoking the name and blessings of the heavenly Buddha of compassion.

Within the form of Buddhism that developed in Tibet, monks use music to "hear the truth" of the Buddha's teachings, to deepen their understanding, and increase their awareness of the world and the nature of existence. All Tibetan Buddhist monks learn vocal music because of its importance both in meditation and in rituals and ceremonies, in which the sermons (*sutras*) of the Buddha and his followers are recited. Of the many types of chant used within the Tibetan monastic tradition, *dbyangs* (pronounced "yung") is the most complex and highly valued. In *dbyangs*, the monks chant the texts of the *sutras* on an extremely low fundamental note, and occasionally sustain a syllable (most notably the sacred word "*aum*" that signifies the sum of all sacred sounds) in such a way that upper overtones become audible. In this recording of Tibetan *dbyangs* chant, you can clearly hear this phenomenon at 0'20". This extraordinary technique enables overtones, which are ordinarily inaudible, to be heard by human ears. The practice symbolizes the Buddhist monks' religious goal: to bring into focus and awareness a world much greater than that which we normally see with our eyes and experience with our bodies, a world without pain and suffering where all opposition and duality is united.[6]

ISLAMIC CANTILLATION (EGYPT, UGANDA)

In the sacred world of Islam, the use of music has long been a matter of debate. Orthodox Muslims prohibit from mosque observances all forms of "music" except Qur'anic recitation and the Call to Prayer (*adhan*), delivered at five prescribed daily prayer times. (These two forms of religious expression are not considered music in Islam, although to non-Muslims they sound like they belong in the category "music." Western scholars use the term "cantillation" to differentiate this category from forms of musical expression that have other contexts and fulfill other purposes.) The Qur'an is the central revelation on which Islam is based. It is experienced by Muslims throughout the world as an auditory phenomenon, recited in classical Arabic by a solo reciter in the manner in which it was revealed to the Prophet Muhammad by Archangel Gabriel. According to generally held beliefs, the principles of recitation are based upon Muhammad's repetition of the sacred words to his companions, who in turn recited them to their followers, and so on until the present day. Qur'an study and memorization is a primary component of religious education for Muslim children. The Qur'an is recited according to a system of articulation that they study meticulously so that every letter of the sacred text is clearly enunciated and free of error.

 The practice of Qur'anic recitation, called *tarteel*, follows strict rules for pronouncing the Arabic syllables, shaping melodic contours, and pausing and breathing during the recitation. While Qur'anic recitation is not considered music, the principles of melody that are associated with this practice are based on the same scale system, *maqamat*, as classical Arabic music. The purpose of using musical pitches is to render the religious words with a beautiful voice. A more elaborate practice called *tajweed,* literally "betterment," is learned by specialists (*qari*) who are identified both for the beauty of their voice and for being particularly skillful in their recitation. *Tajweed* is also characterized by intricate vocal ornaments similar to those in classical music styles. Watch this video clip of Qur'anic recitation by **Sheikh Abdul Basit**, one of the finest and most renowned *qari* of 20th-century Egypt.

The Call to Prayer (*adhan*), a recognizable sonic feature of Islam, is one of its oldest continuing traditions, dating from the life of the Prophet (570–632 CE). Inspired by a dream, Mohammed began the practice of having a caller announce the time of daily prayer with the simple statement of belief at the core of the religion: "God is great, there is one God only, and Mohammed is His prophet." The first *muezzin*, according to legend, was an African slave named Bilal, chosen by the Prophet because of the beauty and power of his voice and the depth of his faith. Traditionally the *muezzin* (a specially-trained singer) stood on a platform at the top of one of the **minarets** (slender towers) that form an essential architectural feature of the mosque. From there, he called the faithful to prayer at the five prescribed daily prayer times: at dawn, just after noon, in the afternoon, just after sunset, and around nightfall. In most parts of the Islamic world, the *adhan* is broadcast live from the mosque over loudspeakers, and recently, recordings of the *adhan* have been used to supplement or replace the live performance.

There is no clearly defined manner in which the Call to Prayer must be delivered, and styles range from simple chanting on two notes to the highly melismatic, covering a wide pitch range. The style of chant heard in Egypt has become popular worldwide, with recordings available to train *muezzins* in Africa and East Asia. Important performance practices of the *adhan* include: it is never accompanied by instruments, rhythmic aspects are de-emphasized, and the *muezzin* is always male. The delivery of the text follows the natural flow of classical Arabic speech, with certain important words elongated through melisma in the more ornate styles, and pauses between lines extended to eliminate all sense of a regular pulse. This is so that the chant is not experienced bodily, as with rhythmic dance music. In this video, from a mosque in Kampala, Uganda, we see the *muezzin* reciting the *adhan* into the

Fig. 10.4 A mosque in western China showing two of its minarets (L), and detail of a loudspeaker on the minaret to the right for broadcasting the Call to Prayer (R)

microphone of a public address system stored in a cabinet behind the *minbar* (equivalent to a pulpit in a Christian church). His voice is broadcast across the neighborhood through the loudspeaker mounted on one of the minarets, visible in the video. Men from the vicinity leave their work and gather for mid-afternoon prayers. The *muezzin* is an employee of the mosque, and performs this duty five times every day, as his father did before him.

The Call to Prayer (*adhan*)

Allahu Akbar	Allah is most great [four times]
Ash-had anna la ilaha illallah	I testify that there is no god but Allah [twice]
Ash-hadu anna Muhammadar rasulullah	I testify that Muhammad is the Prophet of Allah [twice]
Hayya 'ala-salah	Come to prayer [twice]
Hayya 'ala 'l-falah	Come to salvation [twice]
Allāhu akbar	Allah is most great [twice]
La ilaha illallah	There is no god but Allah [once]

DEVOTIONAL SINGING

Sacred chant traditions are among the most conservative practices in many religions. Texts often date from the origins of a religious system and form the basis of, and authority for, belief. They are performed by ritual specialists in ancient languages unspoken by and incomprehensible to lay believers: Roman Catholic priests reciting in Latin, Imams in Qur'anic Arabic, Brahmins in Vedic Sanskrit, and Buddhist monks in Pali. Yet all religions provide opportunities for ordinary people to participate in individual and communal practices through which they express religious emotions, make requests of the divine, and share religious experiences with others in their communities. For example, in a small, remote village in eastern Tibet, women too old for agricultural and childrearing duties spend their afternoons chanting the *Tara Sutra* while spinning the **mani kang** (prayer wheel) located in the center of the village. (Tara is the feminine manifestation of Avalokiteshvara, the Bodhisattva of Compassion.) This is fundamentally a communal exercise, as it takes the participation and effort of all the women to turn the great wheel, which rings a bell at each revolution. These women gather here most days for chatting and socializing as well as offering collective prayers for the benefit of their families and community. In the next section we explore some of the ways ordinary people affirm and celebrate their religious lives and express their personal faith and commitment through devotional singing.

Fig. 10.5   Tibetan women spinning a giant prayer wheel

SAMA, QAWWALI, *AND ZIKR IN ISLAM (TURKEY, INDIA, AZERBAIJAN)*

Within Islam, traditions of sacred poetry and song have developed in such **vernacular** languages as Persian (Farsi), Turkish, Urdu, and modern Arabic, drawing on the poetic and musical forms of the cultures into which Islam spread. Often the term *sama* (literally "attentive listening") is used to describe occasions for experiencing and performing devotional poetry, music, and dance. Ethnomusicologist Jonathan Shannon writes, "Poetry is the supreme art of the Arab peoples with a rich history and vibrant contemporary presence [and] Music has been closely allied with poetry from pre-Islamic times to the present."[7] The devotional poetry of Mevlana Jalaluddin Rumi (1207–1273) has been sung to instrumental accompaniment since the 14th-century, and in his verses references to music form powerful metaphors for spiritual love, beauty, and ecstasy. For instance:

> Today, like every other day, we wake up empty and frightened.
> Don't open the door to the study and begin reading.
> Take down a musical instrument.
>
> Let the beauty we love be what we do.
> There are hundreds of ways to kneel and kiss the ground.

And:

> Don't worry about saving these songs!
> And if one of our instruments breaks,
> it doesn't matter.
>
> We have fallen into the place
> where everything is music.

The strumming and the flute notes
rise into the atmosphere,
and even if the whole world's harp
should burn up, there will still be
hidden instruments playing[8]

Fig. 10.6 Mevlana Jalaluddin Rumi
(1207–1273), from *Collection of Poems
of Molavi* (1980)

Rumi was born in Balkh in what is now Afghanistan, into a
Persian-speaking community. His family settled in Konya,
Turkey (see Map 5–1, p. 74), after traveling west to escape
the ravages of Genghis Khan's Mongol hordes. The son of
a great Islamic scholar and a great scholar himself, Rumi
came under the influence of a wandering dervish, or mystic,
named Shams of Tabriz. Following the death of his teacher
Shams and inspired by the intensity of their relationship, he
began composing one of the longest religious poems in the
history of literature, the *Masnavi,* consisting of 22,000 cou-
plets. These devotional verses, along with the life and teachings of their author, became the basis of the **Mevlevi** Sufi
order, founded in Konya by Rumi's followers after his death. The Mevlevi, known as the "Whirling
Dervishes," practice their whirling dance as a form of *zikr* ("remembrance of God"), discussed below.
(See also Lesson 11.)

Much of the criticism against music and dance in the Islamic world was directed against the
Sufis, members of Islamic mystical sects like the Mevlevi, who were drawn "from all levels of
society, but...above all [from] peasants, workers and poor people [who] sought to escape from
the dullness of everyday life in a heartfelt emotional religion."[9] In India and Pakistan emerged
a highly refined tradition of sung poetry known as *qawwali.* Ethnomusicologist Regula Qureshi
writes:

> All over South Asia there is *Qawwali,* for all over South Asia there are Muslims; where there
> are Muslims, there are Sufis; and where there are Sufis there is *Qawwali,*...the authentic
> spiritual song that transports the mystic toward union with God.... Through the act of
> listening—sama—the Sufi...in opening himself to the powerful message of *Qawwali,* hopes
> for a spiritual experience of intensity and immediacy that transcends his conscious striving.
> The music serves to kindle the flame of his mystical love, to intensify his longing for mystical
> union, and even to transport him to a state of ecstasy and to sustain him there to the limit of
> his spiritual capacity.[10]

Qawwali typically takes place at a Sufi shrine that houses the tomb of a saint, and is a sacred place
that Sufis believe to be charged with spiritual energy (*baraka*). The Nizamuddin Shrine in Old
Delhi, India, is the burial site of the saint it is named for, Nizamuddin Auliya (1238–1325), and
also of his great musician-disciple Amir Khusrow (1253–1325), the inventor of *qawwali.* At the
Nizamuddin shrine, Thursday night is *Qawwali* Night. Professional singers (*qawwals*) perform
sacred songs, creating an environment of religious enthusiasm and inspiring deep religious feelings
in those who congregate there. These singers are members of hereditary professional clans and are
employed by the shrine administration. A typical *qawwali* "party," as the performing ensemble is
called, can consist of between five and ten musicians, often members of the same family or *biradari*
("brotherhood"). A lead singer and several secondary soloists alternate lines of text, with the supporting members joining them on the choruses and providing rhythmic clapping. One or two of the
soloists play the harmonium, and another musician plays *dholak* or *tabla* drums. In this video, there
is a small party consisting of five musicians. The lead singer plays the harmonium; behind him and
to his left sits the *dholak* player. The atmosphere of the shrine is informal compared with that of the
mosque. Tourists brandish their video cameras, women sit right beside the musicians, and a small
boy gives money to the *qawwals,* as is the custom. The greatest modern exponent of *qawwali* was
Pakistani singer **Nusrat Fateh Ali Khan** (1949–1997), who became one of the most recognizable
superstars of World Music with concerts throughout Europe and North America, film scores, and
dozens of recordings to his credit.

Fig. 10.7   Nusrat Fateh Ali Khan performs on the British TV show "Big World Cafe," February 1989

Among Sufi orders throughout Central Asia and elsewhere, believers gather regularly to perform *zikr* (or *dhikr*, "remembrance of God"). This practice can take many forms, from silent reflection on the "ninety-nine names of Allah," to group ceremonies with a strongly rhythmic form of fervent vocalizing, aimed at inducing a state of divine intoxication. In this video, we see women from Azerbaijan performing a strenuous form of *zikr*, with the group repeating one of the Divine Names with rhythmic bodily movements while a solo voice intones a devotional poem. Throughout the Islamic world, the public face of men worshiping together in the mosque hides the more private practices of women, who carry out their religious obligations and express their religious devotions in separate spaces within the mosque, or in the home. Repetitive practices such as these, which often combine rhythm with melody, are found in many religious traditions, from the mantras of Hinduism and Buddhism to the saying of the Rosary of Roman Catholicism.

CHRISTIAN HYMNODY (USA, AUSTRALIA, UGANDA)

As noted in the Introduction to Unit 3, the early Church Fathers were cautiously permissive about the inclusion of music in worship services. Within the central rituals of Christianity—the Mass in particular—prayers and Biblical texts were sung, following the earlier practices of the Jewish synagogue. From the earliest days of Christianity, believers were encouraged to participate in the congregational singing of the Psalms, as described in the quote from St. Basil (see Unit 3 "Introduction"). In addition to these poetic texts from the Old Testament, non-Biblical religious poetry was continuously added to the **liturgy**. These songs of devotion and praise were known from earliest times as "hymns," from the Greek *hymnos* ("an ode to a god or hero").

Over the next two thousand years, music developed as a fundamental and indispensable component of Christian religious life. For many Christians, hymn singing became the ultimate outward expression of their faith. Both the Roman Catholic and Eastern Orthodox churches developed rich repertoires of music, some highly sophisticated and performed by specially trained choirs, some more simple for congregational participation. During the Reformation in the 16th-century, led by Martin Luther, John Calvin, and other reform-minded leaders, a number of Protestant sects split from the Catholic Church, and each developed its own ideas for employing music in religious rituals. Martin Luther was himself a musician, as was King Henry VIII of England, founders of the Lutheran and Anglican/Episcopal Churches respectively. The rich musical traditions of these denominations may be directly related to the strong musical preferences of their founders. In the sects that grew from John Calvin's more austere interpretation of Christian life and worship, such as the

Puritans who colonized New England, music practices were more closely controlled. Simple four-part hymns sung by the congregation without instrumental accompaniment became the only musical worship permitted. One of the most prolific composers of Protestant hymns was the 18th-century poet and composer Isaac Watts (1674–1748), whose more than 750 hymns spread throughout the world. His hymns became so popular that in 1872, the American preacher and abolitionist Henry Ward Beecher wrote,

> When believers analyze their religious emotions, it is common to trace them back to the early hymns of childhood as to the Bible itself. At least until very recently, most English-speaking Protestants who thought about heaven did so more in terms of Dr. Watts than of the Revelation of St. John.[11]

Today, there is enormous diversity in hymn singing during Christian worship. Styles range from the simple four-part harmony of Protestant hymnals from a hundred years ago and more, to "praise and worship" bands using electronic amplification and popular music forms. In this first example of four that we examine, a Mennonite Choir at a funeral sings an unaccompanied hymn, "I Will Meet You in the Morning," in vocal harmony. This style of singing is unaffected by contemporary popular trends, and has deep traditional roots extending back to the early 19th-century. The second example is the most famous anthem by the father of the modern gospel tradition, Thomas A. Dorsey (1899–1993), "Precious Lord, Take My Hand." Dorsey typifies one of the leading trends in Christian worship: the setting of devotional texts to music drawn from popular idioms. Dorsey himself had a career as a leading blues pianist in the 1920s, playing behind the great singer Ma Rainey (1886–1939). He was also a composer and arranger, with more than four hundred blues and jazz songs to his credit. His father had been a minister and Dorsey began a music ministry in Chicago in the 1930s while still working in blues clubs and touring under the name "Georgia Tom." However, in 1932, while he was playing at a revival prayer meeting, he received word that his wife Nettie had died in childbirth. The child died two days later. Stricken with grief and inconsolable, he tried to pray with some friends and to find answers for the tragedy that had befallen him. He said aloud "Lord?" and his friend said, "'No! That's not His name! Say, 'Precious Lord.' And ladies and gentlemen, believe it or not, I started singing right then and there...."[12] The effect of Thomas A. Dorsey's musical revolution, combining simple heartfelt words of faith with the harmonies and rhythms of secular blues and jazz, was one of the most significant in the history of Protestant church music and has had a global influence.

A third example of modern **hymnody** is this evangelical praise and worship song, "Here in My Life," by Australian pastor and singer-songwriter Darlene Zschech. The song closely resembles contemporary popular genres in terms of its musical and performance style, with electronic instruments, drums, light show, and amplified voices. The upbeat music serves to attract younger worshipers and to elicit strong emotions of commitment and self-surrender. Her songs have been sung by millions of Evangelical and Pentecostal Christians worldwide. From Seoul to São Paulo, praise and worship hymn singing has had an enormous influence on forms of Christian worship. In Uganda, young urban Christians, often dislocated from traditional home villages and ways of life, find solidarity in large, modern mega churches. In this typical Sunday morning service at Kampala's Watoto Church, we see the globalizing impact of missionary work in the digital age.

The Roman Catholic Church has remained a vital force in the world despite the schisms of the Reformation that gave rise to the many Protestant denominations. Catholic countries Spain, Portugal, and France led the exploration and conquest of much of Latin America and large parts of Africa and Asia. Missionaries followed in the wake of these military conquests imposing alien forms of music and worship on the new converts. Governing authorities in Rome mandated uniformity of language (Latin) and liturgical music based on Gregorian chant. In Africa, generations-old traditions of drumming and dancing that had provided and affirmed links between the living and the worlds of ancestors and spirits were suppressed as rooted in superstition. The Second Vatican Council (1962–1965) was an attempt to more fully integrate church practices with the modern world, and to provide opportunities for greater participation by worshipers in church rituals. One modification was the change from Latin to vernacular languages in the celebration of the Mass. Another was to permit local and more contemporary musical forms in church worship. These changes in the rituals of the colonizers came about at the same time that all over Africa new countries were forming out of the breakup of

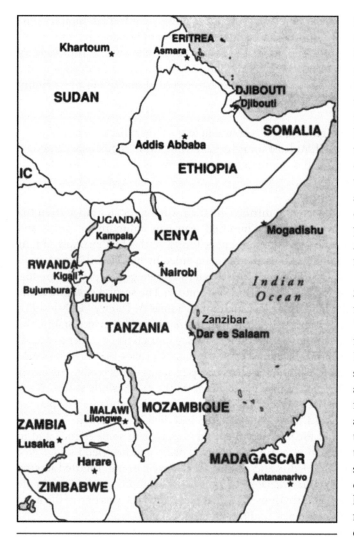

Map 10-1   **East Africa showing Uganda, Ethiopia, and Zanzibar**

Source: *Garland Encyclopedia of World Music*, Volume 1: Africa

the British, French, and Portuguese colonial empires. With independence from colonial rule came a new sense of African identity and assertiveness. For many African Catholics, retaining allegiance to the Church, with its message of love, salvation, and hope for the poor and oppressed, while rejecting the degrading effects of the colonizing powers in whose wake Christianity arrived, created a delicate balancing act. How could one be both devoutly Catholic *and* proudly African? In Uganda, East Africa, resolving this tension produced novel forms of musical worship.

Ethnomusicologist Nicholas Sempijja describes this religious-musical situation as an example of "glocalization,"[13] which we discussed in Lesson 9 with reference to hip-hop. In the two videos linked below, we see secondary school choir students at a Catholic boarding school preparing to compete with other schools in an annual song and dance competition. Two categories in the competition feature unaccompanied hymns sung in four-part harmony. The first category requires two hymns in English, Uganda's official (former colonial) language; the second requires one hymn in the local African language, Luganda. When the festivals were first instituted in the 1970s, songs by such Western composers as Schubert and Mozart were featured.

But by the early 2000s all hymns, including those in Western-style, were written by African composers. In this first video, members of the choir of Archbishop Kiwanuka Secondary School rehearse their
 English language hymn "**I Believe**," written by Reverend Father James Kabuye. In the second, the students rehearse a hymn in the Luganda language, *"Tutende Ddunda"* ("Let Us Praise the Lord").

The third and final category in the competition combines singing, dancing, and dramatic narrative in traditional Luganda style. The stories behind these dramas are Biblical—the fall of the Tower of Babel, or Christ entering Jerusalem on Palm Sunday, for example. But here, native styles of singing and traditional instruments—xylophone, harp, fiddle, panpipes and drums—accompany the exuberant performances. In this video, students at Mbuye Farm and Vocational High School rehearse their traditional offering, showing Christ entering Jerusalem, riding on a donkey. The song, *"Ngenda Yeru-*
 zalemu" ("I am heading to Jerusalem"), is in a style that replicates East African forms of traditional expression, and is also composed by Rev. Fr. James Kabuye.

In this final video taken at the festival itself, we see brief excerpts from the **traditional entries of four schools** performing before the judges and audience members. Each performance begins after a judge rings a bell. From then on, every aspect of the performance is judged: the deportment of the students, the competence of the actors, the enthusiasm of the instrumentalists, the quality of the choreography, and the skill of the dancers. In this Uganda case study, we see music serving as an arena for negotiating issues of cultural identity and religious affiliation and commitment resulting in creative compromises between the local and the global. The traditional forms of ritual expression—music and dance—that had been suppressed with the introduction of Christianity have now become vehicles through which young people negotiate an identity that is both devoutly Catholic and proudly African.

CONCLUSION

In this lesson, we have examined the role music plays as the setting for sacred words—the foundational verses and texts of four world religions: Hinduism, Buddhism, Islam, and Christianity. The chant melodies to which these ancient verses were set are among the oldest surviving musical expressions in the world. They have been performed publicly, in ritual contexts, for generations, and participating in these rituals unites communities in celebration of the mysterious and miraculous origins of their faith. The collective singing of hymns in more contemporary styles allows for overt expressions of joy, enthusiasm, and group solidarity in the here and now. Group singing may also inspire the "**temporary physiological synchrony**" among humans that primatologist Bruce Richman found among the gelada baboons (Lesson 4).

Certainly, we see the synchronized group expression of profound emotion in Darlene Zschech's evangelical ministry, the Azeri women performing *zikr,* and at the Ugandan school festival. In the next lesson, we examine sacred contexts in which music seems to go beyond words...music expressing what words cannot.

KEY CONCEPTS

Nad Brahman	Plainchant	*Zikr*
Sacred chant	Buddhist chant	Christian hymnody
Vocal *vs* instrumental	Islamic cantillation	Second Vatican Council
sacred music	Devotional singing	Missionary
Chant and cantillation	*Sama*	Vernacular languages
Vedic chant	*Qawwali*	

(Q) THINKING ABOUT MUSIC QUESTIONS

1. Musicologist Amnon Shiloah describes the "interminable debate" surrounding music in religious contexts. What are the terms of the debate? Why might music support a religious life, and why might it detract from it? Why was St. Augustine tormented by this question?

2. Why are the *adhan* and Qur'anic recitation (*tajweed* and *tarteel*) not considered "music" even though they *sound* like music, and fit our definition?

3. How did the Second Vatican Council affect Roman Catholic church music in Uganda? Consider how music derived from traditional African rituals came to be used in Christian worship. Are there parallels between this and the phenomenon of "Christian rock"? Incorporate in your response the concept of "re-contextualization"—taking something originally created for one purpose and putting it to a new use in another context.

4. Ethnomusicologist Ter Ellingson wrote: "[Music] enhances, intensifies, and...transforms almost any experience into something felt not only as different but also as somehow better.... When the energies of music and religion are focused on the same object...toward a common meaning and goal, intensification reaches a peak greater...than either might achieve by itself." Do you agree? Think of an example from your own experience, or from the lesson, and explain how it relates to Ellingson's view.

NOTES

1   Ter Ellingson, "Music and Religion," *The Encyclopedia of Religion* (New York: Collier Macmillan, 1987), 166.

2   Pierro Weiss and Richard Taruskin, *Music in the Western World: A History in Documents* (New York: Schirmer, 1984), 15.

3   Several of the ideas and examples in this Introduction come from Ter Ellingson's article "Music and Religion," in *The Encyclopedia of Religion* (New York: Collier Macmillan, 1987).

4   Charles Capwell, "The Music of India," in Bruno Nettl et al., ed., *Excursions in World Music,* 6th ed. (Upper Saddle River, NJ: Pearson Prentice Hall, 2012), 37.

5   St. Basil, *Exegetic Homilies,* trans. S. Agnes Clare Way, cited in Weiss and Taruskin, *Music in the Western World,* 26.

6   Huston Smith, *Requiem for a Faith: Tibetan Buddhism.* Hartley Film Foundation. VHS video, 1979.

7   Jonathan Shannon, *Among the Jasmine Trees: Music and Modernity in Contemporary Syria* (Middletown, CT: Wesleyan University Press, 2009), xviii.

8   Coleman Barks, *The Essential Rumi* (San Francisco: HarperOne, 1995), 34–36.

9   Amnon Shiloah, *Music in the World of Islam,* 42.

10 Regula Qureshi, *Sufi Music of India and Pakistan: Sound, Context and Meaning in Qawwali* (Cambridge: Cambridge University Press, 1986), 1.

11 Esther Rothenbusch Crookshank, "'We're Marching to Zion': Isaac Watts in Early America," in *Wonderful Words of Life: Hymns in American Protestant History and Theology* (Grand Rapids, MI: Wm. B. Eerdmans Publishing Co. 2004), 17.

12 *Say Amen, Somebody.* DVD re-release 1982. Rykodisc, Inc.

13 Nicholas Ssempijja, "Glocalizing Catholicism through Musical Performance: Kampala Archdiocese Post-Secondary Schools Music Festivals" (PhD diss., University of Bergen, 2012).

Lesson 11
Sacred Embodiment and Sacred Enactment

In the previous lesson, we described relationships between sacred music and the words that the music conveys. We noted that in many traditions, music was seen as a suitable envelope or delivery system for conveying sacred texts, verbal doctrines, and avowals of faith. Yet there was also anxiety in some traditions that music might obscure the words, or redirect the attention of the listener away from the texts toward the sensual and aesthetic beauty of music. There are occasions in which the truths proclaimed by religious systems are experienced *within* the body and are enacted *through* the body of the believer. Indeed, for some believers the truths experienced within the body transcend verbal meanings and are believed to *validate* the meanings that the words proclaim. At the United House of Prayer for All People, an evangelical Christian sect founded in 1919 by a charismatic preacher known as "Daddy" Grace (Marcelino Manuel da Graça, 1884–1960), music plays a central role in ecstatic Sunday morning worship services. We see in this video how instrumental music and the dance it inspires can elevate a ritual *beyond* the power of words. Through trombone shout bands, the hallmark of this sect, the members of the congregation collectively "Praise the Lord," as Psalm 150 directs. In this lesson we examine ways in which music acts as a vehicle for accessing and physically experiencing the sacred.

MUSIC AND TRANCE

In popular music terminology, "trance" refers to a style of electronic dance music that dates from the 1990s, but in a religious context the term is used to describe various altered states of consciousness. The outward manifestations of trance encompass a broad range of physical responses, from a hypnotic meditative state and involuntary body movement to extraordinary physical activity and uncontrollable convulsions. While Western medical science has inadequate explanations of this widespread phenomenon, it may be described by various symptoms observable in entranced individuals that include hyperventilation, involuntary movement or loss of control of limbs, the capacity for superhuman feats of endurance, fainting, and uncontrolled emotions. Those who experience these physical phenomena attribute them to the embodiment of sacred entities or energies. The term "spirit possession" refers to the belief that one's body has been temporarily accessed by a divine or demonic spirit entity. A shaman—a term of Central Asian origin—refers to a sacred practitioner or healer who self-induces such a trance state. Many cultures have developed practices and conditions conducive to trance in the context of ceremonial events. Anthropologist David Roche describes a celebration at a Hindu temple as follows:

> The sensory overload common to celebrations in the typical urban Hindu temple [includes] the din of brass bells and large drums, the reflected flashes from oil lamps and sputtering fluorescent lights, the overpowering clouds of incense smoke, the crush of devotees to view the central icon at the auspicious moment, the taste of blessed offerings, and the wafting of flower garlands. When the soundscape also involves ritually encoded music...it can represent both a contributing factor to and evocative symbol of transcendence.... Ritual music...[is] a widespread means by which South Asians access or initiate deep levels of spiritual communication...and trance remains an enduring sign of successful connection to a macrocosmic reality.[1]

Trance and spirit possession phenomena are widely distributed throughout the world. From the South Korean *manshin*, female shamans who transmit messages from the dead and demonstrate the depth of their trance by dancing on knife blades, to the priestesses of Brazilian Candomblé, who become possessed by the gods and goddesses of their West African ancestors, ritual participants consider spirit possession to be proof of successful access to the spirit world. Although such experiences are less common in Western Jewish and Christian practices, some Pentecostal and charismatic congregations promote occasions in which congregants "speak in tongues," "catch the spirit," or otherwise achieve transcendence and ecstasy. Furthermore, music plays an indispensable role in inducing and sustaining trance in the possessed and in creating an atmosphere of heightened emotion among the ritual participants. Indeed, in some traditions, music is itself the sonic bridge that connects the human world with unseen realms.

NADUN (CHINA)

A dramatic example of spirit possession may be found among the mountain villagers in a remote region of north central China. The majority Han ethnic group, which comprises ninety percent of China's population, shares its territory with fifty-five other ethnic groups. One of these, the Tu ethnic minority, has a population of around 250,000, occupying mountainous territory known as the Sanchuan region in northeast Qinghai Province, on the northern bank of the Yellow River. Although most members of this ethnic group, who call themselves Monguor, are nominally Buddhist, they also practice devotional rituals dedicated to local deities. These deities are believed to reside in their midst rather than in distant heavenly realms. Here, as in many parts of rural China, people rely on these local deities for protection. In Minhe County on the Qinghai-Gansu border (see Map 7–3, p.103), a sub-group of Monguor has a distinct language and customs, and calls its branch of the ethnic group Mangghuer. Fifteen Mangghuer farming villages share the protection of the **local deity**, Erlang Ye. While accounts differ among villagers as to who Erlang Ye was, there is agreement that in life he was a

Fig. 11.1 **The local deity Erlang Ye housed in a portable shrine, Mangghuer village, Qinghai province, People's Republic of China**

high government official who performed deeds that were beneficial to the people of the region. After his death, his benevolent influence continues to affect the lives of the local citizens.

Among the Mangghuer, *Nadun* is a two-month long festival dedicated to Erlang Ye that coincides with the harvest season. Like religious festivals elsewhere in rural China, *Nadun* is "performed to thank deities for their protection and to ensure a good harvest, and to avoid incurring the deities' wrath."[2] For most of the year, the image of the deity resides in his main temple in a central village. During the harvest season, the image is placed in a portable shrine (palanquin) that men carry from one village to the next in a cycle of visitations over the two-month period. In each village there is a small temple that houses the visiting deity during a two-day visit. On the second day a ritual is held, after which the deity moves on to the next village. In the remote villages of the Mangghuer, *Nadun* is the most elaborate annual ritual, and each village begins planning for the following year's event the day after the ritual ends.

Australian anthropologist Gerald Roche, on whose research this case study is based, writes: "The noun *nadun* is derived from the verb *nadu*, meaning to play, joke, or to perform or dance, and the term adequately summarizes the basic content of *nadun*: a series of danced performances."[3] The festival has four stages: the image of the deity is carried from the neighboring village and installed in the temple; the deity is entertained with dances and dramatic displays; he makes his presence known through possession; and is finally bidden farewell as his image is carried to the next village. Throughout the entertainment portion of *Nadun*, drums, gongs, and singing are used to accompany a military-style dance and the masked dance dramas that follow. When these entertainments are over, villagers invite the deity to reveal himself by possessing the body of one of the farmers who temporarily becomes a vessel for the god. At the moment of possession, this medium, known as *huala* or *fala*, pierces his cheek with a metal skewer (*qianzi*) to indicate success and demonstrate the god's power. This is the dramatic climax of the event, and if the village *huala* does not attain a state of possession, the participants consider the event a failure.

Fig. 11.2 Men playing gongs and drums entertain the visiting deity (L), and Mangghuer village *huala* dancing with his cheek pierced, Qinghai Province, People's Republic of China (R)

In the body of the entranced *huala,* the deity dances, accepts paper-streamer offerings that the villagers hang on poles, and delivers prophecies for the coming year. During the entire period of entrancement, except while the *huala* is prophesying, the sonic environment is saturated by the deafening sound of gongs and firecrackers. The crashing of the gongs continues as the deity's palanquin is removed from the temple and the deity is escorted out of town and across the valley to the next village. Here the gongs take on a different role—not so much musical instruments as noisemakers, creating a cacophony similar to that produced by firecrackers, which also add to the general commotion. Now watch this video of a *Nadun* celebration in October 2010.

Gerald Roche writes:

> The number of *huala* is decreasing. *Huala* were once the center of religious life in Sanchuan. But now most *huala* are old…and few new *huala* are appearing. When the last *huala* dies, the gods will have left Sanchuan forever. Reflecting on the fate of the *huala* in Sanchuan, one *huala* said: "There won't be any *huala* in the future. Nobody replaces old *huala* when they die. Now many villages don't have a *huala.* Young people don't believe in the gods. So the gods no longer incarnate here."[4]

When the gods no longer visit, what happens to all the songs, dances, dramas, and traditions by which they were entertained? And what will hold together the communities that once spent a year planning for the god's annual visit? The future of the *huala* tradition is uncertain, but for now, the *Nadun* festival continues as a noisy, joyous celebration of the harvest and of the spirits who protect the communities under their watchful care.

BIRA *(ZIMBABWE)*

Among the Shona people of Zimbabwe in southeast Africa, a ritual called **bira** is performed to unite communities with their ancestors, who are believed to mediate between the living and divine sources of power and protection. (See Map 9–2, p. 137.) "We don't go straight to god," explains Zimbabwean musician Thomas Mapfumo. "We have to go through our ancestors, because they are the ones who died long time ago and are the nearest to god. We are not near to god. We are the living ones."[5] In the *bira,* music serves to call the ancestor spirits to possess a medium who is the central figure of the ritual. *Mbira* (thumb piano) and *hosho* (rattle) players play music throughout the night to attract the desired ancestor spirit to the religious gathering made up of family and community members. A *bira* is held at times of illness, drought, or social disharmony, when individuals or whole communities feel vulnerable or under some threat. The ritual provides "a means for villagers to impose the moral values of the society on individuals who have strayed too far from the community's accepted mores," and also instills "a feeling of solidarity [among] the community as villagers ritually unite with their ancestors."[6] The evening ceremony begins with the sharing of ritual beer and progresses to singing, dancing, and handclapping as the musicians perform with ever-greater exuberance. When possession occurs at the climax of the ritual, the medium calls for the musicians to stop playing and then initiates communication between the spirit world and the *bira* participants to discern the cause of illness or misfortune, as explained by ethnomusicologist Paul Berliner:

> When possession does take place at the *bira,* it is often sudden and startling to the uninitiated. The prospective host may be sitting quietly with a glazed look in the eyes; without warning he or she is shaken as if by an epileptic fit, filling the *bira* with cries of anguish. Different spirit mediums have different styles of evidencing their possession by spirits. One medium I have observed shot from his seat with a loud exclamation and the dancers jumped out of his way as his body hit the ground…As he tossed and turned, participants continued to dance around him, careful to stay out of the way of his kicking feet. After fifteen minutes he ceased his cries and his body quieted. Eventually he rose and left the house. He returned shortly after, wearing black cloth in place of his European clothes, and from that point on was the spirit who possessed him…Once the spirit seizes his or her host, the musical proceedings of the *bira* revolve around the medium.[7]

At this point in the ceremony, the musicians must play with greatest intensity so that the spirit doesn't leave the host before speaking words of guidance to the community through the host's mouth.

This video tells the story of **three mbira musicians** in Chaonza village, Zimbabwe, who play their *mbiras* near the graves of their ancestors to honor "their grandfathers or grandmothers who passed away long back, so that they can keep us and they can look after us."[8] It is the music of the *mbiras* that communicates directly with the ancestors and sustains their interest and thus their care for the living. In the *bira* ceremony, it is this music that calls them down and into the medium. The *Nadun* and *bira* trance rituals represent phenomena—shamanism and spirit possession—that demonstrate for a community the reality and accessibility of divine powers. In both cases, music serves important ritual functions: in structuring the events, communicating between worlds, and sustaining a heightened sense, within the community, of anticipation before possession and catharsis afterwards. Music also has the power to inspire and sustain in ordinary people powerful emotional states that are different from those of daily existence. Many people, inspired by music, attain a deep response to the extraordinary nature of the divine in relationship to which ordinary existence becomes endurable (*svikiro*), meaningful, and hopeful. These experiences serve to strengthen the convictions of the faithful.

SACRED DANCE

Perhaps for as long as humans have sought to connect and communicate with sacred beings, people have used movement and dance as a form of worship and to achieve spiritual experiences. In early Judeo-Christian tradition, believers were commanded to praise the Lord with instruments, voices, and dance ("Praise him with the timbrel and dance," Psalm 150); and in various Christian churches today, worship services include liturgical and praise dance. Native Americans have danced their sacred stories and beliefs in numerous and diverse ceremonies, as in the Hopi Corn Dance in Arizona invoking rain, now often performed for tourists. In Tibetan Buddhist monasteries, monks often stage dance performances in courtyards for the local lay people. These performances convey moral teachings and channel spiritual energies. Attending them provides religious merit both for the dancers and the spectators. In this video taken at the Dutsi Til monastery, **Tibetan Buddhist monks of the Karma Kagyu** ("Black Hat") school portray the battle between the *dharma* (Buddha's teachings) and the demon of selfishness, symbolized by a small black clay effigy. Afro-Brazilian and Afro-Caribbean religious practitioners perform sacred dances as a form of worship and preparation for spirit possession. In the **Winti religion of Surinamese Creoles**, drummers play specific rhythms in ceremonies that invoke the West African deities of their ancestors. In this video, women circle the ritual ground in the back courtyard of a Winti leader's home, singing songs that evoke the goddess Legba who guards doorways. One dancer becomes possessed by the goddess, and in trance begins to ritually sweep the courtyard with a broom, Legba's sacred symbol.

Sufis employ ritual movements like the rhythmic head and body motions of the Azeri women performing *zikr* as seen in Lesson 10. In Turkey, Sufi dervishes of the Mevlevi Order, founded by followers of Jalaluddin Rumi in the late 13th century, perform a whirling dance during their sacred *sema* ceremony. The **Mevlevi dervishes** remove their black cloaks, symbolically leaving behind their attachment to this world, and seek direct communion with God by turning with arms extended. The word "dervish" literally means "doorway," and for the Mevlevi, the *sema* is "the doorway into the spiritual world" where "the soul is freed from earthly ties and can commune joyfully with the divine."[9] Musicians accompany the whirling dance on *qanun* (plucked zither), *ud* (plucked lute), *rebab* (fiddle), *ney* (flute), *bendir* (frame drum), and *kudum* (small kettledrums), and the ceremony ends with chanting from the Qur'an. When the Ottoman Empire broke apart following its defeat at the end of the First World War, Kemal Ataturk became the first president of the modern, secular Republic of Turkey. Among his modernization reforms was the banning of the *sema* in 1925. Members of the Mevlevi Order continued the practice in private until, in 1955, it was given official recognition as a "cultural" rather than a religious practice. Since that time the Mevlevi *sema* has been accepted as an important expression of Turkish identity. This short video clip shows a dervish whirling to the accompaniment of a single *qanun* and *bendir* at an **outdoor restaurant** in Istanbul, as families and tourists wait for food service to begin in order to break the sunup-to-sundown fast of Ramadan.

Fig. 11.3 Mevlevi dervishes dance during the *sema* in Istanbul, 2007

Sacred dance may be a form of communal religious worship, as in the examples above, or individual or private devotion; and furthermore may serve as both a sacred and a secular form of artistic expression. In the solo classical *bharatanatyam* dance style of South India, for example, the dancer interprets through elaborate hand gestures religious narratives concerning the deeds of Hindu gods and heroes. Often the theme is the all-consuming love of a woman for the god-man Krishna, symbolic of the yearning of the individual for union with the divine. The art form is rooted in the sacred temple dancing of women, known as **devadasis,** employed by Hindu temples to worship and serve the residing deities. Today, *bharatanatyam* is one of the primary Indian classical dance forms learned by students in India and elsewhere throughout the South Asian diaspora. Like music, dance is controversial in some sacred contexts: embraced by those who view it as a physical manifestation of divine presence and an emotionally powerful form of expression and communication, yet disapproved of by those who find dancing worldly or provocative.

CÔTE D'IVOIRE MASKED DANCE (WEST AFRICA)

Côte d'Ivoire (Ivory Coast) "is the origin of several of the most important and interesting masking traditions in Africa," writes dance scholar Juliana Azoubel.[10] (See Map 6–2, p. 88.) While these masks are prized as art objects by collectors in the West, they serve important ritual functions within their native African communities. Azoubel continues, "Through their embodiment in dance...masks are the way many Ivorians communicate with supernatural forces and bring power to the community."[11] Masked dancers are overtaken by the deities and ancestors that the masks depict. In the dance, parallel worlds become visible and manifest to audience members.

During intense seven-day initiation rites for adolescent boys of the Guro communities in the West-Central region, masked male elders embody powerful beings that provide instruction in the secrets of adult social membership. Some masks are considered dangerous and powerful, and girls and women are forbidden from viewing them. The dancers are usually members of "mask families" that pass down the ritual secrets from generation to generation, although a child from a non-masked family may be "chosen by the ancestors to become a mask." During the initiation rites, the spirit of the mask, Djoanigbe, "is the teacher for the initiates, their spirit guide; and the primary source of enlightenment in their young lives."

Some masks have a more social, entertainment function, as does the mask Zaouli, whose dance is characterized by "rapid-fire movement of the feet." The Zaouli dancer is always male, although the spirit is female. "The cross-gender mask performs on many different occasions to amuse people: during holidays, for entertainment of visitors to the community, to collect food from the community members during the initiation process, and also in some funeral ceremonies."[12] As you can hear in this video clip of Zaouli masked dancing, the music that accompanies and drives the dance is melodically simple and repetitive; the melody consists of only a few notes played on a pair of reed pipes. The drummers' repeating patterns of interlocking phrases complement the complex footwork made audible by the bells on the dancer's feet.

Juliana Azoubel concludes:

11-9

Fig. 11.4 **Zaouli mask from Guro Village, central Côte d'Ivoire**

> More than figures used to decorate walls, masks embodied by a performer can express emotions, feelings, and ideas that serve to orient society; and often use the hand of the spirit to control, discipline, and to order lives. This process is facilitated by the fact that the audience, composed of fellow villagers, has been brought up in this tradition and believes in its history and its power. The mask communicates advice, order, and feelings in a dynamic language of motions and real-life presence.... As masked dance paves the way for spiritual guides to protect society, it is also a critical strategy to preserve, practice, and project cultural meaning into the future.[13]

BON ODORI *(JAPAN)*

In Japan, the major Buddhist festival of **Obon** (or simply *Bon*) is usually held in mid-August and commemorates ancestor spirits that are believed to return to earth at this time. Over several days, many Japanese return to their family home towns to honor the departed spirits of their ancestors by visiting and cleaning graves, making special food offerings in temples and at home altars, and performing sacred dances (*bon odori*). The observance is believed to have developed from a Buddhist scripture about a monk named Mokuren. While meditating, Mokuren visualized his deceased mother starving in the Hell of Hungry Ghosts. She was unable to eat, for whenever she touched food it caught on fire. The monk discovered that his mother was suffering because of her selfish past deeds, and he prayed to the Supreme Buddha to ask how he could help. The Shakyamuni Buddha told him he should:

> make offerings of food from land and sea to his fellow monks at the end of their 90-day retreat which ended in mid-July. Upon following Shakyamuni's instructions, Mokuren danced for joy when his mother and seven generations of his ancestors were freed from their suffering.[14]

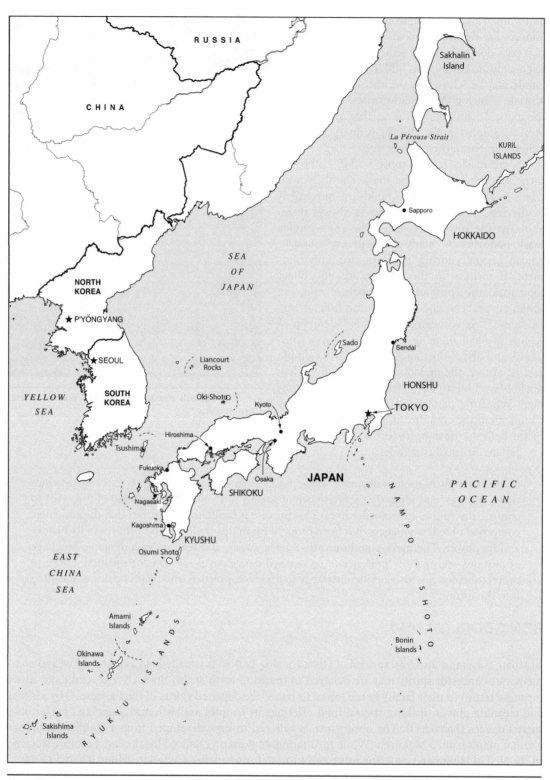

Map 11-1   Japan

Source: *Garland Encyclopedia of World Music* Volume 7: East Asia: China, Japan, and Korea

The *Obon* festival has been held annually in Japan since the mid-7th century. During the *Obon* festival, people hang lanterns outside their homes and temples to welcome the spirits of their ancestors. In temple courtyards and elsewhere, a raised wooden platform (*yagura*) is built specially for the festival, and at evening time musicians and singers perform traditional *Obon* music on the platform while community members and visitors dance around it. *Obon* dances and music vary from one region to another. In some locations, dance troupes perform choreographed dances on or around the *yagura*; in others, dances take place in street parades. Some dances include the use of fans or colorful towels, and others, the playing of small wooden clappers. Throughout Japan, *taiko* drumming frequently accompanies *bon odori*, as seen in video 11–10. The songs sung for *Obon* may have spiritual lyrics, may be local folk songs, or may even be modern popular songs. People attend the celebrations and join in the dancing to express gratitude toward their ancestors. People mark the end of the festival by floating lanterns on lakes and rivers in order to guide the spirits back to their own world.

A music and dance tradition performed during the *Obon* celebrations in Kyoto is the **Rokusai Nembutsu Odori**. *Rokusai* ritual dance is believed to date back to the 10th century when a Buddhist monk and teacher, Kuya Shonin, traveled through the streets of Kyoto (then the capital of Japan) with a bell hung around his neck, spreading the faith by dancing, beating a drum, and chanting the name of the Buddha. In recent times, *Rokusai* groups have formed to preserve and develop this traditional Kyoto performing art. Troupes consist of up to thirty or more musicians and dancers,

Fig. 11.5 *Yagura* platform for *Obon* festival at Tsukiji Hongwanji Temple, Tokyo

Fig. 11.6 *Chudoji Rokusai* group performing at Kiyomizu temple, Kyoto, 2009: the Lion and Spider dance (L), and young members take turns beating four drums (R)

ranging in age from young to old. They play a variety of drums, gongs, bells, and flutes, and perform dances at temples and shrines to enact sacred myths and secular tales in a popular regional folk style.

A typical performance lasting sixty to ninety minutes begins and ends with the chanting of Buddhist prayers (*nembutsu*) and includes a sequence of five or more music and dance pieces. In *yotsu daiko* (four drums), players, starting with the youngest, take turns performing on four drums accompanied by flutes and gongs. A faster drumming piece concludes with the ritual spinning of a *bo* (pole), to ward off evil. Young children participate in dances such as the Circle Monkey Dance (*saru mawashi*), in which the young "monkeys" each play their own small drum as they dance around an adult playing a large drum. The culmination of a *Rokusai Nembutsu* performance is typically the acrobatic Lion and Spider dance (*shishi mai* and *tsuchi gumo*). This enacts a battle between the easy-going, carefree lion, symbolizing Righteousness, and the evil spider that spins numerous webs around his prey. Inevitably the lion, played by two dancers, celebrates victory over the spider. In Japan as elsewhere, the division between the sacred and the secular is growing increasingly blurred, and the continuity of sacred and ritualistic expressive forms frequently relies on the creative development of new, popular styles that communicate more directly and more meaningfully with today's audiences and congregations.

SACRED DRAMA

Sacred dramas are ritual performances of ancient myths or religious stories that frequently include music and dance. They often take place within or outside churches and temples, and are presented in front of an audience or congregation. In medieval Europe, "mystery plays" enacted episodes from the Bible or from the lives of saints or church leaders. These **liturgical dramas** were first created and performed by monks and priests inside church sanctuaries, and were later performed by amateur actors in village squares or on traveling carts. They served to entertain, educate, and inspire their audiences. The music for several of these has survived in Gregorian chant notation.

Unlike the realistic theater of the West, sacred dramas in India, Indonesia, and Sub-Saharan Africa frequently fuse dramatic performance with ritual ceremony. The texts are often minimal or even non-existent, placing central importance on spectacle: gestures, dance movements, shouts and other vocalizations, music, acrobatics, lighting, and sound effects, etc. Sacred dramas are not supposed to reveal ordinary reality. Rather, they reveal the true Reality of the belief system, which is invisible in everyday life. Sacred dramas represent for their audiences the deep past or the beginning times of mythical or celestial realms. Performances are believed to be occasions for visitations by supernatural beings and ancestors, and the suspension of everyday modes of behavior and feeling. There is the expectation of magic, trance, and close encounters with sacred reality. Actors play the roles of gods, goddesses, and archetypal characters. In some dramatic traditions, actors wear decorated masks that depict the nature of the sacred beings they are portraying, and in some cases the masks themselves are believed to embody the power of the deities. Sacred drama is symbolic on many levels, and it can be a deeply transformational process for both actors and audiences.

CALONARANG *(BALI, INDONESIA)*

The island of Bali is predominantly Hindu in contrast to the largely Muslim populations of most other Indonesian islands.

On Bali, Hindu temple ceremonies take place on a daily basis, and frequently include masked dance drama. Such events

Map 11-2   Island of Bali, to the east of Java

Source: *Garland Encyclopedia of World Music*, Volume 4: Southeast Asia

function as religious ritual and as entertainment for their audiences, and are integral to people's daily lives. One such masked dance drama is the *calonarang* or "*Barong* dance." Its current version, presented daily for tourists, is said to have been created in the late 19th century, but the association of the mythological creature *Barong* with healing and exorcism dates back many centuries. On sacred occasions, local drama troupes still perform longer, more ceremonial versions in temple courtyards and other sacred locations. The two principal characters in the drama are the *Barong* and *Rangda*, who represent the forces of good and evil respectively. The *Barong* is a large, shaggy, four-legged creature with the head of a lion or other animal. His striking face has bulging eyes, fangs, and a beard of human hair. *Rangda* is a witch-like woman (played by a man) also with bulging eyes and fangs, a long tongue, long spiky hair, pendulous breasts, and long tubes representing her victims' intestines attached to her costume.

Fig. 11.7   Characters in the Balinese *calonarang* dance drama: the *Barong* (L), and *Rangda* (R)

The *calonarang* performance dramatizes the Balinese worldview of powerful and opposing forces in the universe. It takes place outdoors in an open stage area with a *gamelan* percussion ensemble seated to one side. The demonic character of *Rangda* can inflict great harm, and is simultaneously feared and respected. The *Barong* is believed to have magical and healing powers, and his actions help maintain harmonious balance in the world of human beings. The actions centers around the confrontation, direct or indirect, between these two supernatural antagonists. In this *calonarang* performance at Camphuan Temple in Ubud, we meet *Rangda* and the *Barong* at the outset. During the ritual, the *gamelan* plays continuously, adding an otherworldly aura to the supernatural proceedings. Followers of the *Barong* appear and attack *Rangda* with their knives. *Rangda* places a spell on the attendants, causing them to turn their daggers on themselves. At the drama's end, *Rangda* is temporarily held in check by the power of the *Barong* though she is free to cause further damage and destruction in the future.

For the Balinese, masks both possess and are visible representations of extreme spiritual and magical power. Those who carve them, from wood growing in a spiritually powerful place (such as a temple or cemetery), must perform purification rituals to ensure protection from supernatural forces. The dancers who wear these sacred objects must likewise be spiritually pure before putting on their masks and their costumes, which are extensions of the masks. Unmasked dancers in the drama paint white spots on themselves to protect them from possible attack by harmful spiritual forces.

In extended, ceremonial *calonarang* performances, the *Rangda* dancer invariably goes into trance, while the two *Barong* dancers are less likely to become entranced because of the concentration needed to manipulate the mask and costume. Occasionally, however, *Barong* dancers do fall into trance. Trance-inducing techniques such as inhaling incense, making ritual offerings, and meditating are typically carried out as the *calonarang* dancer prepares for the performance. During the performance audience members may also go into trance, overcome with emotion. Entranced performers believe the force that drives them resides in the mask, and when they come out of trance, revived with holy water, the spiritual forces remain in the mask. This entrancement and the capacity to fall into trance are viewed positively by the Balinese, and thus provide the society with a socially acceptable outlet for extreme behavior. The *calonarang* sacred drama thus brings together the rich artistic traditions of this small Indonesian island—colorful dramatic presentation, vividly costumed dancers, exquisitely carved masks, experienced *gamelan* musicians—with the enactment of religious and mythological beliefs. The *calonarang* is simultaneously an expression of Balinese identity, a continuation of cultural tradition, a performance of sacred ritual and ceremony, and a primary tourist attraction.

Fig. 11.8   Unmasked dancer with protective white spot (L), and Balinese *gamelan* percussion ensemble (R)

KATHAKALI (INDIA)

The subcontinent of India has diverse traditions of dance drama that involve troupes of dancers and musicians, and one of the most well-known is *kathakali* from the southwestern state of Kerala.

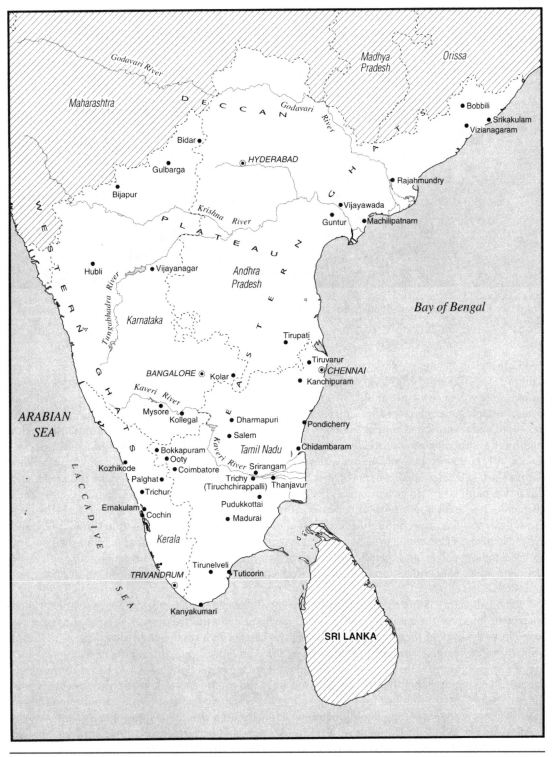

Map 11-3   South India showing the southwestern state of Kerala

Source: Garland Encyclopedia of World Music, Volume 5: South Asia: The Indian Subcontinent.

Fig. 11.9 *Kathakali* actors and musicians on stage in the Sri Vallabha temple, Thiruvalla, Kerala, 2012

Kathakali is a complete performing art involving music, dance, mime, acting, costumes, and face painting. The dramas, many based on scenes from the great Hindu epics, the *Ramayana* and *Mahabharata*, were written by some of Kerala's greatest authors. *Kathakali* traditionally was performed outdoors in staging areas attached to temples, but is now often performed in highly abbreviated form in school auditoriums and tourist hotels. A traditional *kathakali* performance lasts an entire night, beginning at sundown with a recital by the percussionists whose collective din announces the performance. All the actors are male. Actors with special costumes and makeup play the female roles. The flaring skirts, elaborate makeup, and paper face-enlargers (*chutti*) all serve to make the actors and the action more visible from a distance. The makeup color and type help the audience identify each character's role and status—royal or common, human or divine, good or evil. The thick makeup gives the appearance of a mask, but unlike a mask it allows the actor to express emotion through face and eye movements. The makeup process takes from two to three hours; the actor applies his own outline and preliminary colors, and then lies on his back as a makeup artist adds the details and applies the elaborate *chutti,* white ridges forming a frame from cheeks to chin traditionally made of rice paste but nowadays often of paper.

Kathakali actors mime the action and use a highly developed language of hand gestures called **mudras** to interpret the meaning of the lyrics. Two specially-trained singers present the narrative songs from the back of the stage, accompanying themselves on a small gong struck with a stick, and a small pair of cymbals, that serve to keep time. They are joined by a drumming ensemble consisting of a large cylindrical drum (*chenda*) played with sticks, and a double-headed barrel drum (*maddalam*). The singing is highly ornamented, and lines are often repeated, giving the dancing actors time to express their meanings fully. *Kathakali* actors usually come from acting families and begin their arduous years of training in childhood, which includes a strenuous form of martial art known as *kalaripayattu*. While the stories are of a religious nature and performances are supported by temple administrations, *kathakali* is also a form of entertainment that brings the community together to enjoy the music, artistry, drama, and poetry. Traditionally it was believed that the gods also enjoyed *kathakali* and would be present at the performances.

Fig. 11.10 **Green face paint and golden headdresses identify heroes, gods, and kings in *kathakali* (L), and a makeup artist applying designs onto black face paint, portraying evil characters (R)**

Watch this eight-minute clip of *kathakali dancers* beginning with narration by Ravi Shankar, whom we met in Lesson 6. Then follows several scenes from a famous *kathakali* play, *Kalyana Sougandhikam* based on a story from the Hindu epic *The Mahabharata*. Queen Draupadi asks her husband Bhima, son of Vayu the wind god and a hero of enormous strength, to fetch some sacred flowers from a mountaintop grove from which humans are banned. The proud Bhima brags that he can go anywhere and nothing can stop him. He sets out boldly through the forest, frightening animals and knocking down trees. Bhima's half-brother, the divine monkey-god Hanuman, hears his destructive thrashing and decides to teach him a lesson in humility. He transforms himself into an old, decrepit monkey and lies down with his tail across the road, blocking the hero-king's way. Bhima demands that the old monkey move aside, and when the monkey refuses, Bhima attempts to push the tail out of the road with his cudgel. Yet with all his superhuman strength, he can't move the tail. Hanuman then rises from the ground and reveals to Bhima his divinity.

In her Booker Prize-winning novel *The God of Small Things*, author Arundati Roy describes the frustration of the Indian actors forced to perform in hotels for European tourists who know nothing of the great *kathakali* tales they have been trained since childhood to tell. Their traditional audiences now go to the cinema or stay home and watch Indian soap operas on television. Their children prefer the steady employment of banking or engineering to the arduous training required for this art.

The Kathakali Man is the most beautiful of men. Because his body is his soul. His only instrument. From the age of three it has been planed and polished, pared down, harnessed wholly to the task of story-telling. He has magic in him, this man within the painted mask and swirling skirts.

But these days he has become unviable. Unfeasible. Condemned goods. His children deride him. They long to be everything that he is not. He has watched them grow up to become clerks and bus conductors. Class IV non-gazetted officers. With unions of their own.

But he himself, left dangling somewhere between heaven and earth, cannot do what they do. He cannot slide down the aisles of buses, counting change and selling tickets. He cannot answer bells that summon him. He cannot stoop behind trays of tea and Marie biscuits.

In despair he turns to tourism. He enters the market. He hawks the only thing he owns. The stories his body can tell.[15]

The *kathakali* actor in his distinctive makeup has become a symbol of the region. Traveling through Kerala, one cannot avoid seeing the painted face of the *kathakali* dancer on signs, advertisements, and tourist brochures.

CONCLUSION

We have noted in this lesson that religious beliefs, values, and understandings are not only expressed through words; they are enacted, performed, and felt at deep psychological levels. At times, the emotions and actions inspired by religious devotion lie outside of ordinary everyday experience. Often, special times and places are set aside from the rest of life and dedicated to sacred moods that may be cultivated, and to sacred actions that may be performed. Many believe that in these places and times set aside, the invisible forces, deities, ancestors, or angelic influences that are central to religious experience are present. Music often plays a role in creating a boundary between the secular and the sacred while at the same time providing a sonic bridge to the invisible realms that many religions acknowledge and affirm. In the next lesson we examine some of the roles music plays in marking off sacred space and time and creating a context for ritual.

KEY CONCEPTS

Trance	Harvest ritual	Sufi
Spirit possession	Sacred dance	Initiation rite
Shaman	Masked dance drama	Sacred drama
Local deity	Spirit medium	

(Q) THINKING ABOUT MUSIC QUESTIONS

1. Consider the sentence from Lesson 11: "There are occasions in which the truths proclaimed by religious systems are experienced *within* the body and are enacted *through* the body of the believer. Indeed, for some believers the truths experienced within the body transcend verbal meanings and are believed to *validate* the meanings that the words proclaim." Explain this in your own words. Consider it in the context of: a) United House of Prayer trombone shout bands; b) *Nadun*; and c) Mevlevi dervishes.

2. The relationship between religion and social entertainment is in some cases very close (consider the Uganda song festival, the dervish at the restaurant in Turkey, Bon Odori, *Calonarang*). Do you see this as a contradiction?

3. How do you account for the phenomenon of trance, given your own worldview and experience? Have you experienced or encountered similar phenomena? Is there a relationship between the trance states (and music) we encounter in this lesson and the "trance" of popular nightclubs?

4. Individuals and communities respond emotionally and physically to sacred music in a variety of ways. Think of an extraordinary experience that you or someone you know has had, which was triggered or enhanced by music and generated an emotional or physical response in the listener. How did you or your acquaintance respond to the musical sounds, and was the response individual or part of a communal expression?

5. Many religious belief systems are concerned with the relationship between everyday human experience and invisible sacred worlds, beings, and powers that are contacted through prayer and rituals. Music often provides a vehicle or bridge by which people access "the sacred." Consider these three examples—*Nadun, bira,* shout bands—and choose one. What is the music like and what responses does it elicit? Also, how would you describe the nature of the relationship or contact that the music establishes between the human and sacred worlds in your chosen example?

NOTES

1   David Roche, "Music and Trance," in *The Garland Encyclopedia of World Music, V: South Asia*, ed. Alison Arnold (New York: Taylor and Francis, 2000), 288.

2   Gerald Roche, "Nadun: Ritual and the Dynamics of Cultural Diversity in Northwest China's Hehuang Region," PhD diss. (Griffith University, Queensland, Australia, 2010), 64.

3   Gerald Roche, "Nadun," 33.

4   Gerald Roche, "The Gods Incarnate – The Huala of China's Sanchuan Region," 9-minute video documentary, 2013, subtitles, https://www.youtube.com/watch?v=QUjLwtix2_U&list=UUdljWglGBn0P0XIbTJteTpQ

5   Narrative from the *tromba* ceremony in Madagascar, in Jeremy Marre, writer, producer, and director, *The Nature of Music* (Harcourt Films and RM Arts, 1988).

6   Paul Berliner, "Music and Spirit Possession at a Shona Bira," *The Soul of Mbira* (Chicago: University of Chicago Press, 1981), 200–201.

7   Paul Berliner, *The Soul of Mbira,* 204–205.

8   Narration from "Mbira Maestros," a film by Antonio Lino on three Mbira musicians—Chikomborero, Prince, and William—in Chaonza village, Zimbabwe, uploaded August 21, 2010, https://www.youtube.com/watch?v=qja5kJ37lYA.

9   Narration from "Whirling Dervishes," video by Omar's Travels, uploaded August 25, 2009, https://www.youtube.com/watch?v=DnvSqHDJAnc.

10 Juliana Azoubel, "The Côte d'Ivoire Mask Tradition from the Viewpoint of Dance Ethnology: Dancing the Gap between Spirit and Human Worlds," *Journal of Undergraduate Research*, I/6 (2000), http://ufdc.ufl.edu/UF00091523/00030.

11 Juliana Azoubel, "Côte d'Ivoire Mask Tradition," http://ufdc.ufl.edu/UF00091523/00030

12 Juliana Azoubel, "Côte d'Ivoire Mask Tradition," http://ufdc.ufl.edu/UF00091523/00030

13 Juliana Azoubel, "Côte d'Ivoire Mask Tradition," http://ufdc.ufl.edu/UF00091523/00030

14 "History of Bon Odori," accessed January 6, 2012, http://www.angelfire.com/celeb2/obon/page/History.htm.

15 Arundati Roy, *God of Small Things* (New York: Random House, 1997), 230.

Lesson 12
Sacred Space and Sacred Time

In the previous lessons in this unit we have examined the roles music plays in performing sacred texts and inspiring sacred emotions including ecstasy and trance. This lesson concerns how music is used worldwide to set apart sacred spaces, times, and events from everyday, secular experience. On pilgrimages and processions, accompanying music demarcates as sacred the space through which the faithful move. Places where religious practices take place—churches, synagogues, temples, shrines, and pilgrimage sites—have special music associated with them. Some religions recognize and celebrate a single, most holy site—the Ka'aba in Mecca (Islam), St. Peter's Basilica in Rome (Roman Catholicism), Bodh Gaya in North India (Buddhism)—and in these singular locations, sacred sounds, chants, and music can reach their ultimate forms of expression. Holy days (holidays) are distinguished from ordinary days by their own special music. Music not only symbolizes the sacred events but shapes them and people's experience of them in a number of ways. Where there is the belief that sacred places and times are openings between the human world of mundane reality and the divine realms that religions often acknowledge, placate, and celebrate, music can serve as a sonic connection between the two, a channel by which prayers are transmitted upward and blessings flow downward.

SACRED SPACE (INDIA, MYANMAR, CHINA)

Throughout the world, special places have been set apart for ritual activities. Buildings such as temples, mosques, shrines, churches, and synagogues are consecrated for the sacred purposes for which they are used. Members of belief communities sometimes consider natural sites to be sacred. For the ancient Celts, Greeks, and Hindus, groves, streams, and caves were associated with deities and set aside for ritual purposes. On a grander scale, the Greeks believed Mt. Olympus to be the abode of the gods and the place where earth and heaven meet—the *axis mundi*. Tibetan Buddhists spend months circumambulating Mt. Kailasa and Qinghai Lake, continuously chanting "*Aum, Mani Padme Hum*" to receive the blessings that these places and practices bestow. Some sacred places are associated with historical events and serve as pilgrimage destinations: Mecca, Jerusalem, Sarnath—the site of the Buddha's first sermon. Sarnath, in fact, lies near the Ganges River at Banaras, North India, one of the most sacred places in the world for millions of Hindus. For several thousand years, people have made pilgrimages to the banks of this river to bathe in its waters and thus purify themselves of physical and spiritual pollution. Today, however, the river itself is seriously polluted by industrial and agricultural run-off. A ritual of purification, *Ganga puja,* is performed nightly on the *ghats* (steps) that lead down to the water. In this video from 2011, we see seven priests offering prayers and hymns to the sacred river. As one attendee put it, "Our Mother Ganga saved us from harm over many generations; now it is our turn to save her."

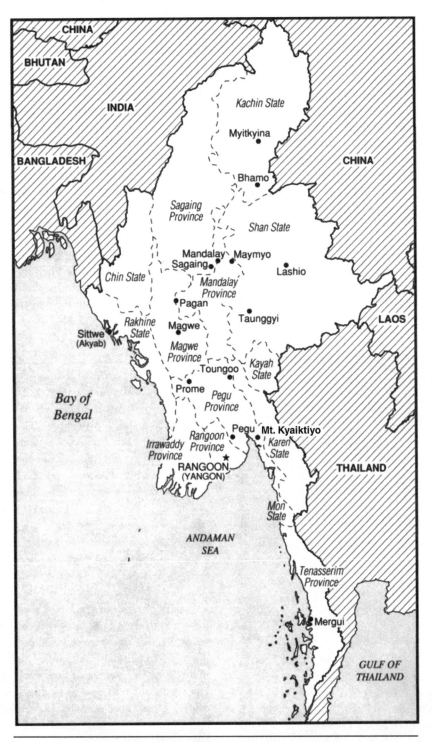

Map 12-1   **Myanmar showing Mt. Kyaiktiyo.**

Source: *Garland Encyclopedia of World Music*, Volume 4: Southeast Asia

Musical sound often differentiates the interiors and exteriors of sacred places. Church bells ringing across the town direct the faithful to the center of ritual activity on Sunday mornings, while organ music inside the church creates a sonic environment permeated with associations of faith and worship that the congregants encounter as they enter. Musical sound is used universally to mark off sacred places; it contributes to creating an environment conducive to worship, and it enriches religiously inspired states of mind. However, sacred musical traditions vary profoundly from place to place, as people match appropriate sounds to the responses to the sacred that their tradition cultivates. These responses range from the meditative and introspective to the ecstatic and celebratory, as the examples below illustrate.

Special sounds mark two Buddhist holy places in Asia. The simplicity of ringing gongs and bells in Myanmar contrasts dramatically with the state-sponsored symphony in China that announces the Buddha's birth.

One of the three most sacred sites in Myanmar is the Golden Rock in Kyaiktiyo. According to one legend, before he died, the Buddha gave a hair from his head to a hermit who tied the hair into his own topknot and wandered for years seeking an appropriate place to enshrine it. When the hermit saw the boulder perched on the edge of the cliff in Kyaiktiyo where it rests today, he realized that it had the same shape as his own head. There he built the pagoda to contain the hair. The rock rests on less than one percent of its surface and seems to be on the verge of rolling off the cliff at any moment into the valley 3000 feet below. A seven-mile climb takes pilgrims and monks to the summit, where they perform various acts of devotion. The entire hilltop is paved with white marble, and positioned around the grounds are white and gold pavilions, shrines, and statues of the Buddha. Worshippers announce their presence before the Buddha by striking large gongs three times (or nine times: three times three), placed for that purpose in front of the statues. The sound of the gongs is believed to purify the air and announce to the world the teachings (*dharma*) of the Buddha. Then the worshipers perform various devotional acts such as lighting incense, bowing, praying, and meditating. Men are allowed to walk down to the rock itself and rub gold leaf, which they have purchased from a nearby vendor, directly onto its surface.

12-2

Fig 12.1   The Golden Rock in Kyaiktiyo, Myanmar (L), and monks rubbing gold leaf onto the Golden Rock (R)

Parties of visiting monks may recite Buddhist scriptures (*sutras*) that are broadcast over loud-speakers. The combination of gongs, resounding at random intervals, and chanting fill the area with an awe-inspiring sound that announces to the approaching pilgrims the sanctity of the place.

A very different kind of sound awaits the visitor to the Great Standing Buddha of Wuxi in China, three hours by train from Shanghai. (See Map 8–4, p. 127.) The cast bronze statue was constructed from 1994 to 1997 at government expense. It is one hundred feet taller than the Statue of Liberty. The giant statue is the centerpiece of a government-supported Buddhist theme park built on the site of a thousand-year-old monastery. Ransacked during the Cultural Revolution (1966–1976), the monastery was rebuilt during the current period of relative tolerance for traditional religious practices that had been suppressed under Chairman Mao Zedong.

As visitors enter the gates of the park, they confront a huge bronze lotus bud atop a column in the middle of a fountain. Banks of loud speakers stand at the four corners. Several times a day, a computerized mechanism within the column causes the bud to open slowly, accompanied by music coordinated with a "dancing water" display in the fountain. The music begins with a deep, unearthly sound of chanting monks digitally mixed with Tuvan throat singing. (See Video 8-3.) As the lotus bud opens, the chanting gives way to a Western-style orchestral score fit for a Hollywood movie. Within the bud the infant Buddha appears, as harps, trumpets, and kettledrums announce the birth of the child who will become "The Enlightened One." When the mechanized display and the music reach their climax, water shoots from the mouths of bronze dragons to wash and anoint the figure, which turns slowly to the four directions with a hand gesture of benediction. The whole Wuxi Buddha show takes almost twenty minutes. The emotional contours of the musical performance, which combines both Asian and Western instruments and elements, engage and guide the viewers through the miracle portrayed in the spectacle. As the bud closes and the music subsides, the water that doused the statue streams out from decorative spigots allowing people to wash, drink, and receive blessings.

12-3

Fig 12.2   The Great Standing Buddha at Wuxi, Jiangsu Province, People's Republic of China (L), and water washing and anointing the infant Buddha statue in the bronze lotus bud fountain at Wuxi (R)

Despite their differences, these examples demonstrate the power of sound to permeate sacred space, thus creating a sonic environment that demarcates them from their secular surroundings.

SACRED JOURNEYS AND PROCESSIONS (CAPE VERDE, INDIA)

As music serves to set apart sacred spaces—temples, churches, synagogues, mosques—so too does it mark the sacred paths and journeys of religious worshipers. Processions and pilgrimages from one sacred place to another are often accompanied by special music, and on such occasions the music sanctifies the roads and highways of the ordinary, secular world and makes the way suitable for the sacred purpose and presence. Group devotional singing transforms a journey into a pilgrimage, and distinguishes the time of pilgrimage from that of ordinary travel. In this video from the Cape Verde Islands, a former Portuguese colony off the northwest coast of Africa, townspeople process to church for a Mass celebrating the installation of new sacred statues that had arrived from Portugal following the destruction of the old ones by vandals. The ringing of the church bell announces the beginning of the Mass. Later in the video, we see a procession on Easter morning, accompanied by the singing of hymns. On Palm Sunday throughout the Christian world, congregations sing hymns and play instruments as they process behind the Cross re-enacting Jesus' joyous entry into Jerusalem at the beginning of Holy Week. The next example shows chanting Daoists in Hong Kong processing from one altar to another, celebrating the Luo Tian Da Jiao ceremony dedicated to world peace; and in Xian, Chinese instruments accompany a procession of Daoists celebrating a new temple.

Map 12-2   **Northern India showing Manali in the state of Himachal Pradesh**

Source: *Garland Encyclopedia of World Music*, Volume 5: South Asia: The Indian Subcontinent

In Agra, North India, a **wedding procession** accompanying the groom astride a horse fills the neighborhood with a loud, hybrid sound—both modern and traditional (see Map 8–3, p.123). A brass band in full uniform marches behind a float on which a portable generator powers a speaker system, and a DJ plays recordings of Bollywood film music. The band tries to play along, but with their traditional role usurped by the new technology, their playing is half-hearted and futile. They seem only to be participating for the flashy instruments and crisp uniforms.

In Manali, a town in the Himalaya Mountains in Himachal Pradesh, North India, the image (*murti*) of sage Vashistha, one of the mythical authors of the Vedas, is worshiped by the townspeople and villagers scattered along the mountain passes. When a wedding is held in a remote village, the *murti* is carried out of the temple to the wedding site so the deity can lend his sacred energy (*shakti*) to the party. But removing the *murti* from the sanctuary of the temple risks compromising its purity as it travels out into the marketplace and along the profane roadway. When the *murti* is neither in the temple nor in the village but is in transition between locations, it is at its most vulnerable. So, the environment is purified with prayers and offerings made by a presiding priest, while horns and drums create a sonic envelope through which the deity will travel outside the temple walls and into the town and beyond. In the video, you will see several parts of the **ritual procession** that lasted three days, including the initial courtyard purification rites (***puja***): the prayers of the priest, the entry of the *murti* into the temple courtyard, the blessing of flowers and food (*prasad*) on a stone altar, and the sharing of the ritually-blessed food among the participants. Finally, the procession moves from the temple courtyard out into the street where a participant falls into trance. Because this is a region popular with tourists, you will also see many cell phones and digital cameras, creating a stark juxtaposition with the ancient forms of the ritual.

SACRED TIME (ETHIOPIA, CHINA, SURINAME)

In many religious traditions, music serves to mark the division between secular and sacred time. In Jewish synagogues and other sacred locations, the **ram's horn** (*shofar*) is blown on the High Holy Days of Rosh Hashanah (Jewish New Year) and Yom Kippur (Day of Atonement). Five times a day in Islamic countries the *adhan* (Call to Prayer) is heard across towns and cities as the **muezzin** announces from the mosque the singular greatness of Allah and bids the faithful to prayer. The *adhan* validates for the faithful the belief that life in this world is continuously interpenetrated by the divine. Sacred seasons are marked around the world by music unheard at other times of the year. In northern Chinese villages, amateur and semi-professional guild musicians practice all year long for performances at the February **Lunar New Year** celebrations. After Thanksgiving in North America, the radio waves, shopping malls, and churches are filled with songs of the Christmas season. During the four days

Fig. 12.3 Blowing of the *shofar* ram's horn (L), and the muezzin calling out to the faithful, *Hayya 'ala-salah* ("Come to Prayer") and *Allāhu Akbar* ("God is Great") (R)

leading up to Ash Wednesday and the beginning of Lent, Christians in Latin America and elsewhere celebrate Carnival with festivities and dancing that will not be enjoyed during the next forty days of the penitential season.

Often sacred times commemorate an occasion when the higher planes of spiritual reality and the secular plane of earth come into close contact. The anniversary of the birth or death of a holy personage or saint is often designated a feast day and time for celebration that may include special music. The two most important holy days for Christians are Christmas and Easter, celebrating the birth and resurrection of Christ respectively. Through song, Christians of the English-speaking world ask the question "What child is this who laid to rest in Mary's arms is sleeping?" And at Easter, "Christ the Lord is risen today…Sing, ye heav'ns, and earth reply, Alleluia!" resounds in thousands of churches. At Sufi shrines in South Asia, the anniversary of the death of the saint that the shrine commemorates is called *Urs,* meaning "wedding." Each year, people gather to celebrate the anniversary of the day the saint united (as in marriage) with the divine. This is the most important time of the year for *qawwali,* the tradition of Sufi song discussed in Lesson 10. Solstices and equinoxes, and planting and harvest times are also marked by religious festivals, as we saw with *Nadun.*

In the Ethiopian Tewahedo Orthodox Church, the 12th day of each month is dedicated to the Archangel Saint Michael. Especially on the 12th day of June, special Masses are performed and the treasures of the church—paintings, icons, crosses, and the replica of the Ark of the Covenant housed in every Tewahedo Orthodox Church—are removed from the inner sanctum and paraded before the worshipers. At Lalibela, the site of eleven 12th-century churches hollowed from a rock escarpment and one of the most sacred places in Ethiopia, eight thousand white-robed worshipers congregate each year on that day to celebrate St. Michael's feast day. Chanting of the Liturgy begins at 6:00 am in the ancient language of **Ge'ez,** which very few understand, including the priests who perform it. The celebrations continue as priests and deacons sway ritualistically, women ululate, and the entire community celebrates the mysteries of their faith. Festivals like these are called "calendrical" because they return each year when their time on the solar or lunar calendar rolls around.

While **calendrical rituals** occur with the regularity of the seasons, **life-cycle rituals** occur at the transition points in people's lives. When an individual moves from one status level or state of being to another—childhood to adulthood or being single to being married, for instance—rituals are performed to affirm and validate the transition. Rites of passage such as birthdays, adolescent initiations, graduations, weddings, and funerals all have appropriate music. In Judaism, when boys and girls reach adolescence, they celebrate their coming of age with a special ritual: the Bar Mitzvah (for boys) and Bat Mitzvah (for girls). In Jewish synagogue services, one of the two officiating leaders is the *hazzan* or cantor, a specially trained ritual musician who leads the congregation in prayer services that contain a number of sung portions. Among the *hazzan's* most important duties is the training of a Bar or Bat Mitzvah candidate in the recitation of selected passages from the Torah (the five Books of Moses) and the Haftarah (the Books of the Prophets). A boy or girl will recite before the congregation, symbolizing his or her transition to adult membership in the community.

Anthropologists refer to "in-between" states—such as when the Manali *murti* is neither in the temple nor in the village—as "liminal," from the Latin word for "threshold." Individuals, societies, and even deities can be in liminal states, and special music is often involved in rituals of liminality. In the *Nadun* festival we examined in Lesson 11, for example, the time between the end of the dances and dramas but before the possession of the medium is liminal: a period of great intensity and anxiety as the community waits to see if it will be favored by the visitation of the deity. At no other time are the gongs beaten with such furious intensity. In sacred contexts, these times create openings during which the divine or the eternal intersects with the mundane, human world. Perhaps funerals are the ultimate rite of passage, and the time between death and burial is often seen as a highly significant liminal period for a community.

In Shaanbei (northern Shaanxi province, China) near the border of Inner Mongolia, the **funeral** of an 89-year-old farmer was a noisy, two-day affair (see Map 8–4, p. 127). The occasion was mostly a joyous one, since the old man had lived a good life, long and prosperous. His wife had died two years earlier, and the local Daoist priest ("**yinyang**") had selected an auspicious gravesite in the high fields that they would ultimately share. The time between his death and his burial next to his wife was liminal, filled with music, chanting, and noise from gongs and firecrackers. There were formal rituals, prayers, and processions; but also food and conversation among family and friends brought together by the event. While his body had already been carried to the gravesite before the ritual commenced, his soul had been captured by the priest and placed in a portable cardboard shrine. The soul would be released with the burning of the shrine and other paper offerings at the gravesite on the second day of the ritual. The music was celebratory and went on all afternoon of the first day. The family and all the villagers then gathered for a midnight procession led by the musicians blowing shawms (*suona*), clanging cymbals, and beating drums. The darkness was punctuated by strings of firecrackers and illuminated by a thousand candles placed along the roadway. Bonfires and lanterns burned high up in the hills above the roadway, tended by the neighboring farmers who had known the man their whole lives. At dawn, a smaller procession set off into the mountains to the burial plot. Two brothers played *suona,* as they did for all such events in the area when they weren't farming themselves, and showed extraordinary stamina throughout the ritual. Using a technique known as circular breathing, they were able to maintain a continuous stream of music, even on the long hike to the gravesite. The priest chanted, and the *suona* brothers played on in celebration of life's continuity and cyclical processes.

A final example of a liminal ritual takes place in a Saramaccan Maroon community deep in the Amazonian rainforest. As described in Lesson 7, the Surinamese Maroons are the descendants of escaped African slaves who live in the deep interior of the rainforest. A three-day ceremony will determine the fate of two widows who were married to the same man. He had died exactly one year before, and his widows had been living in forced seclusion, a liminal state, ever since. Because they were originally from a different village, the elders had to determine whether they could remain in the home of their husband, or must return to their native village, since now their status had changed. For three days, there was disruption of the ordinary routines of life. The two widows were led out each morning to the ritual space at the center of the village, draped in veils and attended by family members. There

Fig. 12.4 Young Maroon masked dancers participate in the three-day ceremony, Amazonian rainforest, Suriname

they sat motionless, awaiting their fate as women relatives and neighbors danced around them. Various deities inhabited a pair of shamans, dressed in blue, who both presided over the activities and contributed to the mayhem. Guns were discharged; children wearing masks danced in a frenzy. At one point, one of the family members charged through the village with a chain saw. At another point young men went into each home, led by the shamans, and threw everything out into the central clearing. Finally, before the elders met, two large river turtles were slaughtered with machetes as blood sacrifices. It was determined the next day that the widows would return to their native village. Order was restored. During the entire three-day ritual, the drummers almost never stopped playing.

STRUCTURING SACRED RITUAL (ZIMBABWE, USA)

As mentioned in the opening of this lesson, not only does music symbolize and frame sacred spaces and times, it also shapes sacred events and people's experience of them in several ways. Many Christian worship services begin with a prelude and end with a **recessional** or postlude; thus music provides a kind of sonic frame that separates the events of the service from the rest of the day's activities. Music not only frames Sunday services but organizes the flow of events within the frame. During the service, along with readings and preaching, worship time is punctuated by a variety of musical practices: congregational hymn-singing, anthems from the choir, a solo on organ or piano while the collection plate is passed. In the worship services of many African American Protestant denominations, music is nearly continuous, underscoring or inspiring emotional intensity as demonstrated by this sermon from Pastor Audrey B. Bronson of Philadelphia.

In the *bira* ceremony of Zimbabwe, which we read about in Lesson 11, music likewise helps structure the sequence of ritual events. The *mbira* musicians begin playing as an unobtrusive background to the socializing that precedes the event. Gradually, the music grows in volume and intensity as the participants become more focused on dancing, singing, and engaging in the ritual activities that will culminate in the possession of the medium. The music reaches its greatest intensity at the moment of the medium's possession by the ancestral spirits. At this point in the ritual the music stops. Following the speaking of the medium, the musicians resume their playing, then gradually their music fades away into the background as the ritual draws to a close. Both the place and the time for the ceremony are framed by the sound of the musicians; and the intensity of the ritual action is controlled by the waxing and waning of musical intensity.

Closer to home, a typical wedding ceremony in North Carolina often begins with a hired string quartet playing "unobtrusively" off to the side of the sanctuary as relatives and guests enter the church, greet each other, get caught up on news and gossip, and settle into the pews. A signal from the back of the church by a designated guest or professional wedding planner to the musicians directs a change in the music. A **processional piece** chosen by the couple, like Pachelbel's *Canon* or Bach's *Jesu, Joy of Man's Desiring,* accompanies the seating of special family members: grandparents and parents. A second processional piece brings the wedding party—bridesmaids, flower girls, and ring bearers—down the aisle to the altar. Again a signal, and the famous Wedding March begins. At this musical cue, all rise and face the back of the sanctuary to watch the veiled bride march to the front of the church in step with the familiar tune. The officiating clergy speaks the appropriate texts—"Dearly Beloved, We are gathered here today, etc." Toward the middle of the ceremony, the string quartet plays a meditative piece or a ballad chosen by the couple as they light a "Unity Candle;" or a friend comes down to the altar area and sings, accompanying herself on the guitar. Finally, when the pastor pronounces the couple "Man and Wife" and they kiss, the string quartet strikes up the recessional march and the happy couple heads for the rear doorway. After they leave, the quartet plays celebratory pieces from Handel's *Water Music* as the guests move toward the exit. At this point, no one is really listening; each is engaged in a private conversation about directions to the reception, or how beautiful the bride looked. The quartet's playing again becomes unobtrusive, but its sonic presence closes the frame. A dance band at the reception takes the couple, their status changed in the eyes of the church and community, back to the secular world of eating, drinking, and dancing.

CONCLUSION

In each of these cases, music serves as a **demarcator**, creating a border between ritual time and space and ordinary everyday experience. Music is a symbol of the sacred occasions, places, actions, and powers with which religious beliefs and practices are associated: the *shofar* signifies High Holy Days, organ music signifies Sunday worship, the bridal march signifies matrimony, the call of the *muezzin* signifies the practice of daily prayer. Beyond the roles of demarcation and symbolism, music serves as a sonic channel of communication with spiritual realms; indeed, music may also be the very manifestation of the sacred. In the United House of Prayer, the trombone choir takes the place of the sermon; Shona *mbira* music serves as the link between the living and the ancestors, and the gongs of *Nadun* call the deity Erlang Ye to manifest himself in the midst of the community by possessing the *huala*.

"In most cultures of the world, throughout the history of humankind," writes Robin Sylvan, a professor of Religious Studies, "this spiritual power of music has been acknowledged, cultivated, and celebrated. It is an important part of our common heritage, one of the great expressions of the human endeavor. We recognize it when we hear it and experience it; we feel the power, even when our culture has no conceptual category for it, even when we are listening to a seemingly trivial popular song."[1] He concludes by quoting ethnomusicologist David McAllester: "We are not all practicing mystics and most of us do not experience God easily. But when we hear music, something like that is happening to us."[2] While sacred music marks off Sunday morning from the rest of the week for Christians, music of a different kind marks Saturday night, with its earthly pleasures of sociability, storytelling, entertainment, and courtship, and lends to the mundane pastimes of the everyday its special powers. Our final unit explores roles music plays in human social life.

KEY CONCEPTS

Sacred space and time	Sonic envelope	Processional/recessional
Sacred journeys and	Calendrical rituals	music
processions	Life-cycle rituals	Demarcator of the sacred
Pilgrimage	Liminal/Liminality	
Wedding procession	Rites of passage	

(Q) THINKING ABOUT MUSIC QUESTIONS

1. In your experience, think of two calendrical rituals and two life-cycle rituals and describe the music associated with each. How does music serve to differentiate these times from ordinary times?

2. Listen again to the sermon of Pastor Audrey Bronson of Philadelphia. Consider the role of music in her manner of delivery. How is music structuring the emotional trajectory of the ritual of which her sermon is the central component? Compare this with the description of the music at the *bira* ritual of Zimbabwe.

3. Explain in your own words the concept of "liminality." Consider the Surinamese Maroon ritual described in this lesson. If liminal time occurs between the end of one state and the beginning of another, how does that relate to this ritual? In what sense are weddings and funerals also rituals of liminality?

4. Think of two examples of sacred musical performance and consider how one relates to sacred space and how the other relates to sacred time. How does the music mark "the sacred" and separate it from the ordinary, secular time and space, and how does music shape and enhance the sacred event or experience?

5. Pretend you are a tourist who has happened upon the procession in Manali, northern India. What roles might music be playing in this ritual, and how would you explain them in a letter to a music teacher, family member, or friend back home?

NOTES

1 Robin Sylvan, *Traces of the Spirit: The Religious Dimensions of Popular Music* (New York: New York University Press, 2002), 44.
2 David McAllester, "Some Thoughts on 'Universals' in World Music," *Ethnomusicology* 15/3 (1971): 380.

UNIT 4
MUSIC AND SOCIAL LIFE

INTRODUCTION

If music plays important roles in the formation and projection of human identity and in the expression of the core beliefs and values of religious life, music is equally important in enhancing human social life. In Unit 4 we focus on music's relationships to those occasions in which people tell stories, communicate through mass media, and gather publicly. Alan Merriam makes the point that because music is incorporated as an integral component of so many social situations, its importance in human life cannot be overestimated. "There is probably no other human cultural activity which is so all-pervasive, and which reaches into, shapes, and often controls so much of human behavior."[1]

Music in some social situations is the primary element and object of people's attention and the reason why they gather. Music in other social situations is not the central feature or catalyst for social gathering, yet is an essential component of the sonic environment and in many cases is indispensable. People attend public concert halls and music theaters, and even fill vast sports stadiums to hear music played out to the crowds over loudspeakers, as at the Salala concert in Madagascar discussed in Lesson 5. In South Korea, young people go on dates to the *norebang* ("sound room"). In these store-front enterprises, often located in the basement of shopping centers, couples rent rooms by the hour and spend the evening singing songs to each other. Their voices, processed with reverb through a karaoke machine, sound like pop stars. Nightclubs and dance halls from Buenos Aires to Bangkok provide evening entertainment for locals and tourists alike, and offer employment to musicians and DJs. In some countries, public social life is more restrained. In Iran, for example, where the Islamic government tightly controls live public music performance, particularly by women, traditional Persian classical music has long thrived in the context of private concerts in people's homes. These restrictions also pertain to Western-style pop music; rock musicians there perform "underground" in urban basements and parking garages, and seek audiences on the internet. In each of these cases music is the primary element that brings people together, even if, as in the last example, the gathering is virtual.

In many social situations, music is present but is not the central feature. Sporting events often involve group singing of patriotic songs, as do political rallies where the speeches of the politicians are the main event. Shopping districts and malls employ musicians or pipe in recorded music to keep shoppers pleasantly engaged in the acts of browsing and buying. At outdoor public celebrations like Carnival in Brazil and the Caribbean, Lunar New Year in China, and the Fourth of July in the United States, special music creates and sustains the festive mood, propelling dancers and marchers down the street and distinguishing these special times sonically from the rest of the year. Many forms of storytelling and theater employ music to enhance the dramatic impact. Narrative is the subject of both Lesson 13, in which we explore the complex roles music plays in Storytelling Traditions, and Lesson 14, which deals with Musical Theater and Film. In Lesson 15 we discuss music associated with Night Life, Public Ceremonies and Festivals, and Sporting Events.

Lesson 13
Music and Storytelling

Throughout much of human history, the core beliefs of a society have been transmitted orally within and across generations through stories that were sung. These often included creation myths, explanatory fables, and tales of the origins of dynasties and their founding heroes. Because remembering and passing on these narratives accurately and compellingly was so important to maintaining the fabric of a society, specially trained and adept storytellers served as a people's collective memory. Particularly before the spread of literacy, epic narrators held important positions, often closely associated with powerful ruling families whose authority these tellers of tales helped to legitimize. In pre-Christian Celtic societies, hereditary poets known as "bards" kept and transmitted the oral histories and genealogies of ruling families in poetic verse. The term "**bard**" later acquired a broader, generic meaning comparable to the medieval European minstrel, the West African *griot*, the Turkish *asik*, and the Ethiopian *azmari*, seen here performing at a traditional Ethiopian coffee house. Accompanying himself on the one-string *masenko*, he improvises verses about the guests, half complimentary, half insulting. Often the wordplay makes the meaning ambiguous and the guest isn't sure whether to be flattered or insulted.

Over centuries, collections of stories, legends, histories, and myths were passed on in oral tradition from one poet-singer to another. They later coalesced into great epic narratives that became central to their societies, and many were eventually written down: the *Mahabharata* and *Ramayana* of India, the Malian (West African) *Epic of Sundjata*, the Tibetan *Epic of King Gesar*, the Japanese *Tale of the Heike*, and the ancient Greek epics the *Iliad* and *Odyssey* attributed to Homer, for example. In some cases the epic was first written as a literary text and subsequently moved into oral tradition. A famous example is the 10th-century CE *Shahnameh* ("Book of Kings") of Firdausi, which recounts the entire history of Persia up to the Islamic conquest in the 7th century CE. It is the national epic of Iran.

While the contexts in which bards have transmitted these epic poems have ranged widely from royal courts to teahouses, and from village squares to performance stages, the rapid social and technological changes of the 20th and 21st centuries have hastened the decline of many of these traditions, and in some cases have resulted in their disappearance. The art of oral epic performance offers little competition in today's high tech world of cinema and videogames, which leave much less to the imagination of their audience. There are nevertheless communities and cultures in which the singing of oral epics still survives. In this lesson we begin with the highly influential research of Albert B. Lord and his mentor and teacher Milman Parry on Balkan epics, and then explore other traditions of sung narrative.

BALKAN BARDS (BOSNIA AND HERZEGOVINA)

In 1960, Harvard University professor of Slavic Languages, Albert B. Lord, published a study of oral epic poetry based on his own research in Yugoslavia (now divided into independent countries) and on that of his teacher, Milman Parry.[2] In his study, *The Singer of Tales*, Lord developed a comprehensive theory of epic recitation that has greatly influenced the way bardic traditions of today are studied, as well as ancient traditions from which came such milestones of world literature as the *Iliad* and *Odyssey*. Lord describes a process of **oral transmission** that is the opposite of Vedic transmission as discussed in Lesson 10. In the case of Vedic recitation, the transmission across generations was strictly controlled so that in ritual performance neither a single syllable nor the manner of its expression would change. Sacred words and actions are repeated with fidelity to a pre-existing template, replicated precisely each time the ritual is performed. By contrast, what Lord and Parry discovered with the Balkan bards was a much more flexible and creative process. While the gist of a story might remain fairly stable over time, the telling was never the same twice. Social occasions for storytelling tended to be informal and of varying time intervals, and stories were skillfully tailored to fit the situation.

Fig. 13.1   Illustration from a 17th-century manuscript of the Persian *Shahnameh*

The Balkan storytellers that Lord and Parry studied were often from storyteller families and they grew up hearing the stories over and over, each time slightly embellished or altered. From these multiple versions, each storyteller developed an individual style based partly on rote learning and partly on imaginative improvisation. From the inherited storehouse of learned and remembered tales, melodies, and rhymes, storytellers would add, delete, and alter as much as their creativity and audiences allowed. Then in turn, the altered versions were passed to the next generation and became the tradition. In cultures in which literacy was rare or non-existent, sung stories, performed in a manner part memorized and part improvised, constituted the ancient oral wisdom and collective memory of the people.

Albert B. Lord describes in detail a learning process by which the Balkan storytellers acquired their extraordinary skill, as exemplified by the following quote from one of his research subjects:

When I was a shepherd boy, they used to come for an evening to my house, or sometimes we would go to someone else's for the evening, somewhere in the village. Then a singer would pick up the gusle [one-string fiddle], and I would listen to the song. The next day when I was with the flock, I would put the song together, word for word, without the gusle, but I would sing it from memory, word for word, just as the singer had sung it…. Then I learned gradually to finger the instrument, and to fit the fingering to the words, and my fingers obeyed better and better...I didn't sing among the men until I had perfected the song, but only among the young fellows in my circle [druzina] not in front of my elders and betters.[3]

The young singer thus begins his training by listening to accomplished storytellers and repeating, as accurately as he can, what he hears. He then attempts to work out story narratives on his own or among his peers, fitting the lines of narration into the fairly rigid grid of meter, melody, and rhyme; and of course, learning how to accompany himself on the single-string fiddle called the *gusle* as he recites. When he can recite an entire story, he tries out his skill before a critical adult audience. From then on, throughout his life, he will add to his stock of tales, and improve his manner of delivery and rapport with his audiences. Competition among rivals continuously raises the stakes. The most accomplished storytellers perform creative feats of imagination and artistry akin to Homer's.

Milman Parry recorded over 3500 disks of South Slavic epic singing in the mid 1930s, including almost 500 disks from a single singer, bard Avdo Međedović of eastern Montenegro. Parry was also able to record a short film of Avdo Međedović, reciting part of a 12,000-line narrative, accompanying himself on the *gusle*.

Avdo Međedović (1875–1953) was raised in a Muslim family in the village of Obrov, eastern Montenegro, then part of the Ottoman Empire. He became a butcher, like his father and grandfather before him, and he never learned to read or write. From a young age, Avdo learned the art of singing through listening to his father and other skilled singers. While his singing voice and *gusle* playing were not virtuosic, he was remarkably creative in singing epic tales of the Ottoman Empire and its heroes. He richly embellished the tales with detailed descriptions, making his versions far longer than those of other epic singers of the time. When once invited by Milman Parry to listen to another epic singer performing a tale he did not know, Avdo sang the epic himself with three times as many verse lines. His own epic song repertoire was extensive, amounting to fifty-eight tales; Parry recorded over 78,000 lines of epic poetry from Avdo, and some fifty-three hours of singing. By all standards, Avdo's abilities as an oral epic singer and poet were indeed extraordinary. For people living in rural towns and isolated villages—a world without televisions, cell phones, computers, or films—listening to the bard sing stories of kings and battles was an event not to be missed. His performances captured the listeners' attention, fired their imagination, and vividly brought to life the characters and heroes of the past.

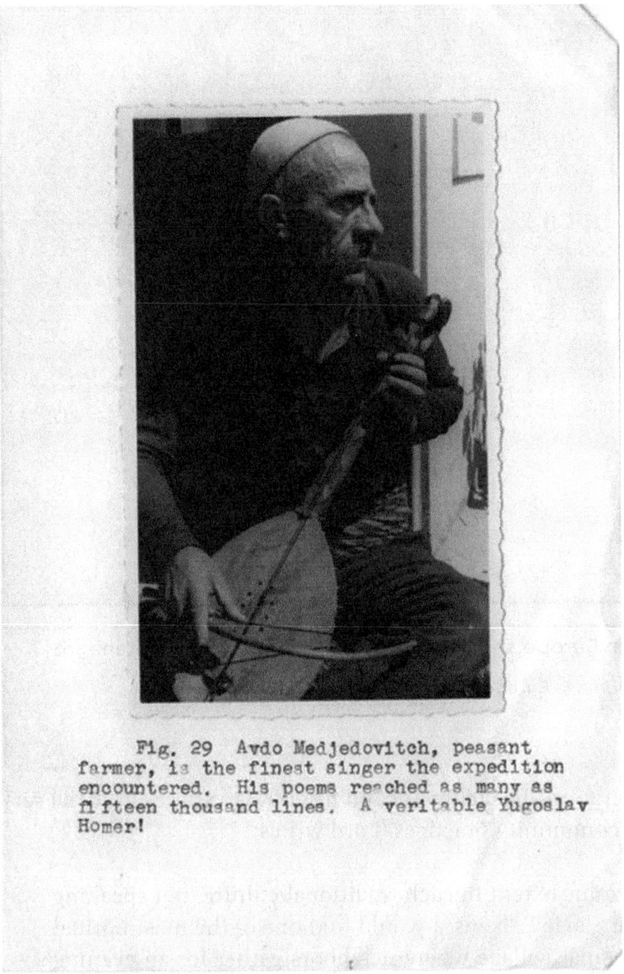

Yet, the extraordinary narrative and musical accomplishments of the "singers of tales" did not occur in a vacuum. The singers and their listeners were part of the same community and all members would have listened to storytellers from early childhood. Furthermore, they would have grown up in communities in which the tradition of epic narration

Fig. 29 Avdo Medjedovitch, peasant farmer, is the finest singer the expedition encountered. His poems reached as many as fifteen thousand lines. A veritable Yugoslav Homer!

Fig. 13.2   Avdo Međedović (ca. 1875–1953) of Montenegro, accompanying himself on the *gusle* (one-string fiddle)

Map 13-1 The Balkan region in Southeastern Europe showing the village of Obrov in Montenegro

Source: *Garland Encyclopedia of World Music*, Volume 8: Europe

had been passed on from generation to generation. The telling of and listening to stories in social settings would have been deeply ingrained in community practices. Lord writes:

> The circumstances will be different to some extent in each traditional culture, but speaking for the one that I know best, that of the Slavic Balkans, I would find one of the most normal places for singing to be the house in a small village where neighbors gather for an evening

and sit and talk and listen to a singer. Epics are sung also at weddings and to help celebrate the Slava, the family feast for its patron saint. Another informal setting is the coffeehouse in Moslem communities, where men gather, especially during Ramadan, and listen, after a day of fasting, to epic songs that may continue for a whole night. The singers and the listeners are all "insiders;" that is, they are part of the same tradition.[4]

Epic singing in the Balkans continues today largely in Serbia and in the mountainous regions along the Adriatic coast. Singers accompany themselves almost exclusively on the *gusle*, and professional singers perform at folk music festivals and fairs, on **public stages**, and in competitions. Modern *guslari*, as the Balkan epic singers are known, sing occasionally from the traditional repertoire, and also perform songs based on more recent events, such as the Yugoslav and Kosovo Wars of the 1990s. Through the 20th century, this geographic region underwent enormous political and social upheavals, from the establishment of the Kingdom of Yugoslavia (1918–1941) to the formation of the Socialist Federal Republic of Yugoslavia (1943–1992), and to its eventual breakup into independent nations accompanied by much bloodshed. Through it all, the ten-syllable epic song remained an important medium for the transmission of culture as well as news and political views. "The **decasyllabic** epic song," writes language professor Ivo Zanic in 2007, "is even today for a large part of the population not only a source of aesthetic pleasure but also an important, sometimes the main, medium through which information about current events is conveyed, on which they build their value system, form political judgments and model their general social conduct."[5] Epic singing has remained relevant to Balkan society for several reasons. One is its value as a symbol of traditional culture for a population uprooted under socialism; between 1948 and 1981, 6.5 million people migrated from the countryside to the city and left their agrarian lifestyle to become industrial workers. A second reason is the involvement of epic singers in election campaigns. Political leaders have invited *guslari* to perform at political rallies where the singers both glorify past heroes and promote political messages. Politicians benefit from the singing of epic songs that support their ideology. They also benefit from the epic singers' reinforcement of a traditional worldview and value system, which provides politicians with a strong connection to their audiences. This political encouragement and support of *gusle* playing and epic singing led to the formation of *gusle* associations, a third reason for the continued vibrancy of epic singing. These *gusle* organizations promote regular performances of epic songs at festivals, on the radio and television, and in competitions. Until the 1980s epic singers were largely male performers; nowadays **women singers** also perform professionally, reflecting recent social changes in the Balkans. As the oral epic performance tradition changes it takes on new meanings for its performers and audiences, yet continues to serve as a powerful symbol of cultural identity.

WEST AFRICAN *JALOLU* (WEST AFRICA, USA)

In several countries of West Africa including Mali, Senegal, and The Gambia, singers called *jalolu* (in Manding languages) or *griots* (the term used by the French colonizers) serve as oral historians, genealogists, and praise singers. (See Map 6–2, p. 88.) *Jalolu* (singular, *jali*) are members of a hereditary profession, born into families that have passed on their inherited knowledge for generations, and identified within their societies by surnames such as Diabate, Kouyate, Jobarteh, Cissokho, and Suso. Since at least the 1200s, with the establishment of the great Malian Empire under the Mandinka warrior king Sunjata Keita (reigned 1235–1255), aristocrats employed *jalolu* to chronicle the deeds and lineages of their families. "The Griots are walking libraries, with knowledge of the past, present and future of our people," writes Foday Musa Suso, a 20th-century *griot* from The Gambia, in his memoir *Jali Kunda*. "When a Griot arrives in a village he is given great respect, because he is the keeper of tradition. He is welcomed, fed, and given a place to stay. It's very important to have a Griot visit your village. Everyone wants to know about their family history. The Griot sings about ancestors of the village, about kings and wars between the kings, and also about living friends and neighbors."[6]

The **praise songs** of the *jali,* sung on public occasions such as birthdays, anniversaries, and ceremonies of state, celebrated and legitimized the claims of their wealthy patrons to high social position.

They also "gave...kings the courage to fight battles. Indeed, battles could be won or lost by the sheer power of the *jali*'s word. Nowadays, they may sing for politicians or businessmen instead of kings, but they function in very similar ways. Their gift of speech has made them ideal 'go-betweens'; they patch up quarrels and feuds, arrange marriages, and negotiate the most delicate economic and political matters. In the words of Toumani Diabaté, one of Mali's most brilliant young *kora* players: 'They are the needle that sews.'"[7] *Griots* in some regions are also called upon to sing "songs of ritual necessary to summon spirits and gain the sympathy of the ancestors."[8] Their role as "go-betweens" extends to connections with spiritual powers. "Even today," writes Foday Musa Suso, "you see Griots travelling with their koras, moving between cities and towns...If you want to buy some cloth, go to the weaver. If you want a hoe, ax or knife, then go to the blacksmith. But if you want to know the history of the people, you must go to the Griots."[9]

Musical instruments associated with the West African *jali* tradition include the *kora* (21-string harp-lute), the *balo* (xylophone), and the *kontingo* (plucked, long-necked lute). *Jalolu* specialize in playing one of these instruments (their choice often dictated by region). In some places they accompany their own singing, while in others the singers and instrumentalists are separate. Women *jalolu* (*griottes* in French) are also often singers, and in some cases have become highly respected artists. A superior woman singer, according to *jali* Nyulo Jebateh, "is not afraid of crowds, not afraid of anything, except God. She can stand before a crowd with all eyes upon her and not become confused (*kijo faro*). She can shout (*feteng*), literally 'split' the air with her voice, but do it with feeling (*wasu*) and sentiment (*balafa*), so that people will sympathize with her."[10] The *jali* typically employs "a fluid set of descriptive phrases, praise names, proverbs, songs, and instrumental patterns, which all feed into a story line or collection of deeds, actions, events, attributes, and social mores. It can be expanded, embellished, or condensed."[11] Both the instrumental and vocal components of a performance contain fixed, repeating patterns and improvisational sections. This is similar to the creative, flexible process that Lord and Parry described in their studies of Balkan bards.

In the West African regions associated with *griots*, music and musicians are among the most profitable export products. Many *jalolu* have settled in the United States, Europe, and elsewhere, and pursue

Fig. 13.3 Kaira Ba with (L to R) Will Ridenhour (*djembe*), Diali Cissokho (*kora*), John Westmoreland (guitar), Austin McCall (percussion), and Jonathan Henderson (upright bass)

careers as concert artists. In the spirit of musical globalization, some join rock and fusion groups creating exciting new hybrid forms. An example is Senegalese musician Diali Cissokho, who now lives in Pittsboro, North Carolina. Diali's lineage stems from two important *jali* clans: his father is Cissokho and his mother is Diabate. Diali met his American wife Hilary Stewart when she was spending a semester abroad in Senegal studying music of the *jali* tradition. She found a *kora* teacher, who became her husband in 2009. Diali emigrated to North Carolina with his new wife in 2010. When he consulted with his family whether to stay within his home community or leave for America, he was told: "Diali, you know what? Music is music. Life is life. But wife is wife. You have to go help your wife."[12] In America, he continues to perform the traditional *kora* songs of his ancestors and also explores new avenues for contemporary expression. In the song *"Lu Mu Mety Mety"* Diali sings an autobiographical song in the traditional style. He tells of his early music education, his family, meeting his wife, and coming to America. This narrative is interspersed with proverb-type phrases like "Everything is in front of us," and "The instruments give us courage." In 2011, he formed the band **Kaira Ba** with a group of North Carolina roots musicians. Kaira Ba (pronounced "KAI rah bah") is a Mandinka word meaning "the great peace" or "peace and love." Their hybrid sound is "at once unique and universal," writes National Public Radio correspondent Frank Stasio.[13] That Diali and his collaborators can fit their styles together like hand and glove is really no miracle. The North Carolinans grew up with jazz, R&B, gospel, and the blues, styles that derived from music brought to North Carolina by West Africans on slave ships four hundred years ago. They all speak a common musical language. Diali continues to maintain close family relationships in Senegal and in 2011 Kaira Ba toured there, finding rapport with their African audiences. Diali believes his music is more than entertainment; it is a means to communicate across cultural boundaries about the richness of his African heritage as well as the plight of its poor.

BLIND STORYTELLERS (ANCIENT GREECE, IRELAND, CHINA, JAPAN)

While the West African *griot* and Balkan bard are oral historians, in many parts of the world storytellers are highly skilled, professional entertainers singing fables, myths, legends, and tales of ordinary people in extraordinary, often amusing situations. Music and storytelling have been among the relatively few professions available to the blind, as farm work and other traditional forms of labor were not practical.

Fig. 13.4 *Homer and his Guide* (1874), William-Adolphe Bouguereau (1825–1905)

This tradition dates back at least as far as the legendary Homer, creator of the epic tales the *Iliad* and the *Odyssey*, and includes ballad singers, epic narrators, and storytellers. In 17th- and 18th-century Ireland, itinerant harp players and storytellers traveled around the country entertaining kings and nobles in their castles and great houses, and blind musicians were common among them. Turlough O'Carolan (1670–1738), who was left blind after contracting smallpox at the age of eighteen, composed over two hundred songs and tunes for his patrons. He is the only Irish harper-composer whose works survive, written down after his death and still played today by traditional Irish musicians and others.

In China and Japan as elsewhere, blind itinerant musicians have eked out a living with their stories and songs. Stephen Jones writes of the *shuoshude*, blind storytellers of north-central China (northern Shaanxi Province):

As...the *shuoshude* arrives in a village, a family in the midst of misfortune, perhaps with a handicapped son or ailing livestock, asks him to set up his altar. He invokes the gods to bless the family as he performs a long historical story of romance and suspense, to the rhythmic clicking of clappers tied to his leg, the rustling of slim strips of

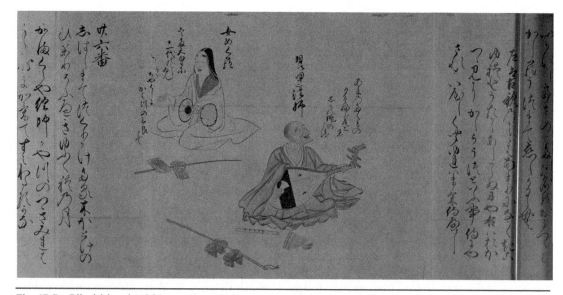

Fig. 13.5   Blind *biwa hoshi* (storysinger), from a scroll housed at the Tokyo National Museum

wood tied to his wrist, and his strumming of the *sanxian* [a three-string fretless plucked lute]. In return, the family gives him a few coins, a bowl or two of noodles, and a bed for the night.[14]

During the Communist Revolution of the 1930s and under the government of Chairman Mao Zedong, these singers were protected, supported, and encouraged to tell new revolutionary stories. One blind storyteller in particular, Han Qixiang (1915–1989), became famous throughout China as the perfect spokesperson for a storytelling propaganda campaign. "He was an illiterate, impoverished peasant (thus socially and economically oppressed), physically handicapped (thus unfortunate and deprived), and extremely talented at his craft (thus potentially a convincing advocate of Communist ideals)," writes Professor Chiang-tai Hung.[15] However since 1982, the post-Maoist age, the once revolutionary storytellers again reverted to the old tales of love and adventure. In 2010, an enterprising concert promoter in Beijing organized a touring company of blind storytellers and street performers led by two famous *shuoshude*. One plays the traditional *sanxian* with clappers and cymbal, the other performs with the *jinghu*, the small two-string fiddle traditionally used to accompany Chinese opera performances. The remaining members of the ensemble would be on the street begging without this opportunity to perform with the troupe.

In Japan since the 8th century, blind Buddhist priests (*moso*) performed in religious rituals on lutes (*biwa*) imported from China. Between 1156 and 1185, the country was torn by a great civil war between two powerful clans, the Heike and Genji, which culminated in the end of the glorious Heian period and the establishment of the Kamakura Shogunate. This period became the subject of great epic narratives like *The Tale of the Heike*. According to a 14th-century account, the courageous deeds of the warriors of both sides were written down and set to music by a blind Buddhist monk named Syobutu. For several hundred years after this, the powerful Todoza organization was responsible for maintaining the integrity of the tradition and for granting performing licenses exclusively to itinerant blind musicians. The tradition reached its peak of popularity in the 16th century. It has been in decline ever since, although it still has a few active practitioners. Watch this video of a present-day storyteller playing the *biwa*.

KOREAN *PANSORI* (KOREA)

A unique form of musical storytelling in Korea is *pansori*, in which a performer tells stories (*madang*) through an alternation of spoken narration and song. While much of the narration is spontaneously improvised and may include topical references and jokes, the songs are pre-composed and passed down from teacher to pupil. The performer sings the songs, takes the parts of the various characters in spoken dialogues, and provides poetic descriptions of locales and action scenes. Traditionally the *pansori* singer, or *kwangdae*, was male; however since the 20th century a number of women have excelled in the art. The term "*pansori*," which was applied around a hundred years ago to genres of storytelling by itinerant entertainers, comes from two terms: "*pan*," an area for activity such as a public square or market place, and "*sori*" meaning sound, indicating that performances often took place outdoors. A complete narrative can take up to six hours, but the stories are frequently excerpted for shorter performances; and the songs are sung independent of the tales in restaurants and teahouses. With only a fan and a handkerchief as props and staging limited to the dimensions of a straw mat, the *kwangdae* can hold an audience enthralled for hours. A drummer (*gosu*), typically male, accompanies the sung portions with the rhythm patterns (*changdan*), performed on *puk* barrel drum, that are characteristic of much of Korea's traditional music. He periodically calls out words of praise and encouragement (*chuimse*) to the singer, provides sound effects, and acts as a straight man or foil during the spoken portions. There is also a great deal of interaction between the storyteller and the audience. Of particular importance to this tradition is the *pansori* "voice" that is cultivated over many years by apprentice singers. Through arduous training and practice, the singer's voice becomes deeply expressive of the great emotional range the stories demand. The *kwangdae* is a highly cultivated and sophisticated artist who, though traditionally from the very bottom of the social hierarchy and often practicing his trade for commoners, was occasionally called upon to perform for the nobility.

The origins of this art form are obscure. Literary references exist since at least the 18th century. The first *pansori* narrative still in existence, and to this day the most popular, is based on an 18th-century story *Chunhyang-ga* (or "Song of Chunhyang") by the aristocrat Yu Jinha (1711–1791): the tale of a wife's devotion to her husband. By the end of the 18th century there were twelve stories in the repertoire of which five survive today. Each exemplifies one of the cardinal social relationships upheld by Confucian ethics: king and subject, father and son, elder brother and younger brother, husband and wife, friend and friend. By the mid-20th century this storytelling tradition was in

Fig. 13.6 *Pansori* performance on a straw mat, at the Busan Cultural Center in Busan, South Korea

decline, after decades of colonial occupation by Japan, World War II and a bitter civil war that divided the peninsula. In 1966, the South Korean government designated *pansori* "Important Intangible Cultural Property Number 5." This was done as part of a program to preserve the cultural legacies of the country. Important performers who had survived these tumultuous times were designated as "Living Cultural Assets" and provided with a small stipend for passing on this art to new generations.

In the 1990s, *pansori* had a revival in South Korea due in part to the great success of the film *Sopyonje*, directed by Im Kwon Taek. A short clip from the film introduced the concept of Korean rhythmic cycles (*changdan*) in Lesson 3. In that scene, a *kwangdae* teaches his two foster children the art of *pansori*. Since the boy has no talent for singing, he is learning to be a drummer. At the beginning of the movie, we meet the main character Yubon performing the climax of *Chunhyang-ga* at the birthday party of a wealthy landowner. Much later in the film, with Yubon's two children grown to adulthood, the wandering family of singer-storytellers has come upon hard times. In this scene, they are singing in a winter marketplace to attract a crowd for a medicine dealer. Their narration is interrupted by a modern brass band playing Western music, with which they cannot compete. The film, which deals primarily with the training of the girl and her coming to artistic maturity through suffering, created great popular interest and brought about a renaissance of the art form. *Sopyonje* is one of the greatest films ever made about the lives of traditional musicians. In 2003, the United Nations Educational, Scientific, and Cultural Organization (UNESCO) proclaimed *Pansori Epic Chant* one of the Masterpieces of the Oral and Intangible Heritage of Humanity; and today, students of the art study in music conservatories and perform in auditoriums and on television.

EPIC OF PABUJI (INDIA)

In the northwest Indian state of Rajasthan, itinerant hereditary storyteller-priests (*bhopas*) present tales from the Epic of Pabuji—a 14th-century hero and folk deity of the region. (See Map 8–3, p. 123.) In this pastoral, desert region of India, Pabuji is the protector of animals. According to the epic, it was Pabuji who first brought camels to Rajasthan, having defeated the demon Ravana and stolen his animals. Later he was martyred while rescuing a herd of cattle on his wedding day. The epic takes thirty-six hours to recite in its entirety, and complete performances—traditionally carried out over five consecutive nights—are rare. A large hand-painted scroll (*par*) of the epic story forms the backdrop to the performance. This scroll is treated as a sacred object, and *bhopa* families make daily offerings to it. The storyteller typically performs at the homes of worshipers of Pabuji who seek his mystical powers in times of misfortune or sickness. The *bhopa* dances and sings the narrative while accompanying himself on a bowed fiddle called a *ravanhatta* ("demon-slayer"). Jingle-bells around his ankles, and also attached to the end of his bow, provide rhythmic accompaniment. His veiled wife (*bhopi*) holds an oil lamp and illuminates the pictures on the scroll of the scene her husband is narrating. The *bhopi*, and sometimes their children, join in singing the refrains that punctuate the narrative. During his performance, the *bhopa* frequently interrupts the **epic narrative**, and tea is served as he tells topical stories and jokes, and leads the audience singing devotional songs (*bhajans*) and film songs. Thus the evening is part religious ritual, part entertainment. Watch this excerpt of an Epic of Pabuji performance.

Fig. 13.7   A Pabuji cloth painting (*par*) dating from 1938, by Jaravcand Josi of Bhilwara, Rajasthan. Tropenmuseum, Amsterdam

On a bus trip through Rajasthan, foreign travelers might see a *bhopa* and *bhopi* waiting by the entrance of a highway tourist restaurant. The *bhopa* offers his services to the tour guide, to sing a tale to the tourists while they eat their lunch. As with *kathakali* (see Lesson 12), changing economic circumstances have required many traditional artists in India and elsewhere to seek opportunities to supplement their incomes by performing for tourists.

CONCLUSION

One of the ways we make sense of our lives—the succession of days and years—is by creating episodes that have beginnings, middles, and endings for the re-telling. We carry into adulthood stories rescued from all that we forget of our childhood. Often these are of extraordinary events like birthdays, trips, victories, injuries, or surprising adventures. Remembering these episodes and sharing them as narratives give us a sense of continuity, self-knowledge, and connection with family and home. Groups also have stories, the telling and retelling of which binds the group together with a shared sense of history and destiny. Why is music so universally incorporated in the telling of these collectively meaningful stories? In the case of the epics we studied in this lesson, music serves as a mnemonic device, aiding bards in memorizing long passages of text. Melody, rhythm, and instrumental accompaniment provide additional levels of entertainment, symbolism, and psychological depth. Music lifts the experience of narrative out of the ordinary in the same ways that music demarcates the sacred: it makes the story extraordinary. In the next lesson, we see how music is joined to other art forms—dance, theater, and spectacle—to create what the German composer Richard Wagner called "complete work of art." We then examine the transformations of music production and consumption brought about by the late 19th- and early 20th-century inventions of sound recording, radio, and cinema. These technologies formed the basis of the modern mass media that provided new scope for musical storytelling.

KEY CONCEPTS

Music and storytelling	Oral and written texts	Musical globalization
Epic narrator/bard	Oral transmission	Blind storytellers
Minstrel	Hereditary profession	"Important Intangible
Epic narratives	Praise song	Cultural Property"

(Q) THINKING ABOUT MUSIC QUESTIONS

1. Discuss similarities between what epic narrators were doing millennia ago and what rap and hip-hop artists do today. Are there significant differences?
2. Consider the art of the epic narrator in terms of the composition/improvisation convergence described in Lesson 3. Describe your understanding of Milman Parry's description of the bardic process in terms of this dichotomy. Explain how and why the art of epic narration is different from the training and practice of Vedic priests (see Lesson 10).
3. Both the Balkan bards and the West African *jalolu* are described as occasionally singing for politicians or businessmen. Why and how do traditional artists sometimes serve powerful interests? Are there musicians in American society serving similar functions?
4. Think of musical storytelling in your own experience, in films, theater, songs. What does music add to the telling of a story? Describe an example.

NOTES

1   Alan Merriam, "Uses and Functions," *The Anthropology of Music* (Evanston, IL.: Northwestern University Press, 1964), 218.

2   Albert Lord, *The Singer of Tales,* ed. Stephen Mitchell and Gregory Nagy (Cambridge, MA: Harvard University Press, 1960, rev. ed. 2000).

3   Albert Lord, *The Singer of Tales,* ed. Stephen Mitchell and Gregory Nagy (Cambridge, MA: Harvard University Press, 1960, rev. ed. 2000), 21.

4   Albert Lord, *The Singer Resumes the Tale* (Ithaca, NY: Cornell University Press, 1995), 2.

5   Ivo Zanic, *Flag on the Mountain: A Political Anthropology of War in Croatia and Bosnia* (London: Saqi Books, 2007), 47.

6   Foday Musa Suso, "Jali Kunda: A Memoir," Matthew Kopa and Iris Brooks, ed., in *Jali Kunda: Griots of West Africa & Beyond*, (Roslyn, NY: Ellipsis Arts, 1996), 1.

7   Lucy Duran, "Mali-Guinea—Mande Music: West Africa's Musical Powerhouse," in Simon Broughton and Mark Ellingham, ed., *World Music: The Rough Guide, Vol.1: Africa, Europe and the Middle East*, (London: Rough Guides Ltd., 2000), 542.

8   Paul Oliver, "Music in West Africa," in *Yonder Come the Blues: The Evolution of a Genre,* 2nd ed. (Cambridge, UK: Cambridge University Press, 2001), 53.

9   Foday Musa Suso, "Jali Kunda: A Memoir," in Matthew Kopa and Iris Brooks, ed., *Jali Kunda: Griots of West Africa & Beyond*, (Roslyn, NY: Ellipsis Arts, 1999), 1.

10 Roderic Knight, "The Style of Mandinka Music: A Study in Extracting Theory from Practice," *Selected Reports in Ethnomusicology*, v (1984), 3–66.

11 Laura Arntson, "Praise Singing in Northern Sierra Leone," in Ruth Stone, ed., *The Garland Encyclopedia of World Music, Vol. 1: Africa*, (New York: Garland, 1997), 490.

12 Sylvia Pfeiffenberger, "Diali Cissokho's Move from Senegal to Pittsboro Sprouted the Music of Kairaba," *Indy Week*, September 11, 2014, http://www.indyweek.com/indyweek/diali-cissokhos-move-from-senegal-to-pittsboro-sprouted-the-music-of-kairaba/Content?oid=2655461

13 Frank Stasio, Press Review, accessed July 25, 2014, http://www.kairabamusic.com/press/.

14 Stephen Jones. "Snapshot: Yellow Earth," in Robert Provine, Yosihiko Tokumaru, and J. Lawrence Witzleben, ed., *The Garland Encyclopedia of World Music, Vol. 7: East Asia: China, Japan, and Korea*, (New York: Routledge, 2002), 258.

15 Chang-tai Hung, "Reeducating a Blind Storyteller: Han Qixiang and the Chinese Communist Storytelling Campaign," *Modern China* 19/4 (Oct. 1993), 395.

Lesson 14
Theater, Opera, Sound Recording, and Film

To participate in storytelling, either as narrator or audience, is to be in at least two worlds simultaneously: the here and now of bodily existence, and the parallel worlds created by the imagination. Anthropologist Clifford Geertz calls the human capacity for abstract thought, "the distinctive characteristic of our mentality."[1] It is because of this capacity that a story can lift us out of the bonds of the immediate into the imagined worlds of the long ago, the make-believe, the far away: the realms that stories create. Stories also reflect back on the reality of the here and now, portraying archetypes, moral teachings, justifications for social hierarchies, and narratives that explain symbolically why things are the way they are. Just as music can create boundaries between secular and sacred space and time (as we noted in Lesson 12), so music provides a vehicle for conveying the spiritual, psychological, and emotional dimensions of a story. This lesson examines ways in which stories are told through music in partnership with other art forms: poetry, dance, theater, and spectacle. Later in this lesson, we discuss the revolutions in electronic media that brought about new forms of theatrical entertainment, culminating in what may be the defining art form of the 20th century, the cinema. The role that music had played for millennia as an essential vehicle for storytelling continues into the 21st century, on streets, stage, and screen.

THEATER

Stories around the world are not only told and sung, they are also danced and dramatized in performance by actors with costumes, masks, and puppets. In many performance traditions, actors do not attempt to imitate or portray everyday human life in a realistic manner. Rather, they attempt to reveal supernatural powers that are believed to lie behind and control human experience. Performances often depict the deeds of deities, kings, and heroes, and enact great battles in which the forces of Good and Evil are locked in endless struggle. The worlds of myth and the sacred, as we noted in Unit 3, are evoked by actors who are highly trained in forms of physical movement and dance. Often they reveal, through their performances, beings that are more than, or other than, human. Many of these actors belong to theatrical families and are trained from childhood in these specialized forms. Other theatrical traditions have more to do with worldly affairs, exploring concerns that are more social and political. While even in Shakespeare's plays the supernatural is not far from the realm of the living, the stories reveal more about human motives than divine ones. In this lesson we discuss several theatrical traditions that use music to enhance the story and engage the audience.

GREEK MASKED DRAMA (ANCIENT GREECE)

All over the world, masks are used in dance dramas and pageants. In ancient Greece, dramas involving masks, musical instruments, and sung or chanted poetry were performed as integral parts of the rites celebrating Dionysus, the God of wine and intoxication. Both chorus members (consisting of twelve to fifteen actors) and leading actors wore masks that changed their identities into the mythic characters of the dramas, and altered and amplified their voices. Plays by Aeschylus, Sophocles, and Euripides, such as *Prometheus Bound*, *Oedipus Trilogy*, and *The Trojan Women* respectively, are studied by high school students throughout North America for their literary merit. However in their original contexts the theatrical and musical elements, which have now been lost, were equally important. Aristotle developed his concept of catharsis from the powerful impact this theater had on its audience members. According to this theory, the purpose of Greek theater was to purify the emotions by experiencing them intensely and yet separated from the circumstances of the individual audience member's life. As we will see later in this lesson, an attempt to recreate music drama in the ancient Greek manner by Renaissance intellectuals led to the development of European opera.

Fig. 14.1 **Masks of Greek tragedy and comedy**   Fig. 14.2 **South Korean *t'al ch'um* masked dancer**

T'AL CH'UM (KOREA)

Korean masked dance dramas (*t'al ch'um*) have been performed outdoors for centuries. These dramas, traditionally enacted by peasant farmers, poked fun at the decadent aristocracy, corrupt monks, and licentious shamans. The performances consist of a series of disconnected vignettes accompanied by native string, wind, and percussion instruments, and can last from a few hours to a full night. The actors improvise much of the dialogue and convey their characters through appropriate gestures and dance movements. All the parts were once played by men, but more recently women play the parts of **courtesan** and shamaness. As the dance drama progresses, the boundary between actor and audience is blurred, and by the end of the evening all present are dancing together. In many parts of the world, masks lend anonymity to members of lower classes, allowing them to mock and satirize the upper class in public without fear of reprisal. Now watch this short documentary on *t'al ch'um*.

LA VIRGEN DEL CARMEN FIESTA *(PERU)*

High in the Andes Mountains near Cuzco, Peru, a four-day masked pageant takes place every year starting on July 15 in the remote town of Paucartambo.

Map 14-1   Paucartambo and Cuzco in southern Peru

Source: *Garland Encyclopedia of World Music*, Volume 2: South America, Mexico, Central America, and the Caribbean

The festival is held in honor of the town's patron saint, *La Virgen del Carmen* (Our Lady of Mount Carmel), the provider of good health and prosperity. Various costumed and masked dance groups enact the story of Paucartambo and its people. The town's population consists primarily of **mestizos** (peoples of mixed Spanish and Native American ancestry) who speak the indigenous language of **Quechua** and are isolated from the majority Spanish-speaking population of Peru. The street festival reenacts the legendary struggle between disciplined jungle Indians and unruly traders from southern Peru over possession of the *Virgen del Carmen* statue. In this struggle, the indigenous peoples of the lowland rainforests (*Qhapac Chunchos*) always defeat the southern highland traders (*Qhapac Qollas*). Groups of townspeople portray their noble ancestors as well as the outsiders in a satirical, comical, and rowdy manner. Each group—Indians, traders, colonial Spanish, black slaves, liquor traders, lawyers, government officials, and clowns—has its own accompanying band, often made up of semiprofessional musicians hired from other towns. These bands have their own distinctive instruments, musical style, and

Fig. 14.3 Masked *Saqra* devil dancer in Peru

dance pieces that reflect the mixed ancestry of the population. Watch this video of the Paucartambo festival showing several of the dance and music groups. First, you will see the procession when the statue is carried through the streets; *La Virgen* is believed to bless every house she passes. The *Qhapac Chunchos* (jungle Indians), wearing feathered headdresses and carrying spears, walk on guard beside the statue, to the accompaniment of indigenous flutes and drums. In front of the statue are the *Qhapac Negros* (black slaves), in whose accompanying band you can hear a *metraca* (ratchet), bass drum, accordion, and *quena* flutes (0'19"). The *Saqras* devil dancers (at 0'39"), also accompanied by a mixed band of European accordions and Andean flutes and drums, wear monster or animal masks and blond wigs to represent the evil European colonizers. Then you will see the *Doctores* (0'56"), lawyers and government officials who exploit the rural population, and the *Majeños* liquor traders (at 1'03") who perform a staggering drunken dance accompanied by a brass band, another symbol of the Spanish colonial rulers.

During the four days of the festival the entire town is taken over by visitors from all over the region and beyond. On the third day, dance groups, musicians, and visitors alike go to the cemetery to visit the graves of former troupe members and to honor the dead (1'20"). Dancers place their masks and props on the gravestones, and music, songs, and dances follow moments of silence and prayer. The festivities continue throughout the day and night, and the video clip ends with the nighttime antics of the *Qhapac Qollas* (llama herders of the southern highlands), sporting white cloth head masks and jumping over street bonfires, twirling fireworks, and riding on flaming carts (1'50"). "For four days a year," writes ethnomusicologist Thomas Turino, "the plaza and cobblestone streets are transformed into a stage for a music drama that turns the normal order of daily life upside down."[2] The Paucartambo festival provides an opportunity for townspeople to honor their beloved saint, but also for the socially powerless to imagine, celebrate, and dwell at least for a short time in a world in which they have the upper hand.

BUNRAKU *(JAPAN)*

Many parts of the world have highly developed traditions of puppet theater. Japanese **bunraku** arose in the 17th century as an urban middle-class popular entertainment form. It developed from the fusing of a tradition of blind storytellers, who accompanied themselves on a plucked lute (*biwa*), with itinerant folk puppet theater. The roles of narrator, accompanist, and puppeteer were distinct, and the louder and more versatile *shamisen* (three-string lute) from Okinawa in the Ryukyu Islands south of Japan replaced the *biwa*. *Bunraku* developed in parallel with **kabuki**, a theatrical form with human actors. The two genres shared stories, competed for audience members, and imitated each other as the *kabuki* actors borrowed movements from the puppets and the puppet designers and puppeteers strove for ever more realistic effects. The puppet theater reached its greatest level of development and popularity in the 18th century, when the primary characters

Fig. 14.4 Puppeteers operate a *bunraku* puppet on stage, in Osaka, Japan (L), and *bunraku* singer-narrator and *shamisen* player (R)

each came to be manipulated by three puppeteers. Still today at the National Bunraku Theatre in Osaka (see Map 11-1, p. 170) the master puppeteer is visible to the audience and controls the puppet's right arm and head, and the other two hooded puppeteers manipulate the left arm, and the feet and legs respectively. Unlike any other puppet tradition in the world, in *bunraku* the puppeteers are on stage with the puppets, fully visible to the audience. Spectators remark that over time they become accustomed to this convention, and the three puppeteers seem to disappear as the audience concentrates on the realistic puppets. Connoisseurs of the art shift their attention back and forth between the puppet itself and the virtuosity of the master puppeteer. A singer-narrator and a *shamisen* player sit on a revolving side stage and provide all the dialogue and musical accompaniment for the *bunraku* play. The *shamisen* closely follows the vocal line, and the singer performs in three different styles: lyrical, declamatory, and most commonly in a half spoken, half sung style. In 2008, **Ningyo Joruri Bunraku Puppet Theatre** was inscribed on the UNESCO Representative list of Intangible Cultural Heritage of Humanity.

Like Indian *kathakali* discussed in Lesson 11, Japanese *bunraku* has faced considerable challenges in its long history, and both now might be considered endangered cultural species. Although *bunraku* has had something of a revival since the 1980s, the traditional crafts of the puppet-head carver, costume designer, and backstage technician are not being passed on to the next generation.

WAYANG KULIT *(JAVA, INDONESIA)*

One of the world's most dynamic, highly developed, musically elaborate, and dramatically complex theatrical traditions is the **wayang kulit** shadow puppet theater of Java, Indonesia. (See Map 7-6, p. 111.) The role of the **dalang** (puppeteer) is similar to the Korean *pansori* singer discussed in Lesson 13, in that he (and recently, she) takes on the different voices of all the characters and is entirely responsible for the narrative and dramatic success of the performance. Yet in addition to telling the story, the *dalang* manipulates leather puppets against a shadow screen, fulfilling the responsibilities of choreographer, director, actor, and producer. His role is one of the most complete and complex in the world's dramatic traditions. As in *kathakali* dance drama in India, many of the stories derive from the Hindu epics *Ramayana* and **Mahabharata**, brought to the Indonesian islands centuries ago and fused with indigenous Javanese mythology. An oil lamp or electric light suspended behind and above the *dalang* projects shadows of the puppets on a screen. Seated on the *dalang*'s side of the screen is an orchestra of musicians accompanying the play on a *gamelan*, an ensemble of instruments consisting mostly of tuned bronze gongs, bronze-keyed metallophones, and drums. Music appropriate to the various stages of the unfolding drama—courtly music, meditative music, and battle music—enhances the power of the narrative. The audience is free to watch the show from either side of the screen, viewing either the musicians and the *dalang*'s intricate manipulations or the shadow drama itself.

The Javanese *gamelan* instruments clearly visible in Figure 14.5b are: (L front) *kempul* (hanging gongs), (R front) *kenong* (suspended gongs), (mid center) *gambang* (xylophone), and (rear

Fig. 14.5a **Leather puppets cast their shadows on the screen in Javanese** *wayang kulit*

Fig. 14.5b Javanese *gamelan* instruments

center) *kendang* (barrel drum). As with *bunraku*, UNESCO placed Wayang Puppet Theatre on the Representative List of the Intangible Cultural Heritage of Humanity in 2008.

WESTERN OPERA

Opera, defined as music drama involving stagecraft (scenery, lighting, props, costumes, makeup) and dialogue that is usually sung throughout, is one of the great art forms of world culture. In the 19th century, the German opera composer Richard Wagner (1813–1883) coined the phrase *Gesamtkunstwerk* ("total art work") to describe an artistic medium that encompasses all others: literature, poetry, music, dance, drama, visual arts, and architecture.

As a distinct genre, opera's origins lie with a group of aristocratic intellectuals living in Florence, Italy, at the end of the 16th century. They met not in public but in the private home of Count Giovanni de' Bardi, and were thus known collectively as the *Camerata* (from *camera*, the Italian word for "room"). This group of philosophers and artists was concerned with the applicability of classical Greek aesthetic ideals to the culture of their own time. They noted that in poetry, sculpture, architecture, and painting, the Florentines of the Renaissance had surpassed their Greek models. Only in one area of artistic production was the current state of art woefully inadequate when compared with the purported accomplishments of their classical forebears. Nothing in their theater could compare with the 6th- and 5th-century BCE Athenian playwrights Aeschylus, Sophocles, and Euripides. It was believed at that time, though doubted by later scholars, that ancient Greek drama was sung, not spoken. Certainly there was music and dance involved; the portion of the stage where the actors sang and danced was known as the "orchestra." However, no music of ancient Greece survived, and the music of Renaissance Italy used for performing texts—Masses, motets, and madrigals—was polyphonic and therefore unsuitable for presenting dramatic speech. How, indeed, could music that combined many voices be used to declaim the speech of a single character?

The solution to the problem of writing music that convincingly projected dramatic speech was a device called *monody,* developed by the *Camerata* members. The most important melodic line was sung by the character, and the other parts that filled out the harmony were simplified and performed by instruments. The narrative moved forward by means of sung dialogue (**recitative**) and songs (arias), which stopped the action, allowing characters to reflect on their situation and show off to the audience their vocal prowess. The mandatory chorus, as in ancient Greek theater,

Fig. 14.6   Richard Wagner (1813–1883) (L), and a scene from Wagner's opera *Das Rheingold* 1869) (R)

 14-1

provided occasional commentary and played the roles of soldiers, townspeople, furies of Hades, etc. The famous aria, "*Tu sei morte*" ("You are dead") from one of the earliest operas, *Orfeo* (1607) by Claudio Monteverdi (1567–1643), demonstrates how, in a single generation, composers were able to combine music and dramatic speech to convey powerfully to the audience both a dramatic situation and the feelings and motives of the characters. Since the earliest operas were attempts to recreate ancient Greek theater, the stories were taken primarily from Greek mythology. The myth of Orpheus (*Orfeo* in Italian) was dramatized numerous times in early opera. The story involves a great musician whose bride Euridice has died on their wedding day, bitten by a snake; it served as a perfect vehicle for a singing actor in emotionally charged circumstances. In this aria, Orpheus declares that he will travel to the land of the dead and use his divinely inspired singing voice to persuade Hades, God of the Underworld, to return his wife to the living world. As the great Monteverdi was perfecting a new form of theater in Venice with his *Orfeo*, William Shakespeare was perfecting the Elizabethan theatre in London, and writing this immortal tribute to Orpheus titled "Orpheus with his Lute":

Orpheus with his lute made trees,
And the mountain tops that freeze,
Bow themselves, when he did sing:
To his music plants and flowers

Fig. 14.7   Claudio Monteverdi (1567–1643)

Ever sprung; as sun and showers
There had made a lasting spring.

Everything that heard him play,
Even the billows of the sea,
Hung their heads, and then lay by.
In sweet music is such art,
Killing care and grief of heart
Fall asleep, or hearing, die.

Shakespeare's Globe Theater employed musicians who played before, during, and after the spoken plays he wrote and produced; and provided fanfares, dancing accompaniments, and other music that the play's action required.

The first public opera house opened in Venice in 1637, and by the middle of the 17th century opera had become the most important form of aristocratic entertainment in much of Europe. In France, a Florentine composer, Jean-Baptiste Lully (in the spelling of his adopted home) adapted the opera to the tastes of the French court, combining the mythological and pastoral themes of Italian opera with the *ballet de cour,* the royal dance and pageantry that were an indispensable feature of court life during the reign of Louis XIV, the Sun King (1638–1713). A century earlier, Florentine Catherine de' Medici had introduced the tradition of ballet to the French court when she became Queen of France in 1547, and there it received lavish patronage. As Paris became the center of ballet, Italian composers had to insert appropriate scenes into their operatic works if they wanted them performed on a Parisian stage.

During the latter half of the 18th century, the themes of opera, most notably those of Wolfgang Amadeus Mozart (1756–1791), broadened to include comedies on contemporary themes including the tensions between the aristocracy and their subjects that would explode at the end of the century in the French Revolution.

The 19th century was the period of greatest development in opera, as national schools arose in Germany, Russia, Bohemia, and Spain (where opera was called *zarzuela*), in addition to Italy, France, and Austria where it was already well established. Two great figures emerged—Richard Wagner and Giuseppe Verdi, both born in the same year of 1813—who would polarize the

Fig. 14.8 Scenes from 19th-century Russian ballet: Odette in Tchaikovsky's *Swan Lake* (1876) (L), and Waltz of the Snowflakes, in *The Nutcracker* (1892) (R)

Fig. 14.9   The masked ball scene of Mozart's opera *Don Giovanni* (1787)

opera-going public and produce works that to this day form the core of the operatic literature. As noted at the beginning of this lesson, Richard Wagner saw music as an equal component of a composite art form through which a modern mythology would be ritually presented. He wrote both words and music for his operas, unlike most other opera composers who worked with playwrights for the text (called *libretto* in Italian). He also designed the scenery and staging effects, and even designed the theater in which his works would be ideally presented. The orchestra was as important as the singers and presented a complex musical mirror to the action on stage. For Giuseppe Verdi (1813–1901), opera was fundamentally about the art of singing, the lyrical and dramatic potential of the human voice. At the end of the 19th century in Italy and elsewhere, a new style emerged called *verismo* ("realism"), in which opera plots were drawn from real life situations, particularly involving the violence and high passions of the underclass. Sailors, clowns, and adulterous peasants all sang their distressing tales for audiences drawn more and more from the urban middle and professional classes.

It would seem that today opera is an anachronism. Few operas have been added to the permanent standard repertoire since the first decades of the 20th century, and opera companies are notoriously conservative. The average age for subscribers to the Metropolitan Opera in New York, North America's oldest and largest company, is sixty. Opera is the most expensive form of live theater, with labor costs for orchestra instrumentalists, stagehands, set designers, etc. in addition to the lead singers who command astronomical fees. Yet composers continue to write them, and young people continue to enroll in opera departments in music conservatories and universities to receive the specialized and arduous vocal training the genre demands. It must be remembered that the form of singing that characterizes opera developed long before the invention of electronic amplification, and since the late 19th century the unaided voice has had to project over an eighty-piece orchestra into a 2000-seat auditorium. New York, San Francisco, Chicago, Houston, and Los Angeles have world-class resident opera companies whose seasons generally sell out; and there are over a hundred smaller regional companies in North America. In Europe, even middle-sized cities have permanent resident companies performing full-season repertoires. Worldwide, there are around seventy fully professional opera companies active in some thirty countries. These artistic institutions are sources of great civic pride. Often resident ballet companies and symphony orchestras share the centrally located opera house, serving as a focal point for social rituals, and a destination for visiting dignitaries much as the medieval cathedral once served. In East Asia, Western opera is becoming extremely popular, with opera houses opening in Malaysia, Singapore, Thailand, South Korea, Japan, and China. In December 2006, New York's Metropolitan

Fig. 14.10   Giuseppe Verdi (1813–1901)

Opera Company premiered an opera, *The First Emperor*, by the Chinese composer Tan Dun who made his reputation in the West with his musical score to the Oscar-winning movie *Crouching Tiger, Hidden Dragon* (2000).

During the 18th and 19th centuries, various parallel genres developed for a more general audience. In London in the 1730s, the **ballad opera** competed with the Italian-language *opera seria* ("serious opera") providing affordable and popular entertainment for working-class patrons. Mozart wrote *The Magic Flute* (1791), a German-language **Singspiel** (music drama with spoken dialogue), for a lower-class, ticket-purchasing audience; his Italian-language operas were written for the Austrian Emperor's court theater. In 19th-century Paris, Jacques Offenbach's (1819–1880) famous *can-can* was danced at the *Opéra Comique* (Comic Opera House) as part of his operatic spoof on the Orpheus legend, *Orpheus in the Underworld* (1858). Spoken dialogue, simpler story lines, and more popularly accessible venues separated these traditions from the Grand Opera of the elite. These are the forebears of the North American musical theater: *The Sound of Music, Phantom of the Opera, Cats, Rent*, etc. Another parallel development in 17th-century Europe was the **oratorio**. This genre developed as a substitute for the opera during the Lenten season when theaters were closed. Plots were drawn from the Old and New Testaments, and costumes and staging were not used. German composer George Frideric Handel (1685–1759) wrote the English-language *Messiah* (1741), with its renowned "*Hallelujah*" chorus, in this genre when his own opera company was facing financial disaster, in part because of the popularity of the competing English ballad opera.

SOUND RECORDING

Developments in music have always been inexorably linked to developments in technology. The smelting of metals, the drawing of wire, the invention of paper and printing, the design of acoustical spaces have all influenced the ways in which music is created, performed, stored, transmitted, and experienced in incalculable ways. However, technological developments over the past hundred and twenty years have had more of an impact on the way music is created and consumed than arguably at any other time in the history of humanity. Prior to the invention of sound recording by the American inventor Thomas Edison in 1877 (the year of the earliest functional phonograph), all music was heard, and only heard, in the presence of the musicians making the musical sounds.

For the first time in history, Edison's machine made possible the separation of the singer from the song. Music thereafter became preservable and portable, and it could be bought and sold as a commodity like a pair of shoes. In 1903, an entire Verdi opera was recorded on forty discs, and by the end of the first decade of the 20th century, the music recording industry was a going concern worldwide. Phonographs and records became common household items by the First World War, at least for the upper classes. Electronic amplification of sound was developed in the 1920s by the engineers at the Western Union Company, as part of telephone technology. Prior to this, phonographs were purely mechanical devices with sound projected by means of a funnel-shaped megaphone. Along with these developments two other parallel technologies would have enormous impact in shaping musical experiences in the 20th century: radio and cinema. In 1910, Lee de Forest, the American inventor of the vacuum tube, broadcast the Italian tenor Enrico Caruso from the stage of the Metropolitan Opera House in New York City to demonstrate the possibility of using radio for entertainment purposes. The history of modern commercial radio began with the broadcast of the 1920 presidential election results over a Pittsburgh HAM (amateur) radio network. Music from phonograph records was played into the microphone between announcements.

Since the early 20th century, the use of electronic amplification in performance, radio broadcast, and recording playback has radically changed the way singers project their voices. Before sound amplification, popular singers employed vocal techniques much like those of opera singers to project their voices in theaters, and they then used these same voices for singing over the radio. Al Jolson (1886–1950), the first to sing in a sound feature film, and Ethel Merman (1908–1984), who made a career in the Broadway theater, retained this style of singing. But a few early pioneers of broadcasting, like Bing Crosby

14-2
14-3

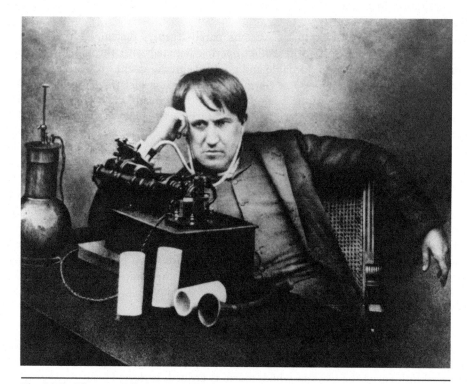

Fig. 14.11   Thomas Edison (1847–1931) and his phonograph, 1889

Fig. 14.12 **Bing Crosby (1903–1977) in 1942**

(1903–1977) and Frank Sinatra (1915–1998), learned how to use the microphone to produce a soft, intimate style of singing that made millions of Americans feel that the **crooners**, as they were called, were singing directly to them in the intimacy of their living rooms. Singers no longer had to fill acoustical spaces; the microphone and loudspeaker did the job for them.

As demonstrated by the enormous cultural importance of singers like Carlos Gardel, Umm Kulthum, and Louis Armstrong, people recognize significant components of their identities reflected in the quality of ideal singing voices. All these singers came of age during the rise of audio and broadcast technologies and their widespread adaptation. Since 1956, the Eurovision Song Contest has been held each year in the member countries of the European Broadcasting Union (EBU). It is one of the oldest and most-watched televised events in the world. Each country selects a song and an artist to represent it in the competition. Winners are chosen by a combination of call-in votes and a panel of music professionals. Since 2001, the Fox Network has had perennial success with *American Idol*, a program modeled after the British *Pop Idol* TV show. Televised song contests like these were designed to give undiscovered singers a chance to break into the music industry. Millions of Americans vote each season by telephone, internet, and text-messaging for their favorite young singer. A number of winners (and runners-up) have since pursued successful stage and screen careers, including Kelly Clarkson, Ruben Studdard, Clay Aiken, Fantasia Barrino, Carrie Underwood; and Jennifer Hudson, a 7th place winner who went on to win an Oscar for her supporting role in *Dreamgirls* (2006). As of 2014, forty-six countries and regions of the world had similar television contests identifying new talent among the citizenry.

Through the history of recording technology, recording and playback devices have steadily decreased in size and increased in storage capacity and portability. Today, a typical MP3 player like the iPod or smartphone can hold an entire library of thousands of songs, and audio files (MP3, M4A, wav, etc.) can be sent almost instantaneously around the world via the internet. Large online music stores like Amazon mp3, iTunes, eMusic, Google Play, Nokia Music Store, and Xbox Music carry downloadable recordings from every continent in the world, and music streaming services such as Spotify and Pandora deliver and recommend audio tracks to millions of users on multiple media devices. The amount and variety of music available to the average American music consumer is simply unimaginable compared to a generation ago. Most of these musical experiences, however, involve consumption rather than creation; and most are mediated, that is, an electronic technology separates and stands between the music maker and the listener. Many young people have had limited experience with the excitement and immediacy of live music performance; and while music accompanies many of their daily activities—driving, walking, eating, studying, exercising— they do not enjoy the satisfaction of playing an instrument, singing in a choir, or attending a concert.

FILM

HOLLYWOOD (USA)

A new form of mass entertainment grew from the invention of the movie camera to rival the printing press. From the beginning of the history of motion pictures in the 1890s, music has formed an integral part of the medium and its history. During the silent film era, live musicians improvised

Fig. 14.13   Poster for the first sound feature film, *The Jazz Singer* **(1927)**

or performed written music to accompany the action cuing the audience's emotional responses, and providing continuity to the succession of images. By the 1920s, musicians were routinely employed in movie theaters, and the music became a sophisticated blend of classical and popular melodies interspersed with newly composed and improvised sections all coordinated with the action on screen. When a studio released a feature film, it sometimes included sheet music notation for local musicians to provide a soundtrack. For example, the great comedian of the silent film era, Charlie Chaplin (1889–1977), composed music scores to accompany all of his silent comedies.

The first "talkie" with synchronized dialogue was the Warner Brothers' film *The Jazz Singer,* released in 1927. Since then, film music composition, sound technology, and cinematic development have been intimately linked. Lavish Hollywood movie musicals date from the late 1930s following the success of *The Wizard of Oz* (1939). At around the same time, the Walt Disney studios were making full-length animated feature films such as *Snow White and the Seven Dwarfs* (1937) and *Pinocchio* (1940), which incorporated songs that became immensely popular. From the 1950s, cinema versions of Broadway musicals brought this distinctly urban form of entertainment out to rural communities, with such successful movies as *South Pacific* (1958), *West Side Story* (1961), and *My Fair Lady* (1964); and more recently *Chicago* (2002) and *Phantom of the Opera* (2004). The large motion picture studios of southern California employed symphony orchestras and European-trained composers who often wrote in the style of grand opera to accompany sweeping sagas like *Gone with the Wind* (1939) and Biblical epics like *The Ten Commandments* (1956) and *Ben Hur* (1959). The 1981 sports drama *Chariots of Fire* sent shock waves through the film music industry when the composer Vangelis created the complete score on a synthesizer, bypassing the entire musical establishment. Since that historic milestone, film scores have been quite eclectic in style and the symphony orchestra has continued to be a mainstay. Indeed, the most successful film composer of our time is John Williams who wrote fully orchestrated scores in the Hollywood epic tradition for *Star Wars, Superman, Jaws, Schindler's List,* and the *Harry Potter* movies. Popular musical styles have also been well represented in film music, including jazz (*Pink Panther*), rock and roll (*Jailhouse Rock, School of Rock,* and *Hard Days Night*), disco (*Saturday Night Fever*), country (*Coal Miner's Daughter*), old timey (*O Brother, Where Art Thou?*), and hip-hop (*Do the Right Thing*), to name a few.

Because music carries and conveys broad and powerful meanings, is richly associative, and evokes deep emotional responses, film viewers have come to rely on musical soundtracks in complex ways to make sense out of the cinematic experience. The producer, director, and film score composer must work together to coordinate the cinematic, narrative, and musical elements of a film. They use several musical devices to enhance audience engagement with the story. These include **diegetic and non-diegetic music,** marker of locale, establishment of mood, **leitmotif,** sheer entertainment value, quotation, and foreshadowing. We discuss these below along with examples from the Hollywood film industry.

Film music is categorized as either diegetic, in which the music and musicians are part of the narrative itself, or non-diegetic, in which the audience understands that the characters neither see the musicians nor hear the music. The purpose of non-diegetic music is clearly supplemental to the narrative, like the score for *Harry Potter* films or music that runs during a film's title and credits. Sometimes background music has an ambiguous source and function. Mira Nair's film *Mississippi Masala* (1991) tells the story of an East Indian immigrant family living in Greenwood, Mississippi. Before moving to the American South, they lived in Uganda, East Africa, where the husband Jay had been a successful lawyer and businessman. The family was caught up in a historical event in 1971, when the ruling tyrant, Idi Amin, gave all Indian and Pakistani residents ninety days to leave the country. They lost nearly everything, and had to start over again as proprietors of a liquor store. At the end of the film, Jay has returned to Uganda alone fifteen years later to pursue a lawsuit suit, unsuccessfully as it happens. As film viewers see him sadly inspecting the ruins of his African home, they hear a blues harmonica in the soundtrack. The scene cuts to his wife in their liquor store in Mississippi reading a letter from him. The camera pans around the store and we see that one of the locals in the shop is actually playing the music. The scene switches back to Africa while the blues music continues, thus having the status of both diegetic in Mississippi and non-diegetic in Uganda. The scene ends with Jay turning his back on the ruined past and walking into the center of Kampala where a street party is going on. In the soundtrack, the African dance music replaces the Mississippi harmonica. Music in this scene is thus both part of the narrative and part of the means by which the narrative is conveyed to the audience. The blues symbolizes Jay's feelings of nostalgia for his adopted home, and the Ugandan dance music symbolizes the beautiful but now alien land he must leave forever. The music serves both as a **marker of locale** (the blues identifying Mississippi and the dance music, Uganda), and as an emotional cue (the blues expressing resignation and acceptance, the dance music a festive joy).

The "Shark Theme" in Steven Spielberg's *Jaws* (1975) is an alternating two-note pattern that performs several functions simultaneously. It is used in the film to evoke terror, to **establish the mood** of horror and suspense, and to propel the sense of dramatic time accelerating. It also functions as a **leitmotif**, a term used to describe a musical/dramatic technique perfected by German opera composer Richard Wagner in which a short musical theme or phrase is consistently associated with a character, a place, an object, or a recurring idea in the plot. Throughout the movie, the theme's recurrence coincides with the presence of hidden danger. When the audience hears the repeating two-note theme it knows the killer shark is in the vicinity, even when the on-screen characters do not. The accelerating rhythm and increase in volume both heighten the dramatic tension and locate the characters and situation in relationship to the imminent danger: the louder and faster the music, the nearer the characters are to calamity. The musical build-up, which parallels the dramatic build-up, also triggers increasing tension, dread, and excitement in the viewers, and the musical and dramatic climax occur simultaneously. Composers of horror movie music are masterful at evoking suspense and terror in a scene that would otherwise be experienced as neutral. As in the *Jaws* example, the audience is sonically alerted to dangers of which the characters in the narrative are unaware.

In the bar scene in George Lucas' first *Star Wars* film (1977), a decidedly non-human quartet plays an almost recognizable version of Dixieland jazz. The bar "musicians" create and sustain the tawdry honky-tonk atmosphere of the space saloon where Ben (Obi-Wan) Kenobi and Luke Skywalker are meeting smuggler Han Solo for the first time to discuss their spaceship mission to the planet Alderaan. The music is diegetic; it does not underscore for the theater audience the emotional charge of the drama unfolding at the bar in the manner of non-diegetic music (like the *Jaws* example). In fact, the musical score only responds to the action when Obi-Wan, defending his charge Luke Skywalker, severs the arm of an attacker. At this climactic moment, the music stops because the musicians are temporarily distracted from their music making. But only momentarily, for soon they strike up the tune again, the violent exchange being nothing terribly out of the ordinary in *this* corner of the galaxy! Despite its grizzly ending, the scene serves as comic relief and the music in the saloon provides **sheer entertainment value** not only for the space travelers but for the cinema audience as well.

Perhaps the most poignant scene in *The Shawshank Redemption* (1994, directed by Frank Darabont) occurs when Andy Dufresne, serving two life sentences at a state prison in Maine for murders he did not commit, locks himself in the warden's office and plays a recording of a duet from Mozart's opera *The Marriage of Figaro* over the public address system. The soaring women's voices coming from the loudspeakers bring the entire Shawshank Prison population to a standstill, stunned by this sudden interruption of intense musical expression. This **quotation** of previously composed music in the film score is the cinematic equivalent of quoted text in a book. For a brief moment, the sublime music allows the prisoners to experience an inner escape, a freedom from the pain and suffering of their incarceration, which is only later articulated verbally by Andy's friend Red in a voiceover. The quotation enhances the emotional drama and **foreshadows** Andy's own eventual escape from Shawshank, both for the audience and for Andy himself. Music often serves this function in cinema, telegraphing to the audience information not available to the characters on the screen, such as impending danger or the resolution of a conflict. It also plays a significant non-diegetic role in deepening the audience's understanding of the prisoners' psychological state through the startling juxtaposition of their bleak prospects and surroundings with Mozart's transcendent melody, symbolizing freedom.

There have been many movies made about musicians such as *Amadeus* (Mozart), *Immortal Beloved* (Beethoven), *Coal Miner's Daughter* (Loretta Lynn), *Sweet Dreams* (Patsy Cline), *Bird* (Charlie Parker), *The Last Waltz* (The Band), *Ray* (Ray Charles), and *Walk the Line* (Johnny Cash), as well as documentaries on music festivals like *Monterey Pop* and *Woodstock*. The relationship between music and film has been one of intense interaction and parallel development. Many of the greatest composers of the 20th century composed for films, including Leonard Bernstein, Aaron Copland, Dmitri Shostakovich, Sergei Prokofiev, Johnny Mercer, and Lennon and McCartney. Recently symphony orchestras have given concert performances of film scores, seeking to broaden their audience base, and songs appearing in films enjoy radio play and often score highly on the "charts."

WORLD CINEMA AND BOLLYWOOD (INDIA)

The first motion picture was filmed by the Lumière Brothers of France in 1894, and within twenty years the technology of cinema had spread throughout the world. By the first decades of the 20th century, film studios and theaters had opened on every continent. Pioneering filmmakers adapted the new medium to different cultures and social contexts with unique conventions and trajectories of development. By the end of the 20th century, more than a hundred countries had established motion picture industries, and since the initiation of the American Academy Awards Foreign Language category in 1956, submissions from forty-six countries have been nominated. Many countries have multiple industries, since they have multilingual societies. Nigeria has the second largest film industry in the world (called Nollywood) and produces films in Yoruba, Hausa, Igbo, and Edo languages for regional audiences. Yet the majority of Nollywood films are produced in English, and their popularity has spread throughout Africa. Besides the government, the Nigerian motion picture industry is the largest employer in the country. It provides, as elsewhere in the world, employment for many musicians, as the hundreds of movies made each year require musical soundtracks to support the narrative.

India produces the largest number of films in the world, in multiple regional languages such as Tamil, Telugu, Bengali, Marathi, and Hindi. Bollywood refers to the Hindi film industry, a combination of the words "Bombay" (the industry's center, now called Mumbai) and "Hollywood." (See Map 8–3, p.123.) While Hindi-language films account for less than fifteen percent of India's total, they are enormously popular and influential both in India and abroad, especially in the Indian diaspora and increasingly among non-Indian audiences. Bollywood films are typically three-hour-long musical extravaganzas that blend melodrama, comedy, violence, action, and romance. Into this eclectic mix are woven at least five or six songs and two or more choreographed dance numbers. A Bollywood film without songs and dances is as rare as a Hollywood film without a music soundtrack. The inclusion of songs and dances dates from the very first Hindi sound film in 1931, *Alam Ara* ("Light of the World"), and is rooted in the musical character of Indian theater itself, from the ancient Sanskrit dramas of the early centuries CE to the performances of India's epic tales (the *Mahabharata* and *Ramayana*), as well as regional folk theaters.

With few exceptions, Indian film songs are sung by professional **playback singers** (ghost singers) and not by film actors and actresses. These playback artists prerecord the songs in sound studios, and film artists lip-synch the song lyrics during filming. Throughout the history of Indian sound cinema, a relatively small number of playback singers have dominated the scene, each recording up to five or more songs per day. Indian audiences from the 1940s and 50s onwards came to love the singing voices of Lata Mangeshkar, Asha Bhosle, Mohammed Rafi, Mukesh, Kishore Kumar, and others, which they heard time and again from the mouths of their favorite actors and actresses. Both Lata Mangeshkar and her sister Asha Bhosle have been recognized in the *Guinness Book of World Records* for having recorded more songs than any other artist in music history.

Film songs have not only played an essential role in the film narrative, developing or commenting on the plot, but they became India's pop music, reaching audiences beyond the cinema via

Fig. 14.14 Bollywood actor Hrithik Roshan dancing at the 15th International Indian Film Academy (IIFA) Awards, Tampa, Florida, 2014

recordings, radio, and television. In the "golden age" of Hindi cinema (1950s–60s), films such as *Awara* ("Tramp"), *Sri 420* ("Mr. 420"), *Jhanak Jhanak Pyal Baje* ("The Ankle Bells Jingle"), *Pyaasa* ("Thirst"), *Mother India*, and *Mughal-e-Azam* ("Mughal Emperor") were enormously successful in large part due to their popular songs. These had simple, memorable melodies, catchy rhythms, and were accompanied by large studio orchestras mixing Western and Indian instruments. In the 1970s and 80s, the trend for historical and romantic dramas of earlier decades gave way to action thrillers and social dramas, such as *Zanjeer* ("Chains"), *Sholay* ("Flames"), and *Pakeezah* ("Pure"). A notable, award-winning film, *Amar, Akbar, Anthony* (1977), represents a common theme in Hindi cinema of religious and ethnic harmony in this often fractious society. The narrative, concerning three brothers separated in childhood and raised as a Hindu, a Muslim, and a Christian respectively, provided the music director team Laxmikant-Pyarelal with the opportunity for a diverse musical score referencing the three religious traditions. In general, disco and other contemporary popular music styles pervaded Bollywood film songs and dances of these two decades. Blockbuster films of more recent years have likewise drawn on new music and dance forms from hip-hop and rap to breakdancing. Among the most successful movies of the 1990s and 2000s were *Hum Aapke Hain Koun!* ("Who am I to You!" 1994), *Dilwale Dulhania Le Jayenge* ("The Brave-hearted will Take Away the Bride," 1995), *Lagaan* ("Land Tax," 2001), *Devdas* (2002), and *3 Idiots* (2009). Bollywood producers release film songs into the music market prior to their movie release dates as promotional material, and music sales serve to enhance box-office sales. As integral components of their film narrative, however, film songs derive much of their meaning from the film itself, and "superhit" movies can greatly increase music sales by later attracting the Bollywood film audience market.

Bollywood songs and films provide entertainment for hundreds of millions of Indian viewers and listeners, both rural and urban. In the 1950s and 60s, a parallel cinema arose in India, producing small-budget, serious art films for a more discerning audience. Satyajit Ray (1921–1992) was a leading film-maker in this movement, who explored in his films and documentaries such topics as India's Hindu society and its colonial history. Unlike Bollywood productions for mass audiences, these art films employed more classical soundtracks generally without songs. For Satyajit Ray's highly-acclaimed

Bengali films, the *Apu Trilogy* (1955–1959), the director worked closely with Pandit Ravi Shankar who composed the scores based on classical *ragas* and Bengali folk melodies; and in 1958 Ray worked with another great Indian *sitar* player, Ustad Vilayat Khan (1928–2004), on the classical film score for his film *Jalsagar* (The Music Room).

CONCLUSION

People attend movies, and theatrical and narrative events like those discussed in this lesson as part of a larger aspect of human social life in which music is deeply implicated in complex ways. Performances bring people together. The phenomenon of watching a movie in solitude on a tablet, smartphone, or home television is quite recent. In the past, attending a movie was a public, social event, like going to the opera, ballet, theater, or even attending a religious ritual. In the next lesson, the final one in our course, we examine the roles music plays on occasions when people gather publicly. For often, when people congregate, music is somewhere on the scene.

KEY CONCEPTS

Rites of Dionysus
Aristotelian catharsis
Social satire
Singer-narrator
Ballet
Opera
Complete work of art
    (*Gesamtkunstwerk*)

Recitative
Aria
Chorus
Public opera house
American musical
    theater
Oratorio
Sound recording

Commodification of music
Digital sound technology
Mediated musical
    experience
Mass entertainment
Film score devices
World cinema

Q THINKING ABOUT MUSIC QUESTIONS

1. Explain in your own words the sentence: "For the first time in history, Edison's machine made possible the separation of the singer from the song." How do you think this impacts the ways people experience music as compared with several generations ago? What are the advantages brought about by the technologies that derive from Edison's original invention? What are the disadvantages?

2. Attend an opera or ballet, or watch a video of one. Think of how the music affects the overall experience. Of the first six of Merriam's Functions—Emotional Expression, Aesthetic Enjoyment, Entertainment, Communication, Symbolic Representation, Physical Response—which ones can you find the music serving? Choose three of the functions and describe in detail how the music fulfills each one.

3. Watch your favorite film and do a similar exercise as question 2. Which of the film soundtrack devices can you identify: diegetic and non-diegetic music, marker of locale, establishment of mood, leitmotif, sheer entertainment value, quotation, and foreshadowing? Choose three and describe in detail how your movie's soundtrack plays these roles.

4. Imagine you are writing the screenplay for a movie about your own life, and you have been asked to suggest specific songs for the soundtrack. Choose a total of at least three songs. Why does each song you have chosen fit a particular stage of your life (infant, child, teenager, college student, etc.)? What information about you will each song reveal to the film audience that the script alone would not provide?

5. Compare your own experience of live music (either as participant or audience) with your experience of mediated music (via smartphone, MP3 player, radio, etc.). How are they the same? How are they different? What have the musical technologies of the 20th and 21st centuries added to the experience of music, and what might they have taken away from it?

NOTES

1   Clifford Geertz, *The Interpretation of Cultures*, new ed. (New York, NY: Basic Books, 2000), 95.
2   Thomas Turino, "The Music of Latin America," in Bruno Nettl et al., ed., *Excursions in World Music*. 5th ed. (Upper Saddle River, NJ: Pearson Prentice Hall, 2008), 271.

Lesson 15
Music in Public Spaces

We are all familiar with the recent phenomenon of people walking along crowded streets or riding on public transportation while listening privately, through earbuds, to music on their iPods and smartphones. In the past, however, private music in public spaces was technologically impossible. Humans are not naturally equipped with the means to close our ears, as we can our eyes, and thus the sounds of vendors calling out their wares, military fanfares, and street entertainers were all inescapable components of the sonic environment. Totalitarian regimes have taken advantage of this by filling public spaces with the sounds of propaganda. The rallies of Adolf Hitler and his Nazi Youth were always accompanied by the martial music of military bands, played at a deafening level. In China after the 1949 establishment of the People's Republic under Chairman Mao, and especially during the Cultural Revolution (1966–1976), more than a million loudspeakers were deployed around the country to saturate the environment with the incessant sound of political slogans and patriotic songs. Earbuds were not available and there was no way to avoid the omnipresent broadcasts from the central government with their insistent message to conform. These represent extreme examples of the way music can be used to fill public spaces, adding its meanings and pervasive presence to the overall "soundscape," as ethnomusicologists call the composite environmental sound of a particular locale. In this final lesson, we examine a variety of soundscapes, and the roles music plays in shaping our experience of social space.

 Busking musicians in popular tourist locations, in subways, and along downtown city streets hope for donations from passersby for their musical efforts. These public entertainers have been part of the urban landscape at least since ancient Roman times. In 1904, English poet Alfred Noyes wrote a long tribute to the pleasures of hearing the sound of a barrel organ—a mechanical, crank-operated instrument popular at the turn of the 20th century. The poem opens:

> There's a barrel-organ carolling across a golden street
> In the City as the sun sinks low;
> And the music's not immortal; but the world has made it sweet
> And fulfilled it with the sunset glow;
> And it pulses through the pleasures of the City and the pain
> That surround the singing organ like a large eternal light;
> And they've given it a glory and a part to play again
> In the Symphony that rules the day and night.

Fig. 15.1 **Barrel organ player in Bruges, Belgium**

Buskers continue to be common sights in many cities and towns. France, Germany, and Italy, in particular, have experienced an influx of musicians from the poorer countries of Eastern Europe who are free to travel in the unified European Union and ply this trade. Seen as little more than beggars by some, street musicians hope that they are heard and understood as important contributors to the public environment.

In suburban shopping malls in North America, recorded music pervades the corridors with pleasant but nondescript tunes, and draws the public into the individual shops with songs pitched to the particular type of clientele each hopes to attract. Just after Thanksgiving, the soundtrack of the mall switches to Christmas holiday music, symbolically and obsessively repeating the message: "Tis the Season...to *shop*!" At harvest time, North Carolina and other states of America put on a great celebration of agriculture, the State Fair. Throughout the fairgrounds sound stages are set up for concerts by local and regional artists, including some of national repute. The ferris wheels, rollercoasters, and merry-go-rounds each have their own pre-recorded soundtrack. Standing at any location in the midst of all this activity, fairgoers hear these sounds and navigate toward their sources to find the various attractions, just as the cooking smells draw them to the fried dough, hot dogs, and turkey legs. Wherever people gather in numbers, music is usually present serving a variety of functions—Entertainment, Symbolism, Communication, etc.—and permeating the environment with its sonic power. As stated in the Unit 4 Introduction, at some of these occasions such as concerts and festivals, music is the central focus of the event; at others, music is a significant part of a larger overall public spectacle or celebration, and at still others, it is merely there in the background. At times, it is the musicians themselves who draw the crowds, as when the Rolling Stones attract thousands for a concert in a sports arena. At other times, it is the crowds that draw the musicians, as in the case of buskers and street entertainers performing along the thoroughfares of urban centers and on market day in provincial towns.

NIGHTLIFE

Nightlife refers to the public activities that people engage in between the hours of work and the hours of sleep. Regimented work schedules dictated by industrial and mercantile economies have affected the life patterns of many people around the world, substituting the agricultural rhythms that follow the sun and the weather with the mechanized time clock. This has created predictable pockets of leisure time—evenings, weekends, vacations—which people can devote to entertainment, socializing, and courtship. Consider Friday nights in particular, when workers have a weekly paycheck in their pockets and an evening and weekend ahead. Urban centers have become the settings for establishments devoted to filling these hours with companionship, alcohol, a relaxation of moral strictures, and music. These establishments include public houses, nightclubs, bars, dance halls, cabarets, movie theaters, playhouses, and restaurants. Many of these use music, either live or pre-recorded, to attract and entertain their clientele. At restaurants the music is often in the background of the dining experience and enhances the ambience of the place and character of the cuisine. At discos and dance halls, live musicians or DJs invite people to the dance floor for what is often a prelude to more serious courtship later on. In Xining, a city in central China with a substantial Tibetan minority population, young Tibetans gather in the large central plaza every Wednesday evening for traditional circle dancing accompanied by recorded and electronically amplified music. Here, Tibetans who have left the countryside, their farms and herds, and are adjusting to the alien world of the city find comfort in socializing with other relocated Tibetans, making new acquaintances and social connections, finding dating partners, and reuniting with distant family members.

SONIDERO BAILES *(MEXICO/USA)*

In the New York City area, DJ dance parties called **sonidero bailes**, held in clubs, community centers, bingo halls, and restaurants, provide a social space where young Mexican immigrants can, in a virtual sense, travel home to Mexico through music, their imagination, and the charismatic person of the DJ or *sonidero*. The *sonideros* spin discs of Columbian-produced *cumbia* dance music amplified and distorted by the high-tech sound systems in which they take "fetishistic pride." The *sonidero* acts "as the voice of a displaced community whose emotions and attentions are constantly shifting between a fragmented reality of 'here' and 'there'—...the US [and] Mexico," writes ethnomusicologist Cathy Ragland. "The sonidero acts as a virtual navigator of the sound experience at the **baile**."[1] With a voice amplified to superhuman proportions, he presides over the evening's events, speaking over the dance music in a running narration of greetings, information, advertising, and self-promotion. "However as the baile progresses, [his] most important and clearly more taxing job is to read into the microphone the personal dedications and salutations which members of the audience and dancers are now giving to him...written...on napkins, scraps of notebook paper,...or whatever is handy."[2] These he reads through the sound system "with creative flair, personality, and conviction." At the end of a half-hour set, the *sonidero's* crew produce recordings of the show that are purchased by the audience members who submitted the dedications. These are then mailed to their relatives in Mexico and elsewhere in the United States. The *sonideros* then travel to Mexico to stage dance parties in which families and friends there record reciprocal greetings and dedications that are sent back to New York.

> The sonidero's constant travel to and from Mexico for performances helps keep Mexico alive in the immigrants' collective imaginations. This sensation is enhanced by the physical presence of the sonidero, who acts as a conduit for communication between individuals on both sides of the border.[3]

Far more than an evening's entertainment or an opportunity to drink and meet friends and make liaisons, the *sonidero baile* binds a community fragmented by poverty, immigration, and cultural displacement. The deafening sounds emanating from the amplifiers constitute "the noise of a community that is determined to maintain family and community cohesion despite being geographically scattered, socially marginalized, and politically powerless."[4]

COURTESANS *(INTERNATIONAL)*

"All over the world, the sensual pleasure of music has made it the natural accompaniment to the other sensual pleasures of life—particularly the very basic ones—food and sex," writes composer and musicologist Gregory Youtz.[5] Many urban areas have designated "pleasure quarters" and "red-light districts," where evening diversions may include the services of women engaged in prostitution. Shakespeare's Globe Theatre was located on the south bank of the Thames River in London, an area associated with illicit as well as theatrical entertainments. The bordellos and whorehouses of the past often employed musicians to entertain clients waiting to be shown a room upstairs. World famous musicians Johannes Brahms and Louis Armstrong began their performance careers in such establishments, the former in Hamburg, the latter in New Orleans.

A strong connection between women, the performing arts, and nocturnal entertainment has existed from ancient to modern times in the role of the courtesan. As "women [who] engage in relatively exclusive exchanges of artistic graces, elevated conversation, and sexual favors with male patrons,"[6] courtesans have differed from prostitutes through their high level of education and their skills as singers, dancers, and instrumentalists. Courtesans have typically belonged to the lower social classes and have been patronized by male members of the upper classes, in some instances using "clothes and makeup to create images of themselves as alluring upper-class women."[7] Referring to the Chinese **min ji**, but applicable broadly, Gregory Youtz writes, "These women ranged from fabulously wealthy and respected queens of urban society, to impoverished and abused victims of the common brothel."[8] From ancient Greece to imperial China, from Renaissance Italy to Edo Japan (17th–19th centuries), the courtesan—the Greek *hetaira*, the Italian *cortigiana*, the Chinese *min ji*, the Korean *gisaeng*, the Japanese *geisha*, the Indian *tawaif*—maintained a high standard of creativity and artistry in music and dance. In some cultural contexts, older members of the profession taught the younger ones the various skills required of them; in others, male music and dance masters taught the girls, sometimes performing with them as accompanists.

In the pleasure districts of Xian, the ancient capital city of Tang Dynasty China (7th–10th centuries),

> courtesans in their houses were organized into guilds, and regulated and taxed as businesses.... [The women in these enterprises] were brought into the profession at the age of eight or nine and trained in the arts of serving food and drink, singing, playing instruments, and dancing. They were also given a basic education in reading, writing, history, and literature because these were necessary to participate in the conversations and the literary-poetic games which were the popular pastimes at gentlemen's gatherings.[9]

In northern India in the late 18th and early 19th centuries, the *tawaif* was responsible for a number of innovations in the music and dance of the region, making available in their salons levels of musical sophistication previously heard only in the royal courts. Their establishments, the *kotha*, were meeting places for wealthy patrons, poets, artists, and intellectuals. First the British colonial authorities and then, after independence, the nationalist bourgeois reform movements suppressed and nearly eradicated all trace of this once vibrant social institution. The descendants of the *tawaif*, a hereditary occupation, are now seeking to revitalize and legitimize their performing arts with the help of non-governmental organizations.

In many cultures of the world, the courtesan appeared importantly as a poetic and literary figure, and unlike most other women, her thoughts and words have come down to us, for she was taught to read and write.

> Courtesans are the elite of prostitutes. Their lives have been lauded by writers of many times and places. In societies where wives were not allowed to interact socially with men, courtesans have been used to fill the gap. They are the only prostitutes to leave their names in histories, and at times they have had a profound effect on politics and the arts.[10]

While the courtesan is often depicted in literature and film as a vibrant and provocative character, changing sexual mores worldwide have made the cultivated female entertainer almost obsolete, and driven underground the sex-trade worker, now often uneducated, trafficked, abused, and from the poorest of the poor.

SPORTING EVENTS (NIGERIA, SOUTH AFRICA)

Sporting events are significant and popular social occasions in many parts of the world. Musicians often take part, entertaining the crowds, stirring emotions in support of athletes, and inspiring group solidarity with songs of unity. In this video clip, musicians perform at a boxing match (*dambe*) in the Hausa region of northern Nigeria. A singer, amplifying his voice with an aluminum cup, announces to the townspeople that the matches are about to begin. Five side-blown *sarewa* flutes accompany him. During the matches themselves, talking drums (*jauje*) inspire the boxers and incite the enthusiasm of the spectators, adding their complex rhythmic patterns to the tumult of the crowd noise. At the very end of the clip, we hear the voice of a praise singer celebrating the victors.

On a much larger scale, American college football has incorporated the tradition of the Half-Time Show, in which marching bands and cheerleaders, baton-twirlers and dancers entertain spectators with their highly choreographed routines. Music served similar functions at the 2010 World Cup Football Tournament in Johannesburg, South Africa. (What everyone else in the world calls "football," Americans call "soccer.") This major international event began with an inaugural World Cup "Kick-off Celebration Concert" in Orlando Stadium in Soweto. The FIFA (Fédération Internationale de Football Association) promotional website stated: "Billed as the greatest entertainment event to date in Africa, the concert will...feature musical performances by international superstars in collaboration with major African artists.... This three-hour celebratory extravaganza, [combining] the two universal passions of football and music before a capacity stadium audience of 30,000, will be broadcast to millions more worldwide."[11]

Fig. 15.2 **Fans blowing *vuvuzelas* at the 2010 World Cup in Johannesburg, South Africa**

Producer of the concert, Kevin Wall, stated, "We believe sports and music transcend cultural, language and geographic barriers, and through the official FIFA World Cup Kick–off Celebration Concert [we will present] the sights and sounds of unity and celebration for an unforgettable, must-see experience."[12] During the games themselves, plastic trumpets (*vuvuzelas*) that have been popular in South Africa for decades were blown by thousand of fans, creating such a deafening din that international sports commentators discussed banning them. Like the talking drums of Nigeria, the **vuvuzelas** at the World Cup created a sound environment that was part of the overall experience of the games. Was this sound music?

OLYMPIC GAMES (KOREA, INTERNATIONAL)

Since the inception of the modern Olympic Games in 1896, opening and closing ceremonies have featured music and dance of the host countries in a display of national identity and collective celebration. At the core of these ceremonies are several mandatory rituals including the opening fanfare, the lighting of the Olympic torch, the Parade of the Athletes, and the performance of national anthems of the participating countries, all of which require the participation of musicians. As the ceremonies evolved over the subsequent century, they became elaborate affairs that allowed considerable creative freedom for the organizing committees to develop performances fit for a world stage. They set the tone of the Games themselves in the spirit of friendly competition, providing a model for international cooperation and world peace. The ceremonies of the 1936 Olympics in Berlin, however, were a skillfully deployed propaganda showcase for Hitler's Third Reich, with stirring militaristic music accompanying persistent straight-arm salutes and cries of "*Sieg Heil*" from the crowds. In 2008, the opening ceremonies of the Summer Olympic Games in Beijing included a performance by 2008 drummers, a perfectly synchronized visual and audible spectacle. The impact of the performance was overwhelming, as it announced the arrival of China at the center of world events with its newly acquired economic and military might.

Among the most artistically inspired ceremonies in the modern history of the Games were those of the 1988 Summer Olympics in Seoul, Republic of Korea. Seoul was an unlikely selection for hosting the Games. Korea had been annexed by Japan in 1910 and at the end of World

Map 15-1   Korea

Source: *Garland Encyclopedia of World Music,* Volume 7: East Asia: China, Japan, and Korea

War II, when it was liberated by the United States military and the Soviet Union's armies, the Korean peninsula was divided at the 38th parallel. As the Cold War developed, the division became entrenched, with rival and hostile governments established in Seoul (in the South) and Pyongyang (in the North), each proxy to the competing world powers. In 1952, the armies of North Korea invaded the South, triggering a war that would end three years later in a stalemate with nearly three million civilian and military casualties. The city of Seoul, capital of the Kingdom of Korea prior to the Japanese annexation, was in ruins, having changed hands four times during the course of the war through fierce street fighting and aerial and artillery bombardment. Yet Seoul was rebuilt, in part through American investment, and by the 1980s was known as "The Miracle on the Han River." When Seoul was selected by the International Olympic Committee over Nagoya, Japan in September 1981, a committee was formed consisting of representatives from the government, sports, the military, and the arts to plan Ceremonies that would celebrate both Korean national identity and the international values represented by the Olympic Games.[13]

During the initial stages, the committee agreed upon three goals that they wished to achieve in the Opening and Closing Ceremonies: first, the presentation should be sufficiently global in scope to appeal to an international audience; second, it should be sufficiently Korean to appeal to the home audience and to communicate to the outside world something essential of Korean identity; and third, it should be fresh and original, embodying "the shock of the new." Three types of music were identified to capture and project these three goals respectively: Western symphonic; traditional Korean (from aristocratic, folk, and religious sources); and electro-disco (internationally popular at the time). Hundreds of composers, writers, choreographers, costume designers, lighting and sound engineers, and stage directors lent their talents to the productions. There was disagreement among the planners as to how to achieve a balance between projecting serious themes of world harmony and reconciliation while providing entertainment for thousands of visitors and millions watching on television. The scenarios and musical scores went through many revisions, accommodating the competing interests and visions of various factions.

While the planners were developing the script for what was becoming a hugely ambitious project, an individual, on his own initiative far from the capital, was hard at work producing what would become the most memorable symbol of the Ceremonies. American ethnomusicologist Margaret Dilling tells "The Story of the World's Biggest Drum":

> There was a man named Kim Kwan-shik who was skilled in the art of drum making. He came from a family of drummakers...that managed a factory for making traditional instruments. One day in September 1981, a year after his father's death, Kim was watching the news on

Fig. 15.3   The world's biggest drum, 1988 Opening Ceremony, Seoul Olympics

TV in Baden-Baden Germany: Korea had been selected to host the 1988 Olympics. He was ecstatic. He clapped his hands, shouting, "Yes, that's it." On the spot, he decided to make the biggest drum in the world, one that could be heard the farthest away, and to dedicate it to the Seoul Olympics. His brothers tried to talk him out of it but he had made up his mind. So began a seven-year saga.[14]

The arrival of the great Dragon Drum of Kim Kwan-shik at the Olympic Stadium signaled the start of the two-week-long international event. According to the explanation developed by the organizing committee and read by the stadium audience in the program:

The Seoul Olympics opens like the dawn of genesis in empty space. Poised in the universe between Heaven and Earth, Humans greet the sun in an act of homage to harmonize the forces of Heaven and Earth, an echo of the role of the king; but the royal seat is filled not by the king but by an enormous drum marked on either head with a swirl of red, blue, and yellow, symbolizing forces which hold the universe in dynamic and delicate balance. The Dragon Drum (*yonggo*) and splendid retinue cut a diagonal across the open space in the morning of the world to the pulse of folk drums and melodies of court music until they reach the foot of the cosmic tree, the link between Heaven and Earth as well as nest for the sun. At the third stroke of the great drum, the sun rises and the cosmic tree reveals itself as the Olympic torch holder. Soon the tree will burn with fire from Olympus and the Games of the XXIVth Olympiad will open a new era of harmony and progress for humanity from the momentary center of the universe—the city of Seoul.[15]

The organizers envisioned the opening sequence of the Ceremony, "Passage at Dawn," in terms of a quasi-religious ritual, using music and ceremony to demarcate a sacred space and time in which the barriers that separate humanity were temporarily overcome and the harmony of Heaven reigned on Earth. Here the music accompanying the procession to the "foot of the cosmic tree" is the most traditionally Korean. So began the ceremonies that included more than 10,000 musicians, dancers, skydivers, and taekwondo athletes—the largest mobilization in Korean history, with the exception of the Korean War.

Music that reflected "the shock of the new" accompanied the extinguishing of the huge Olympic torch at the end of the Closing Ceremony. A computer-generated composition by a Korean composer based in Germany, Kang Sok-hui "filled the night air with voices transmuted electronically from a trumpet, a soprano, a chorus, and a narrator chanting blurred text in long legato lines."[16] Following these eerie, space-age sounds, the organizers chose a daring departure from the fanfares, anthems, disco dances, mass choreography, and pageantry that had occupied most of the Ceremonies. A single bamboo flute (*taegum*) and accompanying drum (*changgo*), alone in the center of the vast arena, play the music of the Korean shaman's dance, *salpuri*. A spotlight soon reveals the graceful movements of a white-robed dancer and her assistants, their images projected onto the stadium video screens. "In her movements is stillness, in her stillness is time suspended."[17] The *salpuri* dance of the traditional Korean shaman serves as a prayer for safe journeys for those who came to Seoul from afar, and an act of cleansing the space, "bringing full circle the opening purification ritual begun in 'Passage at Dawn' "[18] Gradually, the stadium fills with the light of 800 lanterns carried by dancers mingling with the 10,000 athletes on the grounds of the stadium. A chorus takes up the music of Korea's most familiar folk song "*Arirang,*" presented with Western orchestration, harmony, and full symphonic accompaniment, providing a Hollywood-style ending that could only be followed by fireworks. Perhaps nowhere else on Earth at that time was the desire for unity and reconciliation more intense than in divided Korea. That year, the North did not send athletes to compete in the Games.

15-4

PUBLIC CEREMONIES AND FESTIVALS (USA)

Worldwide, music is incorporated in events like presidential inaugurations that serve as public rituals, confirming and reinforcing the established social order. The first inauguration of Barack Obama as President of the United States on January 20th, 2009 drew one of the largest gatherings in recent

American history; nearly two million people were present to witness this solemn ritual. Along with the speeches, the parade, and the pageantry was music that heralded, honored, and celebrated the event. The day before the swearing-in ceremony, performances on the National Mall by such familiar artists as Bruce Springsteen, Shakira, and William (of Black Eyed Peas) were projected onto huge screens and transmitted to televisions across America and around the world. Also shown on these screens, and of great symbolic value, was a film of the late African American singer **Marian Anderson** in a landmark 1939 performance of "My Country, Tis of Thee," on the steps of the Lincoln Memorial. A biographical website devoted to her extraordinary life and career gives the following account of the event:

> Throughout her life, Marian had experienced racism, but the most famous event occurred in 1939. Saul Hurok [her concert manager] tried to rent Washington, D.C.'s Constitutional Hall, the city's foremost center, but was told no dates were available. Washington was segregated and even the hall had segregated seating. In 1935, [the contract for renting the hall was re-written to include] a new clause: "concert by white artists only." Hurok would have walked away with the response he'd received, but a rival manager asked about renting the hall for the same dates and was told they were open. The hall's director told Hurok the truth, even yelling before slamming down the phone, "No Negro will ever appear in this hall while I am manager."
>
> The public was outraged, famous musicians protested, and First Lady Eleanor Roosevelt resigned from the Daughters of the American Revolution (DAR), who owned the hall. Roosevelt, along with Hurok and Walter White of the National Association for the Advancement of Colored People (NAACP), encouraged Secretary of the Interior Harold Ickes to arrange a free open-air concert on the steps of the Lincoln Memorial for Easter Sunday. On April 9, Marian sang before 75,000 people and millions of radio listeners. About her trepidation before the event, she said:
>
> "I said yes, but the yes did not come easily or quickly. I don't like a lot of show, and one could not tell in advance what direction the affair would take. I studied my conscience.... As I thought further, I could see that my significance as an individual was small in this affair. I had become, whether I liked it or not, a symbol, representing my people."
>
> Several weeks later, Marian gave a private concert at the White House, where President Franklin D. Roosevelt was entertaining King George VI and Queen Elizabeth (mother of Elizabeth II) of Britain.[19]

Seventy years later on the Capitol steps on the opposite side of the Mall, America's first African American president was sworn into office. The great R&B singer Aretha Franklin reprised Anderson's performance. Violinist Itzhak Perlman and cellist Yo Yo Ma, two of the most important representatives of the Western Classical tradition, played a commissioned work by John Williams, Hollywood's most successful film score composer; or rather, because of the cold weather, they soundlessly mimed their performance to a pre-recorded rendition. The music was much more than sound and context. It was a powerful symbol of national reconciliation, heritage, and shared values. Taken together, the juxtaposition of multiple musical genres—from rock to gospel to classical, publicly performed in that singular space resonant with the history of the nation—served as a powerful sonic enactment of America's motto, "*E pluribus unum*", "From the many, one."

CULTURE FESTS AND "CELTIC COLOURS" (USA, CANADA)

Also on the National Mall in Washington D.C., between the steps of the Capitol Building and the Washington Monument, hundreds of thousands of visitors attend the two-week long Smithsonian Folklife Festival every summer. As explained on the festival website:

> Initiated in 1967...it has brought more than twenty-three thousand musicians, artists, performers, craftspeople, workers, cooks, storytellers, and others...to demonstrate the skills, knowledge, and aesthetics that embody the creative vitality of community-based traditions.... The Festival has featured exemplary tradition bearers from more than ninety nations, every

region of the United States, scores of ethnic communities, [and] more than a hundred American Indian groups.... In many cases, the Festival has energized local and regional tradition bearers and their communities and, thus, helped to conserve and create cultural resources.[20]

In many parts of the world, cultural festivals like this serve to reinforce local, regional, and global identities and communally shared values. They reinvigorate local musical communities, provide employment for artists who are helping to preserve older and more marginal forms of expression, and encourage young people and neophytes to explore traditions that might otherwise be forgotten, lost to the commercial mainstream. Regional festivals that feature genres of music and dance draw the attention of locals and tourists alike to the particular cultural character of a place and population. In the mountains of North Carolina, the annual Highland Games honor the Scottish heritage of many of the region's inhabitants, while to the east, the Bull Durham Blues Festival honors African American roots. Each summer in the historic and picturesque city of Salzburg, the birthplace of Mozart, classical music lovers from all over Europe and elsewhere attend symphony concerts and operas performed by celebrity musicians. Some festivals celebrate diversity and attempt to project a global identity. The annual Fes Festival of World Sacred Music in Morocco juxtaposes

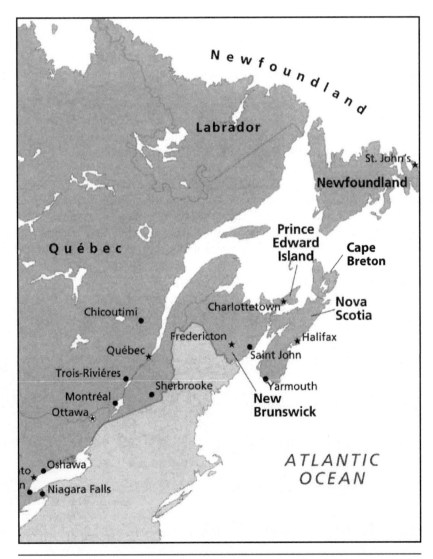

Map 15-2 Eastern Canada showing Cape Breton in Nova Scotia

Source: *Garland Encyclopedia of World Music*, Volume 3: The United States and Canada

religious musical traditions. "The aim of this festival is to harness the arts and spirituality in the service of human and social development, and the relationship between peoples and cultures."[21] In 1980, British progressive rock musician Peter Gabriel laid the groundwork for WOMAD (World of Music, Arts and Dance), an international festival featuring world-renowned popular musicians. Every July, the festival is held over four days in England, with "satellite" festivals held in Australia, New Zealand, Spain, Abu Dhabi, and elsewhere. These festivals bring people together from all over the world "to excite, to inform, and to create awareness of the worth and potential of a multicultural society."[22]

Cape Breton Island, in the Canadian province of Nova Scotia, hosts the "Celtic Colours International Festival" every October in celebration of its Celtic heritage and culture. Over sixty percent of Cape Breton's population claims Scottish or Irish ethnicity, some being descendants of the island's earliest settlers. While Cape Breton is also home to Mi'kmaq First Nations (Native American) people and to French-speaking communities whose early 17th-century ancestors named the region L'Acadie (Acadia), in 1621 British settlers began serious efforts to colonize the land they renamed "New Scotland" (Nova Scotia). After the Treaty of Utrecht (1713) gave control of the Acadian peninsula to the British, many Scots-Irish arrived from New England, and from the late 18th to mid-19th centuries some 50,000 Highland Scots arrived in Cape Breton, expelled from Scotland during the Highland Clearances, an agricultural reform program initiated from London that forced many Scottish smallholding farmers off their land. These immigrants established the Scottish Gaelic language and culture that remain such a strong part of Cape Breton society today. Since the 1950s the provincial government has promoted Scottish culture, introduced Gaelic language into schools, and helped fund the Gaelic College of Celtic Arts and Crafts in St. Ann's. The first "Celtic Colours" international festival took place in 1997, and has attracted tens of thousands of visitors to the island.

The nine-day festival includes dozens of concert performances, *ceilidhs* ("gatherings" with songs, tunes, and dancing), and lectures by renowned musicians, dancers, and storytellers from Cape Breton as well as Scotland, Ireland, Brittany (France), Denmark, the United States, and elsewhere. Festivalgoers can participate in a wide variety of cultural events, from music sessions, square dances, and song circles, to community meals, Gaelic teas, and guided "Celtic" walks and hikes. For some, the festival is an opportunity to celebrate their Scottish or Irish cultural heritage. Open Celtic music sessions such as those at the **Baddeck Yacht Club** and the **Whycocomagh Waterfront Centre** allow visiting musicians to play tunes alongside some of the finest Cape Breton musicians and dancers. For other visitors, the festival is a time to enjoy and experience the diversity of Celtic music traditions; to socialize and network with singers, instrumentalists, and

Fig. 15.4 Welcome sign for festival visitors at the Gaelic College, St. Ann's, Cape Breton (L), and spontaneous step dancing during a music jam session at Whycocomagh Waterfront Center, October 2012 (R)

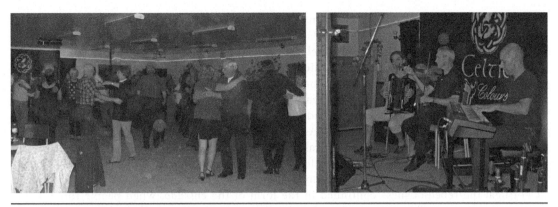

Fig. 15.5 Celtic Colours square dance at the Boisdale Volunteer Fire Department, October 2012 (L), and Boisdale dance musicians playing piano accordion, fiddle, and keyboard (R)

dancers; or simply to explore the island's spectacular scenery as tourists. For festival organizers, the event requires extensive planning, arranging dozens of simultaneous events in communities all over the island. The multiple locations of Celtic Colours events distinguish this international music festival from most others of its kind. The festival's mission statement is: "To promote, celebrate and develop Cape Breton's living Celtic culture and hospitality by producing an international festival during the fall colours that builds relationships across Cape Breton Island and beyond."[23]

ANTI-STRUCTURAL RITUALS AND CARNIVAL (BRAZIL, TRINIDAD)

While the musical performances that take place at the ceremonies and festivals described above are entertaining and aesthetically pleasing, in each case they especially fulfill the last three of Merriam's functions of music: they validate social institutions and religious rituals, contribute to the continuity and stability of culture, and serve to integrate society. Music also accompanies oppositional rallies and celebrations that invert the social order and border on anarchy. The archetypal example of the anarchic and hedonistic festival took place in Bethel, New York, between August 15 and 18, 1969. 400,000 people gathered in the fields of farmer Max Yasgur for "The Woodstock Festival," now considered the world's most famous rock concert. At this event, although music was the focus and magnet that drew the crowds, it also served as catalyst for uniting a large portion of a generation with a set of values—peace, freedom, love, and hope—as the Vietnam War raged and divided the country. According to anthropologist Victor Turner, a healthy, stable society depends on rituals that reinforce structure (like presidential inaugurations) *and* rituals that provide opportunities for "anti-structure" (like Woodstock). He defines the latter as events in which the hierarchies of the rulers and the ruled as well as class structures are temporarily abandoned.[24] In ancient Rome, the festivals in honor of the god Saturn, the Saturnalias, embodied the essential spirit of Turner's **anti-structural rituals**. They were characterized by the overturning of all manner of ordinary conventions of orderly daily life: by drunkenness, licentiousness, and the inversion of social hierarchies.

> Slaves banqueted together with their masters, whom they insulted and admonished. From among them was elected a King of Chaos who, for the period of Saturnalia only, enjoyed full rights to his master's concubines, and gave ridiculous orders that had to be obeyed by everyone.[25]

At the end of these rituals the King of Chaos returned once again to being a lowly slave. Indeed, in the earliest form of the Saturnalia, he was slain as a sacrifice to the god Saturn. Anti-structural rituals like the Roman Saturnalia, according to Turner, contribute to a deep feeling of belonging to a group that transcends one's identification with one's social status. (Recall the Korean masked dance tradition *t'al ch'um* in Lesson 14.)

The roots of Carnival lie in the ancient Greek springtime festival celebrating Dionysus, the god of wine, and in the Roman feasts of Bacchanalia and Saturnalia, which honored the gods of wine and agriculture respectively with revelry, drunkenness, and the reversal of social roles mentioned in the previous paragraph. In medieval Europe, similar festivities took place during the "Feast of Fools" (also called the Feast of Innocents), celebrated between Christmas and Easter in the Christian church calendar. Revelers wearing masks and costumes parodied the holy Mass and made fun of the ecclesiastical hierarchy and religious ethics, while other riotous revelers paraded through town streets dancing and singing. As in the ancient Roman festivals, the inversion of social and in this case religious roles was a central feature. The Roman Catholic Church unsuccessfully attempted to control or ban such festivities for close to a millennium. In 16th-century Italy, "carnivalesque" rebelliousness transformed into masked balls, tournaments, and parades of floats, while in Portugal the rebelliousness continued in the form of the *entrudo,* when people threw flour, eggs, mud, oranges, and lemons at each other; hurled pots and pans out of windows; waged street battles with brooms and spoons; and held gluttonous feasts. These Carnival festivities allowed individuals and communities to engage in unrestrained amusement and boisterous activities in the week before the Christian Lenten season of prayerful reflection and fasting. The term "Carnival" most likely derives from the Latin words *carne vale* meaning "farewell to the flesh," referring to the abstinence from sex and from eating meat during the forty days of Lent that precede Holy Week and Easter Sunday.

Exploration and colonization of the Americas by European powers brought Carnival traditions to the New World. In Brazil, Trinidad, Barbados, and other former Spanish, Portuguese, and French colonies, Roman Catholic colonists held pre-Lenten masquerades and parades. When Europeans brought Africans to the New World to provide labor for sugar cane, coffee, and other plantations, instigating the Atlantic slave trade, elements of African festivals including music, dance, and ritual practices gradually blended with and transformed European colonial culture. African drum rhythms, stilt dancers, stick fighters, and large puppets began to appear in the Carnival parades. In both Europe and Africa, festivities had served to break with daily routines and celebrate life through music, dance, costume, and public display. Religious and other aspects of these festivities, however, held different meanings for the participants. Pre-Lenten European parades and costumes honored pre-Christian mythical characters and historical heroes like Apollo and Aphrodite, or Caesar, Cleopatra, and Nero. African rituals and festivals brought good fortune and healing to the living and soothed the souls of departed ancestors who may have been disgruntled because of some inadvertent insult or transgression. Carnival celebrations in the Americas merged elements of both traditions. They borrowed masks and costumes from Africa, made out of beads, shells, and other natural materials, "with each object or combination of objects representing a certain idea or spiritual force."[26] In Europe, feathers had served as mere decorations and embellishments, while for the Africans they served as symbols of the supernatural, of protection against illness, and of the ability to travel to other worlds and embody sacred beings, as we saw in Lesson 11 with the Zaouli masked dancers. New World Carnival traditions of European landowners, African slaves, and their descendants came to embody and express these multiple meanings.[27] Most North Americans are familiar with the Mardi Gras ("Fat Tuesday") festivities in New Orleans, but the world's largest and most extravagant celebrations of Carnival take place each year in Brazil and on the Caribbean island nation of Trinidad and Tobago.

Carnival in Rio de Janeiro

In the week ending on Shrove Tuesday, tens of thousands of people participate in the spectacular parades, masked balls, street parties, music, and dancing in Rio de Janeiro, São Paulo, and Salvador de Bahia in Brazil.

Immigrants from the Portuguese islands of the Azores, Cape Verde, and Madeira first introduced the pre-Lenten *entrudo* to Brazil in the early 18th century. People of all social strata doused each other

Map 15-3 Brazil

Source: *Garland Encyclopedia of World Music*, Volume 2: South America, Mexico, Central America, and the Caribbean

with buckets of water and threw limes. The authorities eventually outlawed these practices. By the mid 19th-century masquerade balls were held, *cordões* (pageant groups) marched through the streets playing musical instruments, and costumed and masked participants danced in parades. It was from the *cordões* that Carnival groups of musicians and dancers known as *blocos* ("blocks") arose. Today these popular block groups parade through the neighborhoods of Rio de Janeiro for several weeks before the beginning of Lent. While the *blocos* were at first looked down upon by Brazil's social elite for their drunken rowdiness, they paved the way for the samba schools and the official *sambadrome* experience that has become such a significant component of life in Rio de Janeiro.

The quintessential music and dance associated with Brazilian Carnival is the samba, which originated in the dance parties of freed slaves who left the rural plantations and migrated to Rio in the late 19th century. The term is believed to derive from the Angolan word "*semba*", meaning "invitation to dance." Samba is a solo display characterized by gyrating hip movements (**umbigada**) and outstretched arms. The accompanying music has a regular duple meter with syncopated rhythms played by guitars, *cavaquinho* (small four-string guitars), and a percussion ensemble (**bateria**) consisting of bass drums (*surdos*), friction drums (*cuicas*), small tambourines (*pandeiros*), and shakers. At the turn of the 20th century the samba adopted influences from other music and dance genres in Rio including the Afro-Brazilian *maxixe* and *lundu*, the Cuban *habañera*, and the German polka, reflecting the various strands of an immigrant culture. The result was a highly popular musical form that spread to the middle and upper classes, and through recordings and radio broadcasts in the 1920s and 30s quickly gained an international reputation as an icon of Brazilian national identity.

The largest performing groups in the Rio carnival are the samba schools, which first appeared in 1929. These dance clubs are associated with particular neighborhoods, often the poorer shantytowns (*favelas*), although club membership is open to anyone. Samba schools work throughout the year to prepare and rehearse for the annual Carnival parade and competition. Every year each samba school selects its own Carnival theme, such as a tribute to a historic figure or event. Its members, now numbering anywhere up to 5000 people, spend thousands of hours making all the respective floats, props, and costumes. The schools' music composers create new sambas, the choreographers design the dance sequences, and the performers rehearse at length to perfect their spectacular shows. During the Carnival parade the samba schools march down the *sambodromo*, the permanent half-mile avenue near downtown Rio built in 1984, performing in front of the judges and up to 90,000 spectators who fill the bleachers on both sides of the parade route. From 8:00 pm until the morning hours on the four days ending on Shrove Tuesday, samba bands process in turn, each allowed ninety minutes to parade from one end to the other.

A samba school procession begins with costumed individuals who salute the crowds, often followed by a group dressed as early 20th-century Bahian (Afro-Brazilian) women wearing large circular dresses. Marching and dancing on or between the samba school's floats are its various themed groups: vocalists who sing the school's theme song (*samba enredo*) accompanying themselves on the *cavaquinho* (miniature four-string guitar), the *bateria* line of drums and percussion

15-8

Fig. 15.6   **Queen of the Drums, Imperatriz Leopoldinense Samba School, Rio Carnival 2008**

led by the "band godmother," the female flag-holder and her male partner (*mestre-sala* and *porta-bandeira*), and the "old guard" of elderly *sambistas* symbolizing the school's history. Watch this video clip of the **Mocidade Samba School.** This is one of the oldest samba schools in Rio and puts more than 4000 costumed dancers and musicians on the parade ground. The filming of this video began at 3:00 am on the Monday morning of Carnival. In this fierce samba school competition, the participants await the judges' announcement of the winners on Ash Wednesday, and the five winning samba schools perform once more in a Parade of Champions the following Saturday.

Carnival in Trinidad

As the samba schools signify the Rio Carnival in Brazil, three distinctive elements characterize Trinidad's pre-Lenten festival—the steel pan, "**playing *mas***" (masquerade), and **calypso**—all of which are rooted in the island's colonial history. In the mid to late 1700s, when Protestant Great Britain took over many of the French West Indian islands, Trinidad's Spanish rulers invited Caribbean French Catholics to settle on the land. (See Map 8–2, p. 122.) Many French colonists reestablished tobacco, coffee, sugar, and cotton plantations there, and brought African slaves with them. The Spanish ceded Trinidad to Great Britain in 1802, yet "the French community remained in control of the island's economic core and, thus, were able to stamp their cultural characteristics on its ensuing festive developments."[28] Before the emancipation of slaves in 1833, public celebrations of Carnival were confined exclusively to the upper classes. The white community held its masked balls in the plantation houses, and enacted parodies of the emergency procedures of a sugarcane plantation fire (*cannes brulées*, burning sugarcanes) dressed up as black slaves. These festivities included nighttime torch-lit processions accompanied by drumming and singing. After emancipation, freed slaves and other members of the lower classes held their own pre-Lenten *canboulay*. People gathered in tents where a principal singer, called a "chantwell," led them in call and response singing about current events and shared grievances as a way to vent their feelings. They also celebrated in the streets with drumming, dancing, singing, and sexually explicit masquerading. The white community considered this immoral and obscene, calling it the *jamette carnival* from the French term *diametre*, meaning below the *diameter* of respectability. Yet the *canboulay* celebration continues to this day. This pre-dawn ritual is called *J'Ouvert* (from "*jour ouvert*" or daybreak; pronounced "jouvay") and takes place on Carnival Monday. Thousands of revelers cover themselves with mud or oil and parade in the streets to deafening steel band or soca music. In this video, Wendell Manwarren of the Trinidadian rapso band 3Canal ("rapso," a Trinidadian fusion of soca and calypso with American rap) performs and explains a *J'Ouvert* song believed to date from the late 19th century that commemorates and celebrates freedom.

Perhaps the most iconic feature of Trinidad's Carnival is the steel pan. Now the national instrument of Trinidad and Tobago, the pan was invented only in the 20th century. Increasing tension between landowners and laborers in the 1880s led to the British authorities banning drums and religious observances. The black community responded by creating *tamboo-bamboo* **bands** consisting of tunable bamboo sticks, struck on the ground, and bottle and spoon percussion. Black youths later experimented with making musical instruments from metal hubcaps, brake drums, and biscuit tins. This led to the creation of steel pans crafted by hammering out dimples, which produced distinct pitches, on the tops of 55-gallon oil drums. A surfeit of oil drums from American bases on Trinidad during World War II allowed further experimentation, resulting in steel pans capable of producing complete musical scales. By the late 1930s, ensembles of improvised metal instruments of all sorts provided the characteristic musical accompaniment to the Carnival celebrations of the black community.

The sophisticated, multipart **steel bands** of today are the legacy of these early struggles. The family of steel pans includes tenor or lead pans (soprano), double seconds (alto), double guitars (tenor), triple guitars and cellos (baritones), and tenor bass pans (bass). Band members practice year-round for the fierce Carnival competitions that begin weeks before Shrove Tuesday with initial eliminations and semi-finals. Each steel band chooses or composes a "Road March" tune months in advance, and seeks to gain popularity through recordings played in shops, restaurants, taxis, and other public places. The bands, each comprising up to one hundred members, spend months rehearsing longer versions of their Road March in preparation for the Panorama competitions. The Grand Finals take place on the Saturday before Carnival Tuesday in Queens Park Savannah in the capital Port-of-Spain, when the twelve finalists perform before the judges and huge crowds watch the competition for prestigious titles and prizes.

After the steel pan, the second defining feature of Trinidad's Carnival is *mas*, which refers to the numerous masquerade groups that parade and dance through the streets. *Mas* groups are open to any Trinidadians or visitors who wish to buy a costume and join in the parade (to "play *mas*"). Some of the largest groups such as Barbarossa, Legend, and Poison, number up to six thousand or more masqueraders. These groups wear distinctive costumes created around a theme by a designer, and fashioned by volunteers in *mas* camps over the weeks and months preceding the festival. Each is led by a King and Queen wearing huge costumes that often need the support of wheels. They compete for the "King and Queen of the Festival" title. These costume parades are sometimes referred to as "pretty *mas*" in contrast to the rowdy, dirty, muddy *mas* celebrations of *J'Ouvert* that precede them on Carnival Monday morning.

Fig. 15.7 The Petrotrin Katzenjammers steel band performs in the Panorama semifinal competition, Trinidad, 2013 (L), and indentations marking the pitches of the steel pan's concave playing surface (R)

Fig. 15.8 Queen of Carnival competition, Trinidad, 2011 (L), and masqueraders competing in the Red Cross Children's Carnival, Trinidad, 2011 (R)

One of the most prestigious honors awarded each year in Trinidad's Carnival is the "Calypso Monarch" title. Calypso developed from the singing of the chantwell in the 1920s, and is a song genre native to Trinidad and to its Carnival celebrations. Calypsonians compose their own ballad-style songs, usually consisting of humorous, witty lyrics often with pointed social and political commentary. In recent decades, the more upbeat dance music "soca" (or soul calypso) and chutney soca have overtaken calypso in popularity, as discussed in Lesson 8. Nevertheless, calypso remains a distinctive element of Carnival celebrations in Trinidad and calypso competitions are still held annually. The success of women calypso singers in this traditionally all-male genre, along with the introduction of youth competitions and the development of *extempo* calypso—composing and singing of calypsos on the spot on any given subject—are strong indicators of ongoing interest in this traditional song form. Listen to the great Calypso singer, Mighty Sparrow, eight-time winner of Trinidad's Calypso King/ Monarch competition, singing his song "Sparrow Dead" after reading his own premature obituary in the *Jamaica Observer*.

15-1 🔊

In both Brazil and Trinidad, carnival is perhaps the most culturally significant event of the year. For outsiders and tourists, it provides highly visible and dramatic visual and sonic representations of these places that are used by marketers and travel agents to promote them as vacation destinations. At the very heart of these annual celebrations are music and dance, without which the events would not be merely diminished, they would be inconceivable. The saturation of the environment with the special music of Carnival sets this time of year apart from the rest, the din of the *blocos*, *baterias*, and steel bands provides the sonic cover for the extravagant displays and outrageous behaviors that would not be tolerated in public without it.

CONCLUSION

The musical soundscape of human life has been radically altered in the past hundred years by technological innovations and urbanization. While music has never been more available, it has become as never before a consumer good rather than a participatory activity. Forms of musical expression that have been passed down through generations have been forgotten in favor of ephemeral forms of popular music mass-produced in urban studios. Bo Nyed is a middle-aged Tibetan farmer and herder who, in a 2009 interview with a member of the Plateau Music Project, described these radical changes in patterns of musical behavior as follows:

> At that time (1940–1960s) we sang almost constantly as we harvested. We had different songs for every kind of work, and sang songs from morning to night. Even if someone wanted to chase a girl, they needed to sing a love song to show their emotion and never told someone they loved them directly. For example if you had a boyfriend who was very far away from you, he would send a song to tell you he was missing you or something. He would sing that song to a messenger and the messenger would relay that song to someone else. Eventually the girl would get the message and reply in the same way. They used song messages to keep in touch. But now, you cannot see anyone singing these songs to each other. People like pop songs most. Young people prefer to sing modern songs. No one sings local songs anymore; instead they imitate everything they see on TV and in movies. In the past, we were so happy to sing those songs. We didn't get tired when we sang them as we worked. We worked from morning to evening and we sang from morning to evening. Some years ago a local priest asked people if there was anyone who could sing *mgur ma* [a long threshing song]. [I said,] "I sing *mgur ma* the whole day while I cut grass. I'm the only one left who can sing it. Not even my own daughter wants to learn *mgur ma* from me. I never forced her to learn. I never sing modern songs. I have never tried and I never want to. I don't like them at all. My mother really liked to sing. Now everyone is silent; they don't like to sing regardless of where they are and what they are doing. In the past we sang songs wherever we went.[29]

The situation she describes is true throughout the world. Few corners have been left untouched by the digital revolution in musical sound. This poignant account is indicative of a rapidly transforming

Fig. 15.9   Bo Nyed, Tibetan singer-farmer, in 2009

world, impoverished by cultural loss while intoxicated with the expanding possibilities for music innovation that the new technologies promise.

Since December 1968 when an American astronaut first photographed the planet Earth from outer space and the photo appeared on the cover of *LIFE magazine*, humans have been able as never before to envision our world as a single unified whole. This image became a symbol of unity and interdependence among all people. The subsequent period of history saw the development of the internet giving the symbolic power of the image an experiential framework as millions and then billions of people connected to each other through Twitter, Facebook, and other social media sites. Never before have people been more aware of the forces, beliefs, and institutions that both unite us and divide us, providing hope in a self-sustaining future world at peace, or threatening mutual destruction. Music, a mode of expression and communication common to all peoples, can be a source of understanding and communion across the great divides.

Through this text, we have seen how music is integral to all aspects of our lives as an indispensable means of expressing who we are, where we are, what we are, what we believe, what we feel, and sharing this with others. We have explored the functions, exalted and mundane, that music serves in this world. We have noted that different musical styles are intimately connected with the ways individuals and groups express their identities and values. We have seen how fragile some forms of expression are in the wake of rapid social and technological change. In religious contexts, we have examined how music serves as a way of marking out the sacred from the everyday, celebrating and accessing higher powers, and binding individuals and groups together in shared expressions of heightened emotion. Music is the soundtrack of our social lives as we dine, shop, court, and seek entertainment and companionship. As we wrote at the very beginning of this course, "There has never been a time in history when music was more available, more portable, and more pervasive than today." Living at a time when technological, economic, and cultural systems are integrated across the globe as never before makes the creation of an online music text such as this one possible, perhaps for the first time in history. This fact points to a crossroads we are fast approaching, either toward mutual cooperation, respect, and therefore survival, or social disintegration, planetary degradation, and a new Dark Age. Through the rapid shrinking of social space, everyone in the world is at our doorstep, to be welcomed and respected or ignored and silenced. Perhaps through understanding each other's music we can better understand each other. It was, after all, to a musical metaphor that Abraham Lincoln turned when closing his First Inaugural Address in 1861 at another perilous turning point, the outset of the American Civil War: "We are not enemies, but friends. We must not be enemies. Though passion may have strained, it must not break our bonds of affection. The mystic chords of memory, stretching from every battlefield and patriot grave to every living heart and hearthstone all over this broad land, will yet swell the chorus of the Union when again touched, as surely they will be, by the better angels of our nature."

KEY CONCEPTS

Music in public spaces	Community-based	Costume parades
Music in shopping malls	traditions	Music and sporting
Nightlife	Tradition bearer	events
DJ dance parties	Cultural resource	Olympic Games
Courtesans	Anti-structural rituals	Opening and Closing
Presidential inauguration	and Carnival	Ceremonies
Culture festivals	Lent	

Q THINKING ABOUT MUSIC QUESTIONS

1. In the case studies discussed in Lesson 15—presidential inaugurations, *bailes*, folk festivals, sporting events, Carnival—music serves to affirm membership in a collective by contributing to an *experience* of membership at an emotional and physical level. Describe an experience you have had when your individuality was submerged in identification with a group. In what ways did music help to initiate or sustain the experience?

2. Think of a public event you have attended in which music played a part. What was the music like (its musical elements and functions), and how did the music affect you, your behavior, and/or your connection with the other people in attendance?

3. Consider Friedrich Nietzsche's words, "Without music, life would be a mistake." How do these words relate to your own life? What does music contribute to your wellbeing, to your social and/or spiritual life, and to the ways you bond with others?

4. In the conclusion to this lesson, the authors claim "Living at a time when technological, economic, and cultural systems are integrated across the globe makes the creation of an online music text such as this one possible for the first time in history." What is the basis for this claim? Would you agree? Why or why not?

NOTES

1 `Cathy Ragland, "Mexican Deejays and the Transnational Space of Youth Dances in New York and New Jersey," *Ethnomusicology*, 47/3 (2003), 343.

2 Ragland, "Mexican Deejays," 346.

3 Ragland, "Mexican Deejays," 348.

4 Ragland, "Mexican Deejays," 352.

5 Gregory Youtz, *Silk and Bamboo: An Introduction to Chinese Musical Culture*, unpublished manuscript (2000), 156.

6 Bonnie Gordon and Martha Feldman, "Introduction," *The Courtesan's Arts: Cross-Cultural Perspectives* (Oxford: Oxford University Press, 2006), 5.

7 Gordon and Feldman, *The Courtesan's Arts,* 8–9.

8 Youtz, *Silk and Bamboo,* 158.

9 Youtz, *Silk and Bamboo,* 168.

10 Magistra Rosemounde of Mercia, "The History of Prostitution through the Renaissance," accessed July 25, 2014, http://home.comcast.net/~mikibu/Articlefolder/prostitution.htm.

11 "About the Concert," 2010 FIFA World Cup South Africa, http://www.fifa.com/worldcup/archive/southafrica2010/organisation/concert/about.html. Website no longer available.

12 "About the Concert," 2010 FIFA World Cup South Africa.

13 American ethnomusicologist Margaret Walker Dilling sat in on the seven years of planning that preceded the 1988 Games. Her book has provided source material for much of the case study on the Olympic Ceremonies. Margaret W. Dilling, *Stories Inside Stories: Music in the Making of the Korean Olympic Ceremonies* (Berkeley, CA: Institute of East Asian Studies, 2007).

14 Dilling, *Stories Inside Stories,* 1.

15 Dilling, *Stories Inside Stories,* 1.

16 Dilling, *Stories Inside Stories,* 72–73.

17 Dilling, *Stories Inside Stories,* 72–73.

18 Dilling, *Stories Inside Stories,* 74.

19 "Marion Anderson, 'A Dream, A Life, A Legacy'," *Marion Anderson Historical Society,* accessed July 25, 2014, http://marianandersonhistoricalsociety.weebly.com/biography.html.

20 Smithsonian Folklife Festival, *Mission and History,* accessed July 25, 2014, http://www.festival.si.edu/about/mission.aspx.

21 "Our WOMAD Story," World Of Music, Arts and Dance festival website, accessed July 25, 2014, http://womad.org/about/.

22 Fes Festival of World Sacred Music homepage, http://www.fesfestival.com/2013/indexen.php

23 "About Celtic Colours," Celtic Colours Festival website, accessed July 25, 2014, http://www.celtic-colours.com/about-celtic-colours/.

24 Victor Turner, *The Ritual Process: Structure and Anti-Structure* (Piscataway, NJ: Aldine Transaction, [1969] 2008).

25 Maria Julia Goldwasser, "Carnival," in *Encyclopedia of Religion,* ed. Lindsay Jones, Vol. 3, 2nd ed. (Detroit: Macmillan Reference USA, 2005), 1440–1445.

26 "The History of Carnival," accessed July 25, 2014, http://www.allahwe.org/History.html.

27 "History of Carnival"

28 John Cowley, "Carnival in Trinidad.... Evolution and Cultural Meaning," *Musical Traditions* 4 (1985), updated 1/10/02, http://www.mustrad.org.uk/articles/trinidad.htm.

29 Unpublished interview transcript, written and translated by the interviewer Dawa Torbert.

GLOSSARY

Adhan: — Muslim "Call to Prayer". Heard five times a day in Islamic countries of the Middle East and elsewhere.

Aerophone: — Sachs-Hornbostel category of musical instruments comprising those that produce sound primarily from a vibrating body of air, usually in a tube.

Aesthetic: — The comprehension of a phenomenon based upon perception or appreciation of its sensual form and characteristics. Often used in association with the contemplation of beauty or works of art.

Afrikaner: — South African of Dutch, French, or German descent.

Afropop: — African popular music as it is presented and marketed in Europe and North America. Term popularized by the National Public Radio program "Afropop Worldwide," produced by Sean Barlow.

Analysis: — Mode of understanding based on dividing a whole phenomenon into its component parts.

Anti-structural ritual: — Type of ritual event that celebrates the temporary suspension of rules of decorum and the overthrow of social categories and hierarchies in favor of egalitarianism and anarchy.

Apartheid: — System of legalized separation of races in the Republic of South Africa from 1948 to 1994.

Aria: — In European opera, a sustained vocal solo for a single character.

Asik: — Turkish storyteller-singer.

Assimilation: — Process by which immigrants give up the cultural identity of their native country and adopt the language, dress, customs, etc. of their new homeland.

Aum: — Sacred syllable repeated in Hindu and Buddhist meditation practices, said to represent the original vibration of sound in the creation of the universe. Sometimes used as equivalent term for "God."

Aum, mani padme hum: — Tibetan Buddhist prayer (*mantra*) that invokes the Buddha of compassion, Avalokiteshvara.

Avant-garde:	(Literally "forward guard") Most innovative artistic movement, usually associated with 20th-century Modernism.
Avaz:	Persian (Iranian) classical vocal form in free rhythm.
Axis mundi:	(Literally, "axis of the world") World center or connection between earth and heaven.
Azmari:	Ethiopian traditional storyteller, praise singer, or musician-entertainer.
Baile:	Dance party in a Spanish-speaking country or community.
Baithak gana:	(Literally, "seated music") Song genre of the Hindustani (Asian Indian) community in Suriname, South America.
Ballad opera:	18th-century theatrical entertainment in England that appealed to the middle classes, with familiar tunes and spoken dialogue. Distinguished from grand opera with its sophisticated, newly-composed melodies and sung dialogue.
Bandoneon:	Button accordion; primary instrument in the Argentine tango orchestra. Player of the instrument is known as a *bandoneonista.*
Bar Mitzvah:	Coming-of-age ritual for Jewish boys. Comparable ritual for Jewish girls called Bat Mitzvah.
Baraka:	Sufi term for "blessing"; a beneficent emanation of blessings and grace from God.
Bard:	General term in English for epic narrator, storyteller, or poet-singer.
Batería:	The rhythm or percussion section of a Brazilian samba school ensemble.
Bell:	Subcategory of idiophones consisting of a resonant, cup-shaped body struck either by an internal, suspended clapper or external striker or hammer.
Bhava:	Sanskrit term for feeling or emotion; transmitted through the gestures and facial expressions of Indian artists.
Bhopa:	Narrator-priest of Rajasthan who performs the Epic of Pabuji—a regional deity—and its associated rituals.
Bira:	Ritual of the Shona people of Zimbabwe involving music, dance, and spirit possession.
Blocos:	Street bands in cities and towns of Brazil associated with Carnival celebrations.
Bollywood:	Hindi-language film industry based in Mumbai, India—the largest film-producing nation in the world. The term is a combination of Bombay (former name of Mumbai) and Hollywood, center of the American film industry.
Brahmin:	Member of hereditary Hindu priestly caste.
Bunraku:	Japanese puppet theater originating in 16th-century Edo (Tokyo).
Busker:	Street musician who performs and entertains for donations.
Calendrical rituals:	Sacred or secular celebrations that recur each year on the same date. Often associated with agricultural cycle or religious feast days.
Call and response:	Mode of group singing in which parts alternate between a solo leader and a group response. Used in many ritual circumstances, and characteristic of much Sub-Saharan African vocal music.
Calonarang:	Ritualized sacred drama in Bali, Indonesia, that pits the forces of light, personified by the sacred lion Barong, against the witch Rangda,

	personification of darkness. Their battles, staged in temple courtyards and accompanied by a *gamelan* ensemble, are always fought to an inconclusive end.
Calypso:	Afro-Caribbean song genre of Trinidad and Tobago originating in the early 20th century, with roots in West Africa and brought to the New World by slaves imported by French planters. Calypsonians were the most reliable source of news and commentary, through their topical and satirical song lyrics. Hybridized forms include *soca* (soul calypso), *rapso* (rap and calypso), and *chutney soca* (Indo-Trinidadian soul calypso).
Camerata:	Group of Florentine intellectuals who met in the home of Count Giovanni de' Bardi to discuss philosophical and aesthetic issues in the late 16th century that led to reforms of contemporary Italian theater, based on their understanding of Classical Greek theater, and in turn to the invention of Italian opera.
Camposino:	Spanish for "rural peasant". During the *Nueva Canción* movement in Latin America (1960s–80s), musicians sang in support of oppressed and marginalized agricultural laborers.
Canboulay:	Nighttime festivities during Trinidadian Carnival involving the rowdy and satirical re-enactment of sugarcane field fire brigade procedures.
Candomblé:	Afro-Brazilian religion based on worship of Yoruban (West African) deities and frequently involving spirit possession.
Cantillation:	Ritual chanting or vocalization of sacred texts using musical elements like melodic contour and meter.
Capoeira:	Martial art originating in southeastern Africa and brought to Brazil by slaves from Angola. Part dance, part fighting strategy, *capoeira* is accompanied by a musical bow called *berimbau*.
Castrato:	Adult male soprano from mid 16th- to 19th-century Europe whose voice remained in the treble register after the onset of puberty because of surgical castration.
Ceilidh:	Scottish Gaelic term for a social gathering centered around the live performance of traditional music and dance. The equivalent Irish term is *ceili*.
Changdan:	Korean rhythmic mode and drum pattern performed in many aristocratic and folk genres as well as in the *pansori* storytelling tradition.
Chordophone:	Sachs-Hornbostel category of musical instruments comprising those that produce sound from a vibrating string set in motion by striking, plucking, bowing, or rubbing.
Chuimse:	Vocalized shouts and calls of encouragement performed by the drummer (*gosu*) in Korean *pansori* storytelling.
Chutney:	Indo-Caribbean popular music and dance genre based on traditional Indian wedding songs.
Chutney soca:	Indo-Trinidadian popular fusion song and dance genre combining chutney with Afro-Trinidadian "soul calypso."
Chutti:	Paper ridges attached, like a beard, to the chin of a *kathakali* actor using thick rice paste. This face makeup signifies royalty or divinity in the South Indian dance drama.
Circular breathing:	Technique practiced by performers of various aerophones allowing for continuous sound production by exhaling air stored in the cheeks while inhaling through the nose.

Clarinet:	Subcategory of aerophones employing a single vibrating reed.
Communitas:	Subjective experience of group solidarity and transcendence of social, economic, and political divisions during anti-structural rituals. Associated with theories of anthropologist Victor Turner (1920–1983).
Complainte:	French-language long song associated with the first generation of displaced Acadian settlers in Louisiana.
Composition:	Term for music created prior to performance and fixed by notation or other form of preservation. Contrasts with improvisation, the act of spontaneous creation at the time of performance. In many traditions, the two processes are combined.
Conjunct motion:	Melodic contour in which successive pitches are arranged more or less in stepwise order, using consecutive notes of a musical scale.
Context:	Approach to musical inquiry concerned with the natural and human environment in which music occurs.
Cordões:	Groups of outdoor masked revelers in 19th-century Brazilian Carnival festivities; precursors of *blocos.*
Cortigiana:	Courtesan in Italy, 14th–17th centuries.
Courtesan:	Educated female artist-musician and companion of upper-class men. Equivalent term found in many languages suggesting widespread social practice.
Creole:	Term for people of mixed ancestry living in current or former colonial societies; also, for primary languages formed by the fusion of two or more parent languages, usually one European and the other that of a colonized or enslaved population.
Crooner:	American male singer whose voice was characterized by an intimate, conversational tone made possible by the invention of sound amplification. In 1929, Bing Crosby (1903–1977) was awarded the title, "America's Crooner."
Cultural Revolution:	Decade-long social upheaval in the People's Republic of China (1966–1976) when young adults, mobilized under the instigation of aging Communist leader Mao Zedong, attempted to purge society of the "Four Olds": old customs, culture, habits, and ideas. Mass destruction of property and lives took place until the death of Mao in 1976.
Cumbia:	Colombian music and dance genre popular throughout Latin America, particularly among Mexicans living in the United States.
Dalang:	Javanese shadow puppeteer and storyteller in the *wayang kulit* tradition.
Dbyangs:	Form of multiphonic vocal chant practiced by Tibetan Buddhist monks, in which extremely low pitches are sustained while manipulation of oral cavity produces audible upper overtones.
Decasyllabic:	Ten-syllable line structure used in Balkan oral epic narration.
Decibel:	Unit of measurement (dB) for the amplitude or volume of sound.
Demarcator:	A marker of division or boundary between two categories. Music serves as a demarcator between secular and sacred space and time.
Devadasi:	Female dancer/musician dedicated to the service of a deity in traditional South Indian Hindu temples; institution outlawed in 1988.
Diegetic/Non-diegetic:	Music in theater or film whose source is visible to the audience, and is presumed to be audible to characters in the narrative. Non-diegetic refers to music whose source is invisible to the audience and presumed inaudible to the characters in the narrative.

Disjunct motion:	Melodic contour in which successive pitches are arranged with leaps, using non-consecutive notes of a musical scale.
Drone:	A single pitch or combination of pitches that sounds continuously through an entire performance, providing a reference or sonic environment for melodic and rhythmic music. Some instruments are equipped with extra strings or pipes to provide this harmonic feature.
Electrophone:	Sachs-Hornbostel category of musical instruments comprising those that produce sound primarily electronically, either by amplifying a sound produced mechanically (as with the electric guitar) or entirely by electronic or digital means (as with the synthesizer).
Enculturation:	Process by which an individual acquires the norms, characteristics, customs, language, and communicative codes of a culture or group, usually associated with early childhood conditioning but also referring to adaptations made by colonized or immigrant groups.
Entrudo:	16th-century Portuguese form of Carnival mayhem in which people threw flour, eggs, mud, oranges, and lemons at each other; hurled pots and pans out of windows; waged street battles with brooms and spoons; and held gluttonous feasts.
Epic narrative:	Recitation of extended oral narrative poems (epics) based on memorization and improvisation. Performances of epic narratives were particularly important in preliterate societies, since they concern issues central to the identity of a tribe, nation, or similar group. These issues include the lives of gods and heroes, creation myths, and other foundational stories that communicated, across generations, core beliefs and values.
Ethnomusicology:	Academic discipline concerned with the study of music as a component of human culture, emphasizing music's social, environmental, semiotic, and material dimensions, as opposed to its isolated sound components. The field developed from 19th-century attempts by Western scholars to account for non-Western musical practices and repertoires—frequently those encountered through colonial expansion—as well as oral tradition and vernacular repertoires of Western music.
Fado:	Portuguese urban song genre associated with the city of Lisbon conveying feelings of loss, regret, and the hardships of the poor. Dating from the early 19th century, the genre reached an international audience in the 1950s through the success of superstar Amália Rodrigues (1920–1999).
Falsetto:	Upper extension of the adult male singing voice reaching the treble female vocal range. Early rock vocalist Frankie Valli of the Four Seasons made falsetto singing his signature sound.
Fiddle:	Subcategory of chordophones consisting of instruments with strings stretched over a body and neck and played with a bow, thus capable of sustaining a pitch.
Film score:	Music composed specifically to accompany a movie. The musical soundtrack enhances the emotional impact, provides continuity between scenes, establishes the locale, and foreshadows narrative events. It is a near universal component of feature film production.
Flute:	Subcategory of aerophones in which the flow of air is split over an opening in a tube or chamber, causing the air inside to vibrate.
Four-part harmony:	Practice dating from the 14th century and possibly earlier of arranging music in four vocal parts: soprano, alto, tenor, and bass.

Free aerophone:	Subcategory of aerophones, such as the bullroarer, that produces sound by vibrating air not enclosed in a tube or chamber.
Free reed:	Subcategory of aerophones that produces sound when air passes over a reed set in a frame. This technology, used in East Asia from ancient times, was unknown in Europe until the early 19th century when free reed instruments imported from China became the basis for the accordion, harmonica, and reed organ (harmonium).
Gamak:	Term for melodic ornament in the classical music of South Asia (Hindustani and Karnatak).
Gamelan:	Traditional instrumental ensemble of Indonesia, and of the descendants of indentured Javanese laborers in Suriname, consisting mainly of tuned bronze or iron idiophones and drums.
Ge'ez:	Semitic language from the Horn of Africa (Ethiopia and Eritrea), extinct in its spoken vernacular forms and used today only as the liturgical (ritual) language of the Ethiopian Orthodox Tewahedo Church and other Christian denominations of that region.
Geisha:	Japanese professional female artist-entertainer.
Gesamtkunstwerk:	"Complete work of art." Term coined by German composer Richard Wagner (1813–1883) to describe music drama as a combination of music, poetry, drama, stagecraft, and architecture.
Gharana:	In North India, the organization of musicians by lineage or apprenticeship whereby the purity of a musical style is protected, maintained, and passed on across generations.
Gisaeng:	Korean hereditary profession of courtesan artist-entertainer.
Globalization:	Process of progressive integration of the world's political, economic, transportation, communication, and information systems and networks, having profound effect on both cosmopolitan and remote regions, leaving few places unaffected.
Glocalization:	Term for the processes by which globally distributed goods, services, and forms of expression have been adapted and transformed to meet specific local requirements.
Gompa:	Prayer hall in a Buddhist temple or monastery.
Gong:	Subcategory of idiophones consisting of round, flat, metal discs that are struck with a mallet or beater.
Gosu:	Drummer in Korean *pansori* who accompanies storyteller on barrel drum (*puk*) and provides shouts of encouragement (*chuimse*) during performance.
Gregorian Chant:	Repertoire of notated chant melodies, compiled primarily during the 9th and 10th centuries for use in the Roman Catholic Mass Liturgy. Named for Pope Gregory the Great (ca. 540–604) to whom the melodies were attributed. Also known as plainsong or plainchant.
Griot:	French term for West African praise singer/musician. Female *griot* is a *griotte*.
Grooves:	Term coined by ethnomusicologists in the 1990s for repetitive and propulsive dance rhythms. Term comes from the channels cut into a phonograph record in which the needle rides.
Gugak:	Korean traditional music.
Guru-shishya:	Formal relationship between teacher (*guru*) and student (*shishya*) in South Asia through which a spiritual or musical tradition is transmitted and maintained.

Guslari:	Balkan bard or epic narrator; named for the single-stringed fiddle (*gusle*) Balkan storytellers use to accompany their performances.
Harmonic progression:	A series of chords that seem to be directed forward in time toward a resolution or goal. Also called chord progression.
Harp:	Subcategory of chordophones in which strings suspended in a frame lie perpendicular to the resonating chamber.
Harvest celebration:	Calendrical ritual celebrating the harvest, especially in agricultural communities.
Hazzan:	Jewish liturgical singer or cantor.
Hetaira:	Courtesan in ancient Greece.
Heterophony:	Musical texture in which multiple instrumental and/or vocal parts perform the same melody simultaneously, but using different ornaments or variations.
Hindustani:	North Indian classical music tradition derived from the merging of aristocratic styles developed during the Mughal Empire (1526–1857) and Hindu devotional practices. Characterized by extreme melodic and rhythmic virtuosity, and fusion of Hindu and Islamic aesthetic principles. Term also used to identify the South Asian community in Suriname.
Hocket:	Technique for producing a melody by alternating the pitches of two or more instruments or voices.
Homophony:	Musical texture in which a single melody is supported by a harmonizing accompaniment.
Hybridity:	In music, the blending of two or more styles or traditions that may reflect a mixed cultural heritage, or the collaboration of performers of different cultural backgrounds.
Hymnody:	The practice of singing hymns—songs of praise or devotion— primarily in a religious context.
Iqa':	Rhythmic mode or pattern in Arabic music that repeats, with or without variations, throughout all or part of a performance. Patterns may range from as few as two beats to as many as forty-eight.
Idiophone:	Sachs-Hornbostel category of musical instruments comprising those that produce sound from the body of the instrument itself.
Imam:	Worship leader in a mosque and Muslim community.
Improvisation:	Spontaneous musical creation at the time of performance, usually based on conventions within a musical tradition.
Indenture:	Form of servitude in which a servant was bound to a master for a specific time period. On completion of the term, laborers imported from abroad were granted freedom and either return fare home or land in the place of indentureship.
Indigenous:	Native to a particular region or environment.
Indo-Trinidadian:	Trinidadian whose ancestors came from India, usually as indentured laborers.
Interval:	The distance between two pitches, described as melodic if the two pitches are in succession, and harmonic if they are sounded together. Usually measured in terms of scale degrees.
Jali:	(pl. *Jalolu*) Mande language term for hereditary praise singer, poet, and oral historian in the Mande region of northwest Africa.
Jamette Carnival:	Originally a derisive term applied by white planters to the unruly Carnival celebrations of the Afro-Trinidadian population that involved street parades, drumming, dancing, and sexually explicit masquerading.

Janissary band:	Military band of the Ottoman Turks, believed to be the oldest such ensemble in the world.
Jarai:	Tribal language of the Montagnards in the Central Highlands of Vietnam.
Jaran kapang:	Traditional dance by Javanese males on stylized hobbyhorses that involves spirit possession and acrobatics. Practiced also by members of the Javanese diasporic community in Suriname.
J'Ouvert:	Carnival Monday pre-dawn celebration of Afro-Trinidadians in which revelers cover themselves in mud or oil and parade in the streets, accompanied by loud steel band or soca music.
Kabuki:	Theatrical tradition that developed in Edo (Tokyo), Japan in the early 17th century.
Karnatak:	South Indian classical music tradition based on the elaboration of a repertoire of Hindu religious songs primarily composed by three musicians in the early 19th century: Tyagaraja, Shyama Shastri, and Muthuswami Dikshitar.
Katajjaq:	Vocal technique and entertainment genre of Inuit women, almost always performed as a duet. Also known as Inuit throat singing.
Kathakali:	Elaborate dance drama tradition of the South Indian state of Kerala.
Klezmer:	Genre of instrumental ensemble music associated with Jews of Eastern Europe, known for lively dance rhythms and expressive ornamentation.
Kotha:	The first floor of a salon where South Asian courtesans (*tawaif*) entertained upper-class men with song and dance.
Kwangdae:	Storyteller in the Korean *pansori* tradition.
Lamellaphone:	Subcategory of idiophones consisting of thin strips of metal fastened at one end to a frame and plucked with the thumbs at the unattached end. Instruments of this genre include the *mbira, sanza,* and *kalimba,* and are widely distributed throughout Sub-Saharan Africa.
Leitmotif:	A repeating melodic or rhythmic theme associated with a character, situation, or other aspect of the narrative, in opera, music drama, and film music.
Libretto:	In opera, the playbook or script.
Life-cycle rituals:	Rituals that mark transition points in a person's life, like coming-of-age initiations, weddings, and funerals.
Liminal:	(From Latin *limen,* threshold) In-between phase or transition from one state of affairs to another.
Liturgical drama:	A sacred narrative performed in the context of a religious ritual. The medieval Christian morality play is an example.
Liturgy:	Fixed set of spoken or sung texts that are repeated in a ritual setting.
Local deity:	A deity associated with a particular environment or group, often seen as a protector or intercessor for higher, more powerful spiritual forces.
Local nationalism:	Allegiance to one's ethnic group rather than to the nation state, as with Kurds in eastern Turkey.
Lunar New Year:	The first day of the New Year in cultures basing their calendar on the lunar cycle. In East Asia, New Year celebrations fall in late January or February, and in China they are the most extravagant of the year involving fifteen days of music, dance, fireworks, and festivities.

Lute:	(From Arabic *al-'ud*, "wood") Subcategory of chordophones in which strings are stretched across a resonating body and neck, and plucked in contrast to the bowed fiddle.
Lyre:	Subcategory of chordophones related to the harp, in which strings are suspended from a crossbar and fastened perpendicular to the resonating chamber.
Madang:	Tales told by the Korean *pansori* storyteller.
Mahabharata:	Sanskrit epic of ancient India and the source material for various artistic traditions in South and Southeast Asia. The story concerns two families—the Pandavas and the Kauravas—in a battle for succession to the throne of Bharata. Composed by the legendary sage Vyasa, it is ten times longer than the Greek epics *The Iliad* and *The Odyssey* combined.
Mahayana:	(Literally, "The Great Vehicle") Branch of Buddhism that developed in East Asia when teachings of Sakyamuni Buddha spread east from India and combined with the indigenous religions of China. Central to its tenets is veneration of otherworldly Buddhas and Bodhisattvas, beings dedicated to the liberation of others.
Mani kang:	Giant Tibetan Buddhist prayer wheel used in devotional practices. Each turning of the wheel is believed to utter a prayer, thus bestowing merit upon the practitioner.
Maqam:	Modal system for melodic invention in use from northwest Africa through the Middle East and Central Asia to western China.
Maroon:	Descendant of escaped African slaves in the New World. Suriname has the greatest Maroon population in the world because of the inaccessibility of settlements in the Amazonian Rainforest.
Mass media:	Technologies like radio, television, cinema, audio and video recordings, newspapers, and the internet designed to reach a mass audience.
May 4th Movement:	In China, student-led social turmoil and subsequent reform movements following Japan's annexation of the Shandong Peninsula in 1919.
Mediated Music:	As the term is used in ethnomusicology, music distributed and accessed through electronic media.
Melismatic:	In sacred chant, a single syllable stretched over a number of melodic pitches.
Melodic contour:	The shape of a melodic phrase described in terms of the rise and fall of successive pitches.
Melodic mode:	System containing the pitch material used to generate melodies in a music tradition. Examples include *raga* (India), *mugam* (Azerbaijan), and *slendro* (Java).
Membranophone:	Sachs-Hornbostel category of musical instruments comprising those that produce sound from a vibrating membrane. Most membranophones are drums of various shapes and sizes.
Mestizo:	In Latin America, a person of mixed race, especially of Native American and European ancestry.
Mevlevi:	Sufi religious order founded in Konya, Turkey in the 13th century by followers of Mevlana Jalaluddin Rumi (1207–1273). Members of the order are known as "whirling dervishes" after their practice of whirling in the sacred *sema* ceremony.
Minaret:	Tall, slender tower with a balcony near the top, affixed or adjacent to a mosque, from which, historically, the *muezzin* delivered the

	Call to Prayer (*adhan*) five times a day. Today, most minarets broadcast the Call to Prayer through loudspeakers.
Min ji:	Chinese courtesan.
Minstrel:	Itinerant European musician-storyteller.
Monody:	Device invented by members of the Florentine *Camerata* in the late 16th to early 17th centuries for the melodic delivery of dramatic speech with simple instrumental accompaniment. The invention was crucial to the development of Italian opera.
Monophony:	Musical texture comprising a single, unaccompanied melody.
Montagnard:	Member of one of several tribal groups indigenous to the Central Highlands of Vietnam.
Moso:	Blind Buddhist priests who developed the Japanese tradition of epic narration.
Mudra:	A symbolic hand gesture in South Asian dance and religious traditions.
Muezzin:	Appointee of a mosque responsible for performing the Call to Prayer (*adhan*) five times a day.
Mughal Empire:	South Asian dynastic empire established by Babur in 1526 and brought to an end in 1857 when the last Mughal emperor, Bahadur Shah II, was deposed by the British and exiled to Burma. Arts and learning flourished under several Mughal rulers, most notably Akbar the Great (1542–1605).
Murti:	Image of a deity housed in a Hindu temple.
Music therapy:	Branch of medicine dealing with the application of music in therapeutic treatments.
Musical bow:	Subcategory of chordophones consisting of a single string attached at both ends to a bent, flexible stick. The stick, in turn, is often attached to a resonator, which in some cases is the mouth of the performer.
Musical fusion:	The blending of musics from several styles or traditions. The term is usually applied to popular music genres.
Musicking:	Term coined by musicologist Christopher Small in 1998 to refer to music not as an object but as a process ("to music"), including any activities connected with the performance of music.
Musicologist:	Scholar engaged with the academic study of music, usually from an historical or analytical perspective and primarily focusing on Western art music.
Musiki:	Classical Greek term for the arts that fall under the influence of the nine muses.
Muzak:	American company founded in 1934 for delivery of background music to commercial clients. The term has been used to refer to any piped-in environmental music or the system that delivers it.
Nad Brahman:	In Hinduism, the reverence for god as sound. Also, in Indian classical music, an understanding that the universe was created from sound.
Nadun:	Harvest ritual involving spirit possession among the Mangghuer ethnic group in western China.
Naubat:	Royal music ensemble of the Mughal emperors of northern India.
Norebang:	Korean "song room," a private, intimate form of karaoke.
Nueva Canción:	Folk-inspired and politically motivated song movement in Latin America from the 1960s and 70s.

Oboe: Subcategory of aerophones in which air enclosed in a tube is set in motion by the vibration of two reeds.

Obon: A major midsummer festival in Japan commemorating the return to earth of ancestor spirits.

Ocarina: Subcategory of aerophones in which air is blown into a chamber or vessel with several finger holes for changing the pitch. Ancient forms have been found in prehistoric China and Mesoamerica.

Opera: Dramatic work for vocalists and orchestra that includes acting, costumes, and scenery. This secular genre began in late 16th-century Italy.

Oral transmission: Transmission of cultural information—including narratives, histories, genealogies, sacred verses, and music—across generations without the use of writing.

Oratorio: Composition for instruments, chorus, and soloists that presents sacred stories based on Biblical narratives. The genre was developed in mid 17th-century Italy, for performance during Lent when opera houses were closed.

Organologist: Scholar engaged with the academic study of musical instruments.

Ornamentation: Embellishment of pitches using techniques characteristic of a particular style or genre. These include vibrato, trills, shakes, *gamak,* and *tahrir.*

Overtones: Inaudible pitches produced along with an audible fundamental tone that are related to the frequency of the fundamental by simple ratio. These determine the timbre of the audible tone by their relative prevalence.

Panpipe: Subcategory of aerophones consisting of a set of connected hollow tubes or pipes, closed at one end, and arranged in order of length. Blowing across the open end of each pipe produces its respective pitch.

Pansori: Storytelling tradition from Korea.

Par: Large, hand-painted scroll used in the Epic of Pabuji narrative tradition of Rajasthan, North India.

Patronage system: European economic system whereby artists and musicians worked for, and were supported by, church institutions or wealthy aristocratic patrons who controlled their creative output.

Pelog: Seven-tone scale used in Javanese *gamelan* music.

Pentatonic: Five-note scale or mode, used in musical systems of East Asia, Sub-Saharan Africa, and folk traditions of the British Isles among others.

Periodicity: As used in music, the term describes the regular recurrence of rhythmic and melodic patterns that gives stability to musical structures and experiences.

Plainchant: Alternate term for Gregorian chant.

Playback singer: Singer in the Indian film industry who pre-records songs for actors to lip-synch on screen.

Playing *Mas:*   (*Mas,* "masquerades") Participating in Trinidad's Carnival costume parades.

Polyphony: Musical texture of multiple simultaneous melodies.

Polyrhythm: Two or more independent rhythmic patterns played simultaneously (such as 2s against 3s), creating a complex rhythmic texture that often serves as the underpinning for solo improvisation by a lead drummer. Characteristic of Sub-Saharan rhythmic structures.

Praise song:	Improvised song text in praise of a patron. Associated with the *griot* tradition of West Africa.
Processional Music:	Special music, such as a wedding march, to accompany a line of participants entering a ritual space.
Program Music:	Musical depiction of non-music situations, objects, or states of being.
Proletarian:	Member of the working class. A term associated with Marxist ideology.
Primitive Baptist:	Conservative Christian denomination that adheres to Calvinist doctrine forbidding the use of musical instruments in worship services.
Pro-Democracy Movement:	Student-led liberalizing movement in the People's Republic of China, after the death of Mao Zedong in 1976, that culminated in massive public demonstrations at Tiananmen Square in Beijing and subsequent government crackdown and reprisals.
Psalm:	One of 150 sacred and devotional song texts in the Old Testament of the Bible.
Puja:	A Hindu ritual of purification.
Qari:	An expert in Qur'anic recitation.
Qawwali:	Genre of sacred sung poetry in Sufi traditions of northern India and Pakistan performed by professional hereditary musicians primarily at Sufi shrines.
Quechua:	Native peoples of the Central Andean region of South America including Peru and Bolivia, and the languages they speak.
Raga:	Melodic system used in the music of North and South India, as well as parts of Pakistan, Afghanistan, and Bangladesh. Also an individual melodic mode consisting of five to seven pitches arranged in ascending and descending order, and associated with a time of day, season of the year, particular deity, and/or a mood.
Ramayana:	Sanskrit epic of ancient India composed, according to legend, by the sage Valmiki. The story concerns the defeat of demon Ravana by god-king Rama and his loyal general, the monkey king Hanuman. It provides the source material for a number of artistic traditions in South and Southeast Asia.
Raqs sharqi:	Classical Egyptian form of belly dance.
Rasa:	In classical Indian aesthetics, the dominant emotional content of a work of art or musical performance.
Recessional Music:	Special music to accompany a line or group of participants leaving a ritual space.
Recitative:	Sung dialogue in Italian opera, using the inflections and rhythms of spoken language.
Reggae:	Song and dance genre from Jamaica.
Revitalization:	Process by which obsolete or neglected musical traditions gain renewed interest among practitioners and audiences.
Rhythmic mode:	Rhythmic pattern repeated, with or without variations, throughout a performance. Rhythmic modal systems include *tala* (India), *Iqa'* (Middle East), and *changdan* (Korea).
Rishi:	(Sanskrit, "seer; conduit for revelation") Mystics to whom it is believed the Vedas were divinely revealed at least 3500 years ago.
Rokusai Nembutsu Odori:	Japanese music and dance tradition associated with Obon celebrations in the city of Kyoto.

Roots Rhythms:	Rhythmic patterns used in popular dance music genres that derive from earlier forms of sacred ritual music.
Sachs-Hornbostel:	Musical instrument classification system developed in 1914 by ethnomusicologists Erich Moritz von Hornbostel (1877–1935) and Curt Sachs (1881–1959).
Sama:	See *sema*
Sambadromo:	Exhibition venue for samba parades during Brazilian Carnival where teams from samba schools compete before judges.
Samba School:	Brazilian neighborhood-based social clubs in which teams develop themes, songs, and choreography; create costumes and props; and rehearse for Carnival parades at the *sambadromo* exhibition venue.
Sambista:	Experienced participants of Brazil's Carnival samba music and dance traditions.
Sangita:	Sanskrit term for music that includes melody, rhythm, and bodily movement or dance.
Sanskrit:	Liturgical language of Hinduism and ancient literary language of India. It is the original language in which the Vedas were revealed.
Saturnalia:	Ancient Roman festival dedicated to the god Saturn and celebrating the harvest that included the overturning of daily conventions, drunkenness, licentiousness, the overturning of daily conventions, and the inversion of social hierarchies.
Scale:	Stepwise sequence of ascending and descending pitches that form the basis for melodic composition and improvisation.
Sema:	(*Sema*, Turkish; *Sama*, Arabic. Literally, "listening" and "that which is heard") Term refers to sacred ceremonies of various Sufi orders from North Africa to the Indian Subcontinent. In Turkey, refers to the ritual of the Mevlevi whirling dervishes.
Shakti:	Sanskrit for the sacred energy generated by yoga practices and radiating from holy objects such as images of a deity housed in Hindu temples.
Shaman:	Spiritual healer and guide capable of making direct contact with spirits and supernatural forces through self-induced trance. The term was originally applied to Central Asian practitioners; now applied generally.
Sharpeville Massacre:	Civil disturbance in South Africa on March 21, 1960 resulting in the shooting death of 69 black African protesters by police officers. The event gained worldwide media coverage and initiated international condemnation of the Apartheid regime.
Shuoshude:	Blind itinerant musician-storyteller of China.
Singspiel:	German musical theater genre for middle-class audiences that flourished in the 18th and 19th centuries, in which spoken dialogue alternated with songs and ballads.
Slendro:	Five-tone scale used in Javanese *gamelan* music and associated with nighttime *wayang kulit* performances.
Soca:	Popular song genre of Trinidad combining indigenous calypso with elements of Indo-Trinidadian music including fast tempos and heavy percussion accompaniment.
Sonidero bailes:	DJ-led Mexican and Mexican-American dance parties.
"Stimela":	Title of a song by South African jazz trumpeter Hugh Masekela meaning "steam train" in Nguni languages. Released in 1974 during Apartheid, the song describes the hated train that carried black laborers from

all parts of southern Africa to work in the gold and diamond mines around Johannesburg.

Sufi:	Member of an Islamic mystical order.
Sutra:	Sanskrit for a written collection of spiritual sayings or aphorisms in Hinduism or Buddhism.
Sympathetic string:	One of a set of secondary strings, on South Asian chordophones like *sitar, sarod,* and *sarangi,* that vibrate when the primary melodic strings are played, to increase the resonance of the instrument.
Symphony:	Composition for Western orchestra in several sections (movements), originating in 18th-century court entertainments. By the early 19th century, principally due to Beethoven's influence, it had become the most ambitious, complex, and profound form of instrumental music of the Western classical tradition.
T'al ch'um:	Korean genre of masked dance.
Tahrir:	A vocal ornament characteristic of Persian (Iranian) vocal music.
Tajweed:	Rules for correct pronunciation of the Qur'an during recitation.
Tala:	Rhythmic system in South Asian music, and also a single rhythmic mode identified by the number of beats and pattern of accents and rests per cycle.
Tamboo-bamboo band:	Ensemble of idiophones including large tuned bamboo sticks and bottles struck with spoons that developed in Trinidad and Tobago when British authorities outlawed drums in the Afro-Trinidadian community in the 1880s.
Taqsim:	Melodic improvisation in Arabic and Turkish instrumental music based on *maqam* and usually in free meter. May be an introductory or internal section of a performance.
Tara sutra:	Short prayer or mantra addressed to Tara, a female *bodhisattva* (liberated being) who embodies perfect compassion, repeated by Tibetan Buddhists as a devotional practice while turning a prayer wheel.
Tarab:	Arabic term for "enchantment." Ecstatic feeling associated with playing and listening to music. As *taarab*, a genre of East African popular music developed in the 1920s.
Tarteel:	Recitation of the Qur'an with clarity and understanding, according to exact rules of pronunciation.
Tassa drumming:	In Trinidad, an Indo-Caribbean tradition of playing the *tassa* drum (of Indian origin) with sticks in street parades on the Muslim holiday of Hosay as well as at Hindu weddings and other celebrations.
Tawaif:	North Indian courtesan/entertainer who catered to the aristocracy, particularly during the Mughal period.
Techno music:	Electronic instrumental dance party music, developed during the late 1980s.
Temporary physiological synchrony:	Social phenomenon described by primatologist Bruce Richmond in which gelada baboons achieve a state of metabolic and emotional coordination through group vocalizations. Richmond theorized that the same effect might be experienced by primitive or modern humans through collective or choral singing or chanting.
Texture:	Element of music defining the relationship between simultaneous, coordinated parts, such as melody and accompaniment (homophony), and multiple melodic lines (polyphony).

Theravada:	(Literally, "teaching of the elders") Branch of Buddhism that took root in Sri Lanka and Southeast Asia. Most conservative form of Buddhism and least modified by contact with other religions, Theravada puts emphasis on acquisition of merit through individual effort, including service to monastic communities.
Throat singing:	Term used to describe various vocal techniques of Central Asia or the Arctic regions of North America. Techniques in Central Asia involve production of audible whistle-like overtones above a fundamental pitch, while Inuit women of North America produce unique sounds in the neck below the larynx, and in the oral cavity.
Tiananmen Square:	Large, open public space in central Beijing, site of the 1989 student protests of the Pro-Democracy Movement.
Timbre:	Technical term for the quality of a vocal or instrumental sound, also described as tone color.
Tone poem:	Single-movement composition for symphony orchestra with a descriptive title.
Tongsu:	Officially sanctioned popular song genre in the People's Republic of China.
Trance:	Any of a number of psychological states that differ from normal waking consciousness. In a religious context, these range from deep meditation to hyperactive ecstatic states in which the subject is capable of extreme feats of strength or endurance. Music usually aids the initiating or sustaining of trance states, which are often understood as evidence of contact with invisible realms or beings.
Trek Boer:	Native Dutch, French, or German pastoralist who migrated to the interior of South Africa in the 17th or18th centuries.
Trumpet:	Subcategory of aerophones in which the air enclosed in a straight, curved or folded tube is set in motion by the player's vibrating or buzzing lips.
Umbigada:	Gyrating hip movements characteristic of Brazilian samba dance.
Urs:	Annual festival at a South Asian Sufi shrine, commemorating the death anniversary of the saint entombed there. *Sama* or sacred rituals include the singing of *qawwali*.
Veda:	One of four collections of sacred prayers and invocations in ancient India, dating from the 2nd millennium BCE and transmitted to the present through oral tradition. The four Vedas constitute the oldest hymns and revelations of Hinduism.
Verismo:	Late 19th-century style of Italian opera with plots based on real life situations involving the violence and passions of the underclass.
Vernacular language:	Spoken language of a community or population, in contrast to a liturgical language used only in ritual circumstances.
Vibrato:	Vocal or instrumental ornament involving the production of microtonal pitch fluctuations that increase resonance and projection of musical sound.
Virtuosity:	Great technical skill displayed by a musician.
Vodun:	West African traditional religion also practiced by descendants of the African slave trade in Haiti, Puerto Rico, and elsewhere. In the New World, African religious practices blended or syncretized with aspects of Christianity.

Vuvuzela:	South African plastic trumpet that gained notoriety when played incessantly by audience members at the 2010 FIFA World Cup Soccer Tournament games.
Wayang kulit:	Indonesian shadow puppet theater accompanied by a *gamelan* ensemble.
Winti:	Afro-Surinamese religion based upon ancestor worship, spirit possession, and belief in a pantheon of gods (also called *winti*) derived from West Africa.
Yin yang:	In Chinese philosophy, terms referring to opposing forces, such as heat and cold, light and dark, heaven and earth. As a single word, *yinyang*, a Daoist ritual leader and priest.
Yodeling:	Vocal style featuring rapid alternation between low-pitched and high-pitched registers. Associated with herders in the Swiss and Austrian Alps, as well as American country singers in the early 20th century, most notably Jimmie Rodgers.
Zikr:	In Islam, a devotional practice for being mindful of the will of God; forms range from silent recitation of Qur'anic verses to the music and dance of Sufis.
Zither:	Subcategory of chordophones in which strings are stretched across a flat soundboard and typically plucked or strummed.
Zydeco:	Popular dance music genre of Louisiana Creoles combining elements of Cajun, jazz, blues, and R&B.

CREDITS

IMAGE CREDITS

VIDEO CREDITS

LESSON 1

1.2: Buzzing beetle, Kaulong area, southwest New Britain, Papua New Guinea. Birgit Drüppel, *Re-counting Knowledge in Song: Change Reflected in Kaulong Music* (Boroko: Institute of Papua New Guinea Studies, 2009). Courtesy of Birgit Drüppel.

LESSON 2

2.1: Vocal folds. Courtesy of Michael Y. Parker, www.wilmingtonhealth.com; Seth M. Cohen, MD, MPH, and Leda Scearce, MM, MS, CCC-SLP, and Duke Voice Care Center, www.dukevoicecare.org.

2.2: Young voices: 1. Lalibela, Ethiopia, 2012; 2. Yulin, Shaanxi province, PRC, 2006. Courtesy of Jonathan C. Krameri, 3. Freeport, Trinidad, 2008. Courtesy of Alison E. Arnold.

2.3: Quechua traditional ensemble, Cuzco, Peru. Courtesy of Jorge Choquehuillca Huallpa and Familia Choquehuillca.

2.4: *Katajjaq* throat singing by Karen Panigoniak and Maria Illungiayok in Arviat, Nunavut, Canada. Courtesy of Karen Panigoniak.

2.5: Jimmie Rodgers. Courtesy of Jimmie Rodgers Foundation and Museum, Meridian, MS, www.jimmierodgers.com; and the Folklore Alliance International, Kansas City, MO, www.folkalliance.org.

2.6: Tibetan love song. Courtesy of Plateau Music Project, and song collector Tsering Samdrup.

2.7: Old Time Camp Meeting song. Courtesy of Mount Carmel Baptist Church, Atlanta, GA, Pastor Timothy Flemming Sr., www.mtcarmelbaptistchurch.org.

2.8: West African praise singer. Diali Cissokho singing "Lu Mu Mety Mety," accompanying himself on *kora* (harp-lute). Boone, NC, 2010. Courtesy of Diali Cissokho, www.kairabamusic.com.

2.9: Japanese epic narrator. Yoko Hiraoka accompanying herself on *biwa* (four-string lute). Courtesy of Yoko Hiraoka, www.japanesestrings.com

2.10: National Gugak orchestra. From *Gugak: The Korean Traditional Music and Dance,* DVD publication of the National Gugak Center, Seoul, Republic of Korea. Courtesy of the National Gugak Center, www.gugak.go.kr:9001/eng/. © 2011. All rights reserved.

2.11: *Kalumbu* (musical bow) played by Chris Haambwiila. *Zambia Roadside 2,* CD, SWP 041. Courtesy of Michael Baird, founder, SWP Records, www.swprecords.com.

2.12: *Seperewa* (harp-lute) played at the Center for Cultural and African Studies, Nkruma University, Kumasi, Ghana, 2006. Courtesy of Ulf Jägfors.

2.13: Celtic harp. Julie Gorka playing Scottish traditional tune, "Lochaber No More," recorded by Alison E. Arnold, 2014. Courtesy of Julie Gorka.

2.14: Paraguayan harp played by Silvio Solis, recorded in Providence, RI, 2011. Courtesy of Jonathan C. Kramer.

2.15: *Saung gauk* (Burmese harp), played by Zaw Win Maung in Kyaukpadaung, Myanmar, 1998. Courtesy of Gavin Douglas, University of North Carolina, Greensboro.

2.16: Lyre documentary. Courtesy of Michael Levy, www.ancientlyre.com.

2.17: *Krar* (Ethiopian lyre), Totot Traditional Restaurant, Addis Ababa, 2013. Courtesy of Jonathan C. Kramer.

2.18: *Ud* (Arabic lute) played by Naji Hilal, www.najihilal.com, recorded by Jonathan C. Kramer and Alison E. Arnold. Courtesy of Naji Hilal.

2.19: *Tar* (Iranian lute) played by Sahba Motallebi. Courtesy of Sahba Motallebi, www.sahbamusic.com.

2.20: *Setar* (Iranian lute) played by Sahba Motallebi. Courtesy of Sahba Motallebi, www.sahbamusic.com.

2.21: *Sitar* (North Indian lute) played by Harihar Sharan Bhatt at Jawahar Kala Kendra, Jaipur, Rajasthan, India, 2007. Courtesy of Harihar Sharan Bhatt, www.trivet.org.

2.22: *Pipa* (Chinese lute). "Collage 2000" played by Wu Man, www.wumanpipa.org. Courtesy of Brandon Ahlstrom and Shuman Associates, New York, NY.

2.23: Ukulele. Herb Ohta, Sr. playing "Hawaii" on Oahu, HI. Courtesy of Herb Ohta, Sr.

2.24: *Akonting* (Senegalese lute). Remi Diatta playing and singing "Alinom de Caraba." Appreciation to Remi Diatta and Laemouahuma (Daniel) Jatta. Courtesy of Chuck Levy, videographer and publisher, Gainesville, FL. © 2008. All rights reserved.

2.25: Banjo. Chuck Levy playing clawhammer banjo in Gainesville, FL. Courtesy of Chuck Levy, www.banjourneys.com. © 2013. All rights reserved.

2.26: Sergio and Odair Assad playing Astor Piazzolla's "Tango Suite" for two guitars, 1997. Courtesy of Sergio and Odair Assad, www.assadbrothers.com.

2.27: Jimi Hendrix. From *Monterey Pop* by D.A. Pennebaker, courtesy of Pennebaker Hegedus Films, Inc and the Monterey International Pop Festival Foundation, Inc. Available from the Criterion Collection.

2.28: *Kamanche* (spike fiddle). Imamyar Hasanov playing Azerbaijani *Mugham Bayati-Shiraz.* Courtesy of Imamyar Hasanov, www.kamancha.com.

2.29: Ciompi String Quartet: Eric Pritchard and Hsiao-mei Ku (violins), Jonathan Bagg (viola), Fred Raimi (cello), playing Haydn String Quartet Op. 76, 3rd movement. Courtesy of Hsiao-mei Ku and the Ciompi Quartet, www.ciompi.org.

2.30: *Kamanja* (Moroccan viola). Ouled Ben Aguida ensemble performing at a wedding celebration in Safi: Hafida Hasnaouia, lead vocals; Aicha Nousmi, co-lead vocals; Bouch'aib Benshlih, *kamanja*; Boujm'a Benshlih, *darbuka* (goblet drum) and vocals; Miloud Hilali, *ud* (lute); Mustapha Hokaki, *bendir* (frame drum); Hassan Zatani, *bendir.* Courtesy of Alessandra Ciucci.

2.31: *Sarangi* (North Indian fiddle) demonstration by Dhruba Ghosh, 2012. Courtesy of Jasper Berben, Stichting Nieuw Ensemble & Atlas Ensemble, www.nieuw-ensemble.nl/en/.

2.32: *Santouri* (Greek hammered dulcimer). Areti Ketime singing and playing "*Nanourisma*" (traditional lullaby) at the "Tribute to Asia Minor" concert, the Odeon of Herodes Artticus, Greece. Courtesy of Areti Ketime, aretiketime.com.

2.33: *Qanun* (Arabic zither) played by George Sawa. Courtesy of George Dimitri Sawa, georgedimitrisawa.com.

2.34: Harpsichord. The late Rafael Puyana playing Domenico Scarlatti's Sonata K119. Courtesy of Canal de Hauptwerkian.

2.35: *Guqin* (Chinese long zither) played by Dai Xiaolian, Shanghai Conservatory. Courtesy of Dai Xiaolian.

2.36: *Guzheng* (Chinese long zither) played at a teahouse northwest of Beijing, 2007. Courtesy of Alison E. Arnold.

2.37: *Kayagum* (long zither) played by Yi Ji-Young. From *Gugak: The Korean Traditional Music and Dance,* DVD publication of the National Gugak Center, Seoul, Republic of Korea. Courtesy of the National Gugak Center, www. gugak. go. Kr: 9001/eng/ © 2011. All rights reserved. Courtesy of Yi Ji-Young, www.yijiyoung.org.

2.38: Native American wooden flute played by Wolfs Robe. Courtesy of Wolfs Robe, akaflutemanent.com.

2.39: *Enkwanzi* (Ugandan panpipes) played by Haruna Walusimbi of the Nile Beat Artists Traditional Ensemble, www.nilebeatartists.org, 2013. Courtesy of Jonathan C. Kramer.

2.40: Ocarina. Courtesy of Durian Songbird, Songbird Ocarinas, songbirdocarina.com.

2.41: *Nplooj* (leaf) played by a Hmong woman. Courtesy of Mikkel Hornnes.

2.42: *Taepyongso* (Korean oboe). From *Gugak: The Korean Traditional Music and Dance,* DVD publication of the National Gugak Center, Seoul, Republic of Korea. Courtesy of the National Gugak Center, www.gugak.go.kr:9001/eng/. © 2011. All rights reserved.

2.43: *Nadaswaram* (South Indian oboe) played by Indian musicians Kasim and Babu Kalaimamani for the annual Brahmotsavam Festival, Sri Venkateshwara Temple, Cary, NC, 2014. Courtesy of Jonathan C. Kramer.

2.44: *Suona* (Chinese oboe) played in a public park in Urumqi, Xinjiang, 2007. Courtesy of Alison E. Arnold.

2.45: *Cornamusa* (Italian bagpipe). Courtesy of Luca Paciaroni, bagpipes and wind instruments maker, www.varropipemaker.com.

2.46: Clarinet. Mauricio Murcia Bedoya playing Jean Françaix, Clarinet Concerto, 4th movement (1967), with the Orquesta Filarmónica de Bogotá, Colombia, 2007. Courtesy of Mauricio Murcia Bedoya.

2.47: *Launeddas* (Sardinian triple-pipe clarinet). Courtesy of Pitano Perra, www.pitano.it.

2.48: Klezmer. Courtesy of Ahnes Horovitz Binder, manager, Budapest Klezmer Band, budapestklezmerband.webnode.hu.

2.49: *Khaen* (mouth organ) played by Sombat Simlah, Thailand. Courtesy of Mikkel Hornnes.

2.50: Chinese *sheng* (mouth organ) and accordion, with Chen Jun (accordion) and unknown *sheng* player at the American Accordionists' Association Convention, 2008. Courtesy of Linda Soley Reed, President, American Accordionists' Association, www.ameraccord.com.

2.51: English concertina played by Tim Smith, recorded by Alison E. Arnold, 2014. Courtesy of Tim Smith.

2.52: Wanamaker Organ. The Virgil Fox Legacy, virgilfoxlegacy.com. Courtesy of Len Levasseur.

2.53: *Dung-chen* (Tibetan trumpets). Courtesy of Makoto Masaje and Jetokey.

2.54: North Carolina Brass Band. Courtesy of North Carolina Brass Band, Brian Meixner, director. www.ncbrassband.org. Video by permission of Jonathan C. Kramer.

2.55: Bugle. Army Sgt. Keith Clark playing "Taps" at the State Funeral of John F. Kennedy, 1963. Courtesy of Jari Villanueva, www.tapsbugler.com.

2.56: Timpani. Randy Max performing William Kraft, Timpani Concerto No. 1 (1983), with the Rotterdam Philharmonic conducted by Hugh Wolff. Courtesy of Randy Max.

2.57: *Pat waing* (drum circle) played by a senior student group at the Yangon University of Culture, Myanmar. Courtesy of Gavin Douglas.

2.58: West African "talking drum" played by Ayan Bisi Adeleke. Louis Jackson, camera, Ade Panko, director/editor. Courtesy of Louis Jackson III, Creative Improv Productions, Inc.

2.59: *Derbake* (goblet drum) played by Jussef Bichara, director, Escuela Banjara, Chile. Courtesy of Victoria and Jussef Bichara, www.banjara.cl.

2.60: *Changgo* (hourglass drum). Kang Hyo-joo singing *chapka* (narrative song). From *Gugak: The Korean Traditional Music and Dance,* DVD publication of the National Gugak Center, Republic of Korea. Courtesy of the National Gugak Center, www.gugak.go.kr:9001/eng/. © 2011. All rights reserved.

2.61: Powwow drum played by Armour Hill Singers at the Las Vegas powwow. Courtesy of Armour Hill Singers.

2.62: Glen Velez playing the frame drum. Courtesy of Glen Velez, glenvelez.com.

2.63: *Pandeiro* (frame drum) played by Louis-Daniel Joly. Courtesy of Louis-Daniel, founder, Joly, Baratanga Productions, www.baratanga.com.

2.64: *Congas* played by Juan Álamo. Courtesy of Juan Álamo, www.juanalamo.com.

2.65: Church bells in Seville, Spain. Courtesy of Jennifer Westrom.

2.66: Large hanging bell at Sudeoksa Buddhist temple, Republic of Korea. Courtesy of Donald Belmore (DragonDon).

2.67: *Agogo* (iron double bell). Courtesy of Chief Yagbe Awolowo Onilu Agba Awo of Ile-Ife, Osun state, Nigeria.

2.68: Castanets played by Barbara Hennerfeind, with Erik Weisenberger, guitar. Courtesy of Barbara Hennerfeind and Duo Agua y Vino, www.guitarbara.de.

2.69: *Baithak gana* ("seated singing"). Rakieb Waggidhossain (vocalist), Roy Raghu (*dholak*), and Narider Singh (*dantal*) in Paramaribo, Suriname. Courtesy of Jonathan C. Kramer.

2.70: Musical saw. Courtesy of Ian McLean, www.globalvideoprotv.com.

2.71: *Embaire* (Ugandan xylophone) played by the Nile Beat Artists Traditional Ensemble, www. nilebeatartists.org, 2013: Cosmas Takubyaku, *ensaasi,* (shaker), James Isabirye, *enduumi* (small conical drum), Wilson Kalogo, *engoma enene* (large conical drum), Haruna Walusimbi, *omugaabe* (long drum), Okiror and Kitonto, *embaire* (xylophone). Courtesy of Jonathan C. Kramer.

2.72: *Jaltarang* (Indian tuned, water-filled ceramic bowls) played by Ranjana Pradhan, Sydney, Australia, 2006. Courtesy of Damien Reilly, CEO, Blue Pie Productions, www. bluepierecords.com.

2.73: *Endongo* (Ugandan thumb pianos) played by James Isabirye and Haruna Walusimbi of the Nile Beat Artists Traditional Ensemble, www.nilebeatartists.org, 2013. Courtesy of Jonathan C. Kramer.

2.74: *Zil* (finger cymbals) played by belly dancer Christine Dempsey ("Willow"). Courtesy of Christine Dempsey, www.bellydancewillow.com.

2.75: *Rolmo* (Tibetan cymbals). Labrang Monastery, Gansu province, PRC. Courtesy of Alison E. Arnold.

2.76: Soultone cymbals played by drummer Brook Alexander. Soultone Cymbals Extreme Demo Video, 2011. Courtesy of Iki Levy, founder, Soultone Cymbals, www.soultonecymbals.com.

2.77: Hand-held gongs, as used in Beijing opera, Jianxi province, PRC. Courtesy of Jonathan C. Kramer.

2.78: Tuned gong performance in Guilguila, Tanudan, Kalinga, Philippines. Courtesy of Glenn Stallsmith.

2.79: Chinese *tam tam* demonstration. Courtesy of Mark Wessels, director of internet activities, Vic Firth Company, www.vicfirth.com.

2.80: Javanese *gamelan*. Courtesy of Londoireng.

2.81: Steel bands compilation: 1. "Oil Barrels, Steel Drums: Pan in Trinidad and Tobago" (1996). Courtesy of Chris Simon, founder, Sageland Media, www.sagelandmedia.com. © 1996. Museum of International Folk Art; 2. Starlift Children's Steel Orchestra rehearsal, Port of Spain, Trinidad, 2008. Courtesy of Alison E. Arnold.

2.82: Theremin documentary by Carolina Eyck, www.carolinaeyck.com.

2.83: *Shinawi* Korean folk ensemble. From *Gugak: The Korean Traditional Music and Dance,* DVD publication of the National Gugak Center, Seoul, Republic of Korea. Courtesy of the National Gugak Center, www.gugak.go.kr:9001/eng/. © 2011. All rights reserved.

2.84: South Indian violin played by Aishu Venkataraman, accompanied by *kanjira* (tambourine) and *mridangam* (barrel drum). Courtesy of V.R. Venkataraman, www.divinestrings.com.

LESSON 3

3.1: University of Michigan Marching Band. Courtesy of John D. Pasquale. All rights administered by the University of Michigan Board of Regents. University of Michigan Marching Band, © 2014. All rights reserved.

3.2: Souhail Kaspar demonstrating Arabic rhythm pattern on *dumbek* (goblet drum), recorded by Jonathan C. Kramer. Courtesy of Souhail Kaspar, www.neareastmusic.com.

3.3: Belly dance. Souhail Kaspar, *Masterclass at Home Series: Rhythm and Movement for Egyptian Raqs Al-Sharqi,* Vol. 3, DVD. Courtesy of Souhail Kaspar, www.neareastmusic.com.

3.4: Korean rhythmic pattern. From *Sopyonje,* Taehung Pictures, Im Kwon-taek, director. Courtesy of Im Kwon-taek, Im Kwon Taek College of Film and Performing Arts at Dong Seo University, Republic of Korea. © 1993. All rights reserved.

3.5: *Shakuhachi* (Japanese bamboo flute) played by Koji Matsunobu, University of Washington, Seattle campus, March 2008, recorded by Jonathan C. Kramer and Alison E. Arnold. Courtesy of Koji Matsunobu.

3.6: Polyrhythm. From *FOLI (There Is No Movement Without Rhythm)* produced by The Rhythm Project Company and A Moving Company, Thomas Roebers and Floris Leeuwenberg, directors. Courtesy of Thomas Roebers and Floris Leeuwenberg. © 2010. All rights reserved.

3.7: *Bateria* rehearsal in the Mocidade Samba School building, 2013. Courtesy of Paul Hodge, SoloAroundWorld, www.genpolicy.com.

3.8: Prison work gangs. From *Afro-American Work Songs in a Texas Prison*, Folklore Research Films; Pete and Toshi Seeger with Bruce Jackson, producers. Courtesy of Pete Seeger. © 1966. All rights reserved.

3.9: Women hoeing garden rows. Ghanaian Ministry of Food and Agriculture in partnership with Engineers Without Borders Canada. Courtesy of Megan Timmins Putnam, ing. Engineers Without Borders Canada.

3.10: Wedding party in Mali. Courtesy of Jeremy Chevrier, Rootsyrecords.

3.11: Hand and foot drum solo by Nana Kimati Dinizulu, the Dinizulu Center for African Culture and Research, Jamaica, NY. Courtesy of Nana Kimati Dinizulu, Jr., www.dinizulucenter.org.

3.12: *Ghatam* (South Indian clay pot) played by Vikku Vinayakram, with Afro-Swedish band, Mynta. Courtesy of Christian Paulin, www.mynta.net.

3.13: Tito Puente playing "El Sabroso Son," written, composed, and arranged by "La Palabra," aka Rodolfo M. Foster. Courtesy of La Palabra.

3.14: *Gamelan* tuning systems: *Slendro* (five-tone scale) and *Pelog* (seven-tone scale). Courtesy of Mike Simpson, musical director, Inspire-works, www.inspire-works.co.uk/.

3.15: "Singing at a small mosque" video clip from the bonus DVD to the recording entitled *Music of Central Asia vol. 6: Alim and Fargana Qasimov: Spiritual Music of Azerbaijan*, SFW40525, courtesy of Smithsonian Folkways Recordings. Music of Central Asia is a co-production of the Aga Khan Music Initiative and Smithsonian Folkways Recordings. ℗©2007. Used by permission.

3.16: *Muqam* (Uighur modal system). Uighur musicians playing in Kashgar, Xinjiang Province, PRC, 2007. Courtesy of Alison E. Arnold.

3.17: Concert for Bangladesh. Ali Akbar Khan (*sarod*), Ravi Shankar (*sitar*), and Alla Rakha (*tabla*) performing at Madison Square Garden, August 1, 1971. From reissued Apple DVD. © Apple Films Inc.

3.18: "Moon Reflected in the Second Spring." Unknown *erhu* (Chinese two-string fiddle) player. Recorded in Yulin, Shaanxi province, PRC, 2006. Courtesy of Jonathan C. Kramer.

3.19: *Sijo* (traditional Korean art song) sung by Hong Changnam, with National Gugak Center Ensemble. From *Gugak: The Korean Traditional Music and Dance,* DVD publication of the National Gugak Center, Seoul, Republic of Korea. Courtesy of the National Gugak Center, www.gugak.go.kr:9001/eng/. © 2011. All rights reserved.

3.20: *Ajaeng* (Korean seven-string bowed zither) played by Kim Young-gil. From *Gugak: The Korean Traditional Music and Dance,* DVD publication of the National Gugak Center, Seoul, Republic of Korea. Courtesy of the National Gugak Center, www.gugak.go.kr:9001/eng/. © 2011. All rights reserved.

3.21: "Shadanane," by Muttuswami Dikshitar, sung by Vijayalakshmy Subramaniam. Accompanists: Akkarai Subhalakshmi (violin), Neyveli Skandasubramaniam (*mridangam*), Dr. S. Karthick (*ghatam*), Harini Ramakrishnan (*tambura*), Shankari Subramaniam (vocal support). Courtesy of Vijayalakshmy Subramaniam, www.vijayalakshmysubramaniam. com.

3.22: *Taqsim* improvisation on *ud* (Arabic lute) by Naji Hilal, www.najihilal.com, recorded by Jonathan C. Kramer. Courtesy of Naji Hilal.

3.23: "Soeur Monique," by François Couperin, played by Pastór de Lasala on a double Flemish harpsichord made by Carey Beebe, in Neutral Bay, New South Wales, Australia, 1998. Courtesy of Pastór de Lasala.

3.24: *Gaida* (Bulgarian bagpipe) played by the late Dafo Trendafilov in village of Gela, near Shiroka Laka Smolyan, Bulgaria, 2005, filmed by Ivor Davies. Courtesy of Ivor Davies.

3.25: *Tambura* (Indian long-necked lute) played by *dhrupad* singer Shanti Shivani at North Carolina State University, 2011. Courtesy of Shanti Shivani, www.shantishivani.com.

3.26: Limbe Mvano Choir. Blantyre Synod, Church of Central Africa Presbyterian, Malawi. Courtesy of Karen Plater, associate secretary for stewardship, the Presbyterian Church in Canada, www.presbyterian.ca.

3.27: Benedictine nuns of Notre-Dame-l'Annonciation, Abbaye Sainte-Madeleine du Barroux, France. Gregorian chant, Psalm 59, "Commovisti, Domine." Courtesy of Patrick Robles.

3.28: *Gadulka* (Bulgarian fiddle) played by Ivan Iliev Kovachev at Bulgarian folk music workshop in Switzerland. Courtesy of Ivan Iliev Kovachev, www.folkfactory.com, www.audiofactory. com.

3.29: *Rabab* (Afghani plucked lute) played by the late Ustad Rahim Kushnawaz, filmed by John Baily in 1994. From *Ustad Rahim: Herat's Rubab Maestro*, John Baily, producer/director. Distributed by Royal Anthropological Institute, London. Courtesy of John Baily. © 2008. All rights reserved.

3.30: *Bansuri* (Bangladeshi bamboo flute) played by Jalal Ahmad. Courtesy of Nasim Haider.

3.31: "Samai Nahawand" by Simon Shaheen, played by Maya Beiser (cello), Simon Shaheen (*ud*), and Glen Velez (frame drum). From the album *Kinship—Maya Beiser*. Koch International Classics. Courtesy of Maya Beiser. © 2000. All rights reserved.

3.32: "Nhemamusasa" played on *mbiras* (Shona thumb pianos) by Ambuya Beauler Dyoko and Cosmas Magaya. Courtesy of Cosmas Magaya.

3.33:   *Yelli* vocal polyphony, Cameroon. "Traditional *yelli* sung by Loni Julienne and the Baka women of Gbiné, www.gbine.com." Courtesy of Martin Cradick, March Hare Publishing Ltd, www.baka.co.uk, and Global Music Exchange, www.1heart.org.

3.34:   *Isicathamiya.* "*Inkanyezi Nezazi*" ("The Star and the Wiseman") performed by Joseph Shabalala and Ladysmith Black Mambazo. Courtesy of Ladysmith Black Mambazo. © 1998. All rights reserved.

3.35:   "*Shojo No Tsuru*" performed by Yamaguchi Goro (*shakuhachi*), Nakanoshima Keiko (*koto*), and Nakanoshima Kinichi (*shamisen*). Recording by NHK, 1979. Courtesy of John Singer.

3.36:   *Jiangnan sizhu* (Chinese wind and string ensemble) at the Huxinting teahouse in Huangpu district, Shanghai, 2007. Courtesy of Alison E. Arnold.

3.37:   "Large Hadron Rap," lyrics and video production by Kate McAlpine, music by Will Barras, CERN, Geneva, Switzerland. Courtesy of Katherine McAlpine.

3.38:   San Francisco jazz by Steve and Kate Fowler. Courtesy of Steven H. Fowler.

3.39:   Electronic instruments. "*Sonnez la Cloche*" by Karlheinz Essl, performed live during exhibition by Gunter Damisch at Würth Art Room in Böheimkirchen, Austria, on October 3, 2003. Video by Uta Birk. More information at www.essl.at/works/sonnez-la-cloche.html. Courtesy of Karlheinz Essl, Universität für Musik und darstellende Kunst, Wien Institut für Komposition und Elektroakustik.

LESSON 4

4.1:   Humpback whales. Courtesy of Rob Knourek.

4.2:   Gibbons. Courtesy of Lara Mostert, www.monkeyland.co.za, www.saasa.org.za, www.birdsofeden.co.za, www.jukani.co.za.

4.3:   Gelada baboons. Recorded near Debre Birhan, Ethiopia, 2013. Courtesy of Jonathan C. Kramer.

4.4:   Mother-infant interactions between Maren Boudra and baby Sophia. Courtesy of Maren Boudra.

LESSON 5

5.1:   "Mother." Composed and performed by John Lennon and the Plastic Ono Band. Courtesy of Yoko Ono Lennon. © Yoko Ono Lennon.

5.2:   "*Fado Loucura*" performed by Ana Moura. Courtesy of Rita Gouveia, Lisbon, Portugal, www.anamoura.com.pt/indexnm.aspx.

5.3:   Tito Puente salsa band. Courtesy of Milton Esteban, www.miltonesteban.com.

5.4:   Nadia Boulanger. From documentary *Nadia Boulanger: Mademoiselle,* produced by Bruno Monsaingeon. Courtesy of Bruno Monsaingeon, www.brunomonsaingeon.com. © 1977. All rights reserved.

5.5:   Mohammad Reza Shahjarian, Iranian vocalist. Courtesy of Shabnam Ataei, IT manager of Maestro Mohammad Reza Shahjarian, www.mohammadrezashahjarian.com.

5.6:   "*Kyo no shiki*" ("Four Seasons of Kyoto") performed by Satoyuki (*shamisen* lute and vocals) and Naosuzu (dancer). Courtesy of Kiyohito Takenaka, Ritsumeikan University, Kyoto, Japan.

5.7:   Bi Kidude of Zanzibar, performing at the Les Orientales festival, France, 2004. Courtesy of François Mauger, director, Editorial de Mondomix. www.mondomix.com.

5.8:   Steve Riley and the Mamou Playboys. Video by Wilson Savoy. Courtesy of Steve Riley, www.mamouplayboys.com.

5.9:   Remo talking drum. Courtesy of Ayodapo Oyelana, Iyallu Arts, Culture and Tradition of the Yorubas, Nigeria, www.iyailu.com.

5.10:   *Apenti* (Surinamese talking drum), demonstration by Henk Tjon, Paramaribo, 2009. Courtesy of Jonathan C. Kramer.

5.11:   "*Sai Ma*" ("Horse Race") by Huang Haihuai, played on *erhu* by Dai Shenghua, Shanghai Conservatory, 2014. Courtesy of Dai Shenghua and Dai Xiaolian.

5.12:   Getty Videos 89132890.

5.13: *Tassa* drumming. From *Tassa Thunder: Folk Music from India to the Caribbean,* Peter Manuel, director. Courtesy of Peter Manuel. © 2010. All rights reserved.

5.14: South African lullaby. From *Rhythm of Resistance: Black South African Music,* Beats of the Heart Series, Jeremy Marre, director, Harcourt Films. Courtesy of Jeremy Marre. ©1979. All rights reserved.

5.15: Royal Military Tattoo, Edinburgh Castle, Scotland. Courtesy of Barry Ferguson.

5.16: New Orleans jazz funeral parade. From *Jazz Parades: Feet Don't Fail Me Now,* Alan Lomax, producer. From the Alan Lomax Collection at the American Folklife Center, Library of Congress.

5.17: Music therapy infomercial. Courtesy of Joanne V. Loewy, DA, LCAT, MT-BC, Director, The Louis Armstrong Center for Music and Medicine Hospital Mount Sinai Beth Israel, Associate Professor, Albert Einstein College of Medicine.

5.18: Bar Mitzvah. Courtesy of Gregory Rosner.

5.19: Byzantine hymn of Saint Kassia (ca. 805-ca. 865). Performed by Men's Choir of Kimissis Tis Theotokou Greek Orthodox Church, Brooklyn, New York. Courtesy of Archdeacon Panteleimon, director, Archdiocesan School of Byzantine Music; managing director, Archdiocesan Byzantine Choir, Greek Orthodox Archdiocese of America.

5.20: "A Visit to Kirina's New Music School" Filmed and produced by Playing for Change Foundation, Kirina, Mala. Music: "Soundiata" by Boubacar Traoré. Courtesy of Playing for Change Foundation, a multimedia music project started in 2004 by producers Mark Johnson and Whitney Kroenke: www.playingforchange.org. © 2011. All rights reserved.

5.21: "Singing at a house party" video clip from the bonus DVD to the recording entitled *Music of Central Asia,vol. 6: Alim and Fargana Qasimov: Spiritual Music of Azerbaijan,* SFW40525, courtesy of Smithsonian Folkways Recordings. Music of Central Asia is a co-production of the Aga Khan Music Initiative and Smithsonian Folkways Recordings. (p) (c) 2007. Used by permission.

5.22: "*Lanitra Manga Manga*"("Blue, Blue sky) (1994) performed by Salala in Antananarivo, Madagascar, 2005. Courtesy of Olombelo "Ricky" Olombelona.

5.23: "The Internationale." From *The Internationale,* documentary film by Peter Miller and Willow Pond Films. Courtesy of Willow Pond Films, www.willowpondfilms.com. © 2000. All rights reserved.

LESSON 6

6.1: Kajod Wangmo singing a "sky song" in Yulin, PRC, 2006. Courtesy of Jonathan C. Kramer.

6.2: Ravi Shankar (*sitar*) with Alla Rakha (*tabla*). From *Monterey Pop* by D.A. Pennebaker, courtesy of Pennebaker Hegedus Films, Inc and the Monterey International Pop Festival Foundation, Inc. Available from the Criterion Collection.

6.3: Maria Stoyanova playing *gaida* (Bulgarian bagpipe). Courtesy of Timothy Rice, Professor Emeritus, University of California at Los Angeles.

6.4: Celebration of Croatia joining the European Union, 2013. Courtesy of Dino Mihanović, Second Secretary for Political Affairs, Embassy of the Republic of Croatia to the United States of America; and Tomislav Saucha, head of the Croatian government committee in charge of organizing the celebrations.

LESSON 7

7.1: *Bandura* (Ukrainian lute-zither) played by Stepan Shcherbak, Kiev, Ukraine. Courtesy of Leonard (Len) Wicks, www.ody-see.com.

7.2: Tango. Courtesy of Paul Hodge, SoloAroundWorld, www.genpolicy.com.

7.3: Argentine dance orchestras. "Bandoneon & Tango, Buenos Aires" video compilation by Stefan Gergely. Courtesy of Stefan Gergely.

7.4: Otis Redding. "I've Been Loving You Too Long," by Otis Redding and Jerry Butler. From *Monterey Pop* by D.A. Pennebaker, courtesy of Pennebaker Hegedus Films, Inc and the Monterey International Pop Festival Foundation, Inc. Available from the Criterion Collection.

7.5: Janis Joplin. "Ball and Chain" by Willie Mae ("Big Mama") Thornton. From *Monterey Pop* by D.A. Pennebaker, courtesy of Pennebaker Hegedus Films, Inc and the Monterey International Pop Festival Foundation, Inc. Available from the Criterion Collection.

7.6:   Umm Kulthum. From *Umm Kulthum, A Voice Like Egypt,* Michal Goldman, producer. Courtesy of Michal Goldman. © 1998. All rights reserved.

7.7:   *Tibetans* by Acko Choedrag. Courtesy of Acko Choedrag. © 2007. All rights reserved.

7.8:   Acko Choedrag at Kumbum Monastery, Qinghai province, PRC, filmed by Tsering Samdrup. Courtesy of Jonathan C. Kramer.

7.9:   Afro-Surinamese drumming patterns, in Djoemoe, Suriname. Courtesy of Jonathan C. Kramer.

7.10:   Native American dance. Paremuru Native American Culture Organization dance class, Paramaribo, Suriname. Courtesy of Jonathan C. Kramer.

7.11:   Teenage Creole girls performing traditional Afro-Surinamese dance. NAKS (*Na Afrikan Kulturu fu Sranan*) Community Organization, Paramaribo, Suriname. Courtesy of Jonathan C. Kramer.

7.12:   East Indian dance class in Paramaribo, Suriname. Courtesy of Jonathan C. Kramer.

7.13:   *Jaran kapang* (Javanese hobby horse dance). Javanese Arrival Day Celebration, Javanese Cultural Center, Paramaribo, Suriname, 2008. Courtesy of Jonathan C. Kramer.

7.14:   Surinamese *gamelan*. Bangun-Utomo Ensemble, Mariënburg, Suriname. Courtesy of Jonathan C. Kramer.

7.15:   "Playing for Change", a multimedia music project started in 2004 by producers Mark Johnson and Whitney Kroenke, Timeless Media Group, www.playingforchange.com

7.16:   http://www.playingforchange.com/episodes/one-love/. "One Love," Song Around the World, 2009. Playing for Change Foundation.

LESSON 8

8.1:   Johann Pachelbel, *Canon in D* (original instruments version). Courtesy of Voices of Music, www.voicesofmusic.org.

8.2:   Korean *kayagums* with DJ, beatboxing, and break dancing, featuring Sookmyung Kayagum Orchestra. Courtesy of Professor Song Hye-jin, Sookmyung Women's University, director.

8.3:   "A Moment So Close" by Bela Fleck and the Flecktones, recorded live at the Quick Center for the Arts in Fairfield, Connecticut. Featuring the late Kongar-ol Ondar (Tuvan throat singer), Sandip Burman (*tabla* drums), and Victor Wooten (electric bass). Courtesy of Bela Fleck and the Flecktones.

8.4:   Mardi Gras. From *Dance for a Chicken: The Cajun Mardi Gras,* Pat Mire, director. Courtesy of Pat Mire, www.patmire.com. © 1993. All rights reserved.

8.5:   Cajun begging songs in Iota, Louisiana. Courtesy of Eric Breaux.

8.6:   Cajun twin fiddling with Michael Doucet and Mitch Reed, Louisiana. Courtesy of Eric Breaux.

8.7:   Afro-Cajun accordion style. From *Cajun Country: Lache Pas la Patate*! ("Don't Drop the Potato!"), Alan Lomax, producer. From the Alan Lomax Collection at the American Folklife Center, Library of Congress.

8.8:   Steve Riley and the Mamou Playboys. Video by Wilson Savoy. Courtesy of Steve Riley, www.mamouplayboys.com.

8.9:   Community dance at the Montagnard Day Celebrations, Greensboro, NC, 2008. Courtesy of Alison E. Arnold.

8.10:   Montagnard hanging gongs and barrel drum played at a rehearsal in Raleigh, NC, 2008. Courtesy of Alison E. Arnold.

8.11:   *Trung* (Montagnard bamboo xylophone) played by Dock Rmah, Greensboro, NC. Courtesy of Alison E. Arnold.

8.12:   *Goong* (Montagnard tube zither) played by Dock Rmah, Greensboro, NC. Courtesy of Alison E. Arnold.

8.13:   *Ding nam* (Montagnard mouth organ) played by Y Dha Eban, Raleigh, NC. Courtesy of Alison E. Arnold.

8.14:   "*Char Dega*" (Dega Country) composed and performed by Hip Ksor, Raleigh, NC. Courtesy of Alison E. Arnold.

8.15:   "Mondega for the People" performed by Montagnard hip-hop artist Mondega (Bom Siu) at NC State University, 2008. Courtesy of Alison E. Arnold.

8.16:   Chutney wining at Hindu wedding celebration in Trinidad, 2008, with singer Sally Sagram and musicians. Courtesy of Alison E. Arnold.

8.17:   *Calabasse Café*, composed and performed by Mungal Patasar and Pantar. Music video by Aya Vision Ltd., Jason Riley, director. Courtesy of Mungal Patasar. © 2007. All rights reserved.

8.18:   "Awake." Rehearsal with Mungal Patasar and his band Pantar, Trinidad, 2008. Courtesy of Alison E. Arnold.

8.19:   "Nostalgia." From *Mongolian Suite* by Ma Sicong, performed by Hsiao-Mei Ku and the late Benjamin Ward. Recorded in the Nelson Room, Duke University, recorded by Jonathan C. Kramer and Alison E. Arnold. Courtesy of Hsiao-Mei Ku.

8.20:   The Folkloristisch Ensemble, Marléne Lie A. Ling, director, Paramaribo, Suriname. Courtesy of Jonathan C. Kramer.

8.21:   Henk Tjon's funeral. September. 18–19, 2009, Paramaribo, Suriname. Courtesy of Jonathan C. Kramer.

LESSON 9

9.1:   "*Die Stem Van Suid-Afrika.*" South African national anthem during Apartheid. Courtesy of Sean D. Van de Riet.

9.2:   "*Nkosi Sikelel' iAfrika.*" Anthem of the African National Congress during Apartheid. Courtesy of Sean D. Van de Riet.

9.3:   "*Qitik*" ("Dance") by Greenland hip-hop group Nuuk Posse. Courtesy of members of Nuuk Posse.

9.4:   "Do You Want Another Rap?" Courtesy of Ronald Mutebi and Afroberliner Enterprises, Kampala, Uganda.

9.5:   Infomercial (Tibet). Courtesy of Gerald Roche and the Plateau Music Project.

9.6:   Tibetan love song. Courtesy of Tsering Samdrup and the Plateau Music Project.

9.7:   Tibetan nomadic song. Courtesy of Tsering Samdrup and the Plateau Music Project.

LESSON 10

10.1:   Korean Buddhist monk performing syllabic chant accompanying himself with gong strokes. Courtesy of Dr. Jongmae Park and Korean Buddhist Taego order, Loyola Marymount University, Los Angeles, CA.

10.2:   Vedic chant by Brahmin priests seated around a sacred fire. From *Raga: A Film Journey into the Soul of India* (1971), featuring Ravi Shankar, directed by Howard Worth. Originally produced by Ravi Shankar and Gary Haber, edited by Merle Worth. A presentation of the East Meets West Music and the Ravi Shankar Foundation. All rights reserved.

10.3:   Vedic chant transmitted by Nambudiri Brahmins, Kerala, South India. From *Altar of Fire*, Robert Gardner and J.F. Staal, producers. The Film Study Center at Harvard University. Courtesy of the late Robert Gardner. © 1976. All rights reserved.

10.4:   Benedictine nuns of Notre-Dame-l'Annonciation, Abbaye Sainte-Madeleine du Barroux, France. Gregorian chant, Psalm 59, "*Commovisti, Domine.*" Courtesy of Patrick Robles.

10.5:   Theravada Buddhist monks chanting, Wat Sene monastery, Luang Prabhang, Laos. Courtesy of Laos Essential Artistry, www.gotlaos.com.

10.6:   Walking meditation. Buddhist monks in Shanxi province, PRC. Courtesy of Jonathan C. Kramer.

10.7:   Qur'anic recitation (*tarteel*) by Nusaiba Mohammad. Courtesy of Nusaiba Mohammad, Fashion Design and Textiles student, Qur'an teacher, hijab and fashion stylist, also featured in the *Guardian* newspaper UK, Islam Channel, and various TV channels. Also known as @ iamndora on Instagram.

10.8:   Sheikh Abdul Basit 'Abd us-Samad reciting Qur'anic verses. Courtesy of Jazak Allha.

10.9: *Adhan* ("Call to Prayer") recited by the *muezzin* in a mosque in Kampala, Uganda. Courtesy of Jonathan C. Kramer.

10.10: *Tara Sutra* (Buddhist prayers) chanted by Tibetan women as they spin the giant prayer wheel. Courtesy of Jonathan C. Kramer.

10.11: Professional *qawwal* perform sacred songs on *Qawwali* night, Nizamuddin Shrine, Delhi, India. Courtesy of Jonathan C. Kramer.

10.12: Nusrat Fateh Ali Khan and party performing *qawwali* on stage in Paris, 1988. Courtesy of Nusrat Online Team, nusratonline.com.

10.13: Muslim women performing *zikr* ("remembrance of God") in Azerbaijan. Courtesy of Janos Sipos.

10.14: "I Will Meet You in the Morning" sung by a Mennonite choir, 2010. Courtesy of Charles L. Alligood.

10.15: "Precious Lord, Take My Hand" sung by composer Thomas A. Dorsey. From *Say Amen, Somebody* (1982), Rykodisc DVD re-release. Courtesy of George T. Nierenberg, Folk Traditions, Inc.

10.16: "Here in My Life" sung by Darlene Zschech, Hillsong Church. Written by Mia Fieldes, copyright © 2006 Hillsong Music Publishing (APRA)(adm. In the US and Canada at CapitolCMGPublishing.com. Hillsong Worship appears courtesy of Hillsong Church t/a Hillson Music Australia p 2010 Hillsong Church. All rights reserved. Used by permission.

10.17: Watoto Church service, Kampala, Uganda, 2013. Courtesy of Jonathan C. Kramer.

10.18: "I Believe" sung by Archbishop Kiwanuka Senior Secondary School choir, Masaka district, Uganda, 2013. Courtesy of Jonathan C. Kramer.

10.19: "*Tutende Ddunda*" ("Let Us Praise the Lord") sung by Archbishop Kiwanuka Senior Secondary School choir, Masaka district, Uganda, 2013. Courtesy of Jonathan C. Kramer.

10.20: "*Ngenda Yeruzalemu*" ("I am Heading to Jerusalem") sung by Mbuye Farm School choir, Rakai district, Uganda, 2013. Courtesy of Jonathan C. Kramer.

10.21: Four school choirs competing in the Secondary School Sacred Song Competition, Masaka district, Uganda, 2013. Courtesy of Jonathan C. Kramer.

LESSON 11

11.1: Kings of Harmony gospel brass shout band, United House of Prayer, Washington, D.C. From *The Music District*, Susan Levitas, producer. Courtesy of Susan Levitas. © 1996. All rights reserved.

11.2: *Nadun* celebration in Mangghuer farming villages, Qinghai province, PRC. Courtesy of Jonathan C. Kramer.

11.3: Three *mbira* (thumb piano) musicians, Chikomborero Dutiro, Prince Mandere, and William Saviriyo, of Chaonza village, Zimbabwe. From *Mbira Maestros,* documentary film by Antonio Lino. Courtesy of Gilbert Mandere and Antonio Lino. © 2010. All rights reserved.

11.4: Buddhist monks perform the Black Hat dance at the Dutsi Til monastery, Surmang, Tibet, 2002. Courtesy of Ginny Lipson and Holly Gayley of the Konchock Foundation, www.konchok.org.

11.5: Women evoke the goddess Legba in a Winti ceremony, an Afro-Surinamese traditional religion, in Paramaribo, Suriname. Courtesy of Jonathan C. Kramer.

11.6: *Whirling Dervishes,* video documentary by Omar's Travels, 2009. Courtesy of Omar Farooque, Omar's Travels.

11.7: Mevlevi dervishes at an outdoor restaurant in Istanbul, Turkey. Courtesy of Jonathan C. Kramer.

11.8: *Bharatanatyam Margam*, invocatory section of South Indian classical dance performance by Savitha Sastry. Courtesy of Savitha Sastry, www.savithasastry.com and Sai Shree Arts. © 2009. All rights reserved.

11.9: Zaouli masked dance by a Guro male dancer, Côte d'Ivoire, West Africa, 2010. Courtesy of Bidybi.

11.10: *Obon* celebrations. *Bon Odori* dance in Yutenji district, Tokyo, Japan, 2012. Courtesy of Minoru Tanaka.

11.11: Chanting of Buddhist prayers by members of the Chudoji Rokusai group for *Obon* celebrations, Kiyomizu Temple, Kyoto, 2009. Courtesy of Alison E. Arnold.

11.12: *Yotsu daiko* ("four drums") performed by members of the Chudoji Rokusai group at Kiyomizu Temple, Kyoto, 2009. Courtesy of Alison E. Arnold.

11.13: Ritual spinning of a *bo* ("pole") by members of the Chudoji Rokusai group, Kiyomizu Temple, Kyoto, 2009. Courtesy of Alison E. Arnold.

11.14: Lion and Spider dance by members of the Chudoji Rokusai group, Kiyomizu Temple, Kyoto, 2009. Courtesy of Alison E. Arnold.

11.15: *Barong* trance dance at Camphuan Temple, Ubud, Bali. "A subtle layer of energy exchange between the 'Barong' and the 'Kris dancers' is felt by the audience through the emotional state depicted on the Kris Dancer's faces"; *Calonarang* video. Courtesy of Swami Arun, The Yoga Barn. © Swami Arun. All rights reserved.

11.16: *Kathakali* compilation: 1. From *Raga: A Film Journey into the Soul of India* (1971), written by Ravi Shankar, produced and directed by Howard Worth. Courtesy of Cat Celebrezze, East Meets West Music. DVD © 2010. All rights reserved; 2. Margi Theater, Thiruvananthapuram in "Kathakali" from *Symphony Celestial: A Unique Collection, Featuring Ten of India's Fascinating Dance Forms* (2003). Courtesy of Hari Madathipparambil, managing director, Invis Multimedia Pvt. Ltd., invismultimedia. com.

LESSON 12

12.1:   *Ganga puja,* ritual purification of the Ganges river, in Benares, 2011. Courtesy of Jonathan C. Kramer.

12.2:   Sound of the gongs at the Golden Rock at Kyaiktiyo, Myanmar. Courtesy of Walter Kaspar-Sickermann, www.mp.haw-hamburg.de/pers/Kaspar-Sickermann/mm/emm005.html.

12.3:   Great Standing Buddha and the musical water fountain display in Wuxi, PRC. Courtesy of Ting Ting Chen.

12.4:   Two Christian processions in Cape Verde, 1997. From *Viva Cape Verde*, Pacheco e Valadares Produções. © 2002. All rights reserved. Courtesy of Marcia Rego and Hermes Illana.

12.5:   Two Daoist processions: 1. Luo Tian Da Jiao ritual, Hong Kong, 2007. Courtesy of James E. Miller; 2. Celebration of a new temple in Xian. Courtesy of Robert S. Bonati.

12.6:   Hindu wedding procession in Agra, India. Courtesy of Jonathan C. Kramer.

12.7:   Hindu ritual procession in Manali, Himachal Pradesh, India. Courtesy of Jonathan C. Kramer.

12.8:   *Shofar* (ram's horn) blown at sunrise, Jerusalem. Courtesy of Rabbi Rodriguez Sabino.

12.9:   St. Michael's Feast in Lalibela, Ethiopia, 2014. Courtesy of Jonathan C. Kramer.

12.10: Funeral rituals in Shaanbei, Shaanxi province, PRC. Courtesy of Jonathan C. Kramer.

12.11: Three-day Saramaccan Maroon ceremony in Suriname. Courtesy of Jonathan C. Kramer.

LESSON 13

13.1:   Ethiopian *azmari* accompanying himself on the *masenko* (one-string fiddle), Lalibela, 2014. Courtesy of Azmari Gezate and Jonathan C. Kramer.

13.2:   Avđo Međedović, epic singer and *gusle* (one-string fiddle) player of eastern Montenegro. Courtesy of Milman Parry Collection of Oral Literature, Harvard University, Cambridge, MA, chs119.chs.harvard.edu/mpc/.

13.3:   Dane Jurić, Croatian epic singer and *gusle* (one-string fiddle) player. Courtesy of "Brojevni," J. Habrun.

13.4:   Ruža Jolić, Croatian epic singer and *gusle* (one-string fiddle) player. Courtesy of "Brojevni," J. Habrun.

13.5:   West African praise singer. Diali Cissokho singing *"Lu Mu Mety Mety,"* accompanying himself on *kora* (harp-lute). Boone, NC, 2010. Courtesy of Diali Cissokho, www. kairabamusic.com.

13.6:   Kaira Ba performing in Saxapahaw, NC, 2013. Courtesy of Will Ridenhouer and Kaira Ba, www.kairabamusic.com, and Saheed Adeleye, African Rhythms.

LESSON 14

LESSON 15

VIDEO INDEX

Paraguay

2-14: Paraguayan harp

Peru

2-3: Quechua traditional ensemble, Cuzco
14-2: Virgen del Carmen festival, Paucartambo

Suriname

1-1: Competing Amazonian songbirds, Paramaribo
2-69: *Baithak gana* ("seated singing"), Paramaribo
5-10: *Apenti* (Surinamese talking drum)
7-9: Afro-Surinamese drumming patterns
7-10: Native American dance, Paramaribo
7-11: Afro-Surinamese dance, Paramaribo
7-12: East Indian dance, Paramaribo
7-13: *Jaran kapang* (Javanese hobby horse dance), Paramaribo
8-20: The Folkloristisch Ensemble (dance), Paramaribo
8-21: Henk Tjon's funeral, Paramaribo
11-5: Afro-Surinamese *Winti* ceremony
12-11: Saramaccan Maroon ceremony

CARIBBEAN

Jamaica

7-16: "One Love" (original by Bob Marley), Playing for Change version

Puerto Rico

2-64: Congas
3-13: Tito Puente (*timbales*)
5-3: Tito Puente salsa band

Trinidad and Tobago

2-81: Steel bands compilation
5-13: *Tassa* drumming
8-16: Chutney wining
8-17: Mungal Patasar and Pantar music video
8-18: Mungal Patasar and Pantar rehearsal
15-10: *J'Ouvert* carnival song, Port of Spain

ASIA

EAST ASIA

Japan

2-9: Japanese epic narrator
3-5: *Shakuhachi* (Japanese bamboo flute)
3-35: *Sankyoku* (music for three instruments)
5-6: Geisha song and dance
11-10: *Bon Odori* dance for *Obon* celebrations, Tokyo
11-11: Buddhist chant, Kyoto

11-12: Children drumming, *Obon* performance, Kyoto
11-13: Ritual pole spinning, *Obon* performance, Kyoto
11-14: Lion and spider dance, *Obon* performance, Kyoto
13-10: Japanese epic narrator and *biwa* accompaniment
14-3: *Bunraku* puppet theater

People's Republic of China

2-22: *Pipa* (Chinese lute)
2-35: *Guqin* (Chinese long zither)
2-36: *Guzheng* (Chinese long zither)
2-44: *Suona* (Chinese oboe)
2-50: Chinese *sheng* (mouth organ) and accordion
2-70: Musical saw
2-77: Hand-held gongs
2-79: *Tam tam*
3-16: *Muqam* (Uighur modal system)
3-18: Pentatonic Chinese melody on *erhu* (one-string fiddle)
3-36: *Jiangnan sizhu* (Chinese wind and string ensemble)
5-11: "*Sai Ma*" (Horse Race) on *erhu*
8-19: "Nostalgia" by Ma Sicong
10-6: Buddhist walking meditation, Shanxi province
11-2: *Nadun* celebration, Qinghai province
12-3: Musical water fountain display, Buddhist theme park, Wuxi
12-5: Two Daoist processions, Hong Kong and Xian
12-10: Funeral rituals, Shaanbei, Shaanxi province
13-8: *Shuoshude* (blind storyteller), Suide, Shaanxi province
13-9: Touring company of blind musicians, Beijing

Republic of Korea

2-10: National Gugak Orchestra
2-37: *Kayagum* (long zither)
2-42: *Taepyongso* (Korean oboe)
2-60: *Changgo* (hourglass drum)
2-66: Large hanging bell
2-83: *Shinawi* Korean folk ensemble
3-4: Korean rhythmic pattern
3-19: *Sijo* (traditional Korean art song)
3-20: *Ajaeng* (Korean seven-string bowed zither)
8-2: Korean *kayagums* with DJ, beatboxing, and breakdancing
10-1: Korean Buddhist chant
13-11: *Pansori,* excerpt from *Sopyonje* feature film
13-12: *Pansori,* UNESCO video
14-1: *T'al ch'um* masked dance drama

Tibetan Regions

2-6: Tibetan love song
2-53: *Dung-chen* (Tibetan trumpets)
2-75: *Rolmo* (Tibetan cymbals)
6-1: Kajod Wangmo singing "sky song"
7-7: "Tibetans" by Acko Choedrag
7-8: Acko Choedrag at Kumbum Monastery
9-6: Plateau Music Project Infomercial
9-8: Tibetan nomadic song
10-10: *Tara Sutra* (Buddhist prayers)
11-4: Buddhist monks perform Black Hat dance

BY VOICES AND INSTRUMENTS

VOICES

INSTRUMENTS

CHORDOPHONES

AEROPHONES

INDEX

Page numbers in **bold** indicate figures